School of Business

P9-BZD-535

International Marketing Research

Custom Reprint

MKT1210

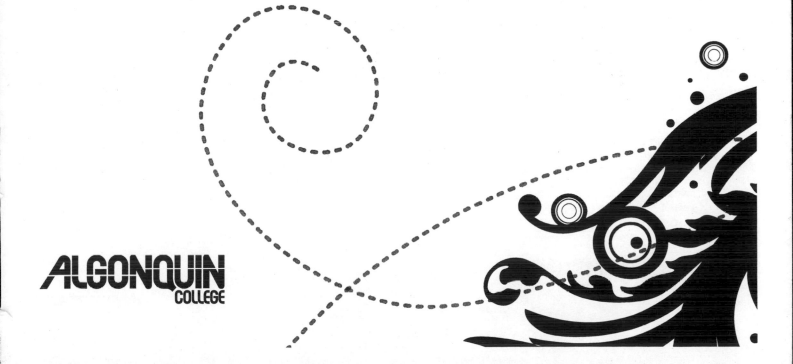

ALGONQUIN COLLEGE

88880079204

Printed by The Print Shop
Algonquin College
2012

International Marketing Research

V. Kumar

Marvin Hurley Professor of Business Administration,
Melcher Faculty Scholar,
Director of Marketing Research Studies, and
Director, Center for International Business
University of Houston, Texas, U.S.A.

Prentice Hall, Upper Saddle River, New Jersey 07458

Acquisitions Editor: Whitney Blake
Editorial Assistant: Michele Foresta
Editor-in-Chief: Natalie Anderson
Assistant Editor: John Larkin
Managing Editor: Bruce Kaplan
Marketing Manager: Shannon Moore
Production Manager: Gail Steier de Acevedo
Production Coordinator: Maureen Wilson
Permissions Coordinator: Monica Stipanov
Manufacturing Buyer: Natacha St. Hill Moore
Senior Manufacturing Manager: Vincent Scelta
Cover Design: Bruce Kenselaar
Full Service Composition: Impressions Book and Journal Services, Inc.

Library of Congress Cataloging-in-Publication Data
Kumar, V.
    International marketing research / V. Kumar.
      p. cm.
    Includes index.
    ISBN 0-13-045386-2
    1. Export marketing. I. Title.
HF1416.K775 2000
65'.8'48—dc21   99-21886
                                   CIP

Prentice-Hall International (UK) Limited, London
Prentice-Hall of Australia Pty. Limited, Sydney
Prentice-Hall of Canada, Inc., Toronto
Prentice-Hall Hispanoamericana, S.A., Mexico
Prentice-Hall of India Private Limited, New Delhi
Prentice Hall of Japan, Inc., Tokyo
Prentice-Hall (Singapore) Pte Ltd.
Editora Prentice-Hall do Brasil, Ltda., Rio de Janeiro

Printed in the United States of America

10 9 8 7 6 5 4

Brief Contents

PART I

Section I

Section II

Section III

PART II

Section IV

Section V

Contents

Section II

Contents

Part I
Section I

CHAPTER

The Nature and Scope of International Marketing Research

INTRODUCTION

One of the most significant economic developments since World War II has been the increasing internationalization of business. Although international trade and business dates back to the days of the Phoenicians and Egyptians, the last five decades have witnessed an increase in volume and complexity of business on a global basis. Both small businesses and big multinationals around the world are increasingly looking at foreign markets for growth opportunities to establish and sustain a competitive edge in the global marketplace. Increasing competition, saturated domestic markets, and cost pressures are further accelerating the globalization of businesses in almost all industries.

Gucci bags, Sony Walkmans, and McDonald's golden arches are seen on the streets of Tokyo, London, Paris, Moscow, and New York. Thai goods wind up on U.S. grocery shelves as Dole canned pineapple and on French farms as livestock feed. The impact of the globalization of businesses is so profound that it has been described as the second Industrial Revolution. Globalization not only means bigger businesses, but also more complex businesses. Understandably, this increase in complexity means the information needs of organizations are also becoming more complex.[1] Consider the following scenarios:

- A Texas-based manufacturer of industrial pumps wants to enter foreign markets. The company has been very successful in the domestic market but has practically no experience or knowledge of international markets. How does the company begin its internationalization process? How does the company select the right foreign market(s) to enter?
- An Australian manufacturer of canned seafood is planning its advertising and distribution strategies for the Western European and Southeast Asian markets. How does the company determine whether its strategies in the domestic market will be effective in the Western European and Southeast Asian markets?

1

- An established multinational company, operating in multiple markets around the world, wants to study its brand image in the various global markets. How can this company conduct such a study?
- A U.S. cake manufacturer introduced its new cake mix in England based on the success of the product with homemakers in the United States. The British, however, thought the cakes were too fancy. The product did not sell very well in England. Could the company have known about this before the product launch in England?

Exhibit 1-1 illustrates the difficulties faced by companies when trying to enter international markets. The answers to these international marketing problems can be obtained from information collected through international marketing research. It has been proven that export companies that train their executives in international business tend to do better than export companies that do not.[2] The complexity of the international marketplace, the extreme national differences, and lack of knowledge of foreign markets add to the importance of international marketing research.[3] Before making

---

EXHIBIT 1-1

Tough Target for Whirlpool in Europe

Nine years ago, Whirlpool Corporation came to Europe believing that the $20 billion appliance market was becoming more American. There were a number of marginal companies operating with slim profit margins and Whirlpool thought that the industry was on the brink of consolidation. America's biggest appliance maker wanted a piece of the cake when this happened. Unfortunately, this did not happen. Two of the bigger competitors matched Whirlpool every step of the way and smaller players managed to hold on. As a consequence, Whirlpool captured only 12 percent of the market and the profit margins are not nearly as high as they expected. The company is also struggling with its second European restructuring.

At the time Whirlpool made the decision to enter the European market, the market was highly regional because of diverse consumer preferences. The Swedes liked galvanized washers to withstand salty air. The British washed clothes more often than the Italians did and wanted quieter washing machines. There was even greater diversity in preferences for stoves.

However, Mr. Whitwam, Whirlpool's chief executive, believed that the differences were overstated and that the market was heading toward a single machine that could be sold anywhere. He expected companies that innovated and found ways to drive costs down would be highly successful; however, the company has faced some rough times in Europe. Whirlpool had to lay off 2,000 employees in Europe in 1995 and posted losses of $13 million for 1996. There have been serious problems with retaining good marketing personnel, and the current state of the appliance business seems no more favorable to Whirlpool than it was nine years ago.

Source: Adapted from Greg Steinmetz and Carl Quintanilla, "Tough Target Whirlpool Expected Easy Going in Europe, and It Got a Big Shock," *Wall Street Journal* (10 April 1998): A1. http://www.whirlpool.com

market entry, product position, or market mix decisions, accurate information about the market size, market needs, and competition must be available. Research helps avoid costly mistakes related to poor strategies or lost opportunities and also helps product development in foreign markets. It has been observed that the field of international marketing research has made substantial progress both in the development of conceptual frameworks for the studies conducted and in the empirical testing of concepts and theories.[4]

The American Marketing Association defines marketing research as *the function that links an organization to its market through information*. This information is used to identify and define marketing opportunities and problems; generate, refine, and evaluate marketing actions; monitor marketing performance; and improve the understanding of marketing as a process. Marketing research specifies the information required to address these issues; designs the method for collecting information; manages and implements the data collection process; interprets the results; and communicates the findings and their implications. Marketing research can be thought of as the application of scientific disciplines to the collection of market data for use in making marketing decisions.[5] It is the means by which marketers obtain consumer and trade responses to their marketing activities. It is a critical marketing function and a useful managerial tool and can be viewed as management's attempt to bring science to marketing.

International marketing research is any one or more of the previous activities conducted in one or more foreign countries. Traditionally, international marketing research has been defined as *research conducted to assist decision making in more than one country*.[6] At the simplest level, international marketing research involves research studies in a single market outside the firm's domestic market. More elaborate and complex are multicountry research programs, which often concern establishing both intercountry priorities and optimizing the intracountry marketing approaches. International marketing research can be defined as *market research conducted either simultaneously or sequentially to facilitate marketing decisions in more than one country*. The focus of this book will predominantly be on multicountry marketing research, whose purpose is to help in solving multicountry marketing problems, as opposed to a purely national marketing problem.

This section gives a brief overview of international marketing research and stresses the importance of research in formulating marketing strategies on a global level. The purpose of this chapter is to inform the reader of the necessity and usefulness of international marketing research. What is international marketing research? Is such a concept valid? If so, how is it different from domestic marketing research? After establishing the need for international marketing research, discussion will focus on the different types of international marketing research and how it helps in the international marketing decision-making process.

INTERNATIONAL MARKETING RESEARCH: IS IT A VALID CONCEPT?[7]

There is a certain tendency among academicians and practitioners to challenge the very concept of international marketing research. The critics of this concept maintain that there is no such thing as international marketing research; that all marketing research is essentially national, and the circumstance that a survey might be carried out in several countries does not essentially alter its national character. This line of argument stems from a preceding argument that there is no such thing as international marketing; however, recent developments in international business should have convinced even the die-hard critics of the unique nature of international marketing.

While not necessarily agreeing with the challenge to the concept of international research, there are many researchers who handle it as if it were a number of separate national surveys that just happen to be similar in nature and take place at the same time. It is not surprising, therefore, that they believe that if you can handle research in one country you can handle it anywhere and that no specific skill or experience is needed. These researchers argue that no particular experience or insight is required for market research overseas and that the basic techniques of doing research internationally are no different from those of doing research in the domestic market.

International marketing involves decisions concerning several countries. Many of these decisions concern priorities and the allocation of resources between countries. Exhibit 1-2 gives the various perspectives of international marketing research. The purpose of international marketing research is to provide information that will serve as a basis for decisions of this type. While some of the information obtained will be of purely national relevance, an international (or multinational or multicountry) survey is distinguished from a national survey, or a collection of national surveys, by the fact that it is undertaken to aid an international marketing decision.

EXHIBIT 1-2

International Marketing Research—Myth or Reality?

There are two ways that international marketing research can be defined: 1) by simply looking at any research activity begun by an entity in one country that wishes to obtain information from another country, and 2) by considering an activity begun by an entity in one country to gather information from many countries simultaneously or sequentially in a coordinated multicountry effort. The latter seems to be a more relevant definition. To develop estimates of the market size of international marketing research, attributes of the market should be examined. The market characteristics include: 1) few client firms organized on a multicountry marketing operations basis, 2) a relatively small number of international marketing research directors, 3) total multicountry research expenditures being relatively small, and 4) a relatively small number of agencies involved in international research. The size of this global market has been exaggerated. Because marketing can only be selectively global, marketing research can only be selectively global as well.

Source: Adapted from Frederick A. Goldstein, "International Marketing Research—Myth or Reality?" *European Research* 15, no. 2 (May 1987): 94–98.

International marketing research is a valid concept insofar as market surveys are carried out that affect decisions concerning more than one country. After all, it is only logical that where marketing strategy is conceived on a multinational basis, marketing research should follow suit. It just does not make sense to base an international marketing program on marketing research fragmented on a country-by-country basis.

WHAT'S DIFFERENT ABOUT INTERNATIONAL MARKETING RESEARCH?

The process of international marketing research is not totally different from domestic marketing research. All the same disciplines that apply to domestic research apply to international research also.[8] The major differences between international marketing research and domestic (single country) research are a) that international research involves national differences between countries arising out of political, legal, economic, social, and cultural differences, and b) that the problem of comparability of research results arises due to these differences.

Importance of National Differences

An international researcher, in contrast to a researcher concerned with only one country, has to deal with a number of countries that may differ considerably in a number of important ways. In contrast to the developed markets in the United States,[9] people in Europe and other regions are used to smaller companies and localized markets. In the United States, the Census Bureau and private vendors provide highly reliable demographic data. The quality of statistics generated in some other countries is very poor. Census geographies and area definitions change very frequently, according to the whims of the national governments or social service organizations. Some other problems include absence of computers and language differences. Language differences make it necessary for a questionnaire to be translated into the foreign language and translated back to English to detect differences in meaning.

The main factors that affect the way in which people from different cultures behave are

> *Cultural Differences:* Culture refers to widely shared norms or patterns of behavior within a large group of people. Buyer behavior is largely determined by culture. Family structure and the role played by each member of the family determines the decision-making process and the family members who influence the decision. For example, Belgium is divided in half, between Flanders in the North and Wallonia in the South. The North uses only margarine while the South consumes butter. Thus, there are differences within a single nation. Culture also shapes the attitudes that consumers have toward certain products and concepts. During the process of researching an advertisement copy across Europe, the researchers got identical responses from the French and German subjects.[10] Both of these groups stated that the advertisement copy contained an abundance of information; however, a deeper probe showed polar differences. The Germans, traditionally known to be

more rational, reacted positively to the copy. The French, who have always been swayed by emotions and more abstract forces, were turned off by the ad copy.

Racial Differences: Differences in cultures mean differences in physical features as well. For example, people from China have a different type of hair compared to those from Africa; therefore, the types of hair care products needed in each place would differ.

Climatic Differences: The presence of different climates in different parts of the world account for a lot of the differences between cultures. For example, the reason why the British drink beer instead of wine is that the climate in the United Kingdom is too cold to grow grapes; therefore, they make alcohol from grain.

Economic Differences: The levels of wealth and taxation also affect consumer behavior in different countries. For example, the reason why the Norwegians consume very little alcohol is that it is prohibitively expensive due to high taxation, not for moralistic reasons, as one may be inclined to assume.

Religious Differences: Certain religions have laid down very specific behavioral patterns. The Jewish rules on dietary behavior is an example. Also, Middle Eastern countries prohibit consumption of alcohol. This national rule must be respected or the offender may be imprisoned or even publicly flogged.

Historical Differences: Historical differences help explain facts such as the playing of cricket in England, as opposed to the game of boules in France. These differences have slowly evolved over time but have a profound effect on consumer behavior. For example, drinking Scotch whiskey is considered prestigious and trendy in Italy, but old-fashioned and almost boring in Scotland.

Differences in Consumption Patterns: There are vast differences in consumption patterns between regions. For example,[11] there is a vast difference in the way different European nations consume alcohol. The French prefer wine, the Germans like beer, and the Spanish drink aperitivos. There are more subtle differences, such as the English drink port after a meal, while in Portugal, port is consumed before a meal.

Differences in Marketing Conditions: If research is being conducted in Hong Kong, people will have to be interviewed through the grill in their front doors because they will not let strangers into their houses. The Japanese are not keen on being contacted over the telephone. The rich in Latin America are hard to interview because they are difficult to approach. Researchers will have to make note of such small differences in different cultures.

Differences in Actual and Potential Target Groups: In countries like England and Germany it is possible to do national samples. Small towns and villages can be included because distances are not very great. In Spain, interviews can be conducted only in cities with populations of over 100,000 people, as the cost of interviewing people in small towns and villages is prohibitively high.[12]

In addition, the international marketing researcher may also have to deal with the following:

- language differences
- differences in the way that products or services are used
- differences in the criteria for assessing products or services
- differences in market research facilities
- differences in market research capabilities

These differences would, of course, be reflected in the results of multicountry research, just as differences between sex, age, or social class groups would be reflected in the results of single-country research. If national differences were relevant only to the outcome of multicountry research, then the procedures involved would be very similar to those pertaining to single-country research; however, national differences can and do have a considerable effect on the formulation of the initial design of a multicountry survey. Unless these differences are understood and appreciated at the planning stage, and allowed for in the design of the survey, the survey may completely fail to achieve its objectives.

While many researchers comment on national differences, the importance of their relevance at the planning stage of international research is frequently not realized. However, it is very easy for a marketing researcher to ignore the differences and get trapped by some of the pitfalls of obtaining marketing intelligence in a foreign country. Exhibit 1-3 describes some of the key pitfalls in international marketing research.

CULTURE[13]

Variations in cultures and cultural values, language barriers, and mistrust of strangers are common. Marketing planning mistakes can result when cultural differences are not recognized, and these mistakes can be appalling, as illustrated by the following:

> *Product:* Pepsodent toothpaste failed in Southeast Asia because it promised white teeth in a culture where black or yellow teeth used to be symbols of status.
> *Promotion:* In Mexico, a Braniff Airlines campaign advertising that passengers could sit in comfortable leather seats was a failure. The translation amounted to "sit naked."
> *Place:* U.S. food manufacturers doing business in the United Kingdom discovered that British culture assigns a different role to supermarkets. Instead of the large American visions they were constructing, the British prefer substantially smaller stores, consistent with values of British housewives who view shopping as a social experience, done in local stores within walking distance of home.
> *Selection of Target Market:* There is little demand in Europe for fabric softener sheets (used in the dryer) because most people use clotheslines.

It is important to understand the definition and the scope of international marketing research because cultural differences play a very important role in distinguishing international marketing research from domestic research. In the world of marketing, culture is defined as *the values, attitudes, beliefs, artifacts and other meaningful symbols represented in the pattern of life adopted by people that help them interpret, evaluate, and communicate as members of a society.*[14] Culture plays a major role in influencing human behavior, and understanding human behavior in a given situation is the job of a marketing researcher. Culture is not a characteristic of individuals; rather, it is an attribute of a society and encompasses all members of that society who have been conditioned by similar education and life experiences. Culture is learned behavior and not inherited. The term can be applied to groups of individuals in a country, society, profession, or social organization.[15] Culture is also an important factor in determining how information processing occurs.[16]

EXHIBIT 1-3

A Practitioner's View of the Key Pitfalls in Conducting International Research

The key pitfalls to avoid when conducting an international marketing research project are

1. *Selecting a domestic research company to do your international research:* Only a handful of domestic research companies are both dedicated to and expert in international research. It is important that international projects be coordinated by a team whose sensitivity and knowledge of foreign markets will ensure a well-executed study. Emphasis should be placed on selecting a research company with a solid reputation and extensive experience in the design, coordination, and analysis of global research.

2. *Rigidly standardizing methodologies across countries:* Attempting to be consistent with a methodological approach across countries is desirable but, among other things, two key questions need to be asked in order to determine whether a particular methodology will yield the best results: (a) Does the culture lend itself to that methodology? For example, relationships in Latin America are based on personal contact. Hence, when conducting business-to-business surveys, personal interviews, though expensive, are more efficient than telephone interviews. (b) Does the local infrastructure hinder the use of that methodology? For example, telephone surveys are very common in the United States, but in Russia the telephone system is notoriously inefficient. For example, the Moscow office for *The Economist* conducted an informal study to determine how ineffective the phone system is. The office kept a log of international calls made in a 30-day period. A total of 786 calls were attempted, of which 754 resulted in no connection, 6 calls were cut off halfway through, and 2 were wrong numbers. Also, the cost of using this inefficient system is exorbitant. To install the phone costs $2,865; one year's service costs $485, and a 1-minute call from Moscow to London costs $3.30.

3. *Interviewing in English around the world:* When conducting business-to-business research, even if the executives in the foreign country speak English, interviewing in English might result in inaccurate responses. Are the subjects comprehending the questions accurately and fully, or are there nuances to the question that are not being understood? Are their answers to open-ended questions without detail and richness due to their apprehension about responding in a non-native language? Moreover, has their attention been diverted to a consideration of accents (theirs and/or the interviewer's) rather than the research questions at hand? Hence, even though translating the questionnaire may be costly and time consuming, it results in more accurate responses.

4. *Setting inappropriate sampling requirements:* Several country-specific variables influence the selection of appropriate sampling procedures in multicountry marketing research. For example, although random sampling is statistically the most reliable technique to use, it may be impractical in a given foreign market. Reasons may include the fact that in many of the less developed countries the literacy rate is very low. Hence, when sampling for surveys that require the respondent to be literate, random sampling might not work.

5. *Lock of consideration given to language:* Translations into the appropriate local languages need to be checked carefully.

When possible, a quality control procedure of "back-translation" should be followed. The prime consideration is to ensure translation of the questionnaire so that there is equivalent meaning and relevance in all the countries where the project is being conducted.

6. *Lack of systematic international communication procedures:* One of the biggest problems of international research is communicating clearly with the local research companies. Do they understand the objectives of the study? Do they understand the sampling criteria? And do they understand what is expected from them? All too often, assumptions are made concerning the above issues that lead to major problems in the study's execution.

7. *Misinterpreting multicountry data across countries:* Analysis of the study's data must focus on the international market from which the data were gathered. Survey comparisons across countries should be made with the understanding of how the particular countries may differ on many key factors, including local market conditions, the maturity of the market, and the local competitive framework for the study category.

8. *Not understanding international differences in conducting qualitative research:* When conducting qualitative research such as focus groups, group discussions, and in-depth interviews, the researcher must be aware of the importance of culture in the discussion process. Not all societies encourage frank and open exchange and disagreement among individuals. Status consciousness may result in situations in which the opinion of one is reflected by all other participants. Disagreement may be seen as impolite, or certain topics may be taboo. Also, in some countries, such as parts of Asia, mixed-sex and -age groups do not yield good information in a consumer group discussion. Younger people, for example, often defer to the opinions of older people. If groups cannot be separated by age and sex, one-to-one interviews should be done.

Source: Adapted from Daphne Chandler, "8 Common Pitfalls of International Research," *The Council of American Survey Research Organizations Journal* (1992): 81.

Hofstede[17] identifies five dimensions of culture: power distance, individualism versus collectivism, masculinity versus femininity, uncertainty avoidance, and long-term orientation. Each of these dimensions helps to explain the differences between various countries.

Power Distance   The power distance dimension can be defined as the extent to which less powerful members of a society accept and expect that power is distributed unequally. In societies where the power distance index is high, everyone has a rightful place in the society. Exercising authority by powerful people and accepting this authority by the less powerful comes naturally. Japan can be considered as an example of a culture with a very high power distance index. The Japanese recognize and accept hierarchy in their personal and professional lives. In many other cultures, like the United States, where the power distance index is very low, authority is not easily accepted and, in fact, the term has a negative connotation. This impacts the way decisions are made and hence impacts the manner in which various groups are targeted for marketing a specific product.

Individualism versus Collectivism   Hofstede defines the contrast between individualism and collectivism (IDV) as people looking after only themselves and their immediate family versus people belonging to in-groups that look after them in exchange for loyalty. Individualistic cultures place a lot of emphasis on the identity of individuals, expression of private opinions, and self-actualization. Collectivistic societies stress identities based on the group or social class to which they belong. Individualistic cultures draw a sharp distinction between private and professional lives, whereas in collectivistic societies there is very little distinction. This makes marketing very different in these cultures. Consider the case of a computer manufacturer targeting the home-computer market in Japan and the United States. The Japanese are very collectivistic and do not believe in working out of their homes; hence, the number of homes in Japan that have computers is very low. In contrast, the United States has a tremendous market for home computers because of the tendency of a lot of people to work out of their homes.

An offshoot of this is the definition of high-context and low-context cultures, which distinguishes cultures according to the degree of context in their communication.[18] Low-context cultures place very high importance on explicit, direct, and unambiguous verbal messages. Most of the Western cultures could be classified as low-context. In contrast, communication in high-context cultures is internalized in the person. There is very little explicit communication. Most high-context communication is economical, fast, and efficient and nonverbal communication plays a major role. The Japanese society is an example of a high-context culture, where people do not appreciate verbosity and eloquence. Understanding this is very important to an international marketing researcher because the research design has to be suitably modified to give an accurate picture of the culture.

Masculinity versus Femininity   Represented as MAS, this dimension can be defined as follows: the dominant values in a masculine society are achievement and success, the dominant values in a feminine society are caring for others and quality of life. Masculine cultures promote an admiration of the strong and the importance of winning. Feminine cultures, on the other hand, advocate sympathy and caring. The Scandinavian cultures such as Sweden and Denmark, and the Netherlands are predominantly feminine cultures and give importance to sensitivity and not being devious. The United States, Japan, and most countries in Latin America score very high on the masculine aspect, with Japan scoring the highest. There is a big difference between the way people in these cultures perceive winning, success, and status and this creates an important dimension for marketing. For instance, many cultures that score high on femininity do not appreciate hard sell. Marketing researchers must bear this in mind when designing the study.

Uncertainty Avoidance   This is defined as the extent to which people feel threatened by uncertainty and ambiguity and try to avoid these situations. People belonging to cultures that score very high on uncertainty avoidance, experience higher levels of anxiety and tend to express their emotions more freely. Cultures that are weak in uncertainty avoidance believe in having fewer rules to define their lives and are not threatened by competition and conflict. Some countries that score high on uncertainty avoidance are Germany, Austria, and Japan. In contrast, Great Britain, Sweden, and Denmark score very low on this dimension. This could probably explain the famous British stoicism, coolness, and lack of emotional display.

Long-term Orientation   Long-term orientation is the extent to which a society exhibits a pragmatic future-oriented perspective rather than a conventional historic or short-term point of view. Any culture that has long-term orientation places a lot of importance on characteristics like persistence, respect for status and position in society, thrift, and a sense of shame. Most Asian countries, China in particular, score very high on this dimension. This could be contrasted with the short-term orientation of many Western countries. These cultures focus on instant gratification and pursuit of material pleasures.

Time is another variable that is culturally sensitive. One of the most important differences faced by researchers in international marketing research is the friction that occurs between parties because their understanding of time is completely out of sync.[19]

The marketing researcher is concerned with the impact that each of these five dimensions has on the perceptions, attitudes, and ultimately on the behavior of consumers in various countries. These factors play an extremely important role in international marketing research simply because it is very difficult for a researcher to comprehend all these aspects and translate them into variables that will aid the marketing function. For the most part, researchers are bound by their own culture and mindsets, which influence the way they view the research problem in different countries. This phenomenon is called the self-reference criterion and is explained in chapter 3. Classification of cultures that are identical in these dimensions will help researchers group countries that are similar and develop identical research methodologies for these countries. Effective marketing strategies can be developed if the researcher is able to identify relevant product attributes that would impact the purchase decision. Exhibit 1-4 talks about the various cultures that make up the world and should be considered important by researchers.

CULTURE CLASSIFICATION MODEL[20]

Assumptions regarding the use of time, the approach to the task at hand, and the role of relationships in making business decisions vary throughout the world. Based on this, countries have been classified into six groups: Northwestern/Central European, North American, Mediterranean European, Latin American, Traditional (includes developing countries, centrally planned, and former centrally planned countries), and Middle Eastern. The importance given to the task at hand relative to relationship building decreases as we move from Northwestern/Central European to Middle Eastern.

North American and Northwestern/Central European cultural groups focus primarily on accomplishing the task at hand as quickly and as efficiently as possible. Typically, the relationship between two parties is not as important as completing the task. If

---

EXHIBIT 1-4

Typical Global Village of 1,000

If the world were a village of 1,000 people, it would include 584 Asians, 124 Africans, 95 (Eastern and Western) Europeans, 84 Latin Americans, 55 former Soviets (including Lithuanians, Latvians, Estonians, and other national groups), 52 North Americans, and 6 Australians and New Zealanders. In the village, 165 people would speak Mandarin, 86 English, 83 Hindi/Urdu, 64 Spanish, 58 Russian, and 37 Arabic. This list accounts for the mother tongues of only half the village. The other half would speak (in descending order of frequency) Bengali, Portuguese, Indonesian, Japanese, German, French, and 200 other languages. In this village of 1,000 there would be 329 Christians (among them 187 Catholics, 84 Protestants, and 31 Orthodox), 178 Muslims, 167 "Nonreligious," 60 Buddhists, 45 Atheists, 32 Hindus, 3 Jews, and 86 of other religions.

One-third of the 1,000 people in the world village would be children, and only 60 would be over the age of 65. With 28 births and 10 deaths, the population of the village next year would be 1,018. In this 1,000 person community, 200 people would receive 75 percent of the income; another 200 would receive only 2 percent of the income. Only 70 people of the 1,000 would own an automobile (although some of the 70 would own more than one car).

The above characterization implies that the world is heterogeneous. It is important to recognize the uniqueness of every religion, culture, and nationality in discussing international marketing research. These differences warrant complete understanding; a researcher has to incorporate these differences when conducting international marketing research.

Source: Adapted from *Houston India Herald,* 9 October 1998, p. 27.

---

the task requires a long period for completion, a relationship has to be built between the parties; however, this is still a business relationship. Meetings are scheduled for a specific time that must be adhered to.

The Mediterranean countries consist of non-Parisian French, Iberian, Italian, and Greek cultures. Starting with this group, all cultures exhibit the concept of the "extended tribe." If an individual is considered to be a part of the same clan, tribe, country, or cultural group, negotiations usually begin with a focus on establishing a common bond. However, this group does not attempt to build kinship with people outside of one's home country. This group also has a polychronic attitude towards time. While they still consider the task to be most important, time is more flexible than in North American and Northwestern/Central Europe. Many different tasks are given focus and attention.

The Latin cultures increase the importance given to relationships and broaden the notion of the extended tribe to include any other Latin or Spanish-speaking country. Though this group is quite capable of doing business with a focus only on the task, this is not their preferred method. If the foreign business representative demonstrates trustworthiness, credibility, and an interest in the culture and tradition of the host country, a relationship can be built over time. These cultures also require that meetings occur more than once, include meals with local people, and time spent in getting to know the host culture.

The Traditional group includes Asian cultures, developing countries, and those countries that have, or recently had, a centrally planned economy. All of these countries have a strong agrarian tradition and this creates reliance on a network of contacts. Relationships play a more important role in these cultures. They do not like to do business with anyone unless a relationship has been established first; hence, to conduct business successfully with people in these cultures, time must be spent developing a relationship with decision makers or people who can provide access to decision makers. Most of these cultures are also high-context cultures and a lot of communication is based on nonverbal cues.

Middle Eastern cultures also place relationships first. The distinction is that blood relationships are more significant than any other kind. Family relationships and relationships with members of the same faith come first. Introductions of outsiders to relatives and trusted friends are highly significant. Persuasion is the least significant part of the process. After a relationship has been established and appropriately maintained, it is necessary to discuss the constraints and parameters of the situation. If the objective is mutually agreeable, the other side will go along as a favor to a friend.

ALTERNATIVE TYPES OF INTERNATIONAL MARKETING RESEARCH

International marketing research can be conducted through descriptive research, comparative research, or theoretical research.

In descriptive research, the researcher examines in depth the attitudes and behavior of consumers in another country or culture. Comparative research, on the other hand, involves comparing attitudes and behavior in two or more countries or cultural contexts, with a view to identifying similarities and differences between them. In theoretical research, the researcher has a predetermined theory or model and it is possible to examine crosscultural generalizability of these theories or models.

Exhibit 1–5 explains consumer types and their prevalence in different nations.

Many international marketing problems can be solved by the use of a single questionnaire or by one sampling and data collection method in all of the countries covered. However, a researcher working on an international problem must consider right at the outset of each survey whether or not it can be dealt with in this way. This alone makes the task different from that of the researcher concerned with one country only. A single-country survey usually involves the use of one set of survey techniques, a sample design applying to the whole area of the survey, and a uniform questionnaire, and produces a homogeneous set of results. A multicountry survey may necessitate the use of more than one data collection technique, a number of different questionnaires, and sample designs varying from one country to another. It also involves the coordination and supervision of work in countries with different languages and differing economic

---

EXHIBIT 1-5

Consumer Types

A survey conducted by Roper Starch Worldwide Inc. indicates that four major types of consumers dominate the world. These four consumer types are

- *Deal Makers,* who constitute 29 percent of the 37,743 respondents from 40 countries. This group concentrates on the buying process. It is a well-educated group with a median age of 32, average affluence and employment.
- *Price Seekers* place primary value on the product and make up 27 percent. They largely consist of retirees, the lowest educational level, females, and have an average level of affluence.
- *Brand Loyalists*—23 percent of the group—are the least affluent. Largely constituted of males, whose median age is 36, this group has average education and employment.
- *Luxury Innovators,* who make up 21 percent, seek new and prestigious brands. They are the most educated and affluent

shoppers and are largely made up of executives and other professionals. This group is mostly male with a median age of 32.

It was found that consumer type was influenced more by the state of development of the nations than by the price, quality, or brand of goods. Prices in competitive markets like Europe and Japan are fixed. Shoppers cannot negotiate and are hence Price Seekers. In developing markets, there is less brand competition and more open markets and bazaars where bargaining is rampant. Deal Makers hold the sway in such markets as Asia, the Middle East, and Latin America. The U.S. market, being more heterogeneous, is dominated by both categories. In the United States the constitution is as follows: Deal Makers 37 percent, Price Seekers 36 percent, Luxury Innovators 17 percent and Brand Loyalists 11 percent.

Source: Adapted from "Portrait of the World," by Kelly Shermach from *Marketing News*, Vol. 29, No. 18, August 28, 1995, pp. 20–21. Reprinted by permission of the American Marketing Association. http://www.roper.com

---

and cultural environments. Moreover, it involves the interpretation and synthesis of sets of individual country results and the very different national factors that may influence these results. Exhibit 1-6 is an example of a multicountry survey in which national differences were not taken into account.

Based on these facts, an international researcher—in contrast to a research operation in one country only—needs considerable skill and experience in three basic areas:

- Experience and knowledge about individual countries and international conditions, and the ability to obtain and assimilate new information about them when faced with a specific research problem.
- The ability to relate this experience and knowledge to a specific research problem and incorporate it into the survey design.
- The ability to synthesize data from different countries and interpret the factors on which they are based so as to produce results that are meaningful and actionable from both a national and an international point of view.

EXHIBIT 1-6

Ask the Right Question

A survey conducted by *Reader's Digest* in the 1970s, among a wealth of other information, gave the impression that the consumption of spaghetti and macaroni was significantly higher in France and West Germany than in Italy. The results for spaghetti and macaroni consumption in the home were

France	90%
West Germany	71%
Italy	63%
Luxembourg	61%
Belgium	45%
Netherlands	45%

Taken at face value, these results suggest that popular notions about Italian habits are quite mistaken, and that spaghetti is really the national dish of France or Germany rather than of Italy. In fact, the public press seized on this particular result as one of the surprising items of information to come out of the survey. However, the relevant question in all countries was concerned with packaged and branded spaghetti, and many Italians buy their spaghetti loose. In a footnote, the *Reader's Digest* report quite properly estimates that if the question had been asked in a different way the result for Italy would have been 98 percent to 100 percent. The trouble was that the question as asked did not provide, as was intended, valid comparison between the food habits of the six nations.

Source: Adapted from Charles S. Mayer, "Multinational Marketing Research: The Magnifying Glass of Methodological Problems," *European Research* 6, no. 2 (March 1978). http://www.readersdigest.com

---

Researchers operating in one country may or may not have these abilities and are certainly not required to use them in their work.

IMPORTANCE OF COMPARABILITY

In addition to the differences already listed, many of the discussions about international research are dominated by a concept not usually mentioned in relation to single-country research. This is the concept of comparability. It seems to be widely agreed that the most important problem that a researcher dealing with two or more countries has to face is to achieve results that are comparable.

The achievement of comparability is absolutely essential to any research that has been set up to provide a basis for an international marketing decision. Whatever the purpose for which it is initiated, the research must be structured in such a way that the results can be used to make valid comparisons between the countries covered. In other words, a multicountry survey must be able to provide answers to marketing problems such as "Which country or countries provide the best opportunities?", "How should marketing expenditure be distributed between various countries?", or "To what extent should the product, or the pack, or the advertising be varied between one country and another?". Exhibit 1-7 provides an example of the importance of data comparability.

EXHIBIT 1-7

Comparability of Data

This example concerns a questionnaire administered to women in seven countries. The information sought at the beginning of the questionnaire was of a very simple type: whether the respondent was married or engaged, whether she had received an engagement ring, and what type of engagement ring was received. The first three questions on the questionnaire used in England were:

1. Are you married?

    If YES, in what year were you married?

    If NO, are you engaged to be married (again)?

If married or engaged:

2. Do you own an engagement ring or did you obtain one or more rings at the time of engagement?

If YES:

3. What type of ring is it/was it?
    a. No stones
    b. Single diamond only
    c. Several diamonds but no other stones
    d. Diamond(s) and other stones
    e. Other stones only

This looks like a very simple list of questions, involving no difficulty of direct translation. However, if the same questions were asked in all seven countries, results would have been meaningless due to the different interpretations of the word "engaged." In England, to be engaged involves a formal or semiformal agreement to marry. In Spain or Italy, it means no more than to have a boyfriend. If we had used the questionnaire as it stood we would have obtained wildly inflated results for the number of women who were engaged, and—what is even more serious—significant under-statements with regard to the ownership of engagement rings in the target group. In Italy and Spain, the questions were modified as follows:

1. Are you thinking of getting married in the near future?

If YES:

2. Has your hand been asked in marriage?

This is a very simple example of the use of different questions to obtain comparable information, while the use of the same questions would have resulted in information that was not comparable.

The differences, however, did not end there. The question "Do you own an engagement ring?" would not have served any purpose in Germany, because many German women receive a plain gold band at the time of engagement which they later transfer to the other hand and use as a wedding ring. Frequently there is an exchange of rings between the couple at the time of engagement and hence a whole battery of questions was required to obtain information for Germany that was equivalent to that for the other six countries.

Another modification that was made was in the list of precoded ring types in Question 3. Although pearl rings were relatively unimportant in most of the countries covered, they accounted for a high proportion of engagement rings in Japan, and a significant proportion in France. To include pearl rings as a separate category in most of the countries might have unnecessarily complicated the list. However, to exclude them in Japan or France would have resulted not only in a loss of information but also in confusion arising from the list of ring types being incomplete.

Research can help in the solution of these or similar problems only if the results are comparable. This means that any differences that emerge are genuine differences and not merely the results of differences in research approaches or capabilities. The job of a research coordinator is not merely to instruct people, give orders, or show maximum precision in the definition of research requirements, but also to ensure that the following differences have been accounted for:

- availability of resources and expertise in the respective fields
- working habits and corporate cultures
- organizational aspects

Comparability is often confused with standardization, and its achievement believed to involve the exact replication of research methods, assuming that comparability of results depends on comparability of techniques. There is a very clear distinction between comparability at the data-collection stage and comparability at the interpretation stage. Of these two, comparability at the interpretation stage is mandatory for multicountry research and something the researcher should strive to achieve. On the other hand, in a number of cases the replication of data collection techniques is neither practical nor necessary for the achievement of comparability at the interpretation stage. There are many examples to show that for information from two or more countries to have the same validity and be comparable, it does not necessarily have to be collected in exactly the same way.

Marketing academicians and practitioners concur that international marketing decisions are made on a multinational basis and many marketing actions involve the use of diverse marketing strategies. International marketing does not necessarily involve standardized procedures or products in all of the countries covered. Also, international marketing research does not necessarily involve the exact replication of research techniques in all of the countries under investigation. It serves little purpose to define multicountry research in a narrow technical sense, namely as the simultaneous application of the same sampling and the same questionnaire techniques across a number of countries.

A lot of effort is devoted in marketing research in an attempt to iron out differences between countries, such as differences in language or social class divisions, so as to achieve a perfect uniformity of data collection. However, the fact is that multicountry research does involve dealing with countries that differ not only in language but also in economic and social structures, behavior, and attitude patterns. These differences must be taken into account in the formulation of the design of a multicountry survey, and they may well necessitate variations in the research methods to be applied in individual countries. To ignore these differences in the interests of a "spurious" comparability is to commit the cardinal sin of so many researchers—both national and international—namely, to take a technique rather than a problem-oriented view of their function. In fact, it is the differences between the countries covered, and the necessity to allow for them, that renders international research a very different type of operation from national research. In essence, research methods in a multicountry research study can differ considerably but still allow comparability on the indirect or interpretative level. The researcher's main concern should be the comparability of the responses that are obtained with *similar* instruments of measurement, instead of *equality* of these instruments of measurement themselves. While comparability of results is regarded as all-important, practitioners in the multicountry research field are increasingly coming to realize that techniques may have to be varied between countries to achieve their objectives.[21] Comparability is concerned with the end, not the means.

The achievement of comparability with different instruments of measurement does, of course, put a greater strain on the skill and experience of the researcher than the achievement of comparability with the same instrument of measurement. It is because of the overriding importance of the achievement of comparability, and the many complications involved, that make this the main criterion by which international marketing research differs from domestic marketing research and by which the advantages and disadvantages of organizing international marketing research is examined.

CLASSIFICATION OF INTERNATIONAL MARKETING RESEARCH

Having made a case for the validity of international marketing research as a concept different from domestic marketing research, we will now address what is classified as international marketing research. As was mentioned earlier, international marketing research encompasses the entire gamut of marketing research studies—from single-country research at one end to more elaborate and complex multicountry research studies at the other end.

Single-Country Research

In several situations in international marketing there arises a need for organizations to conduct research to assist in the formulation and implementation of marketing strategies in a single foreign country market. Typically, this need arises when a marketer based in country X wants to know whether the marketing strategies that work well in the domestic environment can be translated to a country market Y. If the country market of Y has unique characteristics that require adapting the marketing mix strategies to serve the needs of the local consumers better, research will help determine the strategy.

Exhibit 1-8 points to some of the blunders made by companies in marketing their products in a foreign market.[22] Although such single-country research studies present many of the problems involved in a multicountry study, and hence qualify to be classified as international research, the focus of this book is more on multicountry research studies.

Another example of single-country research would be the survey conducted in Greece to study the criteria involved in the selection of credit and charge cards.[23] Literature was obtained by interviewing marketing personnel at major card-issuing companies in Greece, as well as card users. A list of 15 attributes considered important in the selection of a card were identified. A questionnaire was then generated that attempted to identify the importance attached to each of these 15 attributes by cardholders. A five-point itemized Likert-type scale was developed and pilot tested for the purpose. A quota sample of 151 cardholders was randomly selected, taking into

---

EXHIBIT 1-8

What Went Wrong—Big Business Blunders

An American manufacturer of cornflakes tried to introduce its product to the Japanese, but the attempt failed miserably. The reason being the Japanese were simply not interested in the general concept of breakfast.

After learning that ketchup was not available in Japan, a U.S. company is reported to have shipped the Japanese a large quantity of its popular brand name ketchup. The venture bombed. Unfortunately, the firm did not stop to wonder why ketchup was not already marketed in Japan. The large, affluent Japanese market was so tempting the firm feared any delay would permit its competition to spot the "opportunity" and capture the market. A market test would have clearly revealed the reason ketchup was not sold; soy sauce was the preferred condiment.

Kentucky Fried Chicken, when it attempted to enter the Brazilian market, began operations in São Paulo, hoping to eventually open 100 stores. Sales, though, were unexpectedly low. Why? The firm had not thoroughly researched the possible competition. A local variety of low-priced charcoal broiled chicken was available on almost every corner of the city. Because this chicken was locally considered tastier than the Colonel's recipe, Kentucky Fried Chicken hastily revised its plans and tried to sell hamburgers, Mexican tacos, and enchiladas. The company's troubles were not over, however, for these products were practically unknown in Brazil and met with little customer interest.

CPC International met some resistance when it tried to sell its dry Knorr soups in the United States. The company had test marketed the product by serving passersby a small portion of its already prepared warm soup. After the taste test, the individuals were questioned about possible sales. The research revealed U.S. interest, but sales were very low once the packages were placed on grocery store shelves. Further investigation indicated that the market tests had overlooked the American tendency to avoid most dry soups. During the testing, those interviewed were unaware they were tasting dried soup. Finding the taste quite acceptable, the interviewees indicated they would be willing to buy it. Had they known the soup was sold in a dry form and that during preparation it required 15 to 20 minutes of occasional stirring, they would have shown less interest in the product. In this particular case, the preparation was extremely important, and the failure to test for this unique difference resulted in a sluggish market.

Source: David A. Ricks and Dow Jones Irwin, *Big Blunders: Mistakes in Multinational Marketing* (Homewood, IL: Blackwell, 1993). http://www.KFC.com

---

account factors such as sex, income, and age of cardholders. A national media survey in Greece suggested that 62 percent of the cardholders live in the greater Athens area and 32 percent in Thesaloniki, 52 percent of the cardholders are male, 47 percent are high-income earners, and 12 percent are low-income earners. The data were collected by personally interviewing cardholders living in Athens.

Multicountry Research

Multicountry research studies, as the name indicates, involves research conducted in more than one country market. Multicountry research studies can be further classified into three broad categories:[24]

- similar research conducted *independently* in several countries
- research projects conducted *sequentially* in several countries
- research projects conducted *simultaneously* in several countries

Independent Multicountry Research

This is, perhaps, the most common form of international marketing research that can be seen in the industry today. Independent multicountry research studies occur when subsidiaries or branches of multinational companies independently conduct similar research on the same products in a number of countries. Common examples are awareness/penetration checks on international brands and the test marketing of new products. The major disadvantages of this type of international research study are: a) it often leads to duplication of effort (such as questionnaires, etc.) and hence is not very efficient, and b) because such studies are conducted in isolation, it makes comparisons of results across countries more difficult.

Despite these drawbacks, such independent multicountry studies are prevalent because, even in the largest multinational businesses, most market research funds are derived from local budgets. If there is no international marketing research manager, these budgets may be spent entirely independently of each other. Often, no agreed system exists whereby research managers can inform their foreign colleagues of their activities. Where no formal market research position exists in some, or all, of the individual subsidiaries, the position is even worse.

The presence of an international research manager or a coordinator will help in developing a coherent framework for the research planning of the subsidiary operations. Furthermore, even if projects are being conducted independently by the member companies of an international business, a considerable degree of comparability between the findings can be achieved if the international research manager creates or encourages a research philosophy and study guidelines to be observed by colleagues in the countries concerned.

Sequential Multicountry Research

A very attractive way in which to research a range of geographical markets involves a sequential approach. It is attractive in the sense that lessons can be learned in the first one or two markets to be researched and then can be applied to the other countries subsequently involved in the research program. This procedure is often valuable in helping to

- define the limits of the subject matter to be covered
- ensure that operational problems arising with countries researched early in the program are avoided or overcome more easily elsewhere
- ensure that key findings in the earlier studies influence the focus of later ones
- spread the costs of conducting the research over a longer time period

Most typically, the sequential approach is used when a product or service is the subject of a rolling launch across countries. The greatest benefit is derived from this type of study when the research company (if an outside supplier is used) is informed of the total program at the outset and can plan to avoid variations in research procedure from country to country that might give rise to spurious international differences.

Simultaneous Multicountry Research

Simultaneous multicountry research involves conducting marketing research studies in multiple country markets simultaneously, and is, perhaps, the "purest" form of international marketing research studies. It provides the toughest tests of research supplier capability and also raises in its most acute form the question of comparability. The bulk of issues discussed in this book will address this form of international research. Because simultaneous multicountry research is the most complex and involves handling unique problems, having such a form of research study as the focus will ensure that the problems that an international researcher might encounter in conducting other forms of international research are also addressed.

CHALLENGES TO RESEARCH[25]

The situation today is such that marketing researchers are inundated with data and information and do not really know what to do about it. It is very common to hear complaints on aspects such as

- Too much importance is being given to statistics and techniques and not enough time is spent in interpreting the data and adding meaning to it. Researchers today have become very method-oriented and use methods to work back to the problems rather than letting the problems decide the method that would be most suitable.
- Data is becoming unduly important and there is too much reliance on computers and scanner data. Researchers do not spend enough time trying to provide insight for all of this data.
- Users do not typically understand the methods or the reasoning behind adopting those methods in a given context.
- Most marketing researchers see themselves as data collectors rather than as interpreters. It is important to note that the role of the researcher extends far beyond presenting raw findings. The researcher should also add insight and meaning to the data that has been collected.

The importance of international marketing research, as this chapter has stressed, can be demonstrated with an example.[26] Ford Motor Company is a successful international marketer which sometimes depends on foreign earnings to offset a bad year in the United States. But just as everything is not a winner at home, so there are occasional reverses abroad related to marketing research.

In the 1970s, Ford introduced the Fiesta into Thailand. The Fiesta was a low cost utilitarian vehicle, specially designed to be the "Model T for Asia." It was the top seller in the Philippines, but it failed in Thailand. The reason was imperfect marketing research. Ford was unable to gauge the tastes and preferences of Thai consumers who were attracted to the image and performance of Japanese cars. Ford also overestimated the favorable impact of Fiesta's lower price because cars were usually bought on installment plans. Because Thai vehicles are regularly overloaded two to three times beyond their designed capacity, the Fiesta had frequent breakdowns. A sturdier model was introduced, but too late. The Fiesta was locally made and the Thai government never imposed the ban on imports that Ford had expected. This is the kind of information that a company should be able to obtain or face the risk of incurring heavy losses, as was the case with Ford.

Four years before the Fiesta was launched, Ford began to define the concept through market research. Studies showed what consumers wanted in terms of styling and performance, durability, front wheel drive, and so forth. Internal and external designs were consumer tested. Consumer interviews were conducted in five major market countries to choose a name. Similar research was done to develop advertising themes and advertising campaigns. The introduction was successful and Ford's share increased significantly in three of the five markets.

The onus of making the research respectable by presenting the findings in a manner that will be useful for decision making is on the marketing researcher. The focus of this book will be to provide the tools required for a marketing researcher to do this with an international perspective.

THE MARKETING RESEARCHER OF THE TWENTY-FIRST CENTURY[27]

The marketing researcher of the future will be affected by four main factors: speed, the Internet, globalization, and data overload. Speed is becoming increasingly necessary to provide marketing intelligence and insight much more rapidly. The Internet, overnight delivery services, and facsimile transmissions have speeded up delivery of information. This places heavy emphasis on collecting data and getting it to the end users more quickly. Most consumers and all professionals will have access to the Internet by the start of the twenty-first century. This represents a new data collection tool that the market researcher must master to stay competitive. In terms of globalization, researchers are required to learn more about foreign markets, as well as the values and cultural differences represented in the world economy. Lastly, the researcher should be able to add value and insight to numbers without creating confusion for the user by data overload.

The marketing researcher for the twenty-first century should be better trained, must work smarter, and have more varied skills than the researcher of today. Comfort with cyberspace, excellent computer skills, proficiency in statistical methods, and the ability to communicate with speed and precision are necessary traits.

ETHICS IN RESEARCH

In recent times, ethical issues have taken on an importance that was not accorded to them even a few decades ago. Researchers in many developed countries have voluntarily set up ethical standards that will have to be observed in marketing research. This has not caught on in many developing countries; however, it is important for marketing researchers to adhere to certain principles irrespective of the country where the research is being done. The ethical issues that are dealt with in domestic marketing research also apply to international marketing research. Some of the important issues are the following:

- **Respondents' Rights** Respondents should be allowed to participate voluntarily and there should be no coercion from the firm conducting the research. It is also equally important that respondents be informed accurately of the purpose of the study, and where permitted, the sponsors' identity. This becomes vital in cases where telemarketers call up potential customers and try to sell their product on the pretext of conducting surveys. This has created general mistrust of researchers among a vast majority of the population, leading to very high nonresponse ratios. The other aspect is ensuring that the respondent does not come to harm because of taking part in the survey. If confidentiality or anonymity are guaranteed, it is the onus of the researcher to see to it that these are fulfilled, especially if the topic of the research is socially or politically controversial.

- **Sponsors' Rights** The researcher is morally bound to conduct research in the manner that has been agreed upon with the sponsor. This means the researcher has to ensure that data collection is done in a legitimate manner and that the analysis is unbiased and not affected by the needs of the sponsor or any other agency. This becomes particularly important in cases where the research is being conducted to justify some decision or to get some project approved. It is entirely possible that the sponsor or representatives of the sponsoring company may try to influence the research findings. It is the researcher's ethical responsibility to ignore such influences and present the true findings.

The sponsor and the respondent also have a moral obligation not to misuse the trust placed in them. Sponsors should not ask for extensive research designs and quotes as a part of the preliminary screening process and then use this information to conduct the research in-house. They should not expect the researcher to compromise by asking for acceptable but false research results. The respondents should provide true answers once they have consented to take part in the research.

There is widespread implementation of data privacy laws in the European Union. Some of the guidelines are that personal data will be obtained and processed fairly and lawfully and will be used only for the purpose stated at the time of data collection, and that data will also not be kept longer than required and will be protected from unauthorized access, disclosure, alteration, and destruction.[28]

INTERNATIONAL MARKETING RESEARCH IN PRACTICE

This chapter should be able to convince the reader of the importance of conducting international marketing research before making a decision to enter foreign markets. This book will use practical examples to illustrate concepts. This book will also use the example of a hypothetical fast-food chain, Tasty Burgers, based in the United

States and trying to penetrate the global fast-food market. The example will specifically deal with four foreign countries: the United Kingdom, Brazil, India, and Saudi Arabia. Each of the chapters starting from chapter 2 will take the reader through the process of international marketing research as it is practiced.

Summary

For any company to launch operations on a global level, it takes a lot of resources in terms of manpower and finance. As can be understood from this chapter, it is not easy to market a product or a service outside one's own country. This chapter emphasizes the importance of national and cultural differences. If it were not for these differences, this book, and indeed the whole concept of international marketing research, would not exist. The chapter also discusses marketing blunders committed by some very big names in the industry. This proves that no matter how big a player one is, careful consideration should be given to any marketing decision before it is implemented. Various strategic decisions need to be made about the selection of markets, mode of entry, allocation of resources, and method of management. International marketing research guides companies to make these decisions in a more scientific manner and helps them maximize the benefits of going global. This chapter should have convinced the readers of the importance and uniqueness of international marketing research. It is pertinent to mention that the ethical issues do not change for international marketing research and in this aspect it is identical to domestic marketing research.

Questions and Problems

1. How might the following use international marketing research? Be specific.
   a. Foot Locker, a shoe store, opening stores in Russia
   b. Continental Airlines planning to operate flights to Asia
   c. The U.S. National Basketball Association (NBA) promoting basketball in Central America
   d. A major U.S. television network (CBS, NBC, or ABC) reviewing operations in the Far East
   e. Compaq computers looking out for foreign countries for manufacturing
   f. Harrod's, a department store, opening a new store in Sydney, Australia
2. What are some ethical problems that marketing researchers face in designing and conducting field studies in different countries?
3. Most companies have entire international marketing research studies, or portions of entire studies, such as interviewing, done by outside suppliers. What factors will determine whether a firm decides to "make versus buy," that is, conduct a study themselves or contract out most or all of it?
4. Fred Burton, the owner of a small tennis club in Wichita, Kansas, feels that a demand exists for indoor courts in certain European countries which presently is not being served. He is considering employing a marketing research company to conduct a study to ascertain whether a market exists for the indoor facilities.
   a. What factors should Mr. Burton consider before ordering international marketing research to be conducted?
   b. What are the possible pitfalls that the marketing research company must avoid while conducting the study?

c. After obtaining the marketing research recommendations, Mr. Burton decided not to use the information generated by the international marketing research study. Which factors could have influenced his decision not to use the research information?

5. Linda Philips, an engineering student, has designed an innovative piece of equipment to help the physically disabled to communicate. The equipment incorporates a system of electronic signals emitted with a slight turn of the head. This product is currently a success in the United States among health-care organizations. Linda wants to market this product in different countries. Acting as Ms. Phillips' marketing consultant, suggest a course of action to help Linda bring this product to the international market.

Endnotes

1. Subash C. Jain, *International Marketing Management,* 4th ed. (Belmont, CA: Wadsworth Publishing Company, 1993), 368.

2. Adapted from Eugene H. Fram and Riad Ajami, "Globalization of Markets and Shopping Stress: Cross-Country Comparisons," *Business Horizons* 37 (January–February 1994): 17–23.

3. Anthony C. Koh, "An Evaluation of International Marketing Research Planning in United States Export Firms," *Journal of Global Marketing* 3 (1991): 7–25.

4. Preet S. Aulakh and Masaaki Kotabe, "An Assessment of Theoretical and Methodological Development in International Marketing: 1980–1990," *Journal of International Marketing* 1, no. 2 (1993): 5–28.

5. Alvin A. Achenbaum, "The Future Challenge to Market Research," *Marketing Research* 5, no. 2 (1993).

6. Susan P. Douglas and C. Samuel Craig, *International Marketing Research* (Englewood Cliffs, NJ: Prentice Hall, 1983), 24–25.

7. This section adapted from P. D. Barnard, "International Research is Different: The Case for Centralized Control," presented in ESOMAR seminar on International Marketing Research: "Does it Provide What the User Needs?" Brussels, 1976.

8. Author's interview with Research International.

9. Blayne Cutler, "Reaching the Real Europe," *American Demographics* 12, no. 10 (October 1990): 38–43, 54.

10. Margaret Crimp and Len Tiu Wright, *The Marketing Research Process,* 4th ed. (Herfordshire: Prentice Hall, 1995), 63.

11. Jim Williams, "Constant Questions or Constant Meanings? Assessing Inter-Cultural Motivations in Alcoholic Drinks," *Marketing and Research Today* (August 1991): 169–177.

12. Author's interview with Research International.

13. Richard L. Sandhusen, *Global Marketing* (Hauppage, NY: Barron's Educational Series, 1994), 100–101.

14. Geert Hofstede, *Culture's Consequences: International Differences in Work-Related Values* (Beverly Hills, CA: Sage Publications, 1980), 32–33.

15. Marieke de Mooij, *Global Marketing and Advertising—Understanding Cultural Paradoxes* (Thousand Oaks, CA: Sage Publications, 1998), 42–43.

16. Edward T. Hall, *Beyond Culture* (Garden City, NY: Anchor Press/Doubleday, 1976).

17. Marieke de Mooij, *Global Marketing and Advertising—Understanding Cultural Paradoxes* (Thousand Oaks, CA: Sage Publications, 1998), 42–43.

18. Edward T. Hall, *Beyond Culture* (Garden City, NY: Anchor Press/Doubleday, 1976).

19. Edward T. Hall and Mildred Reed Hall, *Understanding Cultural Differences* (Yarmouth, ME: Intercultural Press, 1990).

20. Camille Schuster, and Michael Copeland, *Global Business—Planning for Sales and*

Negotiations (Orlando, FL: Harcourt Brace & Company, 1996), 17–27.

21. This thought was reiterated by almost all major international marketing firms the author interviewed both in the United States and Europe.

22. For a more detailed analysis of KFC's strategies in Japan see the videocassette "The Colonel Goes to Japan."

23. Arthur Meidan and Dimitris Davos, "Credit and Charge Card Selection Criteria in Greece," *International Journal of Bank Marketing* 12, no. 2 (1994): 36–44.

24. Adapted from P. D. Barnard, "The Role and Implementation of International Marketing Research," presented in ESOMAR seminar on International Marketing Research: "Does it Provide What the User Needs?" Brussels, 1976.

25. Alvin A. Achenbaum, "The Future Challenge to Market Research," *Marketing Research* 5, no. 2 (1993).

26. Vern Terpstra, *International Dimensions of Marketing,* 3rd ed. (Belmont, CA: Wadsworth Publishing Company, 1993), 91.

27. "Faster and Smarter," *Marketing Research* 8, no. 3 (winter, 1996).

28. Simon Chadwick, "Data Privacy Legislation All the Rage in Europe," *Marketing News* 27, no. 17 (August 1993): A7.

CHAPTER 2

Marketing Research in the International Environment

INTRODUCTION

Marketing success in international markets requires that industrial firms collect and analyze market and environmental information and formulate strategies that are appropriate to specific country markets.[1] A number of key parameters are to be considered in such strategy formulation. The nature and impact of these strategies will depend on the phase of the internationalization process. The degree of experience and the nature of operations in international markets will also need to be considered. Strategic planning by an international industrial marketing company must integrate dimensions like industrial supplier–customer interaction, the levels of marketing perspective, and the purchase of industrial products and services. The following strategies will need to be clarified:

- Which markets and target segments will be entered.
- Which mode of entry and operation should be adopted for specific target markets.
- What should be the timing for entry when entering a number of markets (considering available company resources and competitive conditions in different countries).
- How marketing resources must be allocated between different levels of marketing management (product/product line level, customer level, and market segment/country market level) to attain desired goals and degree of control over international operations.
- How to establish a control system to monitor performance in the target market strategic business unit (SBU), and so on.

ROLE OF RESEARCH IN INTERNATIONAL MARKETING STRATEGY FORMULATION

Marketing strategy decisions will be based on information about market potential, customer requirements, industry and market trends, present and future competitive behavior, expected sales, market segment size and requirements, and sales and profit performance for customers, products, and territories.[2] In the marketing of industrial products, the following levels of market definition can be identified: customer level (micromarket), segment level (macromarket), country level, and global level (worldwide market, being the aggregate of markets on a segment or country level).

Selection of target customers and market is one of the basic strategies of an international industrial marketer. Choice of target customers and market segments facilitates adequate allocation of resources within the supplier's present and future market portfolio. Perceived importance and risks of markets and internally acquired market knowledge influence strategic choices at the market level. Market opportunities and risks associated with operating in different countries influence market choice at the country level. Global strategies are formulated at the corporate level and necessitate determination of overall allocation of a company's resources across countries, product markets, and target segments. At the customer level, actual and potential customers in each market of operation should be evaluated. The market decision process for each target customer at the stategic business unit level would involve:

1. The analysis of demand (customer's requirements)
2. The analysis of competition offerings (differentiation analysis)
3. The setting of objectives (micromarket share, volume, profit)
4. The definition of a strategy
5. Planning (marketing programs)
6. Implementation
7. Control and evaluation

Formerly, the basic role of market research was "fact finding," but as it is called on to furnish more and more qualitative and analytical information, its function will be finding solutions to problems. This calls for a transition to strategic marketing research. The market researcher should therefore become a source of actionable marketing information with the capability to respond promptly to information requirements of marketing managers and to perform a marketing consultancy function by advising management on actions to be taken. Two prerequisites must be fulfilled in order to enable such strategic transition of marketing research. First, market information must be treated as a vital ingredient of the firm's marketing resources and be managed and matched to marketing managers' requirements. Second, the market research department should be innovative and customer-oriented in the process of satisfying information needs of marketers. The communication gap between managers and researchers in marketing should be bridged at the very outset if any measure of success is to be achieved at all. Exhibit 2-1 points to the formation of strategic alliances in the international marketplace to obtain marketing intelligence.

About one-third of market research expenditure in any country goes into media and market measurement, most of which is continuous and is controlled by truly interna-

---

EXHIBIT 2-1

LIMRA and International Marketing Research

LIMRA is an international organization composed mainly of insurers in Canada, the United States, and 48 other countries. Its reach extends as far as Europe, Australia, New Zealand, South Africa, the Caribbean countries, the Spanish speaking countries, Japan, etc. It is an international network of partnerships based on the ability to share experiences, innovations, failures, and successes with companies around the globe. This exchange takes place on a regional basis through LIMRA conferences and committee meetings, schools, and research work. To facilitate deeper exchange within and between regions, the LIMRA research division has conducted international research on two levels:

- Research in international marketplaces to support and enhance the marketing

efforts of its member companies operating in those places.

- International research to support and enhance the marketing efforts of its entire membership.

LIMRA conducts buyer studies in some of its member countries to determine the characteristics of consumers buying life insurance, such as age, income, occupation, marital status, type of policy, mode of premium payment, amount of premium payment, and face amount. Member companies could assess their strengths and weaknesses by comparing their experiences against the norms (in their country or area of operation). Member companies use this information to evaluate possible expansion into other countries.

Source: Adapted from Helen T. Noniewiof, "LIMRA: An International Partnership," *LIMRA's Marketfacts 10,* (May/June 1991): 3, 6–9. www.LIMRA.com

---

tional operations, such as Nielsen and Europanel.[3] According to Philip Barnard, chief executive of WPP's Research International (RI), "When you look at the remaining 65 percent, most research companies here and abroad would claim to do international work. And indeed they do. The real difference is whether it is something they can do through their own international subsidiaries, as we do, or through loose associations with other companies, or ad hoc partners. Perhaps it comes down to whether clients want to develop a serious strategic relationship with their suppliers, or shop around each time."

ISSUES SPECIFIC TO INTERNATIONAL MARKETING RESEARCH

Figure 2-1 represents some of the decisions that companies have to make before going international. There are several risks associated with these decisions, and companies should be looking at some key indicators before they invest in the process of internationalization.

Type of Decision	Type of Indicators	Sample Indicators
Country Entry Decision		
• Risks	• Political Risk	• Number of Expropriations, Expert Ratings of Stability
	• Financial Risk	• Rate of Inflation, Foreign Exchange Risk, Restrictions on Capital Flow
	• Legal Risk	• Import-Export Restrictions, Restrictions on Ownership
• Opportunities	• Macromarket Potential	• GNP per capita, Growth of GNP, Population, etc.
• Mode of Entry Decisions	• Production and Marketing Costs	• Electricity, Energy Costs, Labor Skills and Costs, etc.
• Product Market Decisions	• Product Market Size	• Sales Volume of Product, Ownership of Product, Sales of Complementary and Competing Goods

FIGURE 2-1 Sample Indicators for Assessing Risks and Opportunities

Source: Adapted from Susan P. Douglas and C. Samuel Craig, "Information for International Marketing Decisions," I. Ingo Walter (ed.), *Handbook of International Business,* Copyright © 1982, John Wiley & Sons, Inc. Reprinted by permission of John Wiley & Sons, Inc.

Even though economies are slowing down, internationalization provides for growth, and not because of the emergence of common markets. Coca-Cola, Unilever, Mars, Shell, and L'Oreal have always taken into account issues related to management across countries. Companies like BSN, Whirlpool, and Marks & Spencer are beginning to define or redefine their global marketing strategies. The major characteristics of the ways of operating and their consequences on the business can be analyzed as follows.

Globalization

As companies restructure and operate internationally, they find little choice when it comes to global marketing and advertising. Brand property analysis, portfolio management, line extension exploitation, name changes, and transfers of brands to other markets are common issues today. Niche marketing opportunities and new ways of segmenting consumers are being studied in this connection.

There is, however, a fine line between globalization and local adaptation. Marketing achievement is assessed in terms of achieving the right balance between integrated central marketing and strategic thinking and a flexible and more decentralized marketing approach adapted to national cultures. Both these approaches are needed. United Distillers and McDonald's seem carved out for this double task, but it is difficult to decide on the right approach—issues vary with industry sector, maturity of markets, and the company's culture.

Major Decisions

Events such as the acquisition of a brand of Italian mineral water by BSN in France, the purchase of shares in British Rail by SNCF, or the adoption of a Pan-European media approach by Unilever make the task of marketers more complex and multidimensional.

Complexity

Gaining familiarity with systems, structures, and cultures radically different from one's own is a complex maneuver. The old international style, where each market was treated in a separate way, was far more simple and akin to being in the export department. Under the new style, companies have restructured, assigning their best people to coordinate international marketing, advertising, media, or research activities. Today, the international researcher's role is to help clients reduce risks by making better decisions. Clients today expect solutions, not just answers, to all problems. This is reflected in all aspects of their requests.

Fragmentation

Specialists and centralized market research departments are becoming fewer and smaller and end users of research are becoming more involved in purchase decisions. Research agencies will need to play a different role advising clients on which research decisions to make and provide recommendations.

In the current recessionary climate, there is more demand for advice and less for ad hoc services. This is true more of emergent rather than traditional industries. Mature industries have developed research departments that tend to commission research from market research agencies and have specialists or experts in research within the companies, but new industries, like telecommunications, would rather use consultants than set up their own research departments. Even traditionally research-staffed companies like automotive or IT (information technology) industries are restructuring activities, reducing head-office staff, and dealing directly with customers.

Speed and Actionability

More time is needed to implement decisions on a larger scale or wider area; that is why information must be provided faster. A large-scale research program introduces a longer chain of decision making because decision making is delegated to higher and higher levels all the time. Complex decisions involving many people take more time, but the time spent on proposals and result delivery is vastly reduced. Quick answers to complex requests are a strong advantage in a competitive bidding situation. In researching specific countries, people like local client representatives and local advertising agencies which are not vested with real control, just with critical involvement when results are produced. As the information becomes more extensive and complex, clients need to have a much greater degree of analysis of that information, but sometimes clients ask for shorter reports, graphically presented, for immediate use.

International marketing research is further complicated by the fact that each country has different political, legal, cultural, and business environments. It is the responsibility of the researcher to get around these differences and determine the true market potential. Figure 2-2 lists the major environmental variables that have tremendous impact on the marketing strategy.

COMPLEXITY OF INTERNATIONAL MARKETING RESEARCH

Quality issues are far more complex for international research suppliers than for those working solely within national markets.[4] For one thing, research facilities and capabilities still vary widely from one country to another and this will continue as new countries join the market research community. For another thing, there are multiple users within a client company often working miles apart and understanding their differing requirements is a key element in providing decent client service. The two main problems in international research may be summed up as follows:

1. Differences in results between countries are so fascinating that superficiality and loss of quality are masked attempts.
2. Attempts to reject smuggled-in additions or to abbreviate an overly long questionnaire often give rise to responses like, "We had no problems when we did this in such-and-such a country. . . ."

International research buyers cannot hope to know in detail the variety of standards used outside their own country. They tend to take certain standards for granted or insist that things be done in an identical manner across countries. This may prove to be costly or detrimental to the research project. Further, it is sometimes unclear as to

FIGURE 2-2 Major Environmental Variables

Variable	Indicators	Importance
• Economic	• GNP, GNP per Capita, Population, Inflation, Unemployment Rate, Interest Rates, etc.	• Measure of Economic Wealth, Macrolevel Indicator of Market Potential, etc.
• Political	• Type of Government, Expert Ratings of Political Stability, No. of Expropriations, etc.	• Measure of Political Stability and Political Risk, Govt's Attitude Toward Business, etc.
• Legal	• Import-Export Laws, Tariffs, Non-tariff Barriers, Taxes, Copyright Laws, etc.	• Measure of Legal Risk, Protectionism, Influences Marketing Mix Strategies, etc.
• Socio-Cultural	• Religion, Language, Literacy, Values, Work Ethics, Role of Family, Gender Roles, etc.	• Measure of High/Low Context Culture, Attitude of People, Differences in Lifestyles
• Infrastructural	• Energy Costs, Extent of Computerization, No. of Telephones, Fax Machines, Presence of Mass Media, etc.	• Measure of Technological Advancement, Influences Marketing Mix Strategies

which aspects of the research process are covered by quality standards. Fieldwork is usually covered, as is the responsibility toward informants and mutual responsibilities between clients and suppliers, but certain other key areas like research design, data processing, qualitative analysis procedures, or executive training are often not covered. This lack of clarification becomes further complicated in international research because maintenance of standards is a responsibility that must be shared between several parties, including clients at the international level, clients at the national level, coordinating suppliers, and subcontracting suppliers.

When multinational research first started, the problem was of inadequate facilities abroad and assurance of transnational comparability, but this was solved when research facilities in other countries quickly came up to the U.S. level. As for comparability, the original concern was to try to ensure exact literal translation of original English questionnaires,[5] but the U.S. headquarters research department could not do this—it had to be done by experienced researchers in the foreign country. Headquarters staff could not even check the translation unless they were fluent in the language and were not familiar with the original English version. Knowledge of the original would create a bias that would work against finding errors. A standard procedure was developed of an outsider retranslating the foreign language version into English. Comparison of the retranslation with the original was clumsy and time consuming, but it worked, and is still standard procedure.

Today, when a U.S. manufacturer wants to study market needs and attitudes for the same product in several countries, it is possible to decentralize the project and have the company offices in each country conduct the research based on guidelines issued by headquarters. This strategy produces a set of country reports of varying quality and format that are difficult to summarize; however, centralization of the project may not be a solution, as the staff in a particular country may have valid concerns that are at variance with those of central management in the United States.

Centralization of the project can add to the complexity with problems of hierarchy and authority because such a study can involve staff at headquarters, staff at foreign offices of the company, foreign survey contractors, and possibly an overall coordinator, such as a U.S. based survey contractor. This can result in an outstanding amount of dispute, delay, and inefficiency. The best way to overcome this problem is through organization. The headquarters research department has to draw up a very detailed schedule of tasks, responsibilities, and reporting channels and obtain the agreement of all concerned before starting the project.

Most international research problems have similar characteristics.[6] These problems are complex issues involving multiple interdependent and interactive variables. They are heavily relationship-oriented, reflect the complexity of the research environment, and are unstructured. This type of difficulty affects all international research, but particularly field research, because field researchers try to understand a problem within its context and do not confine themselves to investigating a narrow area in isolation.

Heavy Behavioral and Relationship Orientation

Both the organization and the elements in its environment try to exert control over each other. A firm and the groups in its environment must constantly work at effectively managing the relationships created. This process of management needs to be researched for a better understanding of how firms operate internationally and what factors differentiate successful operations from unsuccessful ones. Culture, as an important variable, must be taken into account.

Reflection of Complexity of the Environment

The degree of competitive product market, technological and regulatory variations, and the number of relationships with multiple groups within and outside the organization reflect the degree of complexity in organizational environment. These groups control contingencies and strongly influence corporate actions and decisions. Internal and external interdependencies increase and become constraints on the firm's decision makers. There is also the possibility of multiple interest groups in the environment having goals and values that are conflicting. Cultural and ideological differences between nations also increase complexity.

Lack of Structure

Behavioral interaction is necessary to reduce uncertainty and to define the environment. Normal corporate guidelines and courses of action may not be appropriate in ambiguous situations. Normal, well-defined research strategies may not be adequate to capture the problem. Complex, unstructured problems that involve multiple important relationships and that are behaviorally interactive cannot be studied in a quick or easy fashion. This is a challenge that researchers strive to overcome through clinical field research.

COST

New clients keep entering the field of international research and many are reluctant to pay the premium fees charged by the major international networks.[7] If medium-sized companies wish to compete, they must have comparable levels of quality control.

European Comparability

Average research prices in the latest European Society for Opinion and Marketing Research (ESOMAR) work based on certain European countries and in the Latin American study provide a basis for constructing the overall price indices shown in Table 2-1.

The comparisons are based on prices quoted in Latin America for four particular projects which were either closely comparable in their specifications or where the prices quoted could be reasonably calibrated to make meaningful comparisons. Taking an average across these projects (two qualitative and two quantitative) it appears that prices in Latin America are between 40 and 50 percent of European prices for comparable projects. Exhibit 2-2 provides a snapshot of the study conducted to obtain comparative costs.

Some general conclusions emerge that are consistent with the main findings of previous ESOMAR surveys on research prices for Europe carried out in 1982, 1986, 1988, and 1991:

1. The prevalence of relative price variation within countries for different types of studies.

TABLE 2-1 EUROPE and LATIN AMERICA Marketing Research Price Indices Overall Ratings (Based on 4 Comparable Specifications)

		Indices	
Europe	*Latin America*	*Europe*	*Latin America*
Sweden		151	
France		141	
Switzerland		130	
Italy		126	
Ireland		109	
Norway		107	
Germany		103	
Finland		102	
United Kingdom		102	
Denmark		99	
Spain		99	
	Puerto Rico		89
Netherlands		84	
Austria		69	
Belgium		66	
	Brazil		66
Greece		61	
	Argentina		57
Portugal		50	
	Mexico		44
	Bolivia		41
	Central America*		37
	Peru		34
	Colombia		31
	Uruguay		21
	Ecuador		19
	Chile		18
	Paraguay		17

100 = Average price in Europe for the four studies in 1991
The four studies used in this table were:
- Usage & Attitude Survey
- Advertising Test
- Group Discussions Project
- In-Depth Interview Project

*Costa Rica, Guatemala, and Honduras

Source: From "Latin America Marketing Research Prices" by Carol N. Mohn, *Marketing and Research Today*, Nov. 1991. Copyright © ESOMAR® 1999. Permission for using this material has been granted by ESOMAR® (European Society for Opinion and Marketing Research), Amsterdam, The Netherlands. For further information please refer to the ESOMAR® Publications Website: www.esomar.nl.

EXHIBIT 2-2

Marketing Research Cost

A study initiated in the winter of 1990 provides a comparison of research prices across 12 Latin American countries. Pricing market research is an important issue for multinations. The Coca-Cola Company carried out a study to compare prices for eight quantitative and two qualitative studies for soft drinks. Although the approach was different from that of ESOMAR in Europe, it serves to illustrate the overall difference between Europe and Latin America in the levels of prices changed for comparable objects.

PROCEDURE

To develop comparisons, price quotations were obtained by country marketing research managers of the Coca-Cola Company for ten different research studies, all related to soft drinks. Each research manager was asked to quote in U.S. dollars using the current exchange rate adopted by the Coca-Cola Company.

DATA

The purpose was to give a Latin American comparison of research prices, not absolute levels for any single country. Price quotations did not require sophisticated analysis or substantial time investment. Separate project identification seemed sufficient as it drew few requests for clarification from research managers; however, a complete set of ten price quotations was not obtained from each of the 12 countries. There were some omissions, mostly in smaller countries, where certain types of research are currently not available or are conducted by the in-house staff of the Coca-Cola Company. In such cases, research managers were not asked to furnish quotations.

COUNTRIES

The 12 countries covered were: Argentina, Bolivia, Brazil, Central America (Costa Rica, Guatemala, Honduras), Chile, Colombia, Ecuador, Mexico, Paraguay, Peru, Puerto Rico, and Uruguay. Venezuela was excluded, as the country research manager's position was vacant during fieldwork.

FINDING

Price quotations for each study are expressed as indices. For each study, the average price for participating countries was first calculated. Each of these averages was then set at an index of 100 to calculate the ten separate price indices in Table 2-2.

From Table 2-2, it is apparent that Mexico, Argentina, and Puerto Rico have the largest relative research price ranges with Uruguay and Colombia having the smallest.

QUALITATIVE/QUANTITATIVE COMPARISON

As per Table 2-3, the relationship between qualitative and quantitative research differs widely by country. Most dramatic differences occur for Brazil and Peru. Brazil is the most expensive for qualitative research (202), but is much closer to "middle of the road" for quantitative studies. Conversely, Peru is relatively expensive for quantitative

TABLE 2-2   LATIN AMERICA 1990 Marketing Research Price Indices (Average Price = 100)

	Quantitative studies								Qualitative studies	
	1	2	3	4	5	6	7	8	9	10
	Retail Audit	Simulated Purchase Test	Television Commercial Test	Area Probability Consumer Survey	Quota Consumer Survey	Consumer Diary Paid	Household Pantry Check	Product Taste Test	Focus Group Discussion	In-Depth Interview
1. Argentina	60	155	210	78	120	—	357	285	77	178
2. Bolivia	71	103	—	67	105	—	121	14	66	30
3. Brazil	61	98	134	82	141	45	52	119	206	198
4. Central America*	59	92	70	136	87	33	87	83	83	99
5. Chile	117	75	41	66	—	—	82	42	55	12
6. Colombia	53	—	—	74	66	—	—	—	84	94
7. Ecuador	96	—	44	132	—	—	—	—	—	—
8. Mexico	40	128	130	101	70	345	67	118	182	164
9. Paraguay	199	—	—	—	44	15	74	28	28	13
10. Peru	96	—	93	157	—	—	73	125	39	114
11. Puerto Rico	325	—	117	107	233	142	35	—	204	119
12. Uruguay	22	49	61	—	35	20	52	86	77	79
Average Price	100	100	100	100	100	100	100	100	100	100

*Costa Rica, Guatemala, Honduras

— Not available

Source: From "Latin America Marketing Research Prices" by Carol N. Mohn, *Marketing and Research Today*, Nov. 1991. Copyright © ESOMAR® 1999. Permission for using this material has been granted by ESOMAR® (European Society for Opinion and Marketing Research), Amsterdam, The Netherlands. For further information please refer to the ESOMAR® Publications Website: www.esomar.nl.

work (109) compared with its much lower qualitative studies index (76). Each price index is calculated as a simple arithmetic mean of the category indices for that country from Table 2-2.

OVERALL RATINGS

The comparative picture of Table 2-3 represents one way of looking at the data. Table 2-4 shows a further summarization in the form of an "index of indices." The table sorts the countries in descending order by their respective price indices. The key finding is the way prices differ for the same research program. For example, if a program comprising all ten research studies costs "100" in Peru, it would cost about "169" in Argentina, but only "53" in Uruguay. Compensation must undoubtedly be made for research programs weighted more toward the eight quantitative studies than toward the two qualitative ones. However, any Pan-Latin American research program may very well include both quantitative and qualitative parts and it is helpful to consider some type of overview.

From Table 2-4 the 12 countries can be divided into three equal groups, such groups rarely being accepted universally. The first group of relatively expensive research countries includes Argentina,

TABLE 2-3 Indices Quantitative/Qualitative Studies Comparison

Quantitative*		Qualitative**	
Country	Index	Country	Index
1. Argentina	181	1. Brazil	202
2. Puerto Rico	160	2. Mexico	173
3. Mexico	125	3. Puerto Rico	162
4. Peru	109	4. Argentina	128
5. Brazil	92	5. Central America***	91
6. Ecuador	91	6. Ecuador	—
7. Central America***	81	7. Colombia	89
8. Bolivia	80	8. Uruguay	78
9. Paraguay	72	9. Peru	76
10. Chile	70	10. Bolivia	48
11. Colombia	64	11. Chile	34
12. Uruguay	46	12. Paraguay	20
Average	100	Average	100

*Eight studies

**Two studies

***Costa Rica, Guatemala, Honduras

— Not available

Source: From "Latin America Marketing Research Prices" by Carol N. Mohn, *Marketing and Research Today*, Nov. 1991. Copyright © ESOMAR® 1999. Permission for using this material has been granted by ESOMAR® (European Society for Opinion and Marketing Research), Amsterdam, The Netherlands. For further information please refer to the ESOMAR® Publications Website: www.esomar.nl.

TABLE 2-4 LATIN AMERICA 1990 Marketing Research Price Indices Overall Rating*

Country	Index
1. Argentina	169
2. Puerto Rico	160
3. Mexico	135
4. Brazil	114
5. Peru	100
6. Ecuador	91
7. Central America**	83
8. Colombia	74
9. Bolivia	72
10. Chile	61
11. Paraguay	57
12. Uruguay	53
Average	100

*Ten studies

**Costa Rica, Guatemala, Honduras

Source: From "Latin America Marketing Research Prices" by Carol N. Mohn, *Marketing and Research Today*, Nov. 1991. Copyright © ESOMAR® 1999. Permission for using this material has been granted by ESOMAR® (European Society for Opinion and Marketing Research), Amsterdam, The Netherlands. For further information please refer to the ESOMAR® Publications Website: www.esomar.nl.

Puerto Rico, Mexico, and Brazil. A second "middle of the road" group consists of Peru, Ecuador, Central America, and Colombia. The third, relatively inexpensive group is made up of Bolivia, Chile, Paraguay, and Uruguay.

Source: From "Latin America Marketing Research Prices" by Carol N. Mohn, *Marketing and Research Today*, Nov. 1991. Copyright © ESOMAR® 1999. Permission for using this material has been granted by ESOMAR® (European Society for Opinion and Marketing Research), Amsterdam, The Netherlands. For further information please refer to the ESOMAR® Publications Website: www.esomar.nl.

2. As a result, price ranking for quantitative research is very different from that of qualitative research.
3. A meaningful overall country grouping from relatively expensive to relatively inexpensive research is possible.
4. Research pricing indices are useful tools for defining preliminary budgets for multicountry studies.

These conclusions must be considered conditional. They depend on a fairly general assumption, made only for comparative purposes, that a research program of eight quantitative studies and two qualitative studies is a reasonable idea. It is assumed that the qualitative–quantitative relationship is sufficiently representative of marketing research. They also rest on price quotations by one experienced research manager in each country and only for applicable studies of the ten specified. In several years the picture may be different because prices in Latin America will change over time, as they do in Europe, and worldwide.

EQUIVALENCE

Acceptable and consistent quality standards must be maintained in international research. At present it is difficult for international buyers and research coordinators to determine what standards and practices are being used or can be set across countries.[8] The areas wherein quality standards can be applied are qualitative recruitment, interviewing and analysis, quantitative fieldwork, questionnaire editing, back checking, data entry, and record keeping. There is at present considerable variation in the practices and standards maintained. Some suppliers apply very stringent controls and have clear policies for action in case of unsatisfactory or poor quality work. Others appear to apply very low standards or none at all. A survey was conducted to determine practices being used. It generated concern on quite a few topics, such as

1. High incidence of use of panels for qualitative recruitment
2. Negligible amount of training for qualitative recruiters and quantitative interviewers among a minority of suppliers
3. Low levels of verification for coding and punching of quantitative data

4. Very low levels of back checking among a minority of suppliers
5. Retaining data records for less than 6 months or not at all by a high percentage of suppliers

Areas where high standards are more consistently applied are in detailed analysis of qualitative data and comprehensive editing of quantitative data.

Achievement of quality in market research calls for attention to standards in project management and general company management. The industry as such would be well advised to use government-sponsored schemes, such as ISO 9000, to encourage good management practice. Standards vary widely among suppliers and countries. The variations are sometimes understandable and acceptable, given the type of work concerned or the conditions prevailing in a particular county. On other occasions, lapses are experienced from what are considered the most basic principles of good research.

A growing number of international data banks will be developed not just for carrying information on consumer behavior, market volumes, brand shares, and consumer profiles, but also for illustrating similarities or differences in terms of

1. General attitudes, lifestyles, and social-cultural trends
2. Attitudes about specific product fields
3. Needs, motivations, and perceived and ideal images
4. Brand or corporate images and their development
5. Response to advertising and promotion

It is widely accepted that

1. The only way to objectify lengthy, difficult discussions on the differences and specifics of each national market is to measure the reality concerned by applying the same research techniques everywhere
2. These techniques must be normal in order to draw relevant conclusions; for example, the allocation of very high scores and the use of superlatives does not really mean or imply the same thing in Latin countries as it does in Germanic countries
3. Such systematization brings with it the benefits of scale, experience, and comparability, but high development costs will require rapid payback across as many countries as possible

Percentages and mean scores observed in different cultural frameworks do not necessarily have the same meaning. For example, Latin people are more likely to use superlatives or extreme positions on sales. Answers to buying intention questions or attitudinal data must therefore be carefully interpreted.

PERSONNEL[9]

International research means a real commitment in terms of resources, such as:

- *Technological resources.* For example, centralized CATI systems, data processing capacity.
- *Personnel resources.* For example, operations experts (sampling experts, telephone interviewing experts, etc.) and executives with appropriate skills.

- *Systems* (within the company and across networks). Large-scale multinational projects and globalization tend to make us view research data as "hard data" instead of "soft data." There may be a danger here of missing or misinterpreting an important local factor just because it was hidden behind this need for harmonization. There are also certain areas that will always be difficult to approach globally. For example, trying to achieve comparability in approach and results across America, India, and Saudi Arabia is a Herculean task.

On the qualitative side, because research clearly focuses on people and cultures, the danger is far less important. Exploring behaviors, attitudes, and motivations is part of the objectives. Because data on the quantitative side is more concise and people have less time to spend on each single local report, information tends to be treated like facts. It is a worrisome fact that big quantitative reports with management summaries, graphics, and projections are based on research, which fundamentally deals with inconsistent, subjective, and often irrational human beings.

INFORMATION ON THE INTERNATIONAL MARKETING RESEARCH INDUSTRY

For many years, estimates have been provided of the size of national research markets.[10] These estimates have been based on data collected by national market research trade associations and national research societies, along with the work of a few individuals and earlier ESOMAR studies. It has been estimated that in terms of research expenditure, the top three countries are the United States, the United Kingdom, and Germany. Japan ranks fourth.[11] Research in Europe is primarily conducted out of Germany, the United Kingdom, France, Italy, and Spain.[12] The Japanese firms tend to focus more on forecasting, distribution, and sales research.[13]

The top 25 global firms earned $6.6 billion in revenues for 1997, up 9 percent over 1996 as compared to a 10 percent growth the previous year. Of the top 25 global firms, 15 are based in the United States and 44.8 percent of the revenue came from international operations. The trend is that large European-based conglomerates are actively seeking acquisitions in the United States. Exhibit 2-3 gives some information about the top 15 marketing research firms in the world.[14]

RESEARCH ACTIVITIES OF SOME TOP FIRMS[15]

ACNielsen Corporation provides market information, research, and analysis to consumer products and service industries in the areas of retail services, packaged goods, UPC scanning, and mass merchandising. Customized services are provided internationally by wholly owned subsidiaries or through joint ventures.

Cognizant Corporation was created as a conglomerate spin-off from Dun & Bradstreet Corporation. IMS International, one of its subsidiaries, provides information and decision–support services to pharmaceutical and healthcare industries worldwide. Another subsidiary, Nielsen Media Research, Incorporated, provides television audience measurement services in North America.

EXHIBIT 2-3

Top 15 Global Research Organizations

Rank, 1997	Rank, 1996	Organization	Country	Revenue (millions)	Revenue from Other countries (percentage)
1	1	ACNielsen Corp.	USA	$1,391.6	77.7
2	2	Cognizant Corp.	USA	$1,339.1	47.7
3	3	The Kantar Group Ltd.	UK	$539.8	61.4
4	—	Taylor Nelson Sofres	UK	$463.4	47.3
5	4	Information Resources Inc.	USA	$456.3	19.6
6	5	GfK Holding AG.	Germany	$311.7	47.0
7	11	Westat Inc	USA	$182.0	—
8	7	Infratest Burke AG	Germany	$174.7	46.2
9	16	NFO Worldwide Inc.	USA	$190.0	21.4
10	9	The Arbitron Company	USA	$165.2	—
11	14	NOP Information Group	UK	$163.8	32.9
12	8	IPSOS Group S.A.	France	$163.2	63.2
13	12	Maritz Marketing Research, Inc.	USA	$146.0	20.0
14	12	Video Research Ltd.	Japan	$143.5	—
15	17	NPD Group Inc.	USA	$110.3	18.3

Source: "1998 Honomichl Business Report on the Marketing Research Industry," from *Marketing News* Vol. 32, No. 17, August 17, 1998, p. H4. Reprinted by permission of the American Marketing Association.

The Kantar Group Limited is a subsidiary of WPP Group Plc., London, and consists of three market research companies. Research International is a global custom market research company specializing in corporate strategy, branding, communications, product development, product management, customer relationships, trade marketing, and process management. Millward Brown International conducts research on advertising, promotions, brand awareness, advertising awareness, brand equity, sales response modeling, and media research. MRB Group Limited provides a wide range of qualitative and quantitative custom and multiclient studies both at home and abroad.

Taylor Nelson Sofres in London was formed in December 1997 when Taylor Nelson AGB Plc. acquired SOFRES Group S.A. in Paris. Both companies separately provide a range of continuous and ad hoc research services internationally. The combined firm will be offering services in ad hoc studies, consumer panels, media audience measurement, and advertising expenditure measurement. Taylor Nelson Sofres covers a wide range of industries, such as healthcare, consumer products, automotive, telecommunications, media, business services, and finance.

Information Resources, Incorporated, provides syndicated market tracking service that provides weekly sales, price, and store condition information on products sold in a sample of food, drug, and mass merchandise stores. They also provide "Supply Chain" planning software and consulting services that support efficient replenishment programs.

Types of Research

Research can be described under three heads:

1. Type of product category/subject
2. Ad hoc versus continuous research
3. Qualitative versus quantitative research

About 74 percent of total expenditure is directed to consumer studies groups and the balance is accounted for by nonconsumer studies. Within the consumer research field, the studies of fast moving goods are most prominent (approximately 75 percent), followed by media surveys and durable studies. Within nonconsumer research, two-thirds is accounted for by studies of products, services, target groups in the field of semi-government industry, and the pharmaceutical industry. Expenditure on nonconsumer research in the United Kingdom is relatively low compared with other major research markets in Europe.

Of the European expenditure, 55 percent is accounted for by ad hoc studies and 45 percent by continuous studies. Within continuous research, the importance of panel research is substantial (about two-thirds of the total spent on continuous research). Omnibus studies tend to play only a secondary role. Again, 80 percent is derived from quantitative, 15 percent from qualitative, and 5 percent from desk research and secondary activities. Qualitative research is substantially above average in Austria, France, and Ireland. The last category is well above average in Czechoslovakia, Sweden, Yugoslavia, and Turkey.

Data Collection Methods

Within quantitative research, face-to-face studies account for the majority of expenditure (about 60 to 70 percent in Europe). Relatively small countries with a highly developed infrastructure tend to make less use of face-to-face studies in favor of telephone studies (e.g., Denmark and Sweden).

Employment

The market research industry has 30,000 permanent employees and offers freelance employment to well over 100,000 interviewers as well as freelance qualitative researchers, data processing bureaus, and other self-employed consultants and subcontractors.

Research Organizations

There are well over 1,500 market research companies and consulting agencies in Europe, with 300 in France and over 400 in the United Kingdom. About 611 research organizations have a "full information" listing in the ESOMAR Directory.

Research is still in its youth, the majority of the companies having been started in the 1980s. Southern agencies are younger than the others. Some Western European countries of a low average age reflect the large membership of research organizations in recent years.

Television Advertisement Measurement[16]

In the recent past, television audience measurement has become standardized across nations in Europe and is characterized by the usage of electronic measurement systems. Two significant peoplemeter systems are Telecontrol, developed by SRG of Switzerland and AGB, which has interests in several countries such as Italy, Portugal, Greece, Turkey, and Hungary. Another research group, Sofres, has an extensive presence in Portugal, Spain, and South Belgium. ORF-Teletest researches a representative sample of 600 households in Austria through a contractor GFK-Fessel. ACNielsen samples 600 households in the Republic of Ireland based on Nielsen's Euromonitor technology. German television habits are researched by GfK TV—forschung, based on a representative sample of 3833 households using the Telecontrol System. Five hundred Finnish households are equipped with Finnmeters operated by Finnpanel for YLE/MTV. In the Netherlands, Belgium, and Ireland AGB has developed a system by which viewers can indicate their degree of appreciation of the program being telecast. Mediamet researches 1000 households in France through the Telecontral V1 System and another 1000 through the Audimat A2 System. Norsk Rikskringkasting researches television audiences in Norway.

Client Profile

Survey respondents say about 80 percent of their revenues come from advertiser research departments. The rest of their revenues come from ad agency research units (5 percent), media (3 percent), advertiser account services (1.6 percent), and agency media and account services departments and advertiser media departments, both less than 1 percent. More than 10 percent come from a variety of sources collectively labeled "other." Regarding the broad research categories of syndicated and custom research, nearly 74 percent said they were not involved in syndication; 9 percent said syndicated work accounts for 75 to 100 percent of their activity. For customized research, the percentages were roughly reversed. Nearly 80 percent said all their work was customized. Almost 9 percent said custom work accounted for less than 10 percent of their research.

Market research is the voice of the consumer,[17] but interpreting its results correctly costs the marketing profession a lot of time, effort, and money. Hence, whether it is done in-house or by an outside agency, it has become increasingly important in the marketing mix. Some people bank on decisions made by intuition and instinct alone, but in today's markets, there is too much competition, complexity, and cost involved to risk making basic mistakes about what the consumer wants or needs.

Research Services Limited and *Marketing* magazine have prepared a guide on marketing research that can serve as a beacon light to guide researchers through the market research maze. The most commonly used market research tools are desk research and qualitative research (such as syndicated, omnibus, and ad hoc). Some projects need one of these while others may need a combination. Desk research involves the examination of information that already exists in internal records, government publications, newspaper articles, published research reports, and so on. The skill lies in knowing what is available and relevant, where it can be found, and how much it costs. Many companies do their own desk research rather than commission specialized agencies for the task. Qualitative research has boomed in the United

Kingdom during the past 10 years. It provides insight into market brands or advertising campaigns and involves research among limited consumers. A number of techniques besides a structured question format are used. Consumers express themselves in their own terms, but qualitative research relies heavily on interpretation of findings. The different techniques used for qualitative research are

1. Group discussions comprising six to eight people moderated by a skilled qualitative researcher and allowing creative interaction among participants.
2. In-depth interviews conducted one-to-one so that personal circumstances and behavior can be examined and extremely sensitive subjects investigated.
3. Omnibus surveys, by agencies on a syndicated basis with client companies buying questions at a fixed price. Discounts are allowed depending on the number required and for repeat inserts in more than one survey. By sharing costs with others, research is done at a fraction of the normal survey costs. These surveys are ideal for clients wishing to ask a limited number of questions of a large representative population sample.

Besides noting the sample size offered, buyers should take note of the quality of the sample judged in terms of structure and data collection methods. For example, samples can range from preselected addresses from electoral registers with recalls to establish contact with named individuals, to street interviews at certain sampling points with basic quota controls. Sample reliability is more important than choosing the cheapest option. There may also be omnibus surveys for those interested in particular markets, such as motorists, golfers, and mothers with children under two. Advertisement pages of the Market Research Society's newsletter provide a comprehensive list of available services.

An omnibus survey is a regularly scheduled personal interview survey comprised of questions from several separate firms. Omnibus surveys may not always be the right solution, even if only a limited amount of information is wanted from a large sample. Also, they cannot guarantee a position on a questionnaire and subjects covered earlier can influence responses to questions. They become less efficient as the size of the market decreases. Other methods may be more economical for small minority samples than placement of the same questions on successive surveys.

If selected properly, sampling representatives of the defined population will yield statistically reliable research information. Surveys are of two types: random or quota. In either case, the first step is to select districts or sampling points in which interviews will be conducted. All possible areas must be listed and random selection must be made, taking account of region and population size and structure. Other variables, like political status or geodemographics, may be included.

For a random survey, individuals are preselected from a sampling frame like the electoral register. Up to four calls may be made to establish contact with each individual. Most government and large commercial surveys, such as the National Readership Survey (NRS), use random sampling. Random sampling is better theoretically, but is more expensive and time consuming than quota sampling. In quota sampling, the interviewer is given instructions as to the number of people interviewed and their characteristics, such as age, sex, or social class groups. The quotas will reflect the fact that some members of the population are more difficult to approach, such as people working full-time or in younger age groups. Sample size determines accuracy of data.

What the Client Wants to Know

Bodies such as JICNARS (Joint Industry Committee for National Readership Survey), BARB (Broadcaster's Audience Research Bureau), JICRAR (Joint Industry Committee for Radio Audience Research), and BMRC (British Market Research Company) organized the most familiar syndicated research programs in the United Kingdom. These programs measure media audiences and are used in media planning, buying, and selling. The main users of syndicated research want to know what is available, in what form, and at what cost. Although answers are not always straightforward, all syndicated research bodies must be "user friendly" if they want to attract general marketers.

The committee of JICNARS, an organization representing publishers, advertising agencies, and manufacturers, commissions the National Readership Survey (NRS). Research Services Limited (RSL) conducts 28,000 in-home interviews each year with people 15 years old and over. Subscribers to NRS receive regular reports and special data analysis, including schedule evaluation and optimization programs offered by various accredited computer bureaus. The 1989 *JICNARS/RSL Data Book* presented marketing information gleaned from the NRS and other sources. BARB monitors television audiences across all channels for all programs. BARB subscribers receive weekly and monthly reports and have access to data tapes. The research is financed by the BBC, the independent Television Contractors Association (ITCA), and partly by subscriptions. Peoplemeters in 2,900 panel households collect viewing data on individuals four years old and over. Viewing by guests is also recorded. The current contractor is Audits of Great Britain (AGB) whose findings are retrieved overnight from its home-based panelists by telephone line that feeds into its computer. Radio listening information is collected for JICRAR by its current contractor, the Radio Society of Great Britain (RSGB). The 25,000 respondents aged 15 and over and living in independent local radio regions, complete weekly diaries about their radio listening on each day of the week. BMRC's latest venture, the 1988 Businessman Survey, covers newspaper and magazine readership, responsibilities, decision making, and lifestyles of those in professional, business, and administrative occupations. BMRC is a syndicate of publishers and advertising agencies. In 1988, the *Daily Telegraph,* the *Economist, Financial Times,* and the *Times* were the guarantors. The survey is based on 2,000 in-home interviews with business people.

Pros and Cons in Survey Research

There are four principal methods of gathering information: face-to-face interview, telephone interview, mail survey, and observation. There are no general rules as to any best method, best quality data, cheapest, or quickest method. The effectiveness of each depends on several factors. The researcher must identify the issues, weigh the pros and cons, and then make a choice. The issues fall into four main categories:

1. Sampling (coverage and accessibility)
2. Questionnaire (content and length)
3. Control (supervision and flexibility)
4. Timing (speed and precision)

Many clients ask for a proposal from two or three research agencies. Obvious considerations are product area, understanding of the problems, and the nature of the proposed solution(s). The problem becomes complicated when two equally experienced companies define the problem in similar terms, propose very similar solutions, but quote very different price levels. Price should not necessarily be the deciding factor because a high element of research companies' costs involve time (interviewer time, data preparation time, executive time, etc.). A cheaper quote can mean less rigorous procedures (at the data verification and checking stages), minimal executive supervision, or that the company has underestimated the time needed. It is important to realize that market research provides data to enhance and not to replace decision making. Informed decisions are best but consumers are only a part of the picture. Research could be blamed for failure of a project, but it could be that in the absence of complete information, consumers predicted a course that they did not carry through. The packaging, advertising, distribution, facings, and press might have been at fault too.

COORDINATION OF RESEARCH

Central coordination should be staffed with executives who have knowledge of and sensitivity to local issues. Language and mobility should be viewed as strong advantages. Linguists or foreign nationals can smooth relationships with local partners and save time at the central level when a number of issues do not necessarily need to be referred to local agencies to be sorted out. It is often found that the problem in international research is not just to make sure that research colleagues in other countries carry out a research project[18]—highly specific abilities, expertise, and impressive resources must all be coordinated to achieve optimum results.

Adapting the coordination process to client organization structures is critical; the way in which each client company is organized must be taken into account regarding decision making for marketing policies and marketing research investments. The approach in so-called "multinational headquarters" can vary from "proposing" to "imposing" research programs on their national operating companies. *Proposing* is inviting national subsidiaries to adhere to or join in common research programs that are centrally designed but locally financed. The emphasis is on "convincing" and "serving" with full information being provided for the local situation. *Imposing* implies that all national subsidiaries participate in the exercise, unless they succeed in demonstrating the irrelevance of the specific approach concerned as applied to their home market. Budgets are likely to be managed centrally and emphasis is more on "discipline," with local executives being provided with limited information.

The success of these approaches depends on corporate culture, history of the development of the activities in foreign markets, level of evolution in adapting to the reality of the single European market, and so on. In some cases, national marketing and research executives will be involved right from the inception. Local support may be requested from the coordinating agency in analyzing and interpreting data and its conversion into local conclusions. The client's headquarters may favor or finance close cooperation between its national subsidiaries and research partners, but the coordinating agency will remain responsible for standardization and comparability of techniques across borders. In other cases, national client operating companies will be informed but not at all involved in the conception or initial analysis of projects. In still other instances, local contracts will carefully avoid project information being distillated (or not) by client executives within their organization.

The coordinating research agency must know the client's requirements and points of view so that they can define the way in which local agencies are briefed as well as the level of complexity of the task. For example, it is good to know if the client's local operating companies will be invited or ordered to provide customers' names and addresses for a satisfaction study initialized centrally.

The following must be taken into account for presentation of results and reporting:

1. If the client wants a Pan-European picture of the market with an idea as to differences between national markets.
2. If the client is looking for in-depth, truly parallel analyses of each of the national markets covered with additional reports on transnational consolidation.
3. How detailed the transnational analysis should be. For example, superimposition of a transnational nonclassical segmentation on the needs-based segmentation derived from various countries.

The answers to these questions will influence the analysis and presentation of results and formulation of conclusions. For example, the presentation of results of an IMAGE study carried out in eight countries involved

- one full day with all of the clients' marketing teams on Pan-European results
- one full day with each local marketing team on market situations and for reading and analyzing study results in the country concerned, depending on local particularities
- production of a confirmation report focusing on what could lead to global conclusions and what needs specific local treatment

An efficient coordinating function implies and requires

- close cooperation with direct clients
- sharing of in-depth knowledge of structure of the client organization
- spending a lot of time on getting the proper messages through to the organization
- investing more time in analyzing and producing figures, conclusions, and recommendations without ignoring cultural aspects

Using Comparable but Truly Relevant Techniques   It is not enough to instruct people, give orders, or show maximum precision in defining requirements. Design of research and compatibility of data should take into account differences in

- availability of resources and expertise in the field concerned
- working habits and corporate cultures
- organizational aspects
- the best approach for recruiting motivated participants

Thorough Understanding of Subcontractors   Full freedom in the choice of subcontractors is a mixed blessing. It might have the following effects:

- justify trying to buy data at the cheapest price

- generate wasted time because careful briefing and tight control are needed
- limit dedication of the subcontractor
- reduce opportunities for making use of local expertise

It is good to know the relative strengths and weaknesses of the partners involved, their prices, reluctance, and organizational features. This helps to avoid overheads and internal competition.

Exhibit 2-4 emphasizes how marketing research is being used by companies to make strategic decisions.

INTERNATIONAL MARKETING RESEARCH IN PRACTICE

Continuing with the example for Tasty Burgers, the parent company has to first conduct a feasibility study in all of the countries where they are planning to set up operations. This will involve conducting marketing research in the United Kingdom, Brazil, India, and Saudi Arabia. The company has two choices—they can look for a U.S.-based marketing research company that can conduct research in all of these countries or they can hire independent marketing research companies in each of these countries. There are benefits and drawbacks to both of these options.

By hiring one company to conduct research in all of the countries, Tasty Burgers can get standardized information across all countries. This will help them compare potential sales and profit figures and work out an optimum plan to allocate resources among these countries; however, the marketing research company must be an established player in the field of international marketing. All of the national and cultural differences mentioned in the first chapter will come into play, especially in Brazil, India, and Saudi Arabia, countries vastly different from the United States. Hiring a local marketing research company in these countries greatly increases the chance that these subtle differences will be brought to the notice of the management of Tasty Burgers. The flip side is lack of comparability of data across countries. There are differences in units of measurement, exchange rates, and so on, that have to be converted back to American standards for the management to decide if operating in a given country is financially viable.

There are many major research agencies with multinational operations that provide the benefit of coordinating the project from the home country and assuring the client of comparability. At the same time, these agencies also ensure that they have local staff in all of these countries that are familiar with the local culture and traditions and will be in a position to provide better insight about the market. The standard practice is to ask for basic quotes from multiple research agencies, shortlist, and discuss the project with a few of them. The final selection of research suppliers by Tasty Burgers should take into account all of the different aspects of the research project.

Tasty Burgers should also decide the hierarchy within the company. The external research agency should be made accountable to a specific individual or a committee

---

EXHIBIT 2-4

Use of Marketing Research

With about 4,000 mills worldwide, supplying large process machinery to the paper and pulp industry involves a small and very scattered clientele. Finding out exactly what the market needs from its suppliers is still very significant, however. Research of this type has helped Finland's Ahlstrom group develop a successful international growth strategy based on specialist market sectors.

The initial research program comprised two main elements. Interviews were undertaken with Ahlstrom management in North America, Japan, and Western Europe. The aim was not only to assess the views and opinions of management on the integration option but also to obtain a better understanding of paper and pulp equipment products.

The BPRI (Business Psychology Research Institute; www.BPRI.com) project team assumed that because the products are primarily supplied to the pulp and paper industry they must be very similar. In reality, however, there are substantial commercial and technical differences between an individual component (such as a screen plate) and a system (such as a recovery island).

The main part of the research program comprised 80 personal interviews with pulp and paper mills in the three geographic areas. The semi-structured questioning was directed towards establishing key purchasing criteria, the extent to which these varied by product/market, attitudes toward suppliers, and knowledge and awareness of Ahlstrom product range.

In a further important element of the interviewing program, respondents were quizzed about buying a range of products from one supplier and then asked to give their views on the perceived benefits of a more integrated approach from Ahlstrom.

The findings of the research were presented to Ahlstrom based on a series of criteria. Adoption of the integration option was strongly recommended. Additionally, a series of positioning propositions was developed which reflected market needs, stressed Ahlstrom's strengths, and established key points of differentiation from competitors.

Although the basic positioning propositions had been accepted by the newly-formed board of Ahlstrom Machinery, it was clearly essential that the key messages should also command the support of regional and product line managers.

A program of 40 personal interviews was subsequently undertaken to meet this overall objective. The program also served as a means of obtaining reactions to the Ahlstrom Machinery concept and its organization.

The Ahlstrom project demonstrates how the findings of research can be used as an integral part of the development and implementation of a client's business and marketing strategy. BPRI believes that what started as an international industrial research project demonstrated broader implications. First, the basic principles are the same whether you are selling capital goods or consumer goods. Even when the number of units sold annually is limited, as with Ahlstrom, there is still a need for a coordinated marketing approach and more basic requirements, such as finding out what the customer thinks. Second, the project showed that research can play a major role in helping clients make significant strategic decisions and can assist in the development of an organizational structure.

Source: Adapted from David Willen, "How Ahlstrom's Multi-country Survey Defined Positioning," *Business Marketing Digest* 16, no. 3 (3rd quarter 1991): 47–52.

within Tasty Burgers. This will help avoid duplication of effort by both Tasty Burgers and the external agency.

Summary

This chapter gives an overview of the process of international marketing research, focusing on the issues that are specific to international marketing research. It emphasizes the vast difference between domestic and international marketing research. The problems that are faced by researchers in data collection and other stages bear testimony to this fact. In addition, this chapter provides general information and statistics on the international marketing research industry. It is observed that nearly half of the revenue earned by the top 25 marketing research firms comes from international marketing research. In the past there has also been a move for top marketing research firms to form strategic alliances to gain entry into the global market. There has been a steady growth in international marketing research expenditure by firms all over the world.

Questions and Problems

1. What are the important issues that need to be addressed when conducting marketing research in a foreign country?
2. What are the factors that add to the complexity of international marketing research?
3. What are the steps to be taken in coordinating international research?
4. Sketch a marketing plan for Tasty Burgers to market their product in Argentina.

Endnotes

1. Milan Jurse, "Organizing Information for Effective International Industrial Marketing Management," *How to Do It: Managing the Process*, 193–211.
2. Michael D. Hutt and Thomas W. Speh, *Business Marketing Management*, 5th ed. (Orlando, FL: The Dryden Press, 1994).
3. Ken Grofton, "Europe is Beckoning," *Marketing* (27 June 1991): 28–30.
4. Jane Kalim, "Quality Standards: The Push-Me-Pull-You of Marketing Research," *Identifying the Gap*, 11–26.
5. Thomas T. Semon, "Red Tape is Chief Problem in Multinational Research," *Marketing News* 28, no. 4 (14 February 1994): 7.
6. Lorna L. Wright, Henry W. Lane, and Paul W. Beamish, "International Management Research: Lessons From the Field," *Interna-*

tional Studies of Management and Organization 18, no. 3 (fall 1988): 55–71.

7. Jane Kalim, "Quality Standards: The Push-Me-Pull-You of Marketing Research," *Identifying the Gap,* 11–26.

8. Carol Coutts, "Quality Standards in International Research—A Review of Current Practices," *Identifying the Gap,* 27–47.

9. Katherine Passerieu, "What Changes Will be Needed Within the Research Agency?—Radical Change, Evaluation or Head Down?" *Identifying the Gap,* 49–64.

10. Jan Oostveen and Joost Wouters, "The ESOMAR Annual Market Study: The State of the Art of Marketing Research," *Marketing & Research Today* 19, no. 4 (November 1991): 214–218.

11. Kazuo Kobayashi and Peter Draper, "Reviews of Market Research in Japan," *Journal of Advertising Research* (April/May 1990): 13–18.

12. E. H. Demby, "ESOMAR Urges Changes in Reporting Demographics, Issues Worldwide Report," *Marketing News* (8 January 1990): 24–25.

13. Earl Naumann, Donald W. Jackson, Jr., and William G. Wolfe, "Examining the Practices of United States and Japanese Marketing Research Firms," *California Management Review* (summer 1994): 49–69.

14. Jack Honomichl, "1998 Honomichl Business Report on the Marketing Research Industry," *Marketing News* 32, no. 17 (17 August 1998): H4.

15. Ibid.

16. Peter Chisnall, *Marketing Research,* 5th ed. (Berkshire, England: McGraw-Hill Publications, 1997), 269.

17. Anonymous, "Marketing Guide-Market Research," *Marketing* (13 April 1998): 31–34.

18. Jean Quatressooz, "Coordinating International Research Projects—Easy to Say But …," *How to Do It: Managing the Process,* 233–245.

CHAPTER

International Marketing Research Process

INTRODUCTION

International marketing research process provides a systematic, planned approach to the research project and ensures that all aspects are consistent with one another.[1] Research studies evolve through a series of steps, each representing the answer to a key question. Some of the questions that the firm or the researcher should ask include the following:

1. *Why* should research be done?
2. *What* research should be done?
3. *What* are the firm's long-term goals on globalization?
4. *Is it worth* doing the research?
5. *What* information is needed?
6. *How* should the necessary information be obtained?
7. *How* should the research study be designed?
8. *How* can the data be analyzed and interpreted?

The objective of this chapter is to take the reader through the process of international marketing research and explain the logic behind the sequence of steps as depicted in Figure 3-1.

RESEARCH OBJECTIVE

The first step in the research process is to decide why the research should be done—the research purpose. At this stage, most research problems are poorly defined, only partially understood, and do not have a lot of decision alternatives. It is in the best interest of the firm and the researcher to be sure that the research purpose is fully understood. The research purpose comprises a shared understanding (between the manager and the researcher) of the following:

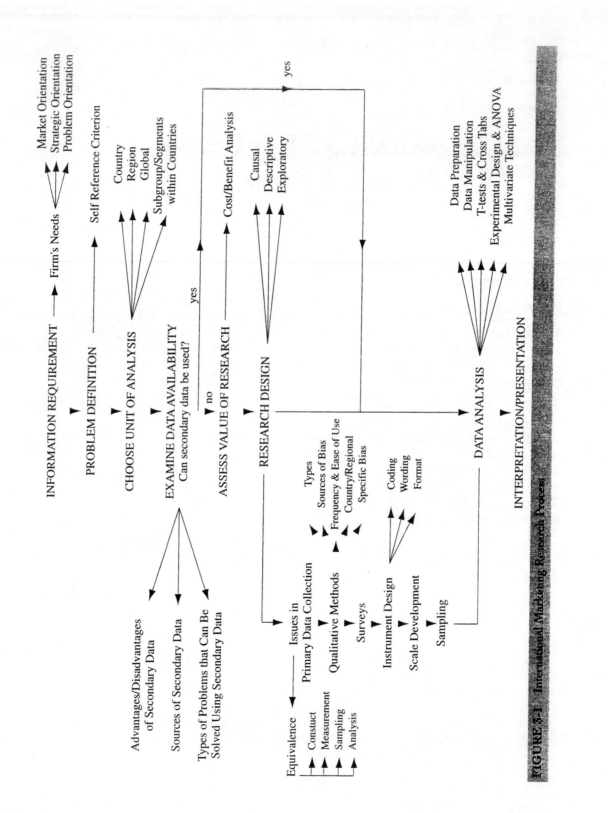

FIGURE 3-1 International Marketing Research Process

1. Problems or opportunities to be studied
   - Which problems or opportunities are anticipated?
   - What is the scope of the problems and the possible reasons?
2. Decision alternatives to be evaluated
   - What are the alternatives being studied?
   - What are the criteria for choosing among alternatives?
   - What is the timing or importance of the decision?
3. Users of the research results
   - Who are the decision makers?
   - Are there any covert purposes?

PROBLEM OR OPPORTUNITY ANALYSIS

Research is often motivated by a problem or opportunity. The firm commissioning the research could be planning on entering a foreign market for the first time, such as McDonald's setting up franchises in China. The firm could be planning to market a new product in another country, like Procter & Gamble introducing disposable diapers in a country where they have already been marketing their haircare products for decades. There could be a sudden drop in sales in a foreign territory. A competitor could be weaning away market share. Any one of these problems could prompt a company to undertake a marketing research study. It is important that the company executives communicate the exact nature of the problem and the decisions they need to make to the researcher. The manager also needs to make sure that the real problem is being addressed. Sometimes the recognized problem is only a symptom or a part of a larger problem. A separate exploratory research project may have to be conducted to isolate the real problem. Exploratory research is explained in detail later in this chapter.

DECISION ALTERNATIVES

It is necessary for the researcher to recognize the fact that the research study has to aid in making decisions. When there are no decision alternatives or when the research results will not have any impact on the decision, the research will have no practical value. The researcher should always be sensitive to the fact that the research can be an exercise in futility and should call a halt when this becomes a certainty. The researcher can clarify the research purpose by asking the following questions:

- What are the alternative actions being considered?
- What are the possible actions that can be taken given the feasible outcomes of the research?

It is also important for the researcher to understand how the decision makers will choose among alternatives. The researcher needs to discuss all possible criteria with the decision makers and choose the one that is most appropriate. The researcher also needs to consider how crucial the decision is to the firm. In today's dynamic global economy, it is very important for companies to time their decisions well. A delay in the decision could mean competition gets ahead and corners a huge chunk of the market share.

RESEARCH USERS

It is very important for the researcher to know who the decision makers are and what they expect of the research project. This will give the researchers a better understanding of the research objective and help them develop a more realistic research proposal. Talking to all of the decision makers will also help the researcher decide if the study is being conducted for covert and sometimes illegitimate reasons.

INFORMATION REQUIREMENT

The next step is to isolate the main issue that needs to be tackled and decide on the information needed to solve the problem. An example would be the efforts of Procter & Gamble to introduce disposable diapers in India. There are a lot of decisions that need to be made by Procter & Gamble in this scenario—how big is the market, what is the ideal price, how can the product be distributed, what promotion strategy should be adopted, etc. At this stage of the research process, the researcher should focus on the main issue—is there a market for disposable diapers in India? Many companies have failed in the international market because they have been sidetracked by small issues and ignored the one main problem that needs to be addressed. For instance, when Coca-Cola Company launched Coke in India, they were not able to overcome the popularity of Thumbs-Up, a local brand. To get a foothold in the market Coca-Cola bought out the bottling operations of Thumbs-Up. Despite this, the market share for Coke did not improve. The company failed to take into consideration the powerful brand loyalty commanded by Thumbs-Up and position their product accordingly. Failure to pin down the root cause of the problem can be very costly in international marketing research.

Once the key issue has been identified, it is necessary to define the research objective. The research objective is a statement, in as precise terminology as possible, of what information is needed. This helps the researcher develop hypotheses that are possible answers to the problem under consideration. The research objective also defines the scope of the research.

The research question asks what specific information is needed to achieve the purpose of the research. In the case of Procter & Gamble, the research objective is to determine if there is a market for disposable diapers in India and, if so, whether it is financially viable to market this product. Some of the research questions could be

- What is the main alternative to disposable diapers used by parents currently?
- Are parents familiar with the cost of disposable diapers?
- Are there any other brands of disposable diapers sold in India currently?
- What is the estimated market size?
- What price are the consumers willing to pay for a disposable diaper?

While defining the problem, researchers face one major stumbling block termed self-reference criterion. It is the tendency of researchers to allow their own values and beliefs to bias their opinion of situations in foreign markets. Apple Computer Company introduced its personal computer in Japan in 1977; however, by 1985 Apple still had only a very small share of the market and the company failed to achieve any significant market penetration. Japanese competitors and IBM had begun to market Japanese-language machines. The Apple computer could only be used by Japanese who understood English very well, thus its market was limited to a small group.[2] It is easy for an American to take the knowledge of English for granted, but to do so in a market like Japan spells disaster for the marketing strategy. It is crucial in international marketing research that the researchers keep an open mind and try to study the problem from the point of view of the foreign market.

The next step in the process is to decide on the information required by the firm to make decisions regarding globalization. There are a number of options available to companies that want to go international. The simplest way would be to export the products to the target country. Some firms (such as McDonald's) decide to license or franchise. Some companies prefer to set up partly or wholly owned subsidiaries. ICI, Britain's largest manufacturing company and one of the world's largest chemical companies, is an excellent example of a foreign-based global company with several business units outside the home country.[3] The researcher should be clear about the motives of the company before designing the study.

The second category of information required will aid in making decisions concerning the strategic orientation of the company. The strategic orientation of the company helps work out the expansion plans in an international market. Some companies look upon their international operations as merely a way of dealing with excess production in their domestic market. These firms do not devise any special strategies for their international markets. Some other companies, however, cater to the specific needs of the foreign markets they operate in. They have independent marketing plans for these markets. Most big car manufacturers follow this policy. They manufacture automobiles keeping in mind the specific needs of the market.

The third category of information required helps find solutions to specific problems like pricing policy, positioning of the product, and the promotional aspects. The researcher will do well to have a clear definition of the problem that needs to be solved. In this stage of the research process, the researcher should watch out for the pitfall of self-reference criterion, previously mentioned. For instance, if Procter & Gamble decided to send an American researcher to India to study the market for disposable diapers, a lot of Indians still use old fashioned alternatives and it would be erroneous for the researcher to assume that every parent is familiar with a disposable diaper. Self-reference criterion can cause researchers to miss out on important problems and lead to fundamental flaws in the research design.

UNIT OF ANALYSIS

One of the most important aspects of international marketing research is deciding on the unit of analysis. The term originates because this is the basic unit considered in the statistical analysis. In an international marketing research problem it is important for a researcher to have a clear idea of the unit of analysis, both at the macro level and micro level. Macro-level units comprise larger segments, such as countries and cities. Micro-level units may consist of firms, customers, and specific market segments. Unit of analysis would also help researchers define the geographic scope analysis. The problem could involve looking for information all over the world, in certain regions or country groupings, or in specific countries or specific cities. Each of these factors is defined as a unit of analysis.

The additional problem faced by researchers in international marketing research projects is in defining a country. Depending on the research problem definition, the country can be defined as a political unit, an economic unit, an organizational unit, a cultural unit, or a linguistic unit. For instance, if the study involves understanding the spending habits of double income families in the United States and the United Kingdom, the unit of analysis would be the individual households. However, if the study were interested in determining if there is any difference in the spending habits of these households in the two countries, the unit of analysis would be the countries themselves. The difference would be the data used in the two cases. In the second case, the average spending for the double income households in both the countries would be considered.

One problem that arises in international marketing research is the definition of various units of analysis. Consider an example of a cosmetic firm wanting to enter several countries simultaneously. The firm wants to target urban working women and asks the researcher to study the market potential in all of these countries. This sounds simple enough until the researcher actually gets down to working on a sampling procedure. How is urban defined? Figure 3-2 gives the definition of urban in various countries around the world. The researcher has to find a way of obtaining equivalent data from each country while meeting the requirements of the sponsor. This is one of the areas where international marketing research differs substantially from domestic research.

Based on the definitions of "urban," the company will have to make a decision regarding how the target markets are to be grouped. If the countries are significantly different from one another with respect to the product, each has to be treated as a separate entity. The country is the most commonly used unit of analysis in international marketing. If there is a reasonable similarity, then these countries can be grouped as one region. For instance, while testing for brand awareness of Coca-Cola, research is done on a global level. Disney, the U.S.-based entertainment company, builds theme parks all over the world. However, the concepts used by them are such that they can be adapted around the world. In some cases, it becomes necessary to devise different marketing plans for different market segments. When launching baby diapers worldwide, Procter & Gamble discovered that Japanese mothers had different needs. Japanese mothers changed their babies' diapers so frequently, thick absorbent diapers were not necessary.[4] Instead, Procter & Gamble designed thin diapers that took up less space in Japanese homes. Similarly, Pepsico uses a different definition of consumption across various countries. In Mexico, Venezuela, and Argentina, the consumers are asked how much of the product was consumed the day prior to the interview. In Germany and Spain the question is based on the number of drinks consumed in a day or a week.[5] It is possible for a company to target specific subgroups within countries. Catholic French-Canadian teenagers are, for example, members of the Catholic subculture and also the French-Canadian subculture. Due to the differences between countries and the nature of the product, companies have different market orientations. This makes it necessary for the researcher to choose the unit of analysis for conducting the study.

Country	Definition of Urban
Albania	Localities of 400 or more inhabitants
Argentina	Localities of 2,000 or more inhabitants
Bermuda	Entire Country
Canada	Areas with 1,000 or more inhabitants and a population density of 400 or more per square kilometer
Congo	Localities of 5,000 or more inhabitants
Denmark	Localities of 200 or more inhabitants
Germany	Localities of 2,000 or more inhabitants
India	Localities of 7,000 or more inhabitants
Japan	Cities (shi) having 50,000 or more inhabitants with 60 percent or more of the houses located in the main built-up areas and 60 percent or more of the population (including their dependents) engaged in manufacturing trade, or other urban type of business. Alternatively, a shi having urban facilities and conditions as defined by the prefectural order is considered urban
Kenya	Agglomerations of at least 2,000 inhabitants
Kuwait	Localities of 10,000 or more inhabitants
Nigeria	Localities of 20,000 or more inhabitants
Norway	Localities of 200 or more inhabitants
Singapore	Entire Country
Switzerland	Localities of 10,000 or more inhabitants
Uganda	Localities of 100 or more inhabitants
USA	Urbanized areas or places of 2,500 or more inhabitants

FIGURE 3-2   Definitions of *Urban*, by Country

Source: Adapted from *World Population 1983* (Washington, D.C.: U.S. Bureau of Census, 1983), 577–86, and Susan P. Douglas and C. Samuel Craig, *International Marketing Research* (Englewood Cliffs, NJ: Prentice Hall, 1983), 80.

DATA AVAILABILITY

Once the unit of analysis has been identified, researchers need to start collecting data. Although data may not be available for all the variables that interest the researcher, secondary data are available from private and public sources at a fraction of the cost for obtaining the primary data. Though it is not possible to list all of the sources of secondary data, some sources are banks, consultants, chambers of commerce, and trade journals. The Internet has now become a powerful tool to obtain secondary data with very little investment of time and money. Secondary data are particularly useful in evaluating country or market environments, whether in making initial market entry decisions or in attempting to assess future trends and developments. The three major uses of secondary data in international marketing research can be summarized as follows:

1. Selecting countries or markets that merit in-depth investigation
2. Making an initial estimate of demand potential in the target market
3. Monitoring environmental change

However, there are some problems associated with the use of secondary data. They can be outdated and inaccurate. It may not always be possible to compare data collected from different countries. The researcher may not be able to find all the data required to complete the study. Chapter 5 explains in detail all aspects of secondary data with regard to international marketing research.

RESEARCH DESIGN

Secondary data are used to arrive at initial hypotheses about the research project. These tentative conclusions are used to conduct a cost-benefit analysis. If the study proves to be financially viable, the researcher starts working on the research design. The choice of the research approach depends on the nature of the research.[6] The types of research can be classified under three broad categories:

1. Exploratory research
2. Descriptive research
3. Causal research

Exploratory research is used when one is seeking insight into the general nature of the problem, the possible decision alternatives, and the relevant variables that need to be considered. A large proportion of marketing research is *descriptive research*. The purpose of descriptive research is to provide an accurate snapshot of some aspect of the market environment. When it is necessary to go beyond inferring that two or more variables are related and the researcher has to show that one variable causes or determines the values of other variables, a *causal research* approach must be used. Chapter 7 focuses on primary data collection techniques and explains in detail the three types of research mentioned here.

An important aspect of this textbook is the extensive coverage of marketing research on the Internet. International marketing research typically requires very high investment in terms of time and money. Due to the paucity of information and lack of understanding of foreign cultures, researchers have to spend a lot of time and resources to gather data and analyze it. The Internet is a very cheap and extensive source of information. Before starting on primary data collection, researchers can locate information about the region of interest and gather useful information, such as the market size and presence of local and global competition. This information might help eliminate many countries in the early stages of the research process. After potential markets have been identified, researchers can then proceed to the next stage. This will help save a lot of time and resources. One word of caution, though—the Internet is still in its infancy and there is no way of checking on the validity of available data and the authenticity of the source; hence, Internet data should be backed by secondary data from traditional sources. Chapter 6 gives a detailed account of the Internet and its uses in international marketing research. Some of the statistics presented in chapter 6 clearly indicate that the Internet is the research tool for the future—for both primary and secondary research.

ISSUES IN PRIMARY DATA COLLECTION

Primary data has to be collected to proceed with the research process. One of the issues that needs to be dealt with in international marketing research is the equivalence of data. First, it has to be ascertained whether the constructs being studied are equivalent. Second, the equivalence of the measures of the concepts being studied has to be assessed. Finally, the equivalence of the sample studied in each country or culture has to be taken into consideration. Figure 3-3 gives a brief description of the three critical types of equivalencies that should be taken into account in international marketing research. These concepts are discussed in later chapters in connection with the research stages that they are applicable to.

QUALITATIVE METHODS

As mentioned earlier in the chapter, exploratory research requires qualitative data collection methods, as it is unstructured and needs data that deal with feelings, attitudes, and past behavior. Qualitative methods are classified into three broad categories: observational methods, projective techniques, and interviews.

Observational techniques are based on watching how respondents behave. In most cases, the respondents are not aware that they are being watched. Sample sizes vary depending on the type of observation and the research subject. Projective techniques require the respondents to perform a specific task, like word association, sentence completion, or interpretation of an action or a picture. In the interview method the respondent is required to verbalize his or her opinion. Qualitative and observational methods are discussed in depth in chapter 8.

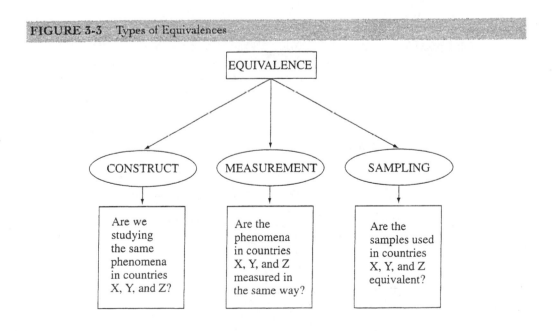

FIGURE 3-3   Types of Equivalences

In any of the previously mentioned types of data collection, there are several sources of bias. The researcher working in a foreign country may not be completely in tune with the environment. Several national and cultural differences can come into play, as discussed in chapter 1. Language differences make it difficult for researchers to translate their intentions verbatim in the foreign language. Chapter 7 deals specifically with collection of primary data and the problems associated with the process.

SURVEYS AND INSTRUMENT DESIGN

Surveys are a popular means of collecting primary data and are conducted using questionnaires that can be self-administered or administered by an interviewer in-person or over the telephone. The first step in designing the questionnaire is to determine the information that needs to be obtained. Information collected through questionnaires can be classified under three major categories: demographic data, behavioral data, and psychographic or lifestyle data. The researcher needs to determine whether the questions should be open-ended or close-ended. It is also necessary to ensure that the translation of the questionnaire in several languages will impart the same meaning to the respondents to ensure comparability of the data.

An important aspect of questionnaire design has been the use of scales to obtain information on attitudes, preferences, and behaviors of the respondents. Scaling is the process of creating a continuum on which the objects are located according to the amount of the measured characteristic they possess. The different types of scales being used are as follows:

- A *nominal scale* is one where the only property is identity and any comparisons of numbers are meaningless. The categories represent mutually exclusive objects and the only operation that can be performed on these kinds of scales is the total count of each category. An example would be the sex or marital status of respondents.
- An *ordinal scale* is one where categories are ranked and arranged in order with regard to some common variable. The only information available about the categories is that there is more or less of a given variable. The amount of difference between the objects is not known. The finishing order of a horse race illustrates this kind of a scale.
- In an *interval scale* the numbers used to rank the objects also represent equal increments of the attribute being measured. The differences between the objects can be compared.
- The *ratio scale* is a kind of interval scale that has a meaningful zero point. This is the only scale that permits comparisons of absolute magnitude.

For an international marketing researcher, the challenge of questionnaire design does not end with choosing the type of scale to be used. In countries where the educational level is low, researchers need to use innovative means to convey the intentions of the survey to the respondents. Researchers also need to watch out for typical tendencies of the respondents that introduce biases in the survey. As mentioned earlier, studies have shown that Japanese tend to be neutral and hence the scale should be designed without a neutral point to force a response from them. On scales measuring lifestyle attributes, Latin Americans tend to overstate their responses; hence the scale should be suitably toned down. Refer to chapter 9 for a detailed explanation of survey methods.

SAMPLING

The first step in sampling is to determine the level at which the sampling is to be conducted; that is, determine the key decision makers for the purchase decision of the product involved. For instance, if the survey is about marketing a cake mix, housewives should be contacted. The next step is to decide the sampling frame. In the international context, getting a list of populations for the sampling frame can present a problem. Telephones are not so widespread in most countries, and the less developed nations do not have comprehensive electoral lists from which the researchers can draw a list of names. More often than not, researchers resort to nonprobability sampling. The researcher then decides on the geographic level at which the sampling is done. The idea is to ensure that all heterogeneous groups in the population will be adequately represented. There are various sampling techniques. They can be broadly classified as nonprobability and probability sampling. Nonprobability sampling includes convenience sampling, judgmental sampling, quota sampling, and snowball sampling. Probability sampling includes simple random sampling, stratified sampling, and cluster sampling. Each of these methods is discussed in detail in chapter 12, which is devoted to sampling.

DATA ANALYSIS

In a multicountry research study the first step in data analysis is preparing the data. The data needs to be coded and edited and the researcher should ensure the quality and reliability of the data. During this stage the researcher checks for ambiguity, interviewer error, inconsistency, lack of cooperation, and ineligible responses. The main issue in coding is to ensure that data are as comparable as possible across samples to aid in multicountry analysis. Once the data has been coded and edited, the researcher has to examine the reliability of the data. The researcher then conducts within-country and across-country analysis. For the purpose of analyzing data, as in domestic research, univariate or multivariate techniques can be used. The various univariate techniques used in data analysis are cross-tabulation, t-tests, and analysis of variance. The different multivariate techniques are analysis of covariance, regression analysis, discriminant analysis, conjoint analysis, cluster analysis, factor analysis, and multidimensional scaling. These topics will be considered in detail in chapters 13 and 14, dealing with simple and advanced data analysis.

INTERPRETATION AND PRESENTATION

The final stage of the research process is very important because here the researchers convey the results of the survey to the decision makers of the firm who commissioned it. The researchers apply their vast knowledge and experience to use the information obtained during the data collection and analysis stages and arrive at conclusions that will aid the decision-making process. The presentation can be written or oral depending on the client preferences. Chapter 16 deals in detail with the finer points of presenting a research study and its results.

NEED FOR INTERNATIONAL MARKETING RESEARCH[7]

Defining the research problem accurately is probably the most important step in any marketing research project, and even more so in international marketing research. Some of the giants of present times have committed marketing blunders—all because marketing research was not conducted accurately. Coca-Cola's classic blunder as explained below stands out as one that will be used time and again to illustrate the importance of marketing research.

Market share for Coke had begun dropping in the 1970s despite widespread advertising and superior distribution. The company then turned to the product itself to look for reasons for this drop in market share. There was strong evidence that taste accounted for this decline. Blind tests had been conducted and the results showed that people preferred Pepsi to Coke. As a consequence, Project Kansas was launched with the objective of scrapping the original formula. Approximately 2,000 people in 10 major markets were interviewed to find out if they would be willing to accept a different Coke. Research showed that most people were more favorable toward a sweeter, less fizzy cola that had a sticky taste due to high sugar content. Blind taste tests were conducted once again and this time the reaction for the new Coke was overwhelming. The majority of the people subjected to this test preferred the new Coke to Pepsi.

The new Coke was launched on April 23, 1985. Word spread quickly. Within 24 hours millions around the world were aware that the Coke formula had been changed. Early results indicated that the response to the new flavor was fantastic. Coke was selling like it never had before.

This success, however, was short-lived. Complaints started trickling in and within a month became a torrent. Media publicity added to the fervor and soon Americans began talking of an old friend who had suddenly betrayed them. Sales for the new Coke started dropping and bottlers began demanding the return of the old Coke.

Finally, on the 11th of July, within four months of introducing the new flavor, the company executives apologized to the public for withdrawing the old Coke. The message was that those who enjoyed the taste of new Coke could continue to do so and those who wanted the old Coke would get it back. The reaction was very favorable and even Wall Street was happy.

This blunder could be blamed on improper marketing research. The decision to introduce the new flavor was based solely on the results of blind taste tests; however, the participants were not told that choosing one flavor would mean they would lose the other. Hence, the test failed to include the emotional attachment that consumers have toward the 99-year-old formula. The target segment that was represented heavily in the taste test, youth, in general prefer sweeter flavors. The researchers overlooked this. The researchers also overlooked the fact that preference for sweet things tends to diminish with use. The taste test focused on the flavor but failed to consider the emotional appeal that the original formula held for the American public.

Gillette committed a similar blunder in the Middle East by launching their shaving products. Despite heavy promotions, there was no improvement in sales. It was only when the product failed that the company realized most men in Middle Eastern countries do not shave.

These examples illustrate the importance of researching a market before deciding to enter. The Coke example is a reminder to researchers how important it is to consider all aspects of a problem and design the research methodology in such a manner that it covers all of these angles.

INTERNATIONAL MARKETING RESEARCH IN PRACTICE

Tasty Burgers will have to define their research problem and work with the research agency to develop the research objectives and formulate a research plan. The first step is to define the research problem. For Tasty Burgers, the objective is to enter international markets that are profitable and present good growth potential. The research question will address specific issues, such as the profit margins that can be expected from various countries, the growth potential in each of these markets, and how to address policies regarding product, pricing, and promotions in each of these markets. An important question that needs to be addressed in this stage is whether the products offered by Tasty Burgers should be standardized or whether they should be customized to suit the local tastes. Decisions should also be made as to whether Tasty Burgers will follow a standardized marketing program; that is, use the same marketing strategies that are being used in the United States or design custom strategies for each separate market. This is called the strategic orientation of the company.

As a first step, the research agency will collect secondary data for all of the markets that Tasty Burgers is interested in. Analyses of secondary data will provide information to shortlist some countries. Information required by Tasty Burgers falls into the following major categories:

- *Customer information:* the consumption patterns, dining out habits, food preferences, religious sentiments that may prohibit consumers from eating certain types of food, and so on
- *Competitor information:* the distribution network, pricing and promotion policies, relations with key suppliers, and so on
- *Country information:* the political risk, the legal system, terms of ownership and repatriation of profits, availability of real estate and competent workforce, investment benefits such as tax breaks, and so on

After the countries have been selected, a cost benefit analysis is done by researchers to justify the costs incurred in conducting the research study. An estimate of profits that can be earned will be weighed against the costs of conducting the research. A decision is made to proceed with the research only if the benefits meet the required standards of Tasty Burgers.

Primary research is undertaken in all the countries that have been selected. The objective of primary research is to gather data to answer all of the research questions. The method of data collection has to be decided depending on the country and culture.

Data that has been collected will then be coded and analyzed. The data analysis technique depends on the quantity and quality of data and the nature of the research problem. Results are interpreted and presented to the client, Tasty Burgers, in the format that was decided upon in the initial stages.

Each chapter in this textbook will deal with relevant sections of this example. Each of the stages mentioned above will be discussed in depth to provide readers with a thorough understanding of the international marketing research process.

Summary

The idea of this chapter is to give the reader a bird's eye view of the international marketing research process. Each of the stages mentioned in this chapter is explained in detail in the successive chapters. The purpose of this chapter is to act like a roadmap, giving the readers a better idea of where they stand as they progress through this textbook. The research purpose is to better define the problem and identify the possible decision alternatives that can be delved into. This is made concrete by writing down the research objective, which defines the scope of the research. The research question enumerates specific information needed to solve the problem. Secondary research helps gather data that is already available so that researchers can further their understanding of the research problem. The next step in the process is gathering primary data. There are many ways primary research data can be collected, such as qualitative research, observation, and surveys. The final stage in the research process is analyzing the data that has been collected and summarizing it in such a manner that it helps decision making.

Questions and Problems

1. Is a research design always necessary before a research study can be conducted?

2. In what ways do exploratory, descriptive, and causal research designs differ? How will these differences influence the relative importance of each research approach at each phase of the marketing program development process described in chapter 1?

3. Smith Computers, Inc., a U.S.-based manufacturer of personal computers has developed a microcomputer, using the new Pentium microchip technology, but at a fraction of the cost of its competitors. The company has an in-house marketing research department and a study has been ordered to assist in developing the marketing program for this product.

    a. Which type of research would be most appropriate for this study?

    b. What are the possible errors that could be made in designing the research project?

    c. The research department has also been given the task of identifying foreign market opportunities for this product. What critical issues must be considered in formulating the research design?

4. What possible problems might be encountered by a domestic research company conducting an international research study?

5. a. How is a cost-benefit analysis useful to management in deciding whether or not to conduct a marketing research study?

   b. What are the two approaches to budgeting for a market research project?

   c. For what situation is each approach most suitable?

6. Sugar Land Creamery is planning to launch its operations in West Europe and South Asia. Does SLC need to create a new menu for each region? What are the specific aspects of the regional cuisine that need to be considered if Sugar Land Creamery wants to develop a unique menu for each region? What type of research design is appropriate? Develop the research purpose, research questions, and hypothesis.

Endnotes

1. This section adapted from David A. Aaker, V. Kumar, and George S. Day, *Marketing Research*, 6th ed. (New York: John Wiley & Sons, 1998).

2. Jean-Pierre Jeannet and Hubert D. Hennessey, *Global Marketing Strategies*, 4th ed. (Boston: Houghton Mifflin Company, 1998), 9–10.

3. Ibid., 17.

4. Susan P. Douglas and Samuel C. Craig, *International Marketing Research*, (Englewood Cliffs, NJ: Prentice Hall, 1983), 33–35.

5. Jean-Pierre Jeannet and Hubert D. Hennessey, *Global Marketing Strategies*, 4th ed. (Boston: Houghton Mifflin Company, 1998), 185.

6. This section is adapted from *Essentials of Marketing Research* 1st ed. by V. Kumar, David A. Aaker, and George S. Day, (New York: John Wiley & Sons, 1999).

7. Robert F. Hartley, *Marketing Mistakes and Successes*, 7th ed. (New York: John Wiley & Sons, 1998), 160–175.

CHAPTER

Preliminary Stages
of the Research Process

4

INTRODUCTION

Chapters 1 and 2 discussed the differences among different cultures and nationalities that make international marketing research complex and challenging. Chapter 3 discussed the process of international marketing research. This chapter focuses on the preliminary stages of the research process. Research is an integral part of any company wanting to go global. Even before the decision to enter foreign markets is made, research helps determine if internationalization is a viable option for the company. Research also helps decide which markets to enter and when and how to enter these markets. Most companies base their product launching and pricing decisions on market research. Each of these aspects of research is dealt with in detail in this chapter.

INFORMATION REQUIREMENTS FOR
INTERNATIONAL MARKETING DECISIONS

International marketing research has often been called *comparative marketing research*, with its principle focus being *the systematic detection, identification, classification, measurement, and interpretation of similarities and differences among entire national systems*. There are five main challenges any marketing manager faces in planning international marketing research:

1. Understanding similarities across countries so as to define a target market
2. A lack of accurate secondary information
3. The high costs of conducting research, especially when primary data is desired
4. Coordinating research across countries, which involves losing control of not only the research process but translations as well
5. Establishing comparability and equivalence in marketing research instruments

Against a background of diversity and change in the strategy and structure of international businesses, information needs are extremely varied. Three broad areas can be identified in which research inputs can be valuable: market orientation, strategic orientation, and problem orientation.[1]

MARKET ORIENTATION

One of the more common uses of marketing research in international ventures is in the screening and identification of potential country markets for possible entry. At this initial stage of its internationalization process a company needs to shortlist and identify one or two potential target markets to enter and decide on the mode of entry.

Internationalization Process[2]

A key factor in determining why firms go international is the type and quality of management. A dynamic management is important when firms take their first international steps. Over the long term, success of a firm in international markets depends on the commitment, attitudes, and perceptions of the management. Researchers have shown that aggressive firms with a long-term view of the business are active in a larger number. Because international markets cannot be penetrated overnight and require vast amounts of market development activity, market research, and sensitivity to foreign market factors, the issue of managerial commitment is crucial. It has also been shown that in most cases, managers of global firms show a higher level of formal education and foreign language fluency than do managers of domestic firms.

However, one factor alone cannot account for success in international markets. Usually a mixture of factors results in firms taking steps in a given direction. These factors are differentiated as proactive and reactive motivations. Proactive motivations represent stimuli to attempt strategic change and include profit advantage, technological advantage, exclusive market information, managerial urge, tax benefits, and economies of scale. Reactive motivations could be in the form of competitive pressures, overproduction in the domestic market, stable or declining sales in the domestic market, excess capacity, saturation in the domestic market, and proximity to customers and ports.

Market Selection

To provide a preliminary understanding of a market or range of markets in one or more countries, only rather limited background data are usually required. Such information would cover

- market size and trends
- market structure/segmentation
- names of companies operating in market (both suppliers and buyers) with indication of their importance
- list of products and prices
- distribution channels
- media availability and rates

Desk research, using published or other easily available sources, is normally adequate for the purpose. Not only are the statistical series of governments and international bodies becoming more numerous and relevant, but also the range of market surveys published by trade associations, chambers of commerce, financial concerns, government trade/commerce departments, the media, consultants, and so on is becoming increasingly wide. A number of commercial organizations offer such market analyses on a regular, syndicated basis at low prices.

Add to these sources the judicious use of trade directories, trade and financial press, and, possibly, information already in the firm, and it is not surprising that companies often feel capable of handling this first market orientation themselves. Market research suppliers are rarely involved at this stage. A more detailed discussion on conducting international marketing research using secondary data can be found in chapter 5 of this book.

Mode of Entry

The nature of a firm's operation in a country market depends on its choice of mode of entry.[3] A mode of entry is an institutional arrangement chosen by the firm to operate in the foreign market. This decision is one of the most critical strategic decisions for the firm; it affects all of the future decisions and operations of the firm in that country market. Because each mode of entry entails a concomitant level of resource commitment, it is difficult to change from one entry mode to another without considerable loss of time and money. The contingency model of decision making consists of a series of stages, as shown in Figure 4-1.

While there is a need for research to determine how to enter or operate in different markets, the degree of interest and commitment to international operations will determine how much time and effort management is willing to spend in investigating foreign market potential and the most appropriate mode of operation. Modes of entry into foreign markets can be broadly classified into four major categories: exporting, licensing (and other forms of contractual agreements), joint ventures, and wholly owned subsidiaries.[4,5]

The first stage of the model involves recognizing the problem and defining it. In the second stage the decision makers ask questions such as, "What factors that affect the modes of entry have to be considered?" and "Where can information on these factors be obtained?" This is the stage where international marketing research comes into play. In stage three managers select the mode of entry with the basic information on hand. In the fourth stage, decision makers collect and process information consistent with the decision strategy they have selected. Some strategies may involve elaborate and costly information collection and processing while some may be based on simple heuristics. The final stage is the actual decision as to which mode of entry to use when entering a foreign market.

Exporting   In the initial stages of its internationalization process, companies typically export indirectly, filling unsolicited orders from abroad via their domestic sales organization. Consequently, little research is likely to be conducted in relation to international markets. More deliberate focus on foreign markets and more effective penetration of international market potential, however, requires a shift to a mode of opera-

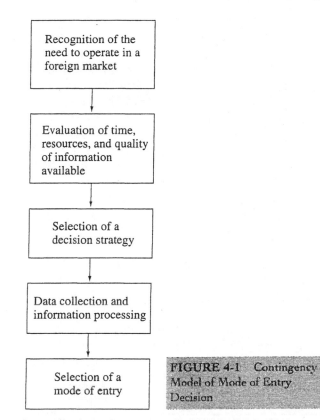

FIGURE 4-1 Contingency Model of Mode of Entry Decision

Source: From "A Contingency Framework for the Mode Entry Decision" by V. Kumar and Velavan Subramaniam from *Journal of World Business*, Vol. 32, No. 1, Spring 1997. Reprinted by permission of JAI Press, Inc.

tion providing more contact with foreign markets, and a greater degree of control over operations in markets abroad. For example, export management companies could be used, a joint venture with a foreign partner, or wholly owned subsidiaries established to market and/or produce the product overseas. Small and medium-sized companies that want to develop export markets without making a substantial commitment of management or financial resources can employ export management companies. These companies arrange the mechanics of exporting, identify markets, find potential buyers, and select distributors. Ultimately, however, as these markets develop, direct contact will need to be established with a separate sales organization for international markets. This then takes over all the complex problems of research to determine which markets to enter, and with what strategy.[6]

Licensing   Licensing, while apparently a low international commitment strategy, also requires research, not only to identify the most appropriate licensee but also, prior to the licensing to decide whether market potential will grow rapidly. In this case, alternative forms of entry, such as joint venture or wholly owned subsidiaries, may be preferred. Franchising, the parallel to licensing in the service industry, also requires research to find potential franchises and to assess how far strategies should be adapted.

Joint Ventures   Joint ventures with local companies in a foreign country also provide a means of reducing the risks associated with foreign market entry. Here, the local partner brings expertise and familiarity with local market conditions. This knowledge reduces the need for research to determine how far products or strategies should be adapted to these conditions. If, however, a company is willing to assume all risks associated with foreign operations, wholly owned subsidiaries may be established. In some cases, these may be independent country units, such as Procter & Gamble's European operations. Research comparable to domestic marketing research is then conducted by the local subsidiary. If, however, products and strategies are to be transferred across national boundaries, some prior research is needed to assess how far standardization will result in loss of market potential.

Wholly Owned Subsidiaries   In other cases, such as in the automobile industry, wholly owned subsidiaries consist of a complex mass of intertwined global operations. The transmissions for the Ford Fiesta were, for example, made in Bordeaux, France; the windshields in Oklahoma; the spark plugs in the United Kingdom; and the bumper-plating in Cologne, Germany. Here, research to establish the global marketing plan and to determine how far programs and strategies should be standardized or adapted to different national environments is more likely to be directed from corporate or regional headquarters, based on input from local subsidiary management.

STRATEGIC ORIENTATION

Whereas the market orientation phase can help a company establish priorities both between markets and countries, more detailed information is required to develop a strategy for entering or extending a presence in a selected market. Data relevant for such a strategic orientation would include

- market shares (estimates will often be available in published material too)
- product awareness/penetration
- buying motivations
- barriers to change and how to overcome them
- brand/product images
- buyer attitudes and profiles
- competitors' weaknesses
- detailed structure of the distribution system and how to take advantage of it

This more detailed market study and diagnosis generally involves primary research; that is, further data collection designed for the particular client (or group of clients). Such studies, which can follow the desk research phase or be combined with it, usually involve interviewing consumers or end users of the products or services to provide a better "feel" for the market. The interviewing may range from a few contacts with key buyers or decision makers in certain industrial sectors to simple habit and attitude studies in consumer goods markets.

Information obtained to help provide a market or strategy orientation when investigating foreign markets primarily gives a picture of the total market, with limited diagnostic data to help formulate plans in marketing, sales, and distribution.

Expansion Strategy[7]

Most firms begin their operations in the domestic market. Over a period of time, some of them expand into international markets. In looking at the internationalization process, one finds that initially the vast majority of the firms are not at all interested in the international marketplace. Over time, a firm may become a partially interested exporter. Most companies that make a transition from uninterested to partially interested exporters are those that have a track record of domestic market expansion. In the next stage, the firm gradually begins to explore international markets, and management is willing to consider the possibility of exporting. After this exploratory stage, the firm becomes an experimental exporter, usually to psychologically close countries; however, management is still far from being committed to international marketing activities.

At the next stage, the firm evaluates the impact that exporting has had on its general activities. It is possible at this stage for the firm to be disappointed with international markets and to decide to withdraw from international activities. More often, the firm continues to exist as a small exporter. The final stage is that of export adaptation. The firm becomes an experienced exporter to a country and adjusts exports to changing exchange rates, tariffs, and other variables. Management is ready to consider the possibility of exporting to additional countries that are psychologically farther away. Revenues from exporting, which were earlier considered as surprise income, will now become a part of the budget. In these conditions, the firm can be considered as a strategic participant in the international market.

The strategies adopted by firms to enter foreign markets fall under two broad categories: the sprinkler strategy and the waterfall strategy.[8] A firm adopting the sprinkler strategy will decide on which markets it plans to enter and simultaneously enter all of these markets. This is a risky method to adopt because of the high cost involved in entering a foreign market. The waterfall strategy is a more conservative approach in which the firm follows a roll out policy, entering the most profitable market first. Depending on the performance of the product in this market, the firm identifies the next best market for entry. This is a strategy more suited for internationalization. It has generally been observed that new products follow a certain pattern of diffusion. For instance, research has shown that after a product has been introduced and accepted in the United States, the next likely market is Germany.[9] Researchers can study the pattern of product diffusion for a given category of products and decide on the roll out strategy. This way the company has the opportunity to cut losses in any market where its products are not accepted.

An example of the waterfall strategy is the expansion of HEB Pantry Foods into Latin America. Because Latin America has not been a kind market to retailing giants, such as Wal-Mart, HEB decided to adopt a cautious approach. For years, Mexicans have been shopping at HEB stores across the border. HEB has a very high level of customer consciousness and is opening its first transnational outlet in Mexico, with a very different product mix more suited to the market conditions in Mexico. If this proves to be a success, HEB may consider other Latin American countries.

Standardization[10]

The most cost-effective method of marketing products or services worldwide is to use the same program in every country, provided environmental conditions favor such an approach. However, local market characteristics exist that may require some form of local adaptation. One of the challenges of international marketing research is to determine the extent of standardization that may be used. The factors that limit standardization may be categorized into four major groups:

1. *Market characteristics.* The physical environment of a market, like the climate, product use conditions, and population size, often force marketers to make the product fit local conditions. Some of the other factors that affect the extent of standardization are income level, exchange rate fluctuations, language, culture, and social factors.
2. *Industry conditions.* The maturity of the market determines the strategy to be followed for introducing and promoting the product. The level of competition, the level of technology, the varying prices of local substitutes, and local production costs can affect the marketing policy.
3. *Marketing institutions.* Practices in distributions systems, availability of outlets, advertising agencies, and presence or absence of mass media channels can affect the extent of standardization.
4. *Legal restrictions.* It is necessary for companies to follow the standards issued by the local governments. Tariffs and taxes make it necessary for the companies to make price adjustments. Restrictions on advertisements affect promotion plans.

In addition, undertaking marketing research in developing countries is significantly different from the way it is conducted in developed countries. The techniques used are the same; however, the application of certain methods differs.[11]

EPRG Framework[12]

EPRG stands for Ethnocentric, Polycentric, Regiocentric or Geocentric, all of which describe the orientation of the management of a firm towards globalization.[13]

The *ethnocentric orientation* is an assumption or belief that the home country is superior. Someone with this orientation sees similarities and believes that products and practices that succeed in the home country are superior and should, therefore, be used everywhere. Overseas operations of such companies are viewed as secondary to domestic and primarily as a means of disposing of surplus domestic production. There is no systematic research conducted overseas and there are no major modifications to products.

The *polycentric orientation* is the belief that each host country is unique and to succeed in each country the firm needs to adapt to each country's unique differences. In this stage, subsidiaries are established overseas and they operate independently. Marketing is organized on a country-to-country basis, with each country having its own unique marketing policy.

In the *regiocentric* or *geocentric orientation*, the company views the region or the whole world as a market and seeks to develop an integrated marketing plan. In this stage, the company sees similarities and differences in markets and countries and seeks to create a global strategy that is fully responsive to local needs and wants. The regiocentric orientation is a geocentric orientation that is limited to a region.

The ethnocentric company is centralized, the polycentric company is decentralized, and the regiocentric or geocentric company is integrated.

PROBLEM ORIENTATION

The third category of information needs brings us to research studies designed specifically to aid in the making of particular decisions. Often, such studies focus only on one or more key elements in the market mix, such as product formulation, price, advertising, package design, or promotions; however, they sometimes involve assessment, directly or indirectly, of the total market or sector through the collection of data to help in market segmentation, target group identification, and detailed brand positioning. New concept or product development work would also feature here. Problem orientation is a feature that all projects in this third category have in common. Usually, companies also face the need to employ a market research company to design and interpret a study involving the collection of primary data.

Problem Definition: Self-Reference Criterion[14]

In addition to objective problems inherent in any marketing research identifying cultural values in global markets, researchers face two subjective problems:[15]

1. Cultural shock or psychological jolts engendered in encountering a wide variety of unfamiliar value systems; and
2. The self-reference criterion (SRC), or the unconscious tendency to assume that everyone else has similar values, attitudes, lifestyles, and so on.

The primary obstacle to success in international marketing is a person's self-reference criterion (SRC). This is an unconscious reference to one's own cultural values, experiences, and knowledge as the basis for decisions. SRC impedes the ability of a researcher to define the problem in its true light. It can prevent the researcher from being aware of the cultural differences and recognizing the importance of these differences. To eliminate the problem of SRC the following four-step framework should be followed:

1. Define the problem in terms of home-country cultural traits, habits, and norms.
2. Define the problem in terms of foreign-country cultural traits, habits, and norms.
3. Isolate the SRC influence in the problem and examine it carefully to see how it complicates the problem.
4. Redefine the problem without the SRC influence and solve for the foreign market situation.

UNIT OF ANALYSIS[16]

After preliminary research has been completed, the company will have an idea of the markets it plans to enter. The firm should then segment the market to get a better understanding of the market dynamics; however, deciding on the geographic boundaries within which to conduct research is becoming extremely complicated. The movement in Europe towards dissolution of national boundaries and coexistence of various cultures within one country makes it difficult for the researcher to decide on a unit of analysis.

In some cases it becomes necessary to conduct research within specific regions in the country. Consider Belgium, which is divided neatly in half, between Flanders in the north and Wallonia in the south.[17] Flemish people use margarine and Walloons use butter. This is everyday product usage American food retailers need to understand. Such region-specific product usage calls for market research on a regional basis. Researchers will have to compare lifestyles of target populations in individual regions before arriving at a marketing plan.

There is a wide gap between consumers in different countries. As discussed in chapter 1, alcohol consumption differs among the various European nations.[18] The French prefer wine, the Germans prefer beer, and the Spaniards like aperitivos. In England, port is drunk after a meal, while in Portugal it is consumed before. Such differences in consumption patterns must be taken into account while conducting marketing research. In this case it becomes necessary to conduct research using the country as the unit of research.

IBM Corporation conducted worldwide research to aid in the designing of Aptiva personal computers.[19] In this case, IBM considered target customers from 40 countries around the world and studied factors like the most preferred location for a computer in a household. Coca-Cola uses a single television advertisement in all of the countries. Research for these products is done on a worldwide basis.

In some cases it becomes necessary to target certain specific groups across countries. For instance, women in China have a different type of hair than women in Africa. A company catering to consumers of hair care products will conduct research targeting women in these countries to understand the varying needs of these markets.

Information needs are also shaped by the nature of the business, with firms in the trading or raw material/extractive industries rarely turning to commercial research suppliers at all. Manufacturing industries have made the greatest use of international marketing research, although there has been considerable growth over the past few years in research demand by companies in the services sector. For example, internationalization of several sectors of the distribution trades has led to greater interest in retailing, transportation, and logistics studies recently.

From the perspective of the research suppliers, marketing companies do not represent the entire target group for their activities. Various forms of social research have grown in importance in the past decade, but when conducted for governments or their agencies, these have largely been confined within national boundaries, for obvious reasons. Increasingly, however, information is being sought on a multicountry basis to provide a yardstick for comparison. The development of international bodies and organs of government has also added to this demand, for example, the EEC Commission's Eurobarometer exercises.

Many companies resist global markets because the problems associated with going global seem insurmountable. Most companies do not seem to acknowledge the fact that their international sales force and the distributors' sales force can be valuable in surmounting cultural and marketing barriers. A couple of decades ago, Webster argued that the "*use of the salespeople for gathering information can be much more critical than their use for promotion*" (1965, 78). Exhibit 4-1 summarizes a study on information

Information Needs in Marketing Research

Research was undertaken by Chonko, Tanner, and Smith to study the information needs of companies and sources used by them operating in an international environment. The study is based on the following assumptions:

- Because of added political and economic risks in operating abroad, accurate and timely marketing information is more important than in domestic marketing.

- Risk of unreliability of international business conducted in the United States and the cost involved make companies eager to find satisfactory alternatives.

- In many cases, salespeople are a company's only link to the customer. So the sales force in any company has almost exclusive access to valuable customer data.

The research is designed to investigate what types of information are being gathered during each phase of the marketing cycle, how it is communicated to marketing offices, if salespeople are given research results, and if so, in what format. In addition, centralization and formality issues are also discussed. The methodology followed will be explained in detail.

THE SAMPLE

The sample consisted of companies who, according to *Standard and Poor's Guide to Business for Corporations,* had revenues of more than $2 million, whose industry entailed personal selling, and who listed names of executives in an international division. The last step was to enable executives to be contacted and asked for by name to ensure higher respondent success rate. No more than two corporations were chosen from any one industry so as to avoid bias. Examples were: office products, pharmaceuticals, cosmetics, home care products, computer systems, raw metals, air travel and tours, foods, insurance, etc. Only those companies originating in the United States were chosen. Foreign companies, even those headquartered or operating in the United States, were excluded. From 26 sample corporations, 23 usable interviews were available. Each executive was screened to test knowledge of international marketing practices of firms.

MEASURES

Phone interviews were used, though more success has been reported with personal interviews. A structured in-depth telephone interview was used that had ten open-ended questions, four of which had three parts each. Six types of information were gathered:

1. Types of information collected in each stage of the product life cycle

2. Problems in gathering and using information

3. System used to gather and relay information

4. Role of expatriates in information gathering

5. Types of decisions used in information gathered by the international sales force

6. Differences in using sales forces internationally versus locally for gathering data.

RESULTS

The three types of decisions used were: sales forecasting, product design, and company/product image. Seventy-one percent of companies surveyed used sales force information for sales forecasting. Only 35 percent used it for product design and 46 percent for company or product image making.

PROBLEMS IN GATHERING AND USING INTERNATIONAL MARKET DATA

One-third of the participants reported situational problems, while 40 percent reported sales force problems. Many felt that data may not be accurate if its use is perceived as too broad or too local to be of value. These problems could arise due to situational limitations or problems with the salesforce.

INFORMATION COLLECTION AND DISSEMINATION

Companies used written questionnaires (32 percent of the sample), informal phone conversations (25 percent of the sample), and continuous communication (26 percent, being written, telephone, and face-to-face). Periodic reports were mentioned most often (30 percent), but only one company used a monthly newsletter. The format in which findings are presented include summarized data (30 percent), along with guidelines and suggestions (30 percent).

It was assumed that executives knew the best way to communicate findings to salespeople but may be unable to implement their system. Respondents were asked what they thought was the optimal technique for communicating findings. It was felt that the frequency with which data was relayed to the marketing office could contribute to success. Daily or weekly communication (telephone and telex) contributed to more timely information and understanding. Of the companies who felt their company's information system was good, their reasons were:

- Open communication between sales force and marketers
- Regular meetings between sales force and marketers
- Continuous exchange of information
- Flexibility of system to meet changing market
- Autonomy of sales force to make independent decisions
- It's one of the best
- We're good at it all
- The sales force is our only touch with the consumers

GROWTH PHASE

Companies use their sales force for gathering information on competition and any new market requirements. Two companies felt this was the most important phase for using a sales force. The first one gathered information on service needs and satisfaction once the product was in place. The second one concentrated on customer likes and dislikes of its product and of competition. Essential market data that salespeople collect during the growth phase include

- Competitor information
- New market requirements
- Customer surveys
- Product quality and features
- Relationship of company with end consumer
- Which areas are most profitable
- Whether or not to expand
- Volume versus start-up costs to determine growth size
- Distributor survey for customer satisfaction index

MATURITY PHASE

Few companies considered themselves mature. One felt use of sales at this point was vital because of considerable investment of capital. Another company felt that it could be an "Early Warning System" for competition. Essential market information that salespeople collect during the maturity phase include

- Competitive information
- Government data on product usage
- Type of businesses using the product
- Improved means of distribution
- Customers' desire for product changes
- New customer needs
- What new products could replace mature product
- Product weaknesses

INTERNATIONAL AND DOMESTIC DIFFERENCES

When asked to elaborate on the common differences between international and domestic sales forces, respondents replied that informational differences found in foreign countries included

- Not as much information available
- Information being harder to obtain
- Information being less reliable, resulting in the need for time-consuming cross-checking
- Because of many complexities and increased competition in the foreign market, there are more types of information needed
- International sales depends more on relations, so there are more areas to monitor and more representatives who need the information
- Our U.S. strategy is to copy, but increased competition internationally

necessitates the need for more market information and market research for more aggressive market strategies

Other respondents noted that the differences lie in the sales force personnel.

USING A U.S. EXPATRIATE

Of the respondents, eight did not use expatriates and ten used both expatriates and foreign salespeople. The use of expatriates is not a universal process. Data indicate that many practices are in use.

CONCLUSIONS AND IMPLICATIONS

Cavusgil (1985), in a study of U.S. export market research, reported that companies typically had information overload and that information was frequently conflicting. The study under focus shows that multinational companies frequently use international salespeople as sources for both marketing intelligence and research data. It was felt that more multinational companies should consider their salespeople for product design information.

In general, salespeople play a more significant role in the market entry stage than in the domestic marketing cycle because of proximity to the markets, a position not easily attainable by marketers located outside the foreign country. The main reasons for multinational companies to rely more on international sales forces than domestic sales forces for market data include

- Foreign published data is often unreliable, necessitating primary information gathering for crosschecking
- U.S. management does not understand foreign customers or foreign sales tech-

niques to make effective educated decisions on market strategy

- International sales in many countries rely more on relations, so more information areas need monitoring and more people in the marketing and sales process need the information

- In a volatile market, close monitoring of the market may only be possible through use of the sales force, since by the time the information was released, it would be obsolete

- The increased complexity and competition in foreign marketing results in more

information being needed to formulate successful marketing strategies

- Too often, domestic strategy is copied, but increased competition in international markets necessitates the need for more information and marketing research by the sales force to design "aggressive" marketing strategies

In the ultimate analysis, multinational companies believe that regular input from the international sales force is needed, and they benefit from the close working relationship between international salespeople and marketers.

Source: Adapted from Lawrence B. Chonko, John F. Tanner, Jr., and Ellen Reid Smith, "Selling and Sales Management in Action: The Sales Force Role in International Marketing Research and Marketing Information Systems," *Journal of Personal Selling & Sales Management* 11, no. 1 (winter 1991).

---

requirements for marketing research. Mellow (1989) recently observed that salespeople are a likely source of information about marketplace problems. Most multinational companies rely on secondary information obtained by hiring outside consultants. In addition to the above problems, language barriers, absence of contacts in foreign data collecting offices, lack of knowledge of government agencies, and gathering footwork locally are other problems.

REGION

Marketers will not be able to look at European consumers in the same way they did before 1992. American marketers cannot expect the same research services in Paris as in Los Angeles, and services will differ between Paris and Barcelona. It is necessary to consider economic integration in Europe to determine its impact on any business. There was a time when consumers in Virginia and New York were as different as those in Greece and Denmark today, but the federation integrated economically independent states. In the same way, Greece and Denmark may come together some day. Europe is not much more diverse than the United States, of which areas as different as Alaska and Hawaii are a part. Most lifestyles and opinion research in Europe is conducted in one country. Only recently, national market research companies have pooled their efforts to compare thoughts or lifestyles of different nations. European consumers have also been segmented by competing market research networks.

It is important to identify market segments across countries. Even if two similar consumers live in two different countries, their perceptions of brand attributes and their importance are the same. For example, Germany may be a more environmentally conscious country than the United Kingdom, but the United Kingdom has its share of green enthusiasts, just as Germany has its share of green detractors.

It is also necessary to track brand images and international advertisement concepts continuously. If the advertisement can change the image in a way that could increase sales, it is considered successful. Even though changing the image may not be the client's or agency's objective 90 percent of the time, ideally this should be the case.

INTERNATIONAL MARKETING RESEARCH IN PRACTICE

Now we will look at the market orientation, strategic orientation, and problem orientation of Tasty Burgers.

While considering the market orientation, it is important to look at several features, as stated in the chapter. One of the first details that should be paid attention to is the market size and number of players in the market. Many U.S. fast-food chains, like McDonald's and Pizza Hut, have already established operations in numerous international locations. The researchers will first look for information on the performance of these companies and their profit figures. The advantage of being a follower rather than a first-mover is that there is an opportunity to learn from the mistakes of other players.

Tasty Burgers should also be concerned about other related industries that supply materials required for the running of a fast-food chain. Because food items are generally perishable, they must identify reliable sources that are also at reasonable proximities from the outlets. Tasty Burgers would have to look for the availability of trays, plates, cutlery, containers, and bags. These items, however, can be transported from distant locations if a need arises.

Another important aspect is the availability of suitable locations in all of these countries. The outlets must be located at places that are frequented by a lot of people, and yet, the real estate prices should not eat into the profits. The company should also consider the product modifications and the pricing required to corner a fair market share.

A decision has to be made about the mode of entry into the markets that are considered profitable. As mentioned in the chapter, there are four possible modes of entry to international markets: exports, licensing/franchising, joint ventures, and partly or wholly owned subsidiaries. The fast-food industry has historically worked on setting up franchises; however, Tasty Burgers should look into legal, political, and cultural issues in each of the countries that have been selected for entry. They must identify partners who are willing to adhere to the moral and ethical standards set by Tasty Burgers in the United States.

Tasty Burgers has to conduct research that answers several strategic questions so as to determine the price and positioning of the product. The first step will be to test if the product will be accepted in its present form or if any modifications have to be made in each of the foreign markets. Local eating habits and religious sentiments have to be taken into account. Researchers will then have to determine the price that consumers are willing to pay for the product. The existing fast-food chains can be used as a point of reference in this matter. The advertising media has to be researched and the most cost-effective way of introducing and promoting Tasty Burgers will have to be worked out.

Based on the research results, Tasty Burgers should decide if they want to use the sprinkler strategy or the waterfall strategy in these countries. Both the strategies have their benefits and drawbacks. If Tasty Burgers adopts the waterfall strategy, they will be rolling out their investments in a phased manner. They can learn from their mistakes in one city and avoid making the same costly blunders in all other cities; however, with this kind of approach, competitors may beat them at opening outlets in new cities that could turn out to be very profitable. With the sprinkler strategy, Tasty Burgers preserves its first mover advantage, but could end up making the same costly mistakes in all of the cities, multiplying their losses many times.

The next stage will be the problem orientation of Tasty Burgers. The corporate attitude dictates this to a great extent. They could set up all of their outlets in these foreign markets exactly the same way as their U.S. outlets—the ethnocentric approach. They could decide to customize their product and management strategies in these countries—the polycentric approach. They could also decide to take it on a case-by-case basis and make changes that are absolutely necessary—the geocentric approach. However, the success of Tasty Burgers depends on their ability to adapt their products to meet consumer preferences in each of these countries, as shown by marketing research.

One factor that could be detrimental to the success of Tasty Burgers is the self-reference criterion. Management cannot work under the assumption that the factors that lead to the success of Tasty Burgers in the United States will help them achieve their goals in international markets.

Summary

This chapter deals with the first stages of the international marketing research process, namely identifying the needs of the firm, defining the problem, and deciding on the unit of analysis. The firm will have to decide on the information requirements for it to set up business in international markets. Once this has been decided, the research objective will have to be drawn and the problem will have to be defined in precise terms, making allowance for biases, like the self-reference criterion. The firm will then have to decide on the unit of analysis—whether it wishes to target one country, one region, or go global. The mode of entry for each of these markets will have to be decided. There are four choices available to companies to set up business in international markets: exporting, licensing, joint ventures, and wholly owned subsidiaries. Another aspect with regard to going international is whether to target many markets simultaneously or follow a more cautious approach and enter one market at a time. Marketing research is used to determine the best alternative. Once a decision to enter has been made, the firm will have to decide on the extent of customization that it needs to make to penetrate local markets in these countries. When making strategic decisions in foreign countries, researchers must bear in mind the problem of self-reference criterion (SRC)—defining problems in a foreign culture in terms of one's native culture. The chapter discusses ways in which SRC can be avoided.

Questions and Problems

1. List the major challenges faced by researchers in obtaining information for international marketing research.

2. Opal Jewelers, a U.S.-based exotic jewelry company, thinks there exists a market for their products in European countries. Explain the steps involved in the process of market selection.

3. Assume that research on market selection stated that France was the best market to start out with. What is the best mode of entry that can be adopted by Opal Jewelers? List any assumptions that have been made to arrive at the mode of entry.

4. What are the information requirements for Opal Jewelers in France during the
   i.   Entry phase
   ii. Growth phase
   iii. Maturity phase
   of the product life cycle?

Endnotes

1. Vern Terpstra and Ravi Sarathy, *International Marketing,* 6th ed. (Orlando, FL: Dryden Press, 1994), 213–218.

2. Michael R. Czinkota and Ilkka A. Ronkainen, *International Marketing,* 5th ed. (Orlando, FL: Harcourt, Brace, and Company, 1998), 296.

3. V. Kumar and Velavan Subramaniam, "A Contingency Framework for the Mode of Entry Decision," *Journal of World Business* 32, no. 1, (spring 1997): 53–72.

4. P. B. Barnard, "The Role and Implementation of International Marketing Research," Research International, Rotterdam, ESOMAR, 67–88.

5. Franklin R. Root, *Entry Strategies for International Markets* (Lexington Books, 1983).

6. S. Tamir Cavusgil and John R. Nevin, "State-of-the-Art in Marketing," *Review of Marketing* (1981), 195–216.

7. Michael R. Czinkota and Ilkka A. Ronkainen, *International Marketing,* 5th ed. (Orlando, FL: Harcourt, Brace, and Company, 1998), 296–301.

8. Shlomo Kalish, Vijay Mahajan, and Eitan Muller, "Waterfall and Sprinkler: New Product Strategies in Competitive Global Markets," *International Journal of Research in Marketing* 12 (1995): 105–119.

9. Ganesh Jaishankar, V. Kumar, and Velavan Subramaniam, "Learning Effect in Multinational Diffusion of Consumer Durables: An Exploratory Investigation," *Journal of the Academy of Marketing Science* 25, no. 3 (1997): 214–228.

10. Erdner Kaynak, "Difficulties in Undertaking Marketing Research in Developing Countries," *European Research* (November 1978): 251–259.

11. This section is adapted from *Global Marketing* by Johny K. Johansson, Chicago: Irwin, 1997.

12. Tiger Li and S. Tamir Cavusgil, "International Marketing: A Classification of Research Streams and Assessment of Their Development Since 1982," *American Marketing Association* (summer 1991): 592–607.

13. Philip R. Cateora, *International Marketing,* 9th ed. (Chicago: Irwin, 1996), 13–15.

14. Richard L. Sandhusen, *Global Marketing* (Hauppagge, NY: Barron's Educational Series, 1994), 109–110.

15. Blayne Cutler, "Reaching the Real Europe," *American Demographics* (October 1990): 38–43.

16. Ibid.

17. Ira Sager, "The Stealth Computer—Annual Design Awards," *Business Week* (2 June 1997): 103.

18. Jim Williams, "Constant Questions or Constant Meanings: Assessing Intercultural Motivations in Alcoholic Drinks," *Marketing and Research Today* (August 1991): 169–177.

CHAPTER

Secondary Data Research

5

INTRODUCTION

Secondary data are data collected by persons or agencies for purposes other than solving the problem at hand. They are one of the most economical and easiest means of accessing information. Because international marketing research projects can work out to be very costly in terms of time and money, researchers should conduct a thorough search for secondary data in the areas of interest to them. Because the amount of data available is overwhelming, researchers have to locate and utilize data that is relevant to their research.

Secondary data can be obtained from the internal records of the company. This is relevant information and is also the cheapest. External sources could include government publications, trade journals, periodicals, newspapers, books, annual reports, store audits, consumer purchase panels, and many more. The usual procedure is to start with the most available, least costly source.

NEED FOR SECONDARY DATA

An important point in the process of international marketing research is that duplication of research work should be avoided. Established sources of information on countries, products, markets, competitors, and potential customers should be checked. At least seven steps are involved before primary international marketing research can be started.[1]

Step 1

Check reference information on countries, products, markets, and competitors. Multi-client studies are referenced by going through the following publications:

a. *MarketSearch, the International Directory of Published Market Research.* This is an annual directory that provides over 18,000 multiclient study references worldwide. It is subdivided by subject based on British SIC classifications.

b. *FINDEX, the Directory of Market Research Reports, Studies, and Surveys.* This directory includes company and industry research from Wall Street, as well as a host of multiclient studies published by research firms the world over. Coverage, however, is more domestic than international.

c. *Marketing Surveys Index (MSI)* includes virtually all international multiclient studies. Updated twice a year by supplements sent via airmail from London, it consists of current news. The subject index is alphabetical, complete, and international.

It is also useful to check some general reference guides, like the following:

a. The European and Far East *Regional Directories* published by the Market Research Society in London.

b. *Croner's A-Z of Business Information Sources.* This directory includes categories for company, product, and market information divided for consumer and industrial/commercial markets, and the scope is clearly international.

c. *Consumer Japan.* This publication covers major consumer markets in Japan with specific information on markets, products, and key commercial organizations.

d. *Consumer Europe.* This resource covers over 500 products bought by consumers in 17 West European countries; it provides market data and trends for six years through 1988 plus forecasts through 1992. It also includes a directory of major companies.

e. *Croner's Europe.* Contains current updates on all European Community proceedings of possible interest to international marketers.

Following are the main sources for European marketing statistics:

a. *International Marketing Data and Statistics* annual publications.

b. *European Marketing Data and Statistics* annual publications.

c. *The International Directory of Marketing Information Sources.*

d. *The European Directory of Non-Official Statistical Sources.*

e. *The European Directory of Marketing Information Sources.* Lists over 2,500 sources of marketing and business information throughout Europe.

f. *The Worldwide Government Directory.* Provides information on 175 governments and 100 international government agencies throughout the world, many of which represent sources of marketing and business information.

Information on international business risk is provided by BERI (Business Environment Risk Intelligence) resources, which include:

a. *BERI's Risk Service.* Provides country risk forecasts for 50 countries throughout the world and is updated three times a year.

b. *BERI's Foreland.* Provides international lenders with risk information on 50 countries with three updates annually.

c. *BERI's Force Reports.* Detailed annual reports on 20 countries, including a *Special Report on Eastern Europe* and another on *Europe 1992.*

d. BERI also offers special services for international risk research, foreign exchange guidance, quick response advice, and specialized risk consultancy.

For updated information on potential international competitors, information is provided by *Kompass Directories, The International Corporate 1000, The City Directory* (the London financial community), *Europe's 15,000 Largest Companies, The London Business Pages,* and, in Canada, *The Canadian Trade Index.* Other sources include:

a. *Business-Line Management, Marketing, and Administration.* This reference lists more than 200 online services worldwide for product and market research and customer analysis.
b. *Business-Line Finance.* This resource includes more than 300 financial databases throughout the world.
c. *Business-Line Company Information.* This reference lists more than 300 databases for company financial information, key personnel, products and services, subsidiaries, and other database categories.

Step 2

Conduct secondary research online and in the library. It is vital to check all secondary information that may help answer client questions about products, markets, opportunities, competitors, and the wisdom of alternative business strategies. The next major step consists of rechecking some of the previously mentioned sources while adding some new ones.

Secondary research of all pertinent published information may be obtained by using in-house online research capabilities at the research firm or client organization. If existing commitments or capabilities make this impossible, it may be necessary to select an outside provider or broker of secondary business research information.

A list of outside firms that conduct secondary research is found is *Burwell's Dictionary of Fee-Based Information Services.* This directory clearly lists information brokers throughout the world and is subdivided by country, state, company, subject, and service. The majority of these information brokers are found in the United States.

Online research is possible through Dialog, Nexis, and other services. The trick is to know which of the hundreds of databases to check for appropriate questions, key words, and subjects. Other online resources include Bibliographical Retrieval Services (BRS), Chemical Abstract Services (CAS), CompuServe, Lexis, and Regulatory Information Service (RIS). Other references include:

a. *Business-Line Management,* which lists more than 200 online services worldwide; *Business-Line Finance,* listing more than 300 financial databases throughout the world; and *Business-Line Company Information,* which provides direction to more than 300 databases of company financial information, key personnel, products, services, subsidiaries, fees, and other database categories.
b. *The City Directory* for London-based financial information sources.
c. *ARK,* which covers 14 major industries in Europe to provide information on more than 2,000 public companies throughout Western Europe.

After identifying the appropriate articles and published references some time will have to be spent in the library reviewing abstracts and other references. Secondary research can cost anywhere from a few hundred dollars for a simple study to $10,000 or more for a complicated project and interpretive report.

Step 3

Select multiclient studies to answer some of the questions at relatively low cost. Because it is neither cost efficient nor wise to purchase every possible multiclient study, additional research is necessary. This research involves contacting publishers of multiclient studies and requesting copies of the content page and the prospectus for each study of interest. The options of purchasing the whole study or just pertinent parts are discussed. Purchase of proprietary add-ons to multiclient studies to answer specific client questions that are not adequately answered by the basic multiclient study is considered. Discounts to purchase multiclient studies below list price are discussed when applicable. Because researchers are resellers of this type of information, discounts are normally available. After contacting and obtaining information from publishers, the clients of the research company are consulted and those studies that seem most appropriate are purchased.

Step 4

Select a foreign firm or firms to assist in the study, or in some cases, perform most of the work and provide some proprietary research. In many cases, in foreign markets, a local firm is needed that can do fieldwork, gather data, and provide some analysis and interpretation.

Selection and use of the foreign firm is critical to overall project success. Certain alternatives may be considered here. Language considerations may require the assistance of a foreign firm. The existing inventory of correspondent firms, companies, and individuals must be examined, as well as qualifications in terms of industry and specific type of study experience. Directories of foreign firms should be checked, like the *International Directory of Market Research Organizations,* which contains information pertaining to over 1,700 marketing research firms in seven different countries of the world. Another useful guide is *Bradford's Directory of Marketing Research Agencies and Management Consultants. The Green Book,* published by the New York Chapter of the American Marketing Association, is useful for details about domestic marketing research firms.

If work is being done on an industrial/business marketing research project in Europe, the membership directories of the Industrial Marketing Research Association (IMRA) and The Federation of European Marketing Research Associations (FEMRA) are useful.

For consumer projects in the United Kingdom, the yearbook of the Market Research Society (MRS) is used. For industrial or business projects in Canada, the membership directory of the Industrial Marketing and Research Association of Canada (IMRAC) is checked. In other countries, use the appropriate association directories, and for Europe use the directory of the European Society for Opinion and Marketing Research (ESOMAR).

Step 5

Solicit proposals for foreign fieldwork and analysis, particularly where foreign languages are involved. At this point, the researcher is able to describe what he or she knows and what type of assistance is needed in the foreign market study. A problem statement or a brief describing exactly what is wanted is prepared. Proposals are solicited from three or four carefully selected foreign firms that have the capability to conduct the study for the client. Confidentiality agreements can be used where appropriate. Once the proposals for foreign fieldwork and assistance are received, it is necessary to recommend a selection procedure and select a subcontractor to complete the foreign work to the client's specifications.

Step 6

Finalize the client proposal, including business reference information, secondary research, multiclient studies, subcontractor fieldwork and analysis, and all other cost elements. By this stage all information to complete the client proposal and begin the remaining steps of the project is available.

Step 7

Begin the primary research study working closely with the client and arranging for frequent interim meetings to ensure that there are no surprises in the report at the end of the project. An interim report covers all of the progress to date in terms of published information resources, findings, conclusions, and recommendations. The proprietary research in the foreign market is completed and becomes part of the final report for the project. The end result may include recommendations on competition entry strategy, joint venture possibilities, distribution alternatives, acquisitions, and other types of strategic partnerships. These aspects are designed to help the client make the right decision on foreign market opportunities. This includes helping the client avoid costly mistakes.

USES OF SECONDARY DATA

Secondary data can be used by researchers in many ways. Some of the uses are by[2]

1. Being a valuable source of new ideas that can be explored later through primary research.
2. Examining available secondary data before collecting primary data, researchers can define the problem and formulate hypotheses about its solution. This provides a better understanding and will also suggest solutions not considered previously.
3. Aiding in the collection of primary data. Examining the methods and techniques employed by researchers to conduct similar research studies may help in planning the present one.
4. Helping define the population, selecting the sample in primary information collection, and defining parameters of primary research.
5. Acting as a reference base against which to compare the validity or accuracy of the primary data. It may be of value in establishing classifications that are compatible with past studies so that trends may be more readily analyzed.

ADVANTAGES OF SECONDARY DATA

The most significant benefits secondary data offer a researcher are savings in cost and time. The process involved in collecting secondary data is fairly simple. The researcher needs to spend some time in a library or on the Internet looking up related sources of data. Even if the data had to be bought from another agency, it would still be cheaper than collecting primary data in a foreign country.

Secondary data can warn the researcher that the project is not feasible or financially viable even before more time and money are spent in primary data collection.

Information about the past history of a country or consumer behavior will not be available through primary data. Secondary data is the only source for such information. For instance, if a researcher were interested in the buying behavior before the Commonwealth of Independent States split up, it would be very difficult to gather primary data; however, some secondary data will be available to assist the researcher.

In some cases, secondary data may be more accurate than primary data. For example, if a company wants information on the sales and profit figures of competitors, it may be easier to get more accurate data from government publications or trade journals than the competitors themselves.

DISADVANTAGES OF SECONDARY DATA

Secondary data does have some disadvantages.[3] A critical shortcoming of secondary data on foreign markets is the lack of availability. The United States and most developed nations have an extensive array of secondary data that are collected through various government and private sources; however, the third world countries do not have agencies that collect data on a regular basis. Hence, accessing even basic information like income, wholesale and retail prices for goods and services, and telephone numbers may prove to be a challenge.

Even if secondary data is available, it may not have the level of accuracy that is needed for confident decision making. Some of the statistics may be too optimistic, reflecting national pride rather than practical reality. In many countries businesses falsely report relevant figures like income and sales to avoid taxation. In some cases errors are intentional, in others they are a result of sloppy recording.[4] It is necessary for researchers to harbor healthy skepticism about secondary data collected from foreign countries regardless of the source of the data.

In a lot of countries, especially the developing countries, data may be outdated and may have been collected on an infrequent and unpredictable schedule. Rapid changes in the global economy make it necessary for data to be current. Even if some countries were collecting reliable data on a regular basis in the recent past, there is no historical data available to compare and study the trends.

Another related problem with secondary data is the method in which data is collected and reported. There is a lot of variation in these aspects between countries. It becomes impossible to compare data between countries when conducting a multicountry study.

Secondary data must be checked and interpreted carefully for it to be of any use to the research study; hence, it is necessary to check the consistency and validity of the data. It is extremely difficult to validate data that has been collected from some countries. The researcher has to find out who collected the data and how it was collected. Further, the researcher also has to investigate if there was any reason for the data to be misrepresented and check if it is internally consistent and logical in light of known sources and market factors. This can be a very challenging task in international marketing research.

PROBLEMS IN COLLECTING SECONDARY DATA

All of the problems that researchers face in domestic marketing research tend to be exacerbated in international marketing research. There is a general dearth of statistical summary data, especially in less-developed countries with primitive statistics and research services. Even in countries that do provide data sources, there is the problem of comparability of data. For instance, in Germany, consumer expenditures are estimated on the basis of tax receipts. In the United Kingdom, however, they are estimated on the basis of a combination of tax receipts, household surveys, and production sources. There could be differences in terms that are used on a day-to-day basis.[5] An example would be the representation of the term 1 billion. In the United States it is numerically represented as 1,000,000,000. In the United Kingdom, however, it is represented as 1,000,000,000,000.

More comparability problems arise in the way different foreign countries process statistical data.[6] Following are the standard age categories for classifying statistical data covering consumer purchases in four different countries:[7]

Venezuela	*Germany*	*Spain*	*Italy*
10–14	14–19	15–24	13–20
15–24	20–29	25–34	21–25
25–34	30–39	35–44	26–35

These differences and difficulties among countries often mean that multiple markets must be researched, including poorer countries where a profit potential is questionable, rather than a single large market, like the United States.

EVALUATING THE VALUE OF RESEARCH

Before proceeding with the research it is necessary to have an estimate for the value of information, that is, the value of obtaining answers to the research questions. This will help the company decide how much, if anything at all, should be spent on the research. The value of research will depend on the importance of the decision that is to be based on the information, the uncertainty surrounding the situation, and the influence of the research information on the decision. It stands to reason that if the decision is likely to have significant impact on the long-term plans of the organization, it would be deemed very valuable. By the same logic, if the outcome is already known with certainty and the research information will not have any impact on the decision, the information will have no value.

These concepts are better illustrated by a simple example. Consider the decision to introduce a new product. The uncertainty in this case is whether or not the product is going to succeed. The probability of success is given as 0.6 and the probability of failure is given as 0.4. Country A and B represent two scenarios faced by the company.

Country A

	Success	*Failure*
Introduce	$4 million	$1 million
Do not introduce	$0	$0

Country B

	Success	*Failure*
Introduce	$4 million	−$2.5 million
Do not introduce	$0	$0

In Country A, irrespective of the uncertainty involved with the success or failure of the product, if the product is introduced, the firm makes money. If the product succeeds in the market, the firm makes $4 million, and if it fails, the company makes $1 million. This is a straightforward decision—the company should introduce the product. Any research conducted to get the exact success and failure probabilities will not add value to the decision. This is a case where research does not have any value.

However, in Country B, the firm cannot make an unequivocal decision to introduce the product. If the product fails in the market, the firm could sustain a loss of $2.5 million. In this scenario, if research information can give perfect information about the success or failure of the product, it can save the company $2.5 million in the event that the product fails. Given the existing information, if the probability of failure is 0.4, the value of perfect information will be 0.4 times $2.5 million, that is, $1 million. Because market information is unlikely to be perfect, the actual value of the information will be less than $1 million.

The value of information will be dependent on the company's opinions on the probability of success and failure of its products.

ELECTRONIC POINT OF SALE SCANNING (EPOS)[8]

Bar-coding, scanning, and computerized information are all part of the new trend in retail auditing. An "intelligent" terminal records the bar code on a product. This information is then fed into a computer and used to compute the bill and record the sale for store-check at a later time. In America and Canada EPOS is widely used for research purposes. Consumer panels are recruited to track purchase patterns. Consumers are asked to present an electronic card at the checkout counter and the sale is recorded. This data helps researchers study buying habits of people across different demographic sections, as well as discerning brand loyalty, switching patterns, and impact of promotions on sales.

Scanner Data in Europe[9]

Scanner-based tracking services will be useful if there are a number of retail locations that engage in scanning. There has been a spurt in the use of scanners in the three major countries in Europe since 1994. In 1994, France had 64 percent coverage, followed by Great Britain with 60 percent, and finally Germany with 23 percent. In the case of France and Great Britain, given a reasonable distribution by chain, store size, and geography, the scan rates are quite adequate to support retail tracking via scanning. In the case of Germany, the low rates are mainly due to the former East Germany, where there is virtually no scanning. Among the next three largest countries in Europe, the Netherlands leads with 44 percent, followed by Italy with 32 percent, and Spain with 30 percent. In the case of the Netherlands, the scanning rate is sufficient to cover supermarkets, but some other supplemental methods are required to cover the smaller stores. Scan rates are also reasonably high in Finland (68 percent), Denmark (63 percent), Belgium (62 percent), Sweden (60 percent), and Norway (37 percent). All of these rates are low compared to the United States, but are generally higher than rates around the rest of the world. The percentage of retail stores using scanners in Europe in 1994 was close to the percentage in the United States in the 1980s, when 100 percent scanner-based tracking services started in the United States.

Presently, there is adequate scanner penetration in most European countries. Many scanner-based tracking services are already operating in Europe. GfK formed a joint venture with IRI in Germany in 1994. In Great Britain, an IRI-led consortium started offering tracking services, which utilized both scanner data and conventional audits and a supplemental all-scan service. Most food products are being checked out by scanners and hence, all-scan service is available to them. Supplemental audits are being phased out as more scanners cover more product groups.

SYNDICATED DATA SOURCES

Syndicated data are collected for a set of information users with a common need. Scanner data, consumer panels, store audits, and so on, are examples of syndicated data. Many research organizations, such as ACNielsen and Information Resources, Inc., provide syndicated data in the United States. For the purpose of marketing research, it becomes necessary for the researcher to identify syndicated data sources for the country of interest. There are many Web sites that provide information on sources of syndicated data in various countries. The ESOMAR Web site—http://www.esomar.org—is one of them.

Global Scan collects detailed brand and category information on more than 1,000 products.[10] Research International (RI) provides continuous panel data for 40 countries in the world.[11] Within RI there are nine ad hoc divisions handling a variety of client accounts. These include fast-moving consumer goods, such as food, drink, and household products, together with more specific market sectors, such as finance, retailing, travel and leisure, and consumer durables. RI Automotive offers both full-service, customized research and a continuous monitor, the *Motorists' Diary Panel*, with data from 4,000 motorists. Exhibit 5-1 describes consumer profiles in Europe and Exhibit 5-2 talks about specific consumer categories in the United Kingdom.

EXHIBIT 5-1

Geodemographic Profiling: MOSAIC and EuroMOSAIC

Consumers can be classified in several ways: on the basis of personal demographics, such as age and income; according to values and attitudes (psychographics); and on the basis of their behavior (behavior graphics). Geodemographic classifications group consumers together on the basis of the neighborhood they live in. The logic behind this is that neighborhoods that are similar across a wide range of demographic measures will offer similar potential across most products, brands, services, and media.

This type of classification has a number of advantages. Marketing researchers can obtain better representativeness and greater coverage for surveys by using preclassified profiles. These lists also offer flexibility, as they can be used for a number of products and various activities. Speed is another big advantage offered by these lists. Availability of ready-made segments will make it easier for marketing researchers to conduct surveys and other research studies. They also make it easy for researchers to extrapolate market potential across similar segments without having to repeat the studies.

Geodemographic classification exists for most countries in Western Europe, North America, and Australia. The size of a typical neighborhood cluster can vary from as little as 15 households in Great Britain to as many as 800 households in Sweden. A given segmentation could include statistics from the census, credit rating agencies, electoral registers, mail-order purchases, car registrations, and many other sources. For instance, in Great Britain, 80 separate measures were used to define 52 distinct MOSAIC types that were organized into 12 cluster groups. On the basis of the zip-code, each household is allocated a MOSAIC code between 1 and 52. The MOSAIC distribution of population in Great Britain is given in Exhibit 5-2. Profiles are a very powerful tool and can be built in a number of ways, such as by

- Profiling the whole customer file against the Great Britain average to establish which MOSAIC types the majority of the consumers are likely to fall in

- Profiling a customer file against a catchment base to establish which MOSAIC types are under- and over-represented compared to the areas in which customers live

- Profiling one segment of a customer file against all customers to establish which MOSAIC types buy each of a range of different products sold

- Profiling the average level of spending and sales to establish which MOSAIC types prove to be the most profitable customers

The emergence of a single European market has meant that a number of companies are adopting marketing strategies for Europe as a whole; hence the profiling system has to expand to encompass all of Europe. EuroMOSAIC is a system that classifies 310 million individuals on the basis of the neighborhoods they live in. International marketing researchers use this profiling to define their population and target segments. EuroMOSAIC identifies ten different lifestyle categories that are consistent across all countries and are derived from 300 or more separate MOSAIC segments describing consumers in different European countries.

Source: "Geodemographic Profiling: MOSAIC and EuroMOSAIC" by Margaret Crimp and Len Tiu Wright from *The Marketing Research Process*, 4th Edition, Herfordshire: Prentice Hall, 1995. Reprinted by permission of Pearson Education Ltd.

EXHIBIT 5-2

MOSAIC Distribution of Population in Great Britain

Code	*MOSAIC Lifestyle Groups*	*Percentage*
L1	High-Income Families	9.9
L2	Suburban Semis	11.0
L3	Blue-Collar Owners	13.0
L4	Low-Rise Council	14.4
L5	Council Flats	6.8
L6	Victorian Low Status	9.4
L7	Town Houses and Flats	9.4
L8	Stylish Singles	5.2
L9	Independent Elders	7.4
L10	Mortgaged Families	6.2
L11	Country Dwellers	7.0
L12	Institutional Areas	0.3

Source: "Geodemographic Profiling: MOSAIC and EuroMOSAIC" by Margaret Crimp and Len Tiu Wright from *The Marketing Research Process*, 4th Edition, Herfordshire: Prentice Hall, 1995. Reprinted by permission of Pearson Education Ltd.

Marketers experience a lot of confusion when trying to learn to decide where to enter the global arena, what to sell, and how to sell it.[12] The organization must collect and analyze pertinent information to support the basic go/no go decision before getting into the issues addressed by conventional marketing research. The key to accomplishing this is to make effective use of secondary research.

To begin with, governments of developed countries offer a wealth of useful data free of cost or for a very nominal charge. One of the most comprehensive sources of information is the National Trade Data Bank maintained by the U.S. Department of Commerce.[13] The best way to go about this is to start with the *Annual Statistical Abstract of the United States*. This abstract contains a host of information, including population totals and trends, population projections, GDP, GNP, and much other useful information. The abstract's source notes provide more detailed information to a marketer. The Trade Information Center is a one-stop shop for providing information collected from 19 federal agencies. International trade specialists are available at the toll free number (1-800-USA-TRADE) and provide assistance and advice to marketers on how to use government information.

Many other countries also provide trade data. If the information is published in the local language, embassies and consulates provide translations. Foreign embassies in Washington D.C. will be able to provide a lot of useful information. There are international magazines targeting people who want to go international with their businesses. The *Statistical Yearbook* published by the United Nations contains trade data on products and information on exports and imports by country. The United Nation's *Statistical Yearbook* also provides information on worldwide demographics.[14] The World Bank's *World Atlas* gives information on population, growth trends, and GDP. The World Bank also publishes a *World Development Report* that summarizes information on indicators such as life expectancy at birth and school enrollment in various countries.[15] The Organization for Economic Cooperation and Development publishes quarterly and annual trade data on its member nations. The International Monetary Fund and the World Bank publish occasional staff papers discussing regional or country-specific issues in depth.

Increasingly, the ability to surf the Internet and its equivalents is essential to amassing pertinent data to support international trade decisions. Electronic databases carry marketing information ranging from latest news on product development to new writings in the academic and trade press and updates in international trade statistics. There are also several profile analysis studies conducted that could help researchers analyze and target the potential customers in a better manner. For instance, the popular belief is that Japan is a homogenous market and that there will either be mass response or no response. Psychographic analysis and segmentation of the Japanese market indicates otherwise. Ten segments have been identified and each of these segments can be targeted with custom programs.[16]

Secondary research will not answer all of the specific questions that a marketer may have, but when it is done right, it is a low cost way to shed light on major decisions that should be made before moving on to the next steps in the research process.

INTERNATIONAL MARKETING RESEARCH IN PRACTICE

Continuing with the example of Tasty Burgers wanting to enter the United Kingdom, Brazil, India, and Saudi Arabia, this chapter takes a look at conducting secondary research. The first step in secondary research is to obtain general data on all of these countries. This would include economic data, such as GNP/GDP and per capita income; political data, such as stability of the government and the legal system in each of these countries; infrastructure availability, such as transportation, communication, and advertising media; the social structure; and the attitude of people towards foreign products. This will give researchers a feel for the viability of each of these countries as potential expansion markets. There are many sources from which this information can be obtained. The embassies of these countries in the United States would be a good place to start. Many magazines and trade journals will also carry information on business climates in foreign countries. Another potentially good source is the Internet. Conducting secondary research on the Internet is explained in great detail in chapter 6. There are many Web sites that contain country statistics and demographics. The onus of verifying the authenticity of the source and the information is on the researcher. It is always best to collect the same information from multiple sources and crosscheck them; this way the possibility of error is minimized. It must be remembered that secondary data will not always be in a format that the researcher wants and, hence, the data may not always be comparable. Some of the sources that can be used have been mentioned earlier in this chapter.

It is also important to obtain information on competing products and other local and foreign fast-food chains that have set up business in these countries. This will help Tasty Burgers decide if the products they offer need to be modified for any of these countries. If other American fast-food chains have already set up business in any of these countries, it is necessary that Tasty Burgers find out their market share and profit margins. This will be required to decide if that particular market can support another fast-food chain. Information about suppliers and distribution networks and potential franchise costs will also have to be obtained. It is possible to sign up for a multiclient study with one of the information providers in America. It may also be beneficial to contact information brokers in each of these countries and contract them to gather data.

The key in secondary research is to consider the costs of gathering data and compare that against the future potential benefits. Secondary data is a useful place to start, but as mentioned earlier, it is neither completely accurate nor is it always available in the exact format that researchers want. A cost benefit analysis has to be performed before deciding the time and resources to be spent in gathering secondary data.

Summary

This chapter deals with secondary data—its sources, advantages, and drawbacks. It is important to note that the sources of secondary data are numerous and this book mentions only a selected few. This chapter should have convinced the reader of the importance of looking into various secondary data sources before launching the research study. Many research studies can be undertaken with the wealth of information available from the company's internal records or other secondary data sources. With the growing power of computers and the Internet, accessing data is becoming very easy. Figure 5-1 displays the screen produced by WorldOpinion, a site dedicated to marketing research all over the world. It is possible for researchers to obtain a list of marketing research companies in the country of interest to them.

Secondary data have many advantages and disadvantages. They are relatively cheap and can be obtained in a short span of time. In many cases, they help decision making without having to resort to primary research. Past history and consumer behavior data can be obtained only through secondary research. On the other hand, there is a lack of adequate secondary data that is authentic. Many developing countries have data that is outdated or inaccurate. There is also the problem of comparison of data that has been collected from different countries. It is important that a cost-benefit study be performed to ensure that the benefits of collecting secondary data outweigh the costs.

Questions and Problems

1. You are opening a new retail store that will sell personal computers and software in a developing country. What secondary data are available in that area to help you decide where to locate the store? Would the same data be relevant to someone opening a convenience copying center?

2. A large chain of building supply yards was aiming to launch at least one new yard in a new country. From past experience, this meant carefully reviewing as many as 20 or 30 possible countries. You have been assigned the task of making this process more systematic. The first step is to specify the types of secondary information that should be available for the market area of each location. The second step is to identify the possible sources of this information and appraise their usefulness.

 **WorldOpinion**

The World's Market Research Web Site

New!

* More resources
* Expanded bookstore

WorldOpinion

- Home
- Latest News
- Directory
- Classifieds
- Calendar
- News Stand
- Stock Watch
- Reference
- Feedback
- Survey Sampling

WorldOpinion's calendar now lists over 500 events!

See the most comprehensive international listing of research and marketing events anywhere.

Join the Talking Research discussion! The first 100 participants are eligible to win a digital camera!

Classifieds: 4,000+ job listings

Searchable database of job openings. -- Submit your ad or resume -- for free!

Latest research news

Breaking News: US Supreme Court rejects statistical sampling for 2000 census. Details.

Among this week's stories:
Collection of online shopping studies ... healthcare studies ... research news from Peru, Kazakhstan, China, UK, US, South Africa, Mexico, Australia, Israel, New Zealand, Ireland ... Lycos gains on Yahoo! ... another mysterious break-in at DC pollster ... UIG buys Audits & Surveys ... Intel, Nielsen MR collaborate ... Gates poll memo significant at Microsoft trial ... online news becoming major info. source ... more.

US area code explosion update

Research conference coverage.

 Information overload? Check **WorldOpinion Quick Facts:** summary statistics on the research industry and the web.

Check WorldOpinion's stock watch for latest prices.

Directory of 6,600 researchers

Over 8,500 research locations in 99 countries.

Submit your directory listing or updates.

Where to find it

A-Z of site content
Site map
First visit? tour the site

Questions?
Comments?

E-mail the editors

WorldOpinion features

Research profiles: interviews with leading researchers.
Research term of the day:
Bivariate Analysis
Notable quote of the week:
impeachment polls: the importance of question wording.

Research resources

Latest research and marketing books
World clock
World weather
International holidays
Exchange rates
Links to research association sites
Links to major researchers' sites
More links for researchers

"A research aficionado's dream come true ... late-breaking research industry news feature **delivers the hottest information faster** than other news services." - Netcom.

FIGURE 5-1 WorldOpinion—The World's Market Research Web Site

3. For each of these products, which industry associations would you contact for secondary data? (a) Foreign convenience dinners, (b) numerically controlled machine tools, (c) irrigation pipe, (d) imported wine, (e) compact disc players, and (f) children's shoes.

4. Obtain data on beer consumption in the United States for the latest available year. Calculate the per capita consumption for the United States and compare it to that of Europe. What accounts for the difference?

5. From secondary data sources, obtain sales for an entire industry and the sales of the major firms in that industry for any year for five Pan-American countries. Compute the market shares of each major firm. Using another source, obtain information on the market shares of these same firms. Are there differences? If so, why?

Endnotes

1. Ian Macfarlane, "Do-it-Yourself Marketing Research," *Management Review* (May 1991): 34–37.

2. David A. Aaker, V. Kumar, and George S. Day, *Marketing Research*, 6th ed. (New York: John Wiley & Sons, 1998).

3. This section is adapted from *International Marketing* by Philip Cateora, 9th ed. (Chicago: Irwin, 1996), 196–198.

4. Tom Lester, "Common Markets," *Marketing* (9 November 1989): 41.

5. Donald B. Pittenger, "Gathering Foreign Demographics is No Easy Task," *Marketing News* (8 January 1991): 23.

6. Adapted from "We are the World," *American Demographics* (May 1990): 42–43.

7. Richard L. Sandhusen, *Global Marketing*, (Hauppagge, NY: Barron's Educational Series, 1994), 49.

8. Peter Chisnall, *Marketing Research*, 5th ed. (Berkshire, England: McGraw-Hill Publications, 1997), 228.

9. Gerry Eskin, "POS Scanner Data: The State of the Art, in Europe and the World," *Marketing and Research Today* (May 1994).

10. "We Are the World," *American Demographics* (May 1990): 42–43.

11. Peter Chisnall, *Marketing Research*, 5th ed. (Berkshire, England: McGraw-Hill Publications, 1997), 217.

12. Michael R. Czinkota, "Take a Short-Cut to Low-Cost Global Research," *Marketing News* (13 March 1995): 3.

13. Available at http://www.stat-usa.gov, also available on CD-ROM.

14. Additional information available at *World Development Report*, Washington D.C. World Bank, an annual publication.

15. For additional information please refer to *International Financial Statistics*, Washington D.C., International Monetary Fund, an annual publication.

16. Lewis C. Winters, "International Psychographics," *Marketing Research* (September 1992): 48–49.

CHAPTER

Marketing Research on the Internet

6

INTRODUCTION

It is now a widely accepted fact that the information technology revolution will have a profound effect on the conduct of international business as we move toward the new millennium.[1] The most important development has been the explosion of international marketing activity on the Internet and the associated emergence of the global information superhighway. There are an estimated 40 million individuals and organizations currently linked to the Net, with connectivity growing at an average of 10 percent per month. A recent study by IBM predicted 500 million users by the turn of the century. The Internet can no longer be considered a "fad" or the preserve of "techies" and "computer nerds." Commercial uses of the Net have become the fastest growing part of the World Wide Web. Used properly, the Internet can be a powerful source of competitive advantage in global markets and an increasing number of companies are developing Internet-based strategies to support overall business development.

As Exhibit 6-1 suggests, the Internet is becoming a powerful marketing tool, fast becoming a household word, and in the foreseeable future will be the marketing tool of the masses. Most companies will be marketing products and services online and a lot of consumers will be looking forward to the convenience of shopping without having to drive to the mall. The home computer, once considered a luxury item, pervades the homes of millions of people across the globe. This has been made possible by the decreasing prices of computers and by the fact that all computers come equipped with a modem. The Internet offers companies many benefits. The cost of advertising on the World Wide Web is reasonably low and the potential audience enjoyed by these Web sites is very high. Hence, it is natural that researchers want to exploit this medium to conduct secondary and primary research. This chapter explains how the Internet can be used in international marketing research.

EXHIBIT 6-1

Attention, Shoppers

A booming fourth quarter—due in part to the presence of more brand name, electronic commerce-enabled retailers than last year—may see Web buyers spend $1 billion on purchases over the Web, bringing the year's total to more than $2 billion. Forrester Research, Inc. predicts that consumers will dish out $17 billion for goods and services on the Web by the year 2000—more than double the $7 billion it was predicting earlier this year. Proving that you can sell a lot of products over the Web, Dell Computer Corporation's popular Web site watched as sales of its computers jumped from $1 million to about $3 million each day. Apple Computer, Inc. launched its own Web site with interim CEO Steve Jobs boasting that Apple's online sales would outstrip Dell's. The Apple Store sold more than $500,000 in its first twelve hours. Then, with less than a month of shopping days to Christmas, Hewlett-Packard took the wraps off a global consortium to boost e-commerce.

Source: Reprinted by permission from *Inter@ctive Week*, December 22, 1997. Copyright © 1997 ZD, Inc.

PSYCHOGRAPHICS OF CYBERHEADS[2]

Researchers are fast discovering that the old psychographic dimensions, such as attitudes toward work and leisure or health and fitness, do not fit today's realities. People's involvement with the media and their responses to and skills at getting information, are the most important predictors today. This information explosion poses a lot of opportunities and challenges for established research tools like the Yankelovich MONITOR. SRI International, an academic and government think tank in the area of marketing research, is working on a project that focuses on the psychographics of Internet users and their attitudes and preferences. Early results of this project reinforce the idea of a dual-tiered society, but one based on knowledge and not income. People who are out of the information highway loop are excluded more because of their limited education than because of the low incomes less-educated people tend to have. Education goes a long way in explaining why half of Web users are Actualizers, the stereotypical upscale, technically oriented academics and professionals who cruise the cyberstreets. Three in four are men and virtually all of them have gone to college. Only 10 percent of the general population belongs to this group. The other half of the Web audience represents 90 percent of the general population and is mostly made up of Strivers, Experiencers, Fulfilleds, and Achievers. They are slightly less male-dominated than Actualizers (64 percent) and nearly as likely to have some college education (89 percent). Because they are already on the Internet but not at the same rates as Actualizers, these four groups represent the next big spurt of growth for the Net and related new media. Appendix 6-1 describes in detail each of these segments. Figure 6-1 gives some relevant figures with respect to these groups.

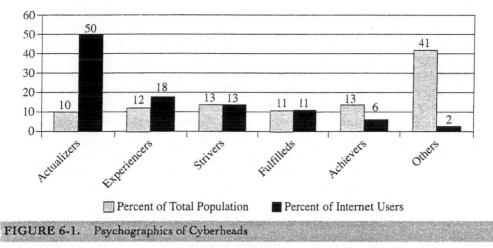

FIGURE 6-1. Psychographics of Cyberheads

Source: http://www.future.sri.com/vals/valsindex.htm/.

THE INTERNET

What is the Internet? Simply put, it is a network of computers. It was originally designed by the government to provide an alternative communication network. The network was designed in a manner that it would continue to operate even if some nodes were destroyed. Large universities were connected to the Internet in the 1970s. In 1995, commercial carriers were granted control of the Internet and the common person gained access to it. Today, the Internet is a network of computer users in homes, schools, organizations, and so on. The protocol used is called TCP/IP. TCP stands for Transmission Control Protocol and IP stands for Internet Protocol. TCP breaks down information into packets for transfer and reassembles them at the destination point. IP ensures that the data is delivered to the right address.

Some of the communication services available for exploring the Internet are:

- *World Wide Web:* This is the most visible part of the Internet. It supports text, graphics, video, and audio and offers user-friendly navigation by simply using "point and click."
- *E-mail:* Allows users to send and receive mail around the world.
- *USENET:* A worldwide system of discussion groups that offers over 10,000 different discussion areas called newsgroups.
- *File Transfer Protocol:* Sends files to and retrieves files from other locations.
- *TELNET:* A program that enables the user to "log in" to a remote host site.

The Internet has now become a popular medium that companies are exploring, surveying, and evaluating. The Internet is being researched in terms of access and usage patterns with the intention of developing the demographic and psychographic profiles of users. Research is also ongoing in an effort to find out why consumers and businesses use the Internet. However, as a marketing tool, the Internet is still in its inception stages and is continually evolving. ACNielsen and ASI-Market Research launched an ongoing study called Net*Views in July 1996 to track products that could be marketed over the Internet. It has been found that some product categories, like electronics, breakfast foods, photographic supplies, and ethnic health and beauty aids, have a lot of potential. A demographic survey conducted over the Internet reveals that its usage is growing rapidly and the users tend to be upscale.

The Internet has been used by companies mainly as a medium of communication. Most companies that are geographically spread out link their offices through the Internet. E-mail is a very cost-effective way of sending and receiving information between offices and also for communicating with vendors, suppliers, and clients. Employees who travel can access information through the Internet. The Internet is the latest medium for marketing products and services. Exhibit 6-2 lists the top ten U.S. Internet access providers. Many traditional catalog companies offer their catalog services over the Internet. Many others use the Internet to advertise their products. Companies are also providing product support, information for vendors and customers, and online sales. The Internet provides researchers with a plethora of information. Marketing researchers can conduct secondary research on the Internet and obtain a wealth of information on various aspects of the country of interest to them. In recent times, it has also become a platform for conducting primary research. Researchers can conduct focus groups or questionnaire surveys over the Internet and the cost is nominal compared to traditional surveys. A San Francisco-based company called I/PRO provides software for measurement and analysis of Web site usage. This enables advertisers and media buyers to select optimal sites.

The World Wide Web has become the latest advertising medium for appealing to the masses. Statistics show that the number of registered commercial domains on the Web grew from 288,788 in May 1996 to 447,738 by August 1996. Exhibit 6-3 lists the number of hosts in different countries around the world. This explosive growth is expected to continue for the next few years. The flip side, however, is that as the nov-

---

EXHIBIT 6-2

Top 10 U.S. Online Access Providers

Service	Type	Users (as of Dec. 31, 1997)
America Online	Online Service	1.54 million (estimated)
The Microsoft Network	Online Service	2.3 million
Prodigy	Online Service	1 million
AT&T WorldNet	Telco-owned ISP	1 million
Netcom	Telco-owned ISP	560,000
EarthLink Network	Independent ISP	550,000
InternetMCI	Telco-Owned ISP	350,000
Erol's Internet	Independent ISP	300,000
GTE Internet Solutions	Telco-owned ISP	265,000
MindSpring	Independent ISP	265,000

Source: Reprinted by permission from *Inter@ctive Week*, February 16, 1998. Copyright © 1997 ZD, Inc.

EXHIBIT 6-3

Number of Hosts Per Country

Domain	Number	Description
.com	4,501,309	U.S. Commercial
.net	2,942,815	U.S. Networks
.jp	955,688	Japan
.uk	878,215	United Kingdom
.de	875,631	Germany
.us	825,048	United States
.au	707,611	Australia
.ca	690,316	Canada
.mil	542,295	U.S. Military
.org	434,654	U.S. Organizations
.gov	418,576	U.S. Government
.nl	341,560	Netherlands
.fi	335,956	Finland
.fr	292,096	France
.se	284,478	Sweden
.it	211,966	Italy
.no	209,034	Norway
.nz	155,678	New Zealand
.ch	148,028	Switzerland
.dk	137,008	Denmark
.kr	132,370	Korea
.es	121,823	Spain
.za	117,475	South Africa
.at	87,408	Austria

Source: Network Wizards, http://www.globalpromote.com/info/domains.html (31 July 1997).

elty wears off, the time spent online by an individual gradually reduces. Advertisers are now forced to think of innovative ways to market their product on the Web. *Inter@ctive Week*[3] reports that 1997 was the first year in which the shoppers took the Internet seriously, and this was backed by the sales of electronic store operators. The momentum carried on to the new year as sales in January 1998 exceeded those of the previous year. This increase in Internet sales is attributed to the increased consumer confidence in Internet security and higher penetration of online services. Several trends have emerged in the recent past. There was a broadening of the types of goods being sold, with apparel as one of the standouts. Retailers say they also notice consumers buying a lot more high-priced items, such as $1,000 televisions and $3,500 treadmills. A survey conducted by PointCast Inc. revealed that more than 30 percent of these people were first time shoppers and many of them said they would shop online

---

EXHIBIT 6-4

Small Businesses Big on E-Commerce

Small businesses are leading the electronic commerce charge and could reap as much as $7.5 billion in sales this year. A New York-based consulting firm, Access Media International Inc. (www.ami-usa.com), reports that more than 2.5 million U.S. small businesses have signed on to the Internet—a surprising 35 percent of all small business in the country. Of those, approximately 900,000 businesses have launched Web sites, and almost half of those are conducting e-commerce, either business-to-consumer sales or business-to-business transactions.

AMI also calculates small businesses invested a record $138 billion in Information Technology and telecommunications products last year, much of which was driven by Internet-related projects. AMI tracked 1,000 companies with fewer than 100 employees for the study; however, it did not include home-based businesses. From a relatively modest $300 million in online sales in 1996, AMI estimates the sector reaped $3.5 billion in sales in 1997 and will surpass $7.5 billion in 1998. AMI believes that by the turn of this century e-commerce sales will reach or exceed $25 billion.

Source: Reprinted by permission from *Inter@ctive Week*, February 16, 1998. Copyright © 1997 ZD, Inc.

---

again. Retailers predict that a lot of big name stores will enter the race for their share of the pie in cyberspace and site designs and marketing will get slicker. Exhibit 6-4 gives readers an idea of the increase in Internet business by small businesses. Many companies have also started studying the various consumer segments that use the Internet on a regular basis. One such classification is listed in Exhibit 6-5.

EXHIBIT 6-5

Segmentation Using Internet Usage

Type of Home Worker	*% Using the Internet*
Home Worker: adult who does any type or amount of job-related or income-producing work at home.	30
After-hours Home Worker: adult in any occupational category (including self-employed proprietors) who brings work home after hours.	35
Self-employed Home Worker: self-employed adult who does any sort of work at home.	23
Telecommuter: adult who works at home during normal business hours at least once a month.	35
Home Business Operator: term preferred by some home workers, mostly self-employed, to describe their home workstyle.	46
Non-Home Worker	8

Source: Internet Marketing & Technology Report 4, no. 2 (February 1998).

Internet marketing is not without its share of problems, though. Due to increased volume, many shoppers cannot get through to some of the more popular sites. Shopping can also be very time consuming and the majority of sites do not have the product in stock when requested. A lot of research is being conducted to find out how information will be priced in the electronic marketplace. Companies have to work out strategies for managing the site better and provide fast and reliable customer service. This will become crucial when competition heats up.

There is also some controversy on the unit used for pricing. Advertisers would prefer to pay for the usage based on the click-through rates rather than on cost-per-thousand. Expenditure on the Web for advertisement has not yet been pegged down to a precise figure; it is, however, estimated to grow to $3 billion by the turn of the century.

ADVANTAGES AND DISADVANTAGES OF THE INTERNET

There are a lot of benefits of advertising on the Internet. It helps advertisers reach a target audience with minimum cost, and because the Internet is interactive, advertisers can request the audience for personal information which will in turn help them design their advertisements better. Many companies have been able to produce custom ads for their audience. Moreover, the Internet offers the additional benefit of handling sales orders. Companies can place their catalogs on the Internet and potential customers who view the ads can place their orders on the Internet. The conversion time is greatly reduced.

One problem with advertising on the Internet is audience measurement. Traditional advertising relies on exposure; however, with the Internet, viewers switch back and forth between different Web sites and the exposure for a given screen may be minimal—the viewer would not have had the chance to read through the entire ad text. This is a problem that a lot of Web advertisers are facing. Some new services have been developed to counter this problem. *AdCount* by NetCount is a tracking service that attempts to measure the effect of Web ads. This software monitors the number of Web cruisers who see a given ad and also the number of these viewers who click on the ad to be connected to the advertiser's own Web site. The software generates reports regarding the daily and weekly click-throughs and ad transfers. It also provides summary reports with comparable statistics on each ad tracked.

HERMES (University of Michigan) and *Project 2000* (Vanderbilt University) are the two academic research endeavors on the activities of the Internet. HERMES looks at the commercial uses of the World Wide Web, such as forecasting consumer and corporate trends. Project 2000 tries to enrich and stimulate generation of knowledge on the role of marketing in the new hypermedia environment. According to HERMES, the usage of the World Wide Web on each of the eight categories is as follows (7 indicates usage all the time and 1 indicates no usage at all):

Reference	6.4
e-Zines	5.8
Commercial product/service information	5.5
Research reports	5.2

Weather	3.6
Financial	3.5
Shopping	2.6

Source: Fifth HERMES/GVU World Wide Web User Survey, April 1996.

Listed below are some examples of how companies use the Internet and the World Wide Web to market their products:

- The Ford Motor Company homepage on the World Wide Web has a listing of all the countries where Ford automobiles are being sold. Potential customers can click on the country of their choice and the various products available are displayed. The site also provides information on the closest Ford dealer and the lease options available to the customer.
- British Airways has a Web page that gives information about flight timings, ongoing promotions, and holiday packages and countries where British Airways services are available. Travelers can check for convenient flight timings before making a reservation.
- Sotheby's site on the World Wide Web has a questionnaire that encourages visitors to give personal information and their tastes and opinions. Responses to the questionnaire will help the art gallery modify its Web page to suit the needs of potential clients. The Web page also provides a list of all the Sotheby's galleries around the world.
- In major cities in the United States, grocery shopping can now be done through the Internet. Peapod, Inc. provides the software to major department chains. This software makes it possible for the customers to order groceries and have them delivered for a cost. This concept is likely to gain popularity in various parts of the world.

The Internet is becoming an inherent part of the marketing process and so it is only natural that it has an impact on the marketing research process. The Internet has been used for both primary and secondary data collection. Exhibit 6-6 lists the top 20 Internet sites for 1997. Critics of the Internet argue that the information found on the Web is of inferior quality. There is also the feeling that the profile of the population that is reached by the Internet is not representative of the target population. There is some truth to these arguments. It has been observed that the majority of people who browse the Web are trendsetters and may not be the ideal group to target for a lot of products and services. As a source of information, the Internet is not a comprehensive source for a lot of topics. Besides, as a medium of communication, it is still in its infancy and evolving very rapidly. Keeping up with the technological developments is a cumbersome task for a lot of people. Despite the obvious disadvantages, it is being used very widely in international marketing research.

SECONDARY RESEARCH ON THE INTERNET

Secondary research has been greatly benefited by the pervasive presence of the Internet. Information for research can be obtained at a company level, industry level (such as databases and directories), or at the macro level (government, organizations, etc.).

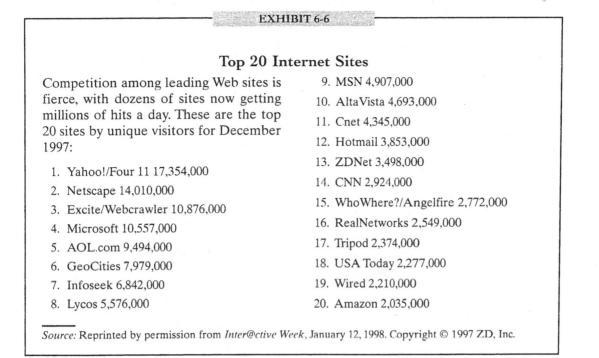

Top 20 Internet Sites

Competition among leading Web sites is fierce, with dozens of sites now getting millions of hits a day. These are the top 20 sites by unique visitors for December 1997:

1. Yahoo!/Four 11 17,354,000
2. Netscape 14,010,000
3. Excite/Webcrawler 10,876,000
4. Microsoft 10,557,000
5. AOL.com 9,494,000
6. GeoCities 7,979,000
7. Infoseek 6,842,000
8. Lycos 5,576,000
9. MSN 4,907,000
10. AltaVista 4,693,000
11. Cnet 4,345,000
12. Hotmail 3,853,000
13. ZDNet 3,498,000
14. CNN 2,924,000
15. WhoWhere?/Angelfire 2,772,000
16. RealNetworks 2,549,000
17. Tripod 2,374,000
18. USA Today 2,277,000
19. Wired 2,210,000
20. Amazon 2,035,000

Source: Reprinted by permission from *Inter@ctive Week*, January 12, 1998. Copyright © 1997 ZD, Inc.

Access to the information can be received directly by using the Internet address (URL) of the site. There are links that provide access to different sites. If the researcher does not have the precise address, search engines and agents can help obtain the information. All of these aspects of the Internet are explained in detail in this section. Increased modem speeds have also made it possible for researchers to access information quickly. Exhibit 6-7 gives details on the modem speeds available.

The usefulness of the Internet is appreciated when conducting secondary research for an international marketing research project. The Nielsen Internet Demographic Survey pointed out that 77 percent of the researchers contacted by the survey used the Internet for secondary research. The survey also revealed that another 45 percent of the respondents use the Internet to gather information about competition.

The Internet is just one of the many sources from which researchers can gather secondary data. Databases like Lexis/Nexis and Knight-Ridder provide information that a lot of businesses rely upon. Commercial online sources, such as CompuServe and America Online, are comprehensive information sources apart from being on the Internet. In terms of speed, the Internet is not the fastest. Information that is available on the Internet is not very well structured and the quality of the information available is mediocre. The Internet has only a limited number of search tools and does not provide extensive user support. The redeeming features of the Internet are its low cost and the broad spectrum of topics on which information is available. This makes it an attractive tool to conduct exploratory or secondary research. Advances in technology are also expected to weed out a lot of operational problems and make it more user friendly. This makes it the most sought after information source in recent times.

EXHIBIT 6-7

Speed Limits

- *56K Modem*—Available now. Speeds of 26,400 to 53,000 bits per second. Internet access at $15 to $35 per month. Regular phone line at approximately $15 per month.

- *Integrated Services Digital Network (ISDN)*—Available now. Speeds of 64,000 to 128,000 bits per second. Internet access at $40 to $100 per month. ISDN line at $58 per month.

- *AccelerNet (UHF-based wireless Internet access)*—Available now. Speeds of 256,000 to 1.54 million bits per second download and 33,600 to 128,000 bits per second upload. Costs of $80 to $850 per month plus phone line or ISDN uplink costs.

- *DirecPC (Satellite-based Internet access)*—Available now. Speeds of 1.54 million bits per second download and 33,600 bits per second upload. Costs of $30 to $130 per month and $229 for satellite-receiving hardware; phone line.

- *Asymmetrical Digital Subscriber Lines (ADSC)*—Available now are speeds of 384,000 to 1.54 million bits per second. Costs of $150 to $250 in trials in Austin. In California, Pacific Bell is offering ADSLs for $89 to $189 per month. About $300 for ADSL modems.

- *Road Runner (Time Warner Cable Internet Access)*—Available now are speeds of 27 million bits per second download and 784,000 bits per second upload. Costs are tentatively fixed at $39.95 a month.

Source: Adapted from *Houston Chronicle,* 26 August 1998, 8C.

Secondary research for international marketing research, however, may be more complicated. The percentage of the world population that does not access the Internet in English is substantial. Efforts must be made to collect information from sites in other languages also. The content and the format will be very different for different countries. Collating and formatting information will be a lot harder. Sometimes it may be necessary to change units or normalize data to enable comparison between regions. Researchers should always check for validity of data and authenticity of the source.

Some of the key statistics in terms of language used on the Internet[4] follow. The United States and Canada represent a market of 290 million consumers, 90 percent of whom speak English as their primary language. Europe represents a market of 380 million consumers, only 15 percent of whom speak English as their first language. Only 28 percent speak English at all. Japan represents a market of 100 million consumers and only 10 percent speak English. Most countries have made an attempt to join the information superhighway; however, there are some that are not on the Internet yet. Some of the bigger countries that do not have Internet connections as of January 1997 are Ethiopia, Myanmar, Sudan, North Korea, Iraq, Afghanistan, Syria, Somalia, Malawi, Tajikistan, Chad, Libya, Laos, Kyrgystan, Turkmenistan, Mauritania, Gabon, Guinea-Bissau, and Gambia.

Forty-five percent of adult Americans have access to the Internet either at work or at home. Sixteen percent of U.S. households use personal computers to access the Internet, 18 percent in Japan, and 12 percent in Hong Kong. In Europe, Germany had the highest Internet usage among home personal computer owners with 11.7 percent, followed by the United Kingdom at 9.5 percent, France at 6.5 percent, and Italy at 5.8 percent. Ninety percent of the white-collar workers use computers in the United States as compared to 53 percent in Europe. Ninety-eight percent of large European organizations are hooked up to the Internet, but only 4 percent of small and mid-sized companies have Internet connections. However, online access within Europe is set for a tenfold increase over the next four years. Access to PCs and other on-line retrieval devices will grow from 3 million in 1997 to 30 million by the end of 2000.

Modem penetration in the United States is 40 percent, but is relatively lower in Europe. There are predictions that the number of personal computers equipped with modems in Europe is set to increase by 735 percent by the year 2000. It is estimated that 35.9 million personal computers in these countries will have Internet/online access via modem, ISDN connections, or cable links by the turn of the millennium.

The number of Internet users is set to triple in the Asia/Pacific region over the next five years. This will mean that there will be more than 28 million users by 2001. In the next five years, nearly 30 percent of households in Japan, Korea, Australia, Taiwan, Singapore, and Hong Kong will have access to the Internet.

Transactions on the Internet have gone up to $6.6 billion in 1997 and are expected to skyrocket to $200 billion by 2000. This alone makes the Internet a very powerful marketing medium that no company can afford to ignore.

Custom Search Services

With the growing popularity of the Internet, a number of companies are offering specialized search services for a fee. This could be either a one-time custom search or regular news deliveries. These custom search services specialize in one or two areas, like telecommunications or food processing, and offer their services in the form of a newsletter. Service charges depend on the frequency with which information is delivered to the client, on the usage, or on the amount of text. An example would be the Dow Jones News/Retrieval Service that scans thousands of business publications from around the world and provides the subscriber with custom financial and business news and information. The user pays a charge for each article viewed. The Service has also configured topic folders that contain information about one specific aspect of business.

Agents

The other tool used by companies to gain access to information is the use of agents. Agents function in different ways. Some of them are available on the Internet and are preprogrammed to perform certain specific tasks. Others are a piece of software that can be purchased by the user, who then has to specify downloading criteria. Most often these searches are scheduled at night so that they do not have to wait for the information. This technology is on the verge of entering mainstream Web search and users can look forward to many innovations in this area.

Besides the above-mentioned sources of information, a number of other sources have set up services that provide free access to information. News agencies such as Reuters, newspapers such as the *New York Times*, and news services such as CNN are very active in this area. On an international level, several news agencies and newspapers from other countries provide this kind of information. The section on search engines will explain how to launch a search to find the addresses of these sources on the World Wide Web. In most cases, the information available on the Web will be the same as that available in the paper version. These sources offer day-to-day information about the country of interest to the researcher. Many news providers have also tried to make their presentation original. The latest in this area, Pointcast, appears instantly on the computer screen. The user does not have to surf the Net for news. Pointcast has dynamic headlines that pop up on the screen and it is completely customizable. Information can be obtained on the stock markets, international events, industry updates, weather around the globe, sports, and even information from CNN, *People,* and *Money* magazines. Pointcast acts as a screen saver and can be downloaded free from the Internet.

Search Engines

The World Wide Web has several search engines that can be used. AltaVista, Excite, Magellan, and Infoseek are some of the commonly used search engines. Conducting a search is a fairly simple task. It is easy to see how secondary research is greatly simplified by the Internet and the search engines. International marketing researchers can conduct a thorough search on the Internet and form initial hypotheses even before stepping out of the borders of their home country. This has a significant impact on keeping the costs down. There are Web sites that provide detailed information, such as the geographic, economic, political, and demographic data about countries of interest. Many countries have also established government agencies that provide free information to businesses wanting to enter those countries. Here are some tips that might prove useful when conducting a search on the Internet:[5]

- Start by typing out a few key words. Try to include all of the obvious choices. For example, if some information is required about Great Britain, type out England, United Kingdom, and Great Britain. Use all of the popular synonyms, as any one of them could be used in the document that is being searched for.
- Beware of search terms with double meanings. For instance, "web spider" could mean what arachnids spin or it could refer to an Internet technology.
- Be precise. Search for "carburetor repairs" and not "car repairs."
- If it is not possible to be precise, use search engines such as Infoseek that make it easy to refine and narrow your search as you go along.
- The search usually results in a number of results as the Web contains many documents with the words used for the search. It is important that the search provide the documents in the correct order with the most relevant first.
- If the information that is sought is not available in the first few pages of the search result, the query should be rephrased.
- If a key word has to be present in the document, use a plus sign in front of it. The query "natural +herbal cosmetics" will return sites that definitely have the word herbal. Natural and cosmetics would be optional. If the query says "herbal –artificial," the search would yield all sites that have herbal but not artificial.
- It is better to use lowercase letters for the search. If the query is for herbal, all sites that contain this word are returned. However, if the query reads Herbal, only those sites that match this exactly will be returned.

- To find a phrase, the query should contain double quotes around the words. The query "Southeast Asia" will yield sites that match the query exactly. It means sites that contain the phrase "south east Asia" will not be returned.
- For specialized searches, specialized search engines may provide faster results.
- Master Boolean logic. "Dolphins OR sharks" finds all the sites containing either of these words. On the other hand, "dolphins AND sharks" will return sites that have both these words.

Conducting a search on the Internet can be done at three different levels: company level, industry level, or macro level. Following are examples of how this information can be used:

1. *Competitive Intelligence Analysis.* Volkswagen wants to capture competitor's marketing action in Brazil. The researcher could study the automotive industry in Brazil.
2. *Industry Analysis.* A major U.S. manufacturer of iced tea wants to enter the Mexican market. This would involve a study of the soft drink market in Mexico.
3. *Buyer Behavior.* A national distribution chain in India has to decide whether it should include consumer-ready food products in its portfolio. A study of the retail food industry will provide some answers.
4. *New Business-to-Business Market.* A consultant firm has to provide the client with a report on potential opportunities in the Venezuelan oil-rig equipment market. This could be expedited by looking up the oil industry on the Internet.

The procedure followed in gathering secondary information for each of the above cases is explained in the following section.

Competitive Intelligence Analysis

Let us consider the case of Volkswagen wanting to capture the marketing action of competitors in Brazil. Conducting secondary research on the Internet is a simple process of following the guidelines mentioned in this chapter. A lot of preliminary information can be obtained from the Internet.

The first step is to decide on a search engine. We choose Excite—readers could opt for a search engine that they are most familiar with. The address for various search engines is mentioned in a separate section. The search engine asks for a search criterion. We look for "brazil automotive." Note that lowercase letters are used. This search yields all the sites that have "Brazil" and "automotive" in them. We then shortlist the ones that seem most useful to our study—ones that give us information about the automobile industry in Brazil or ones that talk about competitor action in Brazil.

We choose to go into "Automotive Fact Sheet: Brazil." Once again, the selection of sites or the order in which they are selected is of no consequence as long as the information is collected. A sample is provided of this document. The next site we look into is called "International Business Practices in Brazil." This document gives information like trade barriers, tariffs, business organizations, commercial policies, foreign investment, incentives, taxation, regulatory agencies, and useful contacts. This site could prove very useful if primary research has to be conducted. The next site we visit is called "Brazil—The Auto Sector." This site is a gold mine in terms of information on the auto industry in Brazil. It give important demographic data, like the population of Brazil, the number of cars sold in Brazil, the manufactures who have a significant presence in Brazil, trade fair information, industry information, and best market opportunities. This site gives us an idea of the major players in the automobile industry in Brazil.

We can now look at individual companies who have a big stake in the Brazilian market. Let us consider Ford. The other sites have given us statistics as to the number of Ford cars sold in Brazil. We know the market share of Ford. We now need to get information on the marketing practices of Ford and the promotional plans offered by them to car buyers. The Excite search engine can be used once again to search for Ford Web sites. Alternately, we could go directly to the Ford site by using the address of their global homepage: www.ford.com. This Web site provides links to different Ford sites around the world. We go into the Brazil Web site. We could also directly access this site by using the address www.ford.com.br. This site provides information on various aspects, like price and features of different Ford models, number and location of Ford dealerships, financing schemes, special promotions, and so on. With this, we should have a fairly thorough idea of the marketing practices followed by Ford.

The same procedure could be followed for each of the other car manufacturers. Secondary search on the Internet is an iterative procedure. Each successive search is further refined until we obtain all of the information we are looking for. The advantage of the Internet is the speed with which a search can be conducted.

Some of the other sites that can be searched are

- www.lanic.utexas.edu—a site on Latin American countries maintained by the University of Texas
- www.mercedes-benz.com.br—Mercedes Benz site for Brazil
- www.fiat.com.br—Fiat site for Brazil.

As mentioned earlier, there are several search engines available and the researcher can use the one that he or she is most comfortable with.

Industry Analysis

Entering a foreign market involves a lot of investment, so most firms prefer to do a thorough study of the market before committing themselves to the project. The iced tea manufacturer has to have a thorough understanding of the Mexican market in terms of the market size, market share of other iced tea manufacturers (if any), the Mexican perception of iced tea, and the popular substitutes that could pose a threat to the market share of iced tea in Mexico. A lot of this information can be collected from the Internet.

We start off by setting up a search on Excite. The search criterion we use is "mexico soft drinks." One of the sites yielded by the search is titled "Euromonitor on Alcoholic and Soft Drinks." We select the topic "Market for Soft Drinks in Mexico." We can also reach this site directly by using the address www.euromonitor.com. The information in this site is provided for a charge. The topics covered are socio-economic background, consumption patterns and shopping habits, prices and inflation, consumer indicators, the retail market, international comparisons, market sectors, packaging of soft drinks, the distribution network, industry structure, trade market share, company profiles, foreign investment, comparative company analysis, and advertising and promotions. This covers all aspects of the soft drink industry in Mexico. The other site that we look into is www.mexonline.com. This site contains information about the government, banks, financial firms, demographic data, and also an educational tape on how to do business in Mexico.

The information from both of these sites should be sufficient to help us get started with the research study and formulate a few hypotheses about the iced tea sales in Mexico.

Buyer Behavior

This case involves studying the retail food market in India to get a better understanding of buyer behavior. It is also necessary to study the distribution setup so that a decision can be made regarding getting the products to the consumer. We start our search with the Web site www.indiaserver.com. There are several options available in the main menu. We go into the search option and type out the search criterion as "retail food industry." The search yields a number of articles and newspaper clips on this topic. An article titled "Food Value Added" gives a summary about the state of the retail food industry in India. There is another document titled "Supermarkets: Has Their Time Come" which gives insight into the evolution of the distribution network in India. A third document titled "Retail Promotion" describes the state of the retail industry in India. There are documents concerning tax cuts on processed foods and other benefits to the food processing industry.

The same site can be used to run another search with "precooked packaged foods." This search yields several more documents on the retail food industry in India. The document titled "Sectoral Focus of the Month" talks about the food processing industry and gives details on processing facilities for fruits, vegetables, meat, and poultry in India. It also talks about technology requirements, government policies, and multinational companies who have set up food processing plants in India. There is a document mentioning the plans for Del Monte, the U.K.-based food-processing company to set up plants in India. "Emerging Food Preservation Technologies" mentions that demand for high quality processed foods is on the rise. Several other sites mention the proliferation of microwaves and increase in demand for precooked spices and curries and processed fruits. All of this is a good indication that there is a tremendous market for consumer-ready foods in India. Some of these sites also mention the possible distribution channels that can be considered.

New Business-to-Business Market

The client is looking for a report on the oil industry in Venezuela. As in the case of previous searches, we look at a search engine to help us get started. We get into Yahoo! and type out "venezuela oil" as the search criterion. Once the list of Web sites appears on the screen, we shortlist some of them based on the titles. The site with the title "Petroleum Guide to Venezuela" looks very promising. This site provides us with a directory of over 1,000 companies serving the oil industry in Venezuela. There are links to sites that provide various auxiliary services, like construction, engineering, consulting, drilling and well service, exploration, technical services, manufacturers and suppliers, oil producing and processing companies, associate services like banking, insurance, legal, government agencies, and the mining industry. This site provides information about all of the aspects of the oil industry.

The next stop is at www.oilonline.com. This site provides general information about the oil industry all over the world. We then look into "International Report." This site provides news clips of major events in the oil industry worldwide. Under the title "World Oil and Gas" there are several links to different locations around the world. We choose Central and South America and then Venezuela. This site provides information on oil, natural gas, coal, electricity, energy efficiency, environment, and profile. General information, like the map of Venezuela, is also available.

The search described above provides us with basic information required to get started on the project. With this data in hand, we can decide on the next step of designing an instrument to collect primary data, if the client wants to proceed with this project.

INTRANETS

Secondary research is further enhanced by the addition of Intranets. Intranets are internal company networks that link various offices of a company around the world. An Intranet user can access the Internet very easily, whereas an Intranet is protected by security codes that prevent outsiders from gaining access. These networks help employees gain access to company information in different parts of the world. The next stage of development will be integrating suppliers, vendors, customers, and branch offices in an Intranet. This will help large corporations with timely communication and distribution of information. This is particularly useful for companies that rely heavily on information to conduct their day-to-day business. Management consultants, software developers, and stock and commodity brokers are some of the people who stand to benefit a lot with the improvements in the Intranet. Information that is considered crucial is stored in the company's internal database and is accessible by all authorized employees around the world. Checking the company's database first saves researchers a lot of time. For instance, Arthur Andersen maintains a database that every consultant can access. At the start of a project, consultants look up this database for similar projects so that a lot of time and expense is avoided by duplication of effort.

Thus, the Internet and the World Wide Web can become an integral part of the information system of a corporation. "Firewalls" can protect outsiders from accessing the information in the Intranet. All the departments of a company can be connected by the Intranet, greatly saving the time taken to communicate back and forth.

With all of these developments in the Internet, it is only natural that users look for increased speed of operation. All of the latest technologies dealing with the Internet look for ways of increasing the bandwidth of the Internet. As more and more users get into the Internet and use it for transferring larger chunks of data, high-speed connections become a necessity. Recent developments have made it possible to transfer audio and video signals live. Many telephone operators, such as MCI and Sprint, are moving toward fiber-optic technology to accommodate transfer of full-screen motion pictures through the Internet. Needless to say, all of these technology improvements will benefit international marketing research. Researchers can conduct focus groups from various parts of the world. This will reduce costs substantially and also give researchers a better understanding of the multiple cultures. Professionals and busy executives who cannot come together in a single location for a focus group will be able to participate over the Internet.

PRIMARY RESEARCH ON THE INTERNET

As can be understood from the previous section, the Internet is being used increasingly in the area of secondary research. Exhibit 6-8 illustrates the use of the Internet as a data collection tool. The use of the Internet has also made primary research easier. Primary research can be conducted on the Internet by two basic methods:

1. *Without Client Involvement.* This involves keeping track of visitors to the Web sites maintained by companies. This method tracks the time spent by visitors in any given Web site, the domain or the country the visitor is browsing from, the type of computer and browser used by the visitor, and the frequency of visits.
2. *With Client Involvement.* This is achieved by e-mail surveys and data collection on the Web site. Questionnaires are sent out and responses are collected via electronic mail.

The starting point for primary research over the Internet is the use of electronic mail surveys. Questionnaires are mailed to respondents at their e-mail addresses. Provision is made in the questionnaires to complete the form online and return it to the researcher. The following advantages are obvious:

- greater speed of delivery
- higher speed of receiving responses
- tremendous cost savings over regular mail
- no intermediaries—usually read only by the recipient
- asynchronous communication.

Electronic mail also has the following disadvantages:

- not completely confidential
- limited to actual e-mail users who may not be representative of the general population
- respondents can give in to creative impulses and make modifications to the questionnaire, like rewriting scales
- typographic problems—some characters cannot be used in an e-mail questionnaire
- if the topic of research is controversial, a lot of responses will be "flames and letter bombs"—of no use to the study.

Participants in the online surveys can interact privately with one another during a focus group. Special symbols called emoticons, which look like facial expressions, obtained by typing certain keys in combination, allow participants to express themselves.

Companies are also collecting information about the people who visit their Web sites. This information can be used for customizing the Web site to suit the needs of their customers. It could also be used by product development, sales, and marketing departments to get more information about the product design and usage. The customer service department can use this facility to receive and redress complaints.

EXHIBIT 6-8

Use of the Internet as a Data Collection Method

The SGA Market Research Paper describes the use of the Internet as a means of conducting commercial surveys and compares this method to the traditional methods of data collection. A study conducted in 1995 showed that e-mail could generate very high response rates in a much shorter time as compared to the postal surveys. It was also found that the quality of responses was much better and the cost savings were significant with e-mail surveys.

The objective of the study was to determine how early adopters of new technology were using the Internet and how their views differed from the population as a whole. The original database of e-mail names was purchased from an Internet magazine publisher. The list included both subscribers to the magazine and others who had interacted with the magazine during the past year. Because the list of e-mail names was limited and many e-mail addresses proved to be invalid, respondents were also contacted using traditional postal media and were requested to complete the online survey that was posted on the Web.

Respondents who were contacted by e-mail were first sent a "pre" e-mail detailing the purpose of the study and requesting their cooperation. This was done to ensure that the respondent did not treat the questionnaire as just another junk e-mail. The questionnaire was e-mailed to all respondents who acknowledged the "pre" e-mail. A reminder questionnaire was sent out after a week and all responses were tabulated. Respondents were also sent the questionnaire by postal mail and a return envelope was enclosed. There was no reminder sent to these respondents. The respondents who were contacted by post were also given the opportunity to complete the online survey.

The questionnaire covered a wide range of topics, such as Internet usage habits, attitudes towards technology, and details regarding the time spent on the Internet and other activities. There were several constraints on the e-mail version of the questionnaire. It could not include any nonstandard characters (such as $), bold, italics, or font size changes. Care had to be taken not to exceed 70 column widths to avoid word wrapping. The respondents had to be informed to ensure that their e-mail viewer was set to a fixed spacing font to make certain that all boxes were aligned. In the case of some respondents the file size proved to be a problem. Some e-mail systems were not equipped to receive a file of the size of the questionnaire (34 K) and hence the questionnaire had to be split into two parts.

Incentives were offered to respondents who completed the survey. A nominal amount was sent to all respondents who completed the survey. They were given the opportunity to donate this money to charity, which proved to be very popular. There was also a prize draw for a wide screen TV for the first 250 respondents.

Time to respond proved to be the biggest advantage of the e-mail survey. Nearly two-thirds of all the questionnaires sent out via e-mail were received back in three days. This included the time required to send out the "pre" e-mail and the time for sending out the survey. In this same time period only one out of 437 postal surveys had been returned. The average postal response time was 11 days. Furthermore, it was observed that all of the e-mail responses were received in the first 7 days and none after that. This suggested that most people read their e-mail boxes very frequently. The overall response from e-mail was 13.5 percent. This could be attributed to the time required to complete the survey (30 to 40 minutes). A shorter questionnaire would have no doubt produced a better response rate. The postal survey produced a response rate of 15.4 percent. It was also observed that the reminder sent out to e-mail respondents did very little to boost the response rate. An interesting feature of the survey was that relatively few people contacted by mail took up the option of completing the survey online. This could be attributed to lack of access to e-mail at the place where the respondents received the questionnaire. (Some were mailed to homes while others were mailed to office addresses.)

The e-mail surveys provided significantly higher response completeness.

Open-ended questions received a more complete and wider range of responses in e-mail surveys; however, the average level of item omission was higher for e-mail surveys and this could be because of the difficulty of completing a survey online. The cost for e-mail surveys was substantially lower than for postal surveys.

The study concluded that the Internet can be used effectively as a data collection method and can offer significant benefits in terms of time and cost savings; however, e-mail may not be the optimum method of contacting potential respondents for Internet surveys. It is better to post the questionnaire on the Web and ask respondents to visit the Web site to complete the survey. This provides a better questionnaire interface and speeds up the response time. The flip side to e-mail surveys is obtaining the list of e-mail addresses. There is no global directory of e-mail names. The respondent base is also not representative of the general population. Hence, Internet surveys may not be the ideal method for all surveys.

Source: Adapted from *SGA Esomar Paper*, 1995 from Http://www.sga.co.uk/esomar.html. Copyright © ESOMAR® 1999. Permission for using this material has been granted by ESOMAR® (European Society for Opinion and Marketing Research), Amsterdam, The Netherlands. For further information please refer to the ESOMAR® Publications Website: www.esomar.nl.

Some Internet Addresses

Search Engines

Alta Vista	http://www.altavista.com
Lycos	http://www.lycos.com
Excite	http://www.excite.com
InfoSeek	http://www.infoseek.com
WebCrawler	http://www.webcrawler.com
Opentext	http://www.opentext.com
Yahoo!	http://www.yahoo.com
Metacrawler	http://www.metacrawler.com
C/Net	http://www.search.com

News Service

Reuters News Media	http://yahoo.com/headlines
The New York Times	http://nytimes.com

Los Angeles Times	http://latimes.com/HOME
CNN	http://www.cnn.com
ClariNet	http://www.clarinet.com
Agent Technology	
WebCompass	http://www.quarterdeck.com
WebWare	http://www.osf.org
Surfbot	http://www.specter.com
Marketing Research	
Innovative Marketing Consultants	http://www.imc-marketing.com
University of Texas	http://www.lanic.utexas.edu
Ford Worldwide	http://www.ford.com/global
MasterCard	http://www.mastercard.com
Nielsen	http://www.nielsen.com
HERMES	http://www-personal umich .edu/~sgupta/hermes
Project 2000	http://www2000.ogsm.Vanderbilt.edu

INTERNATIONAL MARKETING RESEARCH IN PRACTICE

The Internet is one of the most important sources of secondary data. Tasty Burgers could make good use of the Internet to obtain preliminary information on the countries of interest to them. In the previous chapter we outlined the different kinds of secondary data that are required to make a preliminary judgment on the four countries. Economic data include variables such as GDP, GNP, per capita income, and purchasing power parity. Social data include legal systems, social structures, and infrastructure, such as transportation, communication, and media services. Demographic data would cover population, population density in a given region, income ranges, and standard of living. There are many Web sites that provide these data. A search engine could be used to identify these sites. One such site is the CIA World Factbook, which is available at http://www.odci.gov/cia/publications/factbook. This site provides basic data for all countries of interest and is also well updated. There are several Web sites maintained by the Indian and Brazilian statistical institutes that can be identified by using "indian statistics" or "brazilian statistics" as the search criterion. It is also possible to obtain information about the fast-food industry and suppliers of breads, vegetables, and meats in each of these markets.

It is important to interject a word of caution for those who use the Internet as a source of information. There is no control in terms of the information that is posted on the Web; hence, the authenticity of the source and the information must always be verified.

Summary

The Internet was originally designed for use by the U.S. government. Today, it is a major network of computers connecting schools, libraries, organizations, and individuals. There are many options available for users to obtain information from the Internet.

The Internet has contributed to increasing the speed of communication and decreasing the cost. Marketing research is one of the disciplines where use of the Internet is on the rise. It can be used for both primary and secondary research.

This chapter provides a brief overview of the history and relevant statistics pertaining to the Internet. Methods of conducting secondary research using the search engines are explained in detail. Some of the relevant Web sites are also listed. Conducting primary research on the Internet is beginning to become popular and this chapter takes a look at some of the methods.

APPENDIX 6-1[6]

Actualizers are successful, sophisticated, active, "take-charge" people with high self-esteem and abundant resources. They are interested in growth and seek to develop, explore, and express themselves in a variety of ways—sometimes guided by principles, and sometimes by a desire to have an effect, to make a change. Image is important to Actualizers, not as evidence of status or power, but as an expression of taste, independence, and character. Actualizers are among the established and emerging leaders in business and government, yet they continue to seek challenges. They have a wide range of interests, are concerned with social issues, and are open to change. Their lives are characterized by richness and diversity. Their possessions and recreation reflect a cultivated taste for the finer things in life.

Fulfilleds are mature, satisfied, comfortable, reflective people who value order, knowledge, and responsibility. Most are well-educated and in (or recently retired from) professional occupations. They are well-informed about world and national events and are alert to opportunities to broaden their knowledge. Content with their career, family, and station in life, their leisure activities tend to center around the home. Fulfilleds have a moderate respect for the status quo institutions of authority and social decorum, but are open-minded to new ideas and social change. Fulfilleds tend to base their decisions on firmly held principles and consequently appear calm and self-assured. While their incomes allow them many choices, Fulfilleds are conservative, practical consumers; they look for durability, functionality, and value in the products they buy.

Achievers are successful career and work-oriented people who like to, and generally do, feel in control of their lives. They value consensus, predictability, and stability over risk, intimacy, and self-discovery. They are deeply committed to work and family. Work provides them with a sense of duty, material rewards, and prestige. Their social lives reflect this focus and are structured around family, church, and career. Achievers live conventional lives, are politically conservative, and respect authority and the status quo. Image is important to them; they favor established, prestige products and services that demonstrate success to their peers.

Experiencers are young, vital, enthusiastic, impulsive, and rebellious. They seek variety and excitement, savoring the new, offbeat, and risky. Still in the process of formulating life values and patterns of behavior, they quickly become enthusiastic about new possibilities, but are equally quick to cool. At this stage in their lives, they are politically uncommitted, uninformed, and highly ambivalent about what they believe. Experiencers combine an abstract disdain for conformity with an outsider's awe of others' wealth, prestige, and power. Their energy finds an outlet in exercise, sports, outdoor recreation, and social activities. Experiencers are avid consumers and spend much of their income on clothing, fast food, music, movies, and videos.

Believers are conservative, conventional people with concrete beliefs based on traditional, established codes: family, church, community, and the nation. Many believers express moral codes that are deeply rooted and literally interpreted. They follow established routines, organized in large part around the home, family, social, or religious organizations to which they belong. As consumers, Believers are conservative and predictable, favoring American products and established brands. Their income, education, and energy are modest, but sufficient to meet their needs.

Strivers seek motivation, self-definition, and approval from the world around them. They are striving to find a secure place in life. They are unsure of themselves and are low on economic, social, and psychological resources. Strivers are concerned about the opinions and approval of others. Money defines success for Strivers, who don't have enough of it, and often feel that life has given them a raw deal. Strivers are impulsive and easily bored. Many of them seek to be stylish. They emulate those who own more impressive possessions, but what they wish for is often beyond their reach.

Makers are practical people who have constructive skills and value self-sufficiency. They live within a traditional context of family, practical work, and physical recreation and have little interest in what lies outside that context. Makers experience the world by working on it—building a house, raising children, fixing a car, or canning vegetables—and have enough skill, income, and energy to carry out their projects successfully. Makers are politically conservative, suspicious of new ideas, respectful of government authority and organized labor, but resentful of government intrusion on private rights. They are unimpressed by material possessions other than those with a practical or functional purpose (such as tools, utility vehicles, and fishing equipment).

Strugglers lives are constricted. Chronically poor, ill-educated, low-skilled, without strong social bonds, elderly, and concerned about their health, they are often resigned and passive. Because they are limited by the need to meet the urgent needs of the present moment, they do not show a strong self-orientation. Their chief concerns are for security and safety. Strugglers are cautious consumers. They represent a very modest market for most products and services, but are loyal to favorite brands. *Source:* Adapted from www.future.sri.com/vals/valsindex.html

Questions and Problems

1. John Smith has to make a holiday trip from Seoul to Los Angeles. He searched on the Internet for the lowest price offering and bought his ticket. Demonstrate the search process that John used to get his ticket.

2. Assume your family is interested in visiting the NASA Space Center in Houston. They would like to gather more facts about the place before they embark on a trip. How can you assist them in this process?

3. Design a customer satisfaction questionnaire and e-mail it to your friends. Ask them to respond to your survey by filling out the questionnaire and e-mailing it back to you.

4. You are hired as an intern in the marketing research department of a chemical plant in the United States. The firm is interested in expanding its worldwide operations and is interested in country-specific information regarding the land use for agriculture. How will you obtain this information on the Internet?

5. Pick any company of your choice, and:
   a. Identify its Web site
   b. Browse through the Web site
   c. List the type of information that is available
   d. Identify any country-specific or international operators of the firm.

Endnotes

1. Jim Hamill, "The Internet and International Marketing," *International Marketing Review* 14, no. 5 (1997): 300–323.

2. Rebecca Piirto, "Frontiers of Psychographics," *Marketing 98/99* (CT: Dushkin/McGraw-Hill, 1998) 88–92.

3. Mel Duvall, "Web Registers Still Ringing in '98," *Inter@ctive Week* 5, no. 2 (19 January 1998): 48.

4. "bluesky international marketing" http://www.blueskyinc.com/keyfind.htm, (IDC Research, Inc., 1996).

5. Adapted from "Power Search Tips," *Internet World* (December 1997): 86.

6. Adapted from http://future.sri.com/vals/valsindex.html.

CHAPTER

7

Primary Data Research

INTRODUCTION

This chapter focuses on the collection of primary data for international marketing research. We address the different types of primary research, the various issues involved in collecting primary data, the biases that can occur, and the benefits and costs of collecting primary data. Primary data may be required for various reasons. It could be used to aid in a specific project, like launching a product overseas. Some companies collect primary data from their international markets on a continuous basis to plan corporate strategy. Primary research, unlike secondary research, is carried out for a specific purpose. Exhibit 7-1 illustrates how primary research can help companies save millions.

Researchers for international marketing research projects make limited use of primary data. This could be attributed to several reasons. The main reason for use of primary data being less widespread is the cost involved in collecting the data. The management could have doubts about the competence and reliability of the research companies in foreign countries and could hesitate to commission the study; however, large corporations that anticipate huge revenues from these foreign markets conduct primary research, as they are able to justify the cost with the expected revenues.

It is important for researchers to be aware of the data collection methods that work in different countries. Due to differences in availability of infrastructure, cultural differences, geographic limitations, and language barriers, not all data collection methods work in all countries. Because the process of primary data collection is a costly and involved procedure, researchers should obtain some preliminary information on the country of interest before starting out with collecting primary data. As mentioned in chapter 5, secondary research helps. Various organizations publish information that could be used to decide the data collection methods beforehand. Table 7-1 is a table published by the ESOMAR that provides information on the most popular methods of data collection in five European countries. Researchers should look for data of this nature for all countries or regions of interest.

EXHIBIT 7-1

International Marketing Research to the Rescue

In the late 1980s Hilton was in trouble. Renaming its hotels had devalued the core brand, but market research came to the rescue. There had been virtually no significant research by Hilton International for more than a decade. The brand was now being challenged by international competition from the likes of Sheraton, Hyatt, and Marriott and facing changing demands of the consumers it sought to serve. So, in 1988, a program was initiated to establish its standing in the United States, Germany, Australia, and Japan. Hilton scored higher than its competitors in terms of awareness, but there were areas of weaknesses. The sub-brand Hilton National created for existing hotels and Hilton International performed very poorly in terms of awareness compared to the parent Hilton name. Also, the Hilton International logo was the least known of the seven logos tested. Another adverse factor was that Hilton was perceived as unfriendly and complacent.

A global "Take Me to Hilton" campaign rolled out in 1989 and was translated into nine languages, to be viewed by 54 million people. Another similar research in 1991 proved that Hilton had improved its ratings in terms of awareness in all the countries and increased in market share substantially, too.

The moral of the story is clear. Primary research plays a major role even in the most entrepreneurial of organizations. Management decisions in many cases may seem like pure instinct. Primary research can provide a suitable counter-balance. It offers a means to monitor the consequences, and when appropriate, provides a mechanism for reviewing and refining the course of action.

Source: Adapted from Robin Cobb, "The Essential Market Monitor," *Marketing* 26 (28 January 1993).

TABLE 7-1. European Data Collection Methods (Percent of Use)

	France	*The Netherlands*	*Sweden*	*Switzerland*	*United Kingdom*
Mail	4	33	23	8	9
Telephone	15	18	44	21	16
Central location/street	52	37	—	—	—
Home/work	—	—	8	44	54
Groups	13	—	5	6	11
In-depth interviews	12	12	2	8	—
Secondary	4	—	4	8	—
Other	0	0	14	5	10

Source: "ESOMAR Urges Changes in Reporting Demographics, Issues Worldwide Report," by Emanuel H. Demby from *Marketing News* January 8, 1990 p. 24. Reprinted by permission of the American Marketing Association.

TYPES OF PRIMARY RESEARCH

Primary research can be of three types: exploratory research, descriptive research, and causal research. The difference is in the requirements in terms of time and expense. The purpose of each of these types of research is also different, and their utility to companies can vary from purely tactical to strategic and long term. A vast majority of the international marketing research studies are descriptive in nature. Often, exploratory research is insufficient to make important corporate decisions and causal research is too time consuming. Most companies are satisfied with obtaining a thorough understanding of the market, which enables them to make reasonably accurate decisions. This section deals with the three types of primary data collection in detail.

Exploratory research is most appropriate when the primary objective is to identify problems, to define problems more precisely, or to investigate the possibility of new alternative courses of action. Exploratory research can also aid in formulating hypotheses regarding potential problems or opportunities present in the decision situation. In some cases, this could be the only step in further research activity. Exploratory research is characterized by the need for great flexibility and versatility. The researcher has very little knowledge about the situation being researched and needs to be able to adapt quickly to newly emerging situations in order to make research worthwhile. Exploratory research focuses on qualitative rather than quantitative data collection and the researcher is looking for quick answers to the research problem on hand. As a result, this type of research is less rigorous and therefore less reliable then descriptive and causal research. Exploratory research is used when the objective is to define the problem or provide an overview of the situation. It is more economical in terms of time and money. Exploratory research is used extensively in international marketing research. When researchers are asked to solve a problem or identify an opportunity in a foreign country they are not familiar with, they have to resort to exploratory research to learn and understand that culture.

Descriptive research aims at providing a description of the existing market phenomena. Such research is often used to determine the frequency of occurrence of market events, such as frequency of customers visiting a store, machines needing to be replaced, or lawyers being consulted. Descriptive research can also be used, in a noncausal fashion, to the degree to which marketing variables are related to one another. Based on this determination, predictions can be made about regarding future occurrences in the market. In an international setting, the researcher typically uses descriptive research to look for similarities and differences between markets and consumer groups. Similarities can then be exploited through standardization, whereas differences can help in formulating adaptive business strategy.

Descriptive studies require large quantities of data, as the need for accurate portrayal of the population studied is more stringent. Hypotheses are preformulated and subsequently tested with the collected data. The research design needs to be carefully planned and structured. The intent of descriptive research is to maximize accuracy and minimize systematic error. The researcher aims to increase the reliability by keeping the measurement process as free from random error as possible.

Casual research aims at identifying the precise cause-and-effect relationships present in the market. The level of precision is higher than that for other types of research because reasonable unambiguous conclusions regarding causality must be presented. Hence, causal research is often the most demanding in terms of time and financial resources. To extract causality from a variety of unrelated factors, researchers often need to resort to longitudinal and experimental measures. Longitudinal measures are required because after-the-fact measurement alone cannot fully explain the effect of causality. Experimentation is necessary to introduce systematic variation of factors and then measure the effect of these variations. Causal research is useful only if the research objective is to identify these interrelationships and if this knowledge makes a contribution to the corporate decision making process.

Experimental design is based on the principle of manipulating a treatment variable and observing changes in a response variable. This enables the researcher to draw conclusions about causality, especially if the experiment has been controlled for all other factors that can cause changes in the response variable. In establishing causal relationship between variables, it is necessary to determine which variable is the cause and which is the result. While looking for causal relationships the researcher should look for evidences of strong associations between the action taken and the observed outcome and that the action preceded the outcome. The researcher should also be capable of eliminating every other possible or probable cause for the observed outcome. The other important factor to be considered is the time lag between the cause and the effect. In many international marketing situations, the results are not apparent immediately. Even though experimental designs are applicable to all social and cultural backgrounds, it is very difficult to design an experiment that is comparable or equivalent in all countries and cultures. Experiments, by their very nature, incorporate cultural differences in terms of marketing practices, distribution channels, and purchase patterns. Hence, transferring the same design across countries could result in erroneous results. The data must be adjusted to account for built-in national and cultural biases.[1]

Experimental designs are generally divided into two categories: true experimental and quasi-experimental designs. True experimental designs use random assignment of subjects to groups, while quasi-experimental designs do not. The main objective in both types of designs is to control and minimize threats to internal validity, which include effects of mortality, testing, history, selection, and maturation. This helps researchers rule out competing hypotheses. As true experimental designs use random assignment of subjects, they control for internal validity to a great extent. Quasi-experimental designs are used in situations where random assignment of subjects is not feasible or practical. In these cases the researcher should be aware of the factors that can be potential threats to internal validity and should control for them. Field experiments allow the researcher to make causal inferences in a real-world situation. The natural setting provides greater generalizability to the results.

Some of the common experimental designs used in international marketing research follow.

Two-Group After-Only Design

This design uses a test group, which is subjected to the experimental treatment, and a control group, which is used for comparison purposes. Members are assigned to the experimental group and the test group in a random fashion. The researcher can measure the differences in the test group and control group and get an understanding of the impact of the treatment. Because the subjects are randomly assigned to the test and control group, when the sample size is large enough, the two groups will be matched in all dimensions. Because no measurements are taken before the treatment is applied, there can be no bias because of testing effect.

A randomized two-group after-only design can be represented as

$$
\begin{array}{llll}
\text{EG} & \text{R} & \text{X} & \text{O}_1 \\
\text{CG} & \text{R} & & \text{O}_2
\end{array}
$$

where R indicates that subjects are randomly assigned to the test and control groups. Randomization works very well in cases where the sample size is large enough such that the test and control groups are similar; however, this method does not eliminate biases created due to history and maturation effects. Hence, the two-group before-after design is used to control for this.

Two-Group Before-After Design

As was done in the previous design, there are two groups—an experimental group and a control group. In this design, measurements are taken from both the groups before and after the treatment has been applied. This method reveals the effect of the experimental treatment on the test group. A two-group before-after design is denoted as

$$
\begin{array}{lllll}
\text{EG} & \text{R} & \text{O}_1 & \text{X} & \text{O}_2 \\
\text{CG} & \text{R} & \text{O}_3 & & \text{O}_4
\end{array}
$$

where the control group helps control for history and maturation effects and also controls for the reactive effect of O_1 on O_2. The disadvantage with this method is that it may sensitize the members of the experimental group to the procedure and cause them to behave in an unnatural manner.

Solomon Four-Group Design

The Solomon four-group design offers a possible solution to the problems faced in the two previous designs. This procedure uses four groups—two experimental groups and two control groups. Observations are made for one experimental group and one control group before the treatment. The treatment is then applied to both of the experimental groups. Observations are then made for all four groups. This controls for all the biases in the experimental procedure and gives a clear picture of the effect of the experiment. This experiment can be denoted as

$$
\begin{array}{lllll}
\text{EG} & \text{R} & \text{O}_1 & \text{X} & \text{O}_2 \\
\text{CG} & \text{R} & \text{O}_3 & & \text{O}_4 \\
\text{EG} & \text{R} & & \text{X} & \text{O}_5 \\
\text{CG} & \text{R} & & & \text{O}_6
\end{array}
$$

This method is very expensive, as the sample size required is twice that for the other designs.

Quasi-experimental designs include procedures such as trend analysis and time-series measures. In these methods there is no random assigning of subjects.

An example of an experimental design was the study conducted to evaluate the impact shelf facings have on the sales of a given product, which in this case was fruit juice. In the United States, most grocery stores display these products in four columns. Hence, the shelf facings were changed to three and five columns and the change in sales was observed. The researchers made sure that there were no other variables, such as change in price and competitors' promotions going on in the stores that could have a confounding effect on the experiment. The same procedure was to be conducted in the United Kingdom and Japan; however, the key to conducting experiments in the international scenario is adopting the procedure to suit the country characteristics. In the United Kingdom, the average number of columns for display of fruit juice is three. Hence, the experiment changed this to two and four and made a note of the difference in sales. The average number of columns for display in Japan is two, and this was changed to one and three. Suitable changes have to be made in the experimental procedure to make it meaningful in that specific country context.

Problems in Experimental Design[2]

International field experiments are unusual because the organizational settings in which such research is feasible are hard to find, and the complexities that are present in the United States are greater in an international setting. When combined with the influence of cultural differences, this can lead to various problems, some of which are the following:

- A lack of familiarity with the research process on the part of the subject group or the organization can mean that experimental research is seen as an attempt to impose the researcher's values on the subjects. It can be particularly difficult to gain access to the organization under these circumstances.
- The administrative aspects of conducting research, such as gathering information and being present at the site, may, in themselves, be unusual and constitute a form of treatment that confounds the effect of the intended treatment. This is even more likely in international settings than in domestic settings because research projects are unusual in the former.
- The researcher is often different from the subject population in terms of education, status, prestige, and so on. In some cases, the researcher is seen as an authority figure, and subjects may then respond by trying to please the researcher by giving the "right" response or alternatively try to thwart the researcher by giving the "wrong" response.
- The researcher may be considered of a lower status in some cases because of race, sex, or age. In such cases, subjects may refuse to cooperate or may deliberately try to distort the results.
- It may be desirable for the experiment to be carried out by the organization members in order to implement treatment as naturally as possible. If they are unfamiliar with the research process, it may be difficult for such people to understand the need to follow procedures rigorously.
- Differing customs and conditions may have unexpected results. It is relatively easy in a familiar environment to isolate possible confounds to an experiment; in an

unfamiliar environment, the researcher may be unaware of variables that are important, and may overlook them.

- Obtaining subjects' consent for research and debriefing them regarding the purpose of the research may be difficult if they are not familiar with the research process or the theory that is being tested.

Biases in Experimental Design

Researchers encounter biases in experimental designs, which contribute to distorting the results. Some of the more common biases are the following:[3]

History Effect: Events external to the experiment that affect the responses of the people involved in the experiment.

Mortality: Members of a group leave the group in large numbers, hence, groups that start out as matched groups may not remain that way as the experiment progresses.

Selection: There could be a conscious or unconscious bias in selecting the subjects so that the groups are not matched or there is a predisposition toward subjects with certain traits.

Testing Effect: If the subjects are aware that they are being tested in some manner, they may exhibit behavior that is not natural to them.

Measurement or Instrument Error: There could be differences in measuring the before and after findings or there could be a change of instrument during the course of the experiment. This could lead to changes in measurements.

ISSUES IN PRIMARY DATA COLLECTION

Collecting primary data does not always mean that researchers have to set foot in the country that is being studied. The data could be collected from within the United States by talking to students from the nation of interest, the local embassy personnel, tourists, or even experts in the United States who have in-depth knowledge about that country. One word of caution—even though the information collected may be technically correct, it should not be considered representative of the general population. This can be used in exploratory research to get a feel for the problem and to formulate hypotheses.

Once the decision has been made to visit the country of interest, the researcher must be very clear on the information that needs to be collected. The target segment should be very specific. For instance, if the research is meant for working women, parts of the country with a maximum concentration of working women must be concentrated upon. The idea is to collect the maximum amount of useful information with minimum expense of time and effort. At this juncture, it is prudent to mention that the researcher should also be very clear on the decision making process. If the study is on selling financial services, the researcher should have a clear idea of whether the decision is made jointly by a married couple or if the male partner decides for the family.

The researcher should have an idea of the client's capabilities and limitations before deciding on the data sources. Many clients tend to place a lot of faith in their own employees and sometimes this could backfire on the researcher. An employee of the client's firm claiming to know all about another nation may not be the best source for information. The same goes for friends who offer to help. As there is no financial obligation on the part of this person, the information could be substandard or even erroneous. The researcher will have to carry this cross at a later stage in the research process.

EMIC versus ETIC Dilemma

One of the major problems faced by an international marketing researcher is that of comparability of data. It is common fact that each country is unique and people of different nationalities exhibit different values, attitudes, and behaviors. Hence, the researcher is required to design the study in a manner that suits the specific country of interest. This may be useful in gathering accurate data about one country; however, in a multicountry study, this will make data across countries incomparable. For the sake of comparability of data, researchers may design standard techniques to be used across countries. This could, however, result in loss of precision.

Given the preceding dilemma, two schools of international marketing research have emerged. The EMIC school believes in the uniqueness of each country and culture and emphasizes studying the peculiarities of each country, identifying and understanding the uniqueness. The study is typically culture-specific and inferences have to be made about crosscultural similarities and differences in a subjective manner. At the other end of the spectrum is the ETIC school, which is primarily concerned with identifying the universal values, attitudes, and behavior. The research techniques in this case are culture-free, making comparisons across cultures easy and objective. Applying the same techniques across cultures can, however, lead to methodological problems. These schools of thought represent the two polar extremes on the continuum of crosscultural research methodology. The researcher tends toward one or the other depending on the purpose of the research and the number of countries or cultures studied.

Both these ideologies are correct in their own way. For a multicountry study to be useful, information should be comparable. At the same time, if a research study has to be useful to users in the country where it is conducted, the uniqueness that comes with the data has to be retained. The ideal survey instrument would encompass both the EMIC and ETIC schools of thought. This can be accomplished by getting the local users involved in the research study right from the beginning. The research design should not be totally standardized. It has to make allowances for peculiarities of each country. This becomes very important when "soft" data, like lifestyle and attitudes, are researched.

TYPES OF PRIMARY SOURCES

Selection of a specific research technique depends on a lot of factors, such as the following:

- The purpose for which the data is collected. Standardized techniques can be used for collecting objective data, but may not be very useful in collecting subjective data.

- Researchers need to use open-ended questions to get unstructured data.
- The environment in which the data is to be collected affects the technique to be used. Researchers can control the environment in which the data is to be collected or they can collect it from the real world.
- The type of data sought—historical data or future intentions to purchase a product.
- National and cultural differences and individual preferences also affect the research technique adopted. For instance, researchers in the United States prefer the survey method. Japanese researchers prefer to collect data from the dealers and other channel members.[4]

Interviews

Interviews are a popular form of collecting primary data. Interviewing the right person who is knowledgeable about the topic can be of great value to the researcher. Interviews are used to obtain in-depth information on a specific topic. Interviews can be conducted over the telephone or in person. Telephone interviews are useful in countries that have a large network of telephone service. The cost of interviewing over the telephone is minimal and no field staff is necessary. Broad coverage of the sample population is possible with very little investment of time and money. Personal interviewing is the most flexible means of obtaining information. Error due to nonresponse is very low in this method. It is also the most expensive method of data collection. Researchers should watch out for interviewer bias in both of the above techniques.

Focus Groups

Focus groups are another popular method of collecting primary data. A group of knowledgeable people is gathered for a limited time period to discuss a specific topic. As it involves a lot of individuals, many hidden issues surface, something that would not have happened in an individual interview. Discussions are recorded on tape and subsequently analyzed in detail. Focus groups provide more qualitative data and information on subjective matter like attitudes, perceptions, and other covert factors. In the international setting, the researcher must understand the cultural traits and adapt the process accordingly to stimulate a frank and open exchange of ideas.

Observational Techniques

Observational techniques require the researcher to play the role of a nonparticipating observer of activity and behavior. Observation can be personal or conducted through some mechanical devices. It can be obtrusive or nonobtrusive. In international marketing research, observational techniques are mainly used to develop an understanding of practices that have not been previously encountered. These techniques can also help researchers understand phenomena that would be difficult to assess with other techniques. For instance, while redesigning the Aptiva, IBM sent photographers to over 2,000 households all over the world to observe and photograph the way computers were stored in homes.[5] This data would be difficult to gather through any other method. Toyota used observation techniques to improve on the Corolla.[6] They conducted a discreet survey of women trying to open their car, get in, and operate it. They found that a lot of women had problems opening the door and operating various dials on the dashboard. Armed with this knowledge, engineers at Toyota redesigned some features in the car to help overcome these difficulties. Observational techniques have their pitfalls. Once the subject is aware of being observed, the reactions may not be normal.

Surveys

Surveys are the most popular form of gathering primary data. Surveys are usually conducted with the help of questionnaires that are administered personally, through mail, or by telephone. In international marketing research, survey techniques encounter a lot of stumbling blocks. Surveys are conducted with the assumption that the target population is able to understand and respond to the questionnaire. This may not always be the case. Most third world countries do not have widespread availability of telephones, which makes telephone surveys impossible. A lot of these countries do not have an organized postal system and mailing addresses of the majority of the sample population may not be available. In Venezuela, for example, houses do not have numbers, but have individual names. Reaching a respondent at the right address could be a cumbersome task. Mail surveys have also been subjected to a lot of scams. In some countries the postal employees pocket the incentive that has been mailed with the questionnaire. In Italy, for instance, a lot of mail got delivered to paper mills for recycling. Despite all of these problems, survey remains the most popular method of collecting data for international marketing research.

PROBLEMS WITH COLLECTION OF PRIMARY DATA

The problems with collection of primary data can be broadly classified under three main categories: methodological problems, practical problems, and operational problems.[7] We will now discuss each category in detail.

Methodological Problems

Cultural Bias

Each researcher brings into his or her study a set of values, beliefs, and assumptions that are molded by his or her culture. Even when they are aware of this bias, it is very difficult for them to guard against it. For example, while studying international negotiations, Wright designed a background questionnaire to study responses as to how respondents in two countries viewed success in negotiation. The questions being based on North American research findings, an open-ended option was provided to every section so that respondents could add their own items. Fewer than 3 percent of the North American respondents took advantage of the open-ended option, whereas 20 percent of the Southeast Asian respondents did.

Each country therefore has its own sets of beliefs, values and assumptions, logic patterns, and thinking. These are well documented in Nakamura's "Ways of Thinking of Eastern People," Kaplan's "Cultural Thought Patterns in Intercultural Education," and Bloom's "The Linguistic Shaping of Thought."

Language Problems

Most North American research is conducted in English, but in international research use of the English language alone may create problems such as no response or short, uninformative answers, misunderstanding, and difficulty in gaining access to local government officials or local partners. Also, people who speak a second language fluently think differently in another language. The researcher may get subtly different answers to the same question, depending on the language it was posed in.

Translation can overcome these problems, but the terms often do not translate directly. If a translator or interpreter is used, that person must be fluent in both languages and be familiar with the particular research area. The researcher and translator must meet before beginning the research. Translation is also important for the interview protocol, which is the outline of questions to be used. When "back" translations are used, it is found that there are as many mistakes, if not more, as in the original translations.

Wright used an alternative technique, having a panel of four or five native speakers. She studied each question word by word with this panel, explained what she meant, and checked whether the translated question meant what she intended. The corrected version was then checked once more with the panel to ensure that the meaning had not been changed. Even after this, it was found that the construction of sentences was awkward and the phraseology tended to portray a different meaning. To correct this, the final translation was given to a teacher of Indonesian (as a mother tongue) to rephrase. The same process was followed with Thai. The panel double-checked the final version to ensure that no change in meaning had occurred.

Incomplete Research Design

Certain companies may not fit into the research design developed by the researcher. The first challenge is to locate enough good and bad performers with other characteristics necessary to satisfy the research design. Choice of research sites is very important. They should be chosen to keep as many variables as possible constant. A 2×2 matrix is often a good format. For example, in researching the factors in a successful negotiation, Wright chose two companies, both of which had successful and unsuccessful negotiations in the last 5 years. Variables outside the ones being researched were thus held as constant as possible.

The problem of identification is often the problem of sample size. Methodological debate over research with large samples versus research with small samples and lack of potential research sites within a country to satisfy a project design are common problems encountered. In the absence of adequate sites or lack of access to them, the researcher must consider other solutions. For example, if eight sites are desired, but only four can be accessed, alternative solutions must be sought. One strategy is to proceed with the companies that have given access and simultaneously begin the search for additional sites, but this entails thinking through which are the most important variables to control and establishing a hierarchy. This should be used to guide the search for new sites and to make decisions about accepting them. Flexibility must be built in, with fallback positions clearly outlined.

The Problem of Access

In order to learn how organizations cope with restrictive investment policies, localization pressures, and initiating and managing joint ventures in the developing world, they must get into the field and talk with the principal actors in these situations. Assuming that an appropriate sample of companies has been identified, the next problem is to gain access to them as research sites. Depending on how sensitive the research question is, the access problem can be heightened.

To access people in organizations, the first step is to locate the appropriate person in corporate headquarters. Cooperation and probability of success are enhanced if the researcher can enter the company at the top. The initial letter should be directed to the president or vice president of the international organization. It is possible that such people may not be available, the issue may be too sensitive to expose to an outsider, or the organization may not fit the research design at all. Many companies may be unwilling to contribute to academic research. The research proposal must be expressed in terms acceptable to executives and must try to confer a practical benefit on respondents. Business rather than academic terms must be used. For example, company executives are not interested in whether the researcher is using multiple regression, factor analysis, or content analysis. It has been found useful to offer the interviewee a summary of the results when the study is complete.

The viewpoints of the host country government, the local partners, the local general manager, local employees, and so on, must be kept in mind. Each party will have a different logic guiding its actions, but local government officials and joint venture partners may be less accessible and probably less interested in academic research than even North American organizations. Accessing individuals may also prove to be problematic in some countries. In Mexico, the upper socio-economic classes are difficult to reach because of barriers like the housing structure of the walls, gates, and the intervening servants.[8]

Confidentiality and Trust

Confidential data of sensitive nature, relating to, say, the functioning of a sovereign nation or pertaining to local operating problems or intercompany conflicts, may need to be researched. The researcher must convince concerned parties that he or she will not violate their trust. The promise of confidentiality and the keeping of the promise are very important. Confidentiality usually involves keeping actual names of companies or people secret. This prevents the researcher from evaluating the work completely, but this weakness is insignificant because otherwise, one would never be able to gain access for research purposes. Further, companies should believe that the researcher is actually preserving confidentiality.

Researchers must also be sensitive to the time required for interviews and answering questionnaires. The interviewee should be apprised of the purpose of the research at the beginning of the interview. Permission to take notes or use a tape recorder should be asked, though a negative answer may often be forthcoming. Notes must be updated as soon as possible after the interview. A thank you letter and other materials promised should be sent immediately after the interview. Apart from common courtesy, the letter reminds the interviewee of a potential situation that should have been discussed during the interview, such as follow up telephone calls or an additional visit for clarification.

The Problem of Analysis and Communication of Results

After recording the narrative history, a preliminary analysis should be made to ensure that all questions regarding completeness of data are answered. This may uncover areas for further probing or even force the researcher to modify the framework appropriately.

During the final analysis the researcher will search the data for performance-related patterns. Because most of the information is qualitative data from questionnaires, there is a terrific responsibility for the researcher to write well. Good writing is essential in narrative histories and observed patterns. Qualitative techniques, such as content analysis, may also be used.

Practical Problems

Time

Quick, competent studies of adaptation are rare. For example, in research on joint ventures in developing countries, the first 10 months were spent on conceptual development, gaining access to sites, and a pilot survey. This was followed by 5 months of data collection for the main project. Research on international project negotiation takes about as long. A rough checklist has been made to outline the progression of an international field research project. A rule of thumb followed for research is to calculate the anticipated time and then double it. There will be periods of downtime when interviewing, for example, because the researcher has to work around executives' busy schedules.

Expense

Time eventually translates into expense. Field research is the most expensive kind of international research, therefore, it has to be as efficient as possible. A well thought out research design is necessary before launching an actual data collection. If traditional academic sources are not sufficient, nontraditional sources must be considered. In Canada, the Canadian International Development Agency and External Affairs and in the United States, the U.S. Agency for International Development could be considered.

Operational Problems

1. An initial problem could be securing research permission, especially in developing countries. Some countries take 3 to 6 months to grant permission, particularly if the research topic is a sensitive one for the nation or if it requires travel outside the capital city. A sister organization in the country—a university or a management institution—could help with the process.
2. Telephones may not work. A personal visit to the office to request an appointment may work better. If funding permits, hiring someone to do the telephoning and training them well may be the keys to success. The trade-offs must be considered, such as the fact that a foreign voice can often get an appointment that a local person would have difficulty getting, or a local person may be better able to secure appointments than a foreign researcher.
3. Mail systems are unreliable in some countries. Letters may be lost or delayed. Even courier service is not foolproof. The letter may reach the wrong person in the organization. A project carried out by a certain team of researchers showed that the actual addressee did not receive almost 25 percent of letters sent by courier though they had been signed for at the organization.

4. Travel to research sites can be difficult. Poor road conditions, bad traffic, infrequent or expensive air travel, and hazards of travelling by bus may be other problems.

5. Actual and perceived physical risk to researchers is also present. It is important not to look too prosperous—merge with the locals in terms of dress. It would serve well to inquire about the safety of areas where one travels by foot, etc.

6. Keeping a close eye on possessions and placing one's address prominently on one's briefcase are important.

7. The researcher also has to work around problems like people having died, moved elsewhere, or not wanting to talk about certain things the researcher is interested in.

8. The computer used by the researcher at home may be incompatible with the one he uses in the field. Even if made by the same company, there may be incompatibility among software packages. For example, a researcher using the software SCRIPT in a mainframe in Canada, but WordStar on a microcomputer in the field, had endless problems in translation.

In the ultimate analysis, clinical field research involves issues of access, trust, schedules, confidentiality, and feedback of transcribed interviews. Clinical research may not suit everyone, but there may be a fit between a method and a researcher's personality. The implementation phase may be fraught with ambiguity, anxiety, and frustration.

ADVANTAGES AND DISADVANTAGES OF PRIMARY DATA COLLECTION

As compared to secondary data, primary data have a lot of advantages and disadvantages. This section of the chapter deals with them in detail.

Primary data are accurate and precise as they are collected with the specific project in mind. In case of secondary data, they have been collected for purposes other than the research study and, hence, will be useful in giving only a general idea. Secondary data cannot be used to make strategic decisions. Inferences and conclusions can be drawn only with the help of primary data. Also, secondary data are collected in different formats in different countries and are in some cases not comparable. This makes it difficult for researchers to use secondary data in multicountry research. Primary data can be collected in a manner that is preferred for the specific research study.

The one major disadvantage with primary data is the resources involved in collecting it. Companies have to invest significant amounts of time, manpower, and capital into gathering primary data of acceptable quality. This is more pronounced in international marketing research as the national and cultural differences mentioned earlier have a significant impact on the data collection methods.

ESTABLISHING EQUIVALENCE IN INTERNATIONAL MARKETING RESEARCH[9]

In multicountry research it is important for the researcher to be able to compare data across countries, hence, it becomes necessary to examine the various aspects of the data collection process and establish their equivalence. They are listed in Figure 7-1.

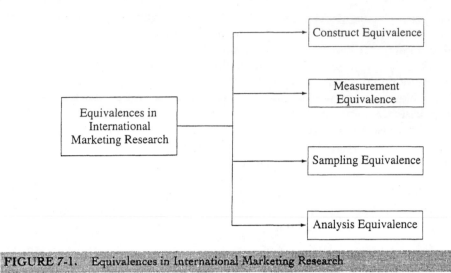

Construct equivalence deals with the function of the product or service that is being researched and not the method used in collecting the information. Different countries that are being studied must have the same perception or use for the product that is being researched. If this is not the case, comparison of data becomes meaningless. If, for example, we are studying the bicycle market, we need to understand that they come under the category of recreational sports in the United States; however, in India and China, they are considered as a basic means of transportation. In Japan, people substitute noncarbonated drinks for fruit juices, whereas in the United States these two categories are considered distinct products.[10] Researchers need to be concerned with the information that is needed for the study and not with the means used to collect the same. For instance, telephone interviews may be used in the United States. In a third world country, researchers may have to resort to mail interviews or personal interviews to obtain the same information. This is explained in detail in the chapter on designing questionnaires.

Measurement equivalence is concerned with the scales used for measuring various aspects of the research study. In a multicountry study, researchers need to modify the units of measurement. In Great Britain and most Commonwealth nations, the standard for measurement is the metric scale. This change of units will have to be taken care of when designing the research instrument. It has generally been observed that it is easier to establish measurement equivalence between demographic variables than between psychographic variables. While in the United States, researchers use a five- or seven-point scale, it is very common to use a twenty-point scale in France. The chapter on development of scales considers this in detail.

Sampling equivalence concerns the decision making process. If, for instance, the study is on purchasing habits regarding toys, researchers need to understand that in the United States, children decide the toys they want to buy. In another country, the parents could make this decision. Hence, to obtain useful information children should be interviewed in the United States and parents should be interviewed in the other country. This will be explained in detail in the chapter on Sampling.

Analysis equivalence is the fourth and last aspect of equivalence that an international marketing researcher should be concerned about. When doing data analysis, the researcher should take into account the different biases that might exist in different cultures. Different cultures differ widely in their assessment of situations and problems. Accordingly, they tend to choose different ratings on a given scale. For instance, the Japanese have a tendency to choose the neutral point, so it is prudent to avoid a scale with a neutral point to obtain useful information. Americans do not typically go into details with open-ended questions. Latin Americans and Italians tend to exaggerate their response. These factors must be kept in mind when designing the scales for measurement. The chapter on data analysis deals with this aspect.

To establish equivalence with respect to all four aspects mentioned above, researchers normally conduct comparisons of results across countries, while simultaneously analyzing and checking for reliability.

The main difference between a domestic and an international marketing research study is the need to establish equivalence as far as construct, measurement, and sampling are concerned. This is easier said than done in cases of international marketing research. For starters, it is very difficult to compare across cultures. People from different nations have different values, beliefs, and lifestyles and in general view the world very differently. It would be impractical to hope that a Frenchman and a Korean would agree to all of the same ideas. In many cases, homogeneity in ideas and values is not even possible within a single country, so it may be necessary for the researcher to adapt the research design to collect comparable data from various countries.

In many cases, researchers try to follow one methodology in all the countries that are being studied. If, for instance, telephone surveys were used as the means of collecting primary data, this would be a very effective method in the developed nations, where most households have a telephone and the list of telephone numbers is easily accessible. Unfortunately, this may prove to be a very costly method in the developing countries where the cost of making a telephone call is very high. Moreover, not all households have a telephone connection and reaching the target sample may not be possible. In such countries, the methodology will have to be adapted. The goal is to ensure that the data are comparable. Comparability of the research instrument comes a distant second.

The same principles could be applied to measurement and sampling equivalence. The scales used to measure various aspects should be modified according to the country where they are to be used. The sampling frame should also be modified. For instance, if a company was interested in researching the office supplies market, in the United States all information regarding buying behavior could be collected by talking to the office secretary; however, in some cultures that are still highly bureaucratic, it may be necessary to interview someone higher up in the corporate ladder. To obtain information that is comparable, researchers should understand the decision-making process and target the right sample.

Establishing equivalence for an international marketing research study is a mammoth task that calls for a lot of judgmental decisions on the part of the researcher. The researcher will have to call upon past experience to decide the methodology that will work in the country of interest. A survey was conducted to study the stress levels at workplaces in different cities and it was stated that Hong Kong was the most stressful city. The importance of establishing equivalence in terms of construct, measurement, sample, and analysis could be illustrated by the results of this survey. The survey compared cities like New York and London to Hong Kong and opinions of working men and women were obtained. Due to a great deal of diversity among the people surveyed, definition of stress is bound to vary widely. A New Yorker could consider the commute stressful, whereas a person in Hong Kong could consider peer pressure to be the most stressful aspect of the job. It is also important that the samples in all these cities be equivalent. This could prove very tricky because a physician in London may not have the same work pressure that a physician in New York has. Hence, it is important that the researcher consider all of these aspects before coming to a conclusion.

INTERNATIONAL MARKETING RESEARCH IN PRACTICE

Tasty Burgers will have a reasonably clear picture of the market size in each of the four countries—the United Kingdom, Brazil, India, and Saudi Arabia—with the secondary data available to them. This will help them eliminate some markets where secondary data clearly indicate there is no potential for growth; however, it is very important to conduct primary research for those markets where they plan to expand. Primary data, as defined in this chapter, is data that has been collected specifically for this project and should be able to provide answers to all the research questions.

The first step is to analyze the extent of information available about a given market. Usually there is a plethora of information available for developed countries, hence, researchers should have in-depth information about the United Kingdom. However, in cases of developing countries, such as Brazil and India, reliable demographic and economic data are not easily available. Even if they were available they would not have been updated in the recent past. Saudi Arabia is another country where there is a dearth of information. In these cases it becomes necessary to perform exploratory research to test the viability of the project in these countries. A detailed study involves time and resources, which should be allocated only if exploratory research proves that there is market potential.

Exploratory research will involve studying the major cities in each of these countries and determining which one of these cities would be a good place to set up the first outlet. Researchers could study the existing fast-food market in each of these countries and determine the products for which there is a great demand. An informal survey of clientele in other fast-food chains could be conducted to find out if they are satisfied with the products being offered by competitors. The survey could be used to find out if the theme used by Tasty Burgers would sell in each of these markets.

Descriptive research involves thorough investigation into all of the aspects that are required to set up business in each of these countries. The most efficient and reliable forms of data collection methods will have to be decided for each of the countries. It may not be possible to use the same method of data collection, as there are significant national and cultural differences among these countries. Care should be taken to ensure that construct, measurement, and sampling equivalence are maintained. The subsequent chapters on measurement scales, sampling, and designing questionnaires will discuss how this can be achieved.

Summary

This chapter deals with collecting primary data for international marketing research. Depending on the research purpose, a choice is made among exploratory, descriptive, and causal research. Exploratory research is most appropriate when the primary objective is to identify problems, define problems more precisely, or investigate the possibility of new alternative courses of action. Descriptive research aims at providing a description of the existing market phenomena. Causal research aims at identifying the precise cause-and-effect relationships present in the market. The different methods of collecting primary data, like qualitative methods, surveys, and observational methods are described in detail. The chapter also deals with the problems that are specific to primary data collection in international research and are categorized under three major headings: methodological problems, practical problems, and operational problems. The chapter also outlines the advantages and disadvantages of primary data. The most important aspect of primary data collection is establishing equivalence. There are various aspects to establishing equivalence and each aspect is explained in great detail in the following chapters.

Questions and Problems

1. List the different types of primary research and describe them briefly.
2. Coca-Cola wants to conduct a blind taste test in the Philippines to test the preference of Coke over Pepsi. In the blind taste test the respondents are asked to taste unlabeled colas and report their preference. Evaluate the validity of this experiment.
3. What are the factors that affect experimental designs in international marketing research?
4. Compare and contrast EMIC and ETIC schools of thought.
5. What are some of the different methods of collecting primary data?
6. What are the problems involved in collecting primary data?
7. Define and describe the components of establishing equivalence in international marketing research.

Endnotes

1. Charles S. Mayer, "Multinational Marketing Research: The Magnifying Glass of Methodological Problems," *European Research* (March 1978): 77–83.
2. Betty Jane Punnet, "Designing Field Experiments for Management Research Outside North America," *International Studies of Management and Organization* XVIII, no. 3 (1988): 44–54.
3. Richard L. Sandhusen, *Global Marketing* (Hauppagge, NY: Barron's Educational Series, 1994), 67–69.
4. Czinkota and Ronkainen, *International Marketing* 5th ed. (FL: Dryden Press, 1998), 256.
5. Ira Sager, "The Stealth Computer-Annual Design Awards," *Business Week* (2 June 1997): 103.
6. Michael Czinkota and Masaki Kotabe, "Product Development in the Proper Context," *Product and Process Innovation:* (November–December 1991): 33–37.
7. Dr. Ugar Yavas and Dr. Erdner Kaynak, "Current Status of Marketing Research in Developing Countries: Problems and

PART I   Section II

Opportunities," *Journal of International Marketing and Marketing Research.* 5, no. 2 (June 1980): 79–89.

8. Jane Kalim, "Quality Standards: The Push-Me-Pull-You of Marketing Research," *Identifying the Gap*, 11–26.

9. Susan P. Douglas and C. Samuel Craig, *International Marketing Research* (Englewood Cliffs, NJ: Prentice Hall, 1983), 78–82.

10. Charles S. Mayer, "The Lessons of Multi-National Marketing Research," *Business Horizons* (December 1978): 10.

CHAPTER

Qualitative and Observational Research

8

INTRODUCTION[1]

In most international marketing research studies, it is not possible to find secondary data that will help solve all of the research problems. Collecting primary data becomes a necessity. In most cases, the researcher does not have enough information to formulate the research question. It becomes imperative that the researcher conduct exploratory research to get a better understanding of the problem. Qualitative and observational data help the researcher get a better feel for the problem before launching into the actual research process.

NEED FOR QUALITATIVE RESEARCH

The purpose of qualitative research is to find out what is in a consumer's mind. In the early 1960s Playtex experienced a downturn in the girdle market. The market research firm hired to investigate the cause for this downturn discovered that women wanted a more natural look and girdles did not fit the changing perceptions of their bodies. Another study conducted by Chrysler found that people were buying cars less for status and more as a means of self-expression. In the international context, qualitative research takes on an added meaning as the regional and cultural differences accentuate the attitudinal variations among people. A cosmetic company sponsored a focus group to study the attitude of men in various countries toward perfumes. The researcher who studied Italian men found that while respondents waxed lyrical about their preference for subtle, delicate fragrances, they were all actually using overpowering fragrances.[2] The contradiction in behavior was duly noted and used in subsequent stages of the research process. These are some examples of qualitative studies that can have far-reaching impact on the marketing decisions made by firms.[3]

Qualitative data are collected to know more about things that cannot be directly measured and observed. Feelings, thoughts, attitudes, intentions, and past behavior are

141

some of the things that cannot be directly measured and can be obtained only through qualitative data collection methods. The basic assumption behind qualitative methods is that an individual's organization of a relatively unstructured stimulus indicates the person's basic perception of the phenomenon and his or her reaction to it. The more unstructured and ambiguous a stimulus is, the more the subjects can and will project their emotions, needs, motives, attitudes, and values. The structure of a stimulus is the degree of choice available to the subject. A highly structured stimulus gives the subject very clear alternatives and leaves very little choice to the subject, whereas a stimulus of low structure has a wide range of alternatives.

Qualitative methods are less structured and more intense than questionnaire-based interviews. There is a longer and more flexible relationship with the respondent, so that the resulting data give the researcher greater insight and newer perspectives. Qualitative research relies on a small sample which may not be representative of the target population. Qualitative research can be used for various purposes. In exploratory research it can be used to define a problem in greater detail. It is used to generate hypotheses that can be researched in detail. It is used by researchers to test new product concepts and for pretesting questionnaires. In international research, qualitative research is used to learn the consumers' vantage point and vocabulary and to get a better understanding of the way decisions are made and products are used in a foreign culture.

All too often, researchers tend to view qualitative research as an alternative to and a competitor with, quantitative research. It has to be understood that each merely represents different tools available to the researcher. Quantitative research addresses the who, what, when, and where of consumer behavior. Qualitative research tends to focus on the why—the reasons behind the overt behavior. There is also a popular fallacy in the research community that qualitative research can be used only for the purpose of exploratory research. Qualitative research aims to understand consumer behavior instead of measuring it, so it is typically used to increase researchers' knowledge, clarify issues, define problems, formulate hypotheses, and generate ideas. It helps researchers understand cultural and personal meanings attached to objects and experiences.[4]

TYPES OF QUALITATIVE RESEARCH[5]

There are different methods of conducting qualitative methods and this section explains each of them in detail. The methods differ from one another in terms of the structure imposed on data collection, the environment in which the data is collected (real shopping world or simulated), the extent to which the respondent is aware of the study, and the sample size.

Individual Interviews

Individual interviews are conducted face-to-face with the respondent so the subject matter can be explored in detail. In-depth interviews are of two basic types:

1. *Nondirective interviews.* The respondent is given the freedom to respond within the bounds of the topics of interest to the interviewer. Success in such interviews depends on establishing a relaxed atmosphere and the ability of the interviewer to

probe the respondent and guide the discussion back to the topic in case of any digression. These sessions may last 1 to 2 hours and may be recorded for interpreting at a later time.

2. *Semistructured or focused individual interviews.* The interviewer attempts to cover a specific list of topics or subareas. The timing, exact wording, and time allotted to each question is left to the interviewer's discretion. These types of interviews are useful with busy executives to obtain basic information on the subject of interest. The open nature of the interviews allows the interviewer to pursue a discussion in detail if required.

Three techniques have been widely used in conducting in-depth interviews. The first technique is called *laddering.* In this technique the questions progress from product characteristics to user characteristics. The technique attempts to use tangible product aspects to elicit responses from the customers with regard to the intangible aspects, like feelings and attitudes. The second technique is called *hidden-issue questioning.* The focus in these interviews is not on the socially shared values, but rather on personal "sore spots"—not on general lifestyles, but on deeply felt personal concerns. The third technique, *symbolic analysis,* attempts to analyze the symbolic meaning of objects by comparing them with their opposites.

Conducting personal interviews over the telephone is beginning to gain greater acceptance in countries that have an extensive telephone network. Respondents are becoming more receptive to the idea of saving time by giving the interview over the telephone. It is also far more economical for the firm conducting the study. Increasingly, the computer is also being used for interviews. The interviewer conducts the interview with a headset and keys the responses directly into the computer. The responses can be printed out at a later time. Some computer programs provide frequency counts and averages for responses to the close-ended questions.

Focus Groups

A focus group discussion is the process of obtaining possible ideas or solutions to a marketing problem from a group of respondents by discussing it. The participants are representative of the target markets and emphasis is placed on the group interaction. Each participant is encouraged to express views on the topic of discussion and elaborate on or react to the views of other participants. The discussion is moderated by an interviewer who stimulates the discussion and guides the group back to the topic at hand whenever there is a digression.

Focus group discussions offer more stimulation than interviews and are known to elicit more spontaneity and candor. Focus groups are used to

- generate and test ideas for new products, product concepts, and product positioning
- generate hypotheses that can be studied in later research
- collect information that can be used for designing questionnaires
- check if marketing strategies are transferable across countries.

Focus groups can be of different types. Exploratory focus groups are used to generate hypotheses for testing or concepts for future research. Experiencing focus groups allows the researcher to experience the emotional framework in which the product is being used. Clinical focus groups are used to gain insight into the true motivations and feelings in the consumers' minds that are subconscious in nature. Clinical focus groups require a moderator with expertise in psychology and sociology.

As a rule, three to four group sessions are usually sufficient to get most of the information on the topic of interest. The first discussion reveals a lot of information to the analyst. The second and subsequent discussions produce a lot of information, but not much of it is new. Exceptions to this occur if there are distinct segments to cover and these segments lead to widely varying opinions on the topic being discussed. In the international setting, it is important for moderators to be conversant with the language and also the patterns of social interaction and the nonverbal clues used by people in that part of the world. The moderator should also bear in mind other practices peculiar to that region. For instance, in the Middle East women do not have as much freedom as women in the Western world. In some Asian countries, the moderator must take special interest in introductions if the discussion is to be truly open and candid. In international marketing research, the role of the moderator becomes crucial, as he or she tends to reflect the norms, attitudes, and response patterns typical of a specific cultural context and these attitudes and responses may be projected into the findings.[6]

The moderator first looks at the research purpose and the research questions. A checklist is then prepared on the specific issues to be covered in the discussion. The moderator uses this checklist as a general guide to prevent digression by the group. The usual method of introducing topics is to start with something general and gradually proceed to specific topics. The group selected for the discussion should provide for both the similarity and contrast within a group. It is necessary to combine participants from different social classes and age groups because of differences in their perceptions, experiences, and verbal skills. Recruiting a focus group requires a great deal of understanding of the topic and of the potential members of the group. For instance, in the United Kingdom, conducting focus group sessions for ethnically sensitive topics poses quite a challenge.[7] While it is necessary to ensure that the group is representative of the population that is being targeted, it is impossible to recruit a perfectly "Asian" focus group. Creating a group of three Hindus, two Sikhs, two Moslems, and a Christian is asking for problems. Young West Indians in groups can also be very difficult to research as they strive very hard to keep their street identity intact. Though the usual group size is about 8 to 12 members, smaller group sizes may also be used.

The moderator in a focus group should possess a few critical skills. These include the ability to:[8]

- establish a quick rapport so that the group gets to the topic of interest in as little time as possible
- demonstrate genuine interest in the views of the group members
- avoid use of technical jargon and sophisticated terminology that will turn off the participants
- be flexible in implementing the interview agenda so that the group does not lose its spontaneity
- introduce and maintain a smooth flow in the discussion
- exert control over the group so that no one individual or subgroup dominates the discussion

- be familiar with the language and its idiomatic usage and also be familiar with nonverbal cues peculiar to that specific nation or culture

For a focus group to deliver useful results the analyst must be culturally sensitive, more so in international marketing research. The analyst should keep in mind the dynamics that are peculiar to the specific nation or culture. Certain cultures may be excessively conservative in their approach to a new idea or a concept. For instance, the French have been proven to resist innovations of any kind. In some cases the participants may be excessively critical of one thing and uncritical of something else. The Japanese hesitate to criticize new product ideas. There is also a very strong group mentality among the Asian culture while most Americans tend to be individualistic. In Asia, this translates to the group rejecting somebody that does not "belong." Care should be taken to address this issue while selecting the panel members. Even though each country is unique in its cultural characteristics, there are some common differences that should be addressed:[9]

- *Timeframe.* Many companies in the United States and Canada are used to completing the research project in a relatively short period of time. This is not possible with international research. Lead times tend to be much longer, more so in the Far East. A good estimate would be to calculate the time required for the research in the United States and double it for Europe. It would be even longer for Asia.
- *Structure.* Most focus group panels consist of four to six people, versus eight to ten in the United States. The focus group interviews themselves last for almost 4 hours. Specific instructions have to be given to research organizations that are coordinating the project in the foreign country.
- *Recruiting and Rescreening.* Panelists for focus groups in the United States are screened and recruited in a rigid manner. These processes must be monitored very carefully.
- *Approach.* Foreign moderators are not as structured and as authoritative as U.S. moderators. This can result in long periods of silence and digression. This is because foreign moderators feel it is necessary to allow the group to settle down and establish trust to build up the necessary comfort. Foreign focus groups tend to use fewer external stimuli, such as photos and visual aids.

Focus groups have become very popular in the recent past. The technology used to conduct focus group interviews has also improved tremendously. Conference rooms with one-way mirrors are used to allow researchers to observe the group dynamics so nonverbal cues may be observed and recorded. Telephone focus groups are conducted for participants who are extremely busy. These are conducted through a conference calling facility. Two-way focus groups are also becoming common. In this case, one group listens and learns from a related group.

Projective Techniques

The central feature of all projective techniques is the presentation of an ambiguous, unstructured object, activity, or person that a respondent is asked to interpret and explain.[10] The more ambiguous the stimulus, the more the respondents have to project themselves into the task, thereby revealing hidden feelings and opinions. These techniques are used when the researchers believe that the respondents cannot or will not respond to direct questions about certain behaviors and attitudes. Some people strive to give the socially correct answer all the time to avoid a bad self-image. Sometimes the respondent may be too polite to correct the interviewer. In all of the preceding cases, researchers make use of projective techniques to get down to the real reason behind consumer behavior.

There are different categories of projective techniques. The *word-association technique* asks the respondents to give the first word or phrase that comes to mind after the researcher presents a word or phrase. The researcher reads out a list of words quickly to avoid the respondents' defense mechanism from setting in. Responses are analyzed by calculating the frequency with which any word is given as a response, the amount of time that elapses before a response is given, and the number of respondents who do not respond at all to a test within a reasonable amount of time. Word association tests produce hundreds of words and ideas. They can be used to conduct associative research on competitive brands. They can also be used to obtain reactions to potential brand names and advertising slogans. *Completion tests* involve giving the respondent an incomplete and ambiguous sentence, which is to be completed with a phrase. The sentences are usually in the third person and the respondent is encouraged to respond with the first thought that comes to mind. In the *picture interpretation technique* the respondent is shown an ambiguous picture and asked to describe it. This technique is very flexible, as the picture can be readily adapted to many kinds of marketing problems. *Third-person techniques* involve asking respondents how friends, neighbors, or the average person would think or react to a situation. The respondents will, to some extent, project their own attitudes on to this third person and reveal more of their true feelings. In *role-playing*, the respondent assumes the role or behavior of another person and in the process may project their own attitudes into the role that they are playing.

Protocol

In the protocol method the respondent is asked to think aloud while a decision is being made or a problem is being solved. This serves as a record of the respondent's thought process. These methods are designed to specifically prevent the researcher from imposing his views on the respondent. The respondent is free to make the decision based on factors that are important to him or her. The common method used is to record the respondent's opinions as he or she is in the process of making the decision. If the researcher is looking for information on buying behavior in a grocery store, he accompanies the respondent as the latter goes through the shopping process. The respondent is asked to talk aloud as the purchase decision is made. In some cases, respondents are given a recorder so that they can talk into it as they shop. This may not be so effective as most people feel embarrassed to talk into a microphone while they shop.

TYPES OF OBSERVATIONAL METHODS

Observation can produce insights into customer behavior that other methods cannot. It can be used to study a wide variety of topics ranging from shopping behavior to patterns in pedestrian traffic. Observational methods can be very useful in producing new ideas for product development, product complements, and substitutes. For instance, it was observed that clients at a community mental health center engaged in odd behavior, parking far from the facility, even though ample parking was available nearby. When they were asked about this, clients admitted that they did not want to be seen entering the facility. The center then redesigned the entrance and changed the signs.[11]

These methods are limited to providing information on current behavior. Observational methods are less expensive than other methods and very accurate. In some cases observation may be the only alternative available to the researcher. There are different types of observation and they are discussed briefly in the following paragraphs.

Direct Observation

Direct observation is when an observer disguised as a shopper watches shoppers approach a product category. The observer gathers information on aspects like the time spent in the display area, the ease of finding the product, and whether the customer reads the package. In some cases the observer is asked to mingle with the customers to find out if they have any problems with service. Better results are obtained if the customers are not aware that they are being watched so that they perform the shopping activities without being self-conscious.

Contrived Observation

Contrived observation involves studying the behavior of people placed in a contrived observation situation. This will reveal some of their beliefs, attitudes, and motives. A variation of the same method uses teams of observers disguised as customers observing the interaction between the customer and the personnel handling the service desk. Though this method has been useful in providing insights into aspects like discriminatory treatment of minorities, there have been some questions about the ethics involved in this method.

Content Analysis

Content analysis is used to analyze written material into meaningful units using carefully applied rules. It is defined as the objective, systematic, and quantitative description of the manifest of the content of communication and includes observation as well as analysis. The material may be analyzed in terms of words, characters, themes, space and time measures, or topics. The categories for classifying and analyzing the material are developed and the written matter is broken down according to prescribed rules. For instance, this method can be used to analyze advertisements.

Physical Trace Measures

Physical trace measures involve recording the natural "residue" of behavior. For instance, if the researcher was interested in finding out the alcohol consumption in a town without checking the retail store sales, the number of empty bottles from the garbage will give a rough estimate of the alcohol consumption. This method may not work in all the countries of interest to the researcher because the developing countries do not have an organized garbage disposal system. Hence, it is necessary for the researcher to first determine if tracing physical evidence will be helpful in the study.

Humanistic Inquiry

Humanistic inquiry involves immersing the researcher in the system that is being studied rather than the traditional method where the researcher is a dispassionate observer. The researcher maintains one log for recording the hypotheses formed during the process. The second set of notes is a methodological log where investigative techniques used during the process are recorded. An external auditor is employed to determine if the interpretation of the data gathered has been impartial.

Behavior Recording Devices

Behavior recording devices have been developed to overcome deficiencies of human observers. Some of these devices do not require the direct participation of the respondents. The peoplemeter developed by ACNielsen is attached to a television set to record continually which channel the set is tuned to. If the variables to be observed are beyond human capacity, special devices have to be used. Eye movement recorders are popular and have been used to record the experience of viewing pictures of advertisements, packages, signs, or shelf displays. These devices help in observing the time spent by the respondent with the various elements of the visual stimulus. Voice-pitch analysis examines variations in the pitch of the respondent's voice and the greater the variation the greater is the emotional involvement of the respondent.

ADVANTAGES AND DISADVANTAGES OF QUALITATIVE AND OBSERVATIONAL METHODS

Each of the qualitative and observational methods described above has both benefits and shortcomings. It is the researcher's decision to choose one method over another. Most researchers prefer to use the same methodology for obtaining data in all the countries that are being studied. While choosing a method, the researcher will have to keep in mind traits and habits that are peculiar to each country and choose the one method that will get the best results. In some cases, researchers may even have to settle for using different instruments in different countries to obtain comparable data.

Interviews are a very good source of obtaining information. In face-to-face interviews, the interviewer has the flexibility to probe the respondent and direct the interview in a manner that will help the study best. This method is very effective with busy executives who are the decision makers and will be able to give authentic information for the study. Advances in technology have made possible telephone interviews that are very cost effective and provide the researcher with a wealth of information. The drawback in this method is that it is dependent on the interviewing skills and the personal biases of the researcher. The interviewer must be sufficiently skilled to establish a good rapport with the respondent and pursue a line of questioning that will provide the best results. Another problem in this method is recording the responses. Some respondents do not like to be tape-recorded, and the interviewer has to be fast enough to record all of the important details of the response. In the international context, interviews must be used with discretion. For instance, the Japanese do not like being interviewed over the telephone. In Hong Kong, the researcher will not be allowed inside the home. Interviews will have to be conducted through an aperture in the front door. In the Middle East, women will not give any interviews, especially to male interviewers. The researcher will have to take care not to flout any traditions.

Focus group sessions are very successful if the number of participants is restricted to between five and nine and all of the participants are allowed to express their opinions. Because most people are comfortable in a group, they are a lot more candid in focus groups than in interviews; however, the moderator should watch out for a few stumbling blocks. Sometimes, one or two members of the panel get very aggressive and force their views on the remaining panel members. This should be stopped before any real damage is done. Focus groups can also yield misleading results if conducted poorly. As is usually the case, in the international setting, researchers will have to be aware of the importance of culture in the discussion process. In the Eastern countries, researchers will have to spend some time in detailed introductions. Only after the panel members know one another will they get comfortable enough to be candid with their views. In many cultures, members are conscious of their social status and disagreement is considered impolite. Exhibit 8-1 illustrates the use of focus groups for gathering information.

In international marketing research, *projective techniques* are very useful, as they do not impose a specific cultural referent on the respondent; however, interpretation of the results is highly subjective. It is very difficult to establish rules regarding coding and analyzing for these methods. Comparing across nations may also prove to be a challenge.

Protocols are very useful in providing information regarding effectiveness of advertising and promotional campaigns. They let the researchers know exactly what the customers think of a marketing strategy. They also give an insight into the different uses that customers have for a single product and the substitutes that are used frequently. Protocols help examine the importance that customers attach to factors like store layout, shelf displays, interaction with store personnel, crowding at the checkout counters, and so on. They also help researchers understand the terminology used by consumers in relation to a product. Protocols have their disadvantages. They are very unstructured. The onus of interpreting them and attributing national and cultural differences is on the researcher. On many occasions the customer may not verbalize the entire thought process and so the researcher ends up with partial information.

Observational methods are costly and time consuming. People tend to react differently if they discover that they are being observed. They also have the added restriction that researchers cannot measure motives, attitudes, or intentions. Hence, they cannot be very useful in diagnostic studies. The interpretation of the results is highly subjective and is entirely dependent on the observer. There is the added complexity of the usage of multiple languages. It may also be very difficult to execute some of the methods mentioned earlier in some countries. If the researchers were planning on using physical evidence in a developing country, the research would yield incorrect results, as garbage disposal is not an organized activity in many of these countries. It may be very difficult to convince a retailer in Japan to consent to a covert observation of customers.

EXHIBIT 8-1

Use of Focus Groups in Marketing Research

Started in 1982, Productivity Products International, Inc. grew to be a leading marketer of object-oriented computer programs; however, executives at PPI felt that the name did not do much to enhance the image of the company as one that helps build software faster. The company opted for a name change to correct two major flaws in the customer perception. The first was that people were more familiar with "C," the language on which its products were based, than with PPI itself. The second was that executives felt the name evoked negative responses. Software programmers, who influence the decision to buy this product, tend to focus more on quality, creativity, and creation rather than productivity. Hence, the company started searching for a new name in 1987 and hired Identica, a New York-based identity consulting and marketing firm.

Researchers from Identica conducted one-to-one interviews with selected customers and prospects. They also spoke to lower level employees. This completed, consultants from Identica held brainstorming sessions to generate a list of 400 names. This list was further narrowed down to 15, then 8, and finally 4. They then launched a legal search to eliminate any names that may already be in use. Two finalists emerged—"Tersus" and "Stepstone."

A focus group was conducted to decide between the two. The group consisted of six PPI employees, two outsiders, a program engineer, and a software salesperson who was also a shareholder of PPI. "Tersus" in Latin means "polished" or "to the point," but the group rejected this because it sounded too close to "terse" which is not very complimentary. The new name was Stepstone, Inc.

Source: Adapted from Tom Eisenhart, "What's in a Name? Plenty," *Business Marketing* 73, no. 10 (October 1998): 88–94.

FREQUENCY AND EASE OF USE

The choice of the research method depends largely on the research purpose, environment, and researcher. If the researcher wishes to gain insight into the problem or understand the differences with respect to domestic research, qualitative methods would be preferred. Protocols are used if the research study focuses on the decision-making process rather than the actual behavior itself. Protocols can also be conducted in a laboratory or any other controlled atmosphere and are used in situations where it is not practical to conduct the study in the real world. Interviews are very frequently used in international marketing studies, primarily because of the complexity introduced due to national and cultural differences. Interviews are very structured and help the researcher in retaining control over the data to be collected.

Observation techniques are used frequently when the researcher is conducting exploratory research to become familiar with the shopping habits in a foreign country; however, in some cultures people are averse to being observed. It has also been the experience of researchers that customers tend to behave differently when they are aware of being observed, therefore, many researchers prefer to observe discreetly. Observation methods are generally useful in studying how people purchase in different environments, especially when the process differs considerably between the different countries that are being studied. If the researcher is not familiar with the usage patterns in a certain country, observational methods serve to educate the researcher and help decide the best method of collecting data.

CULTURAL INFLUENCES

Designing the research instrument for an international marketing research project is tricky. Researchers should make sure that they understand the product usage and other acceptable substitutes to the product before they launch the data collection process. The research instrument should be able to provide the researchers with useful data about the specific country while at the same time being comparable to the data collected from other countries. Questions can be structured or unstructured—this is dependent on the culture. It has been observed that Eastern cultures provide good information on open-ended questions, whereas Americans prefer to avoid such questions; however, open-ended questions are subject to interpretation by the researcher and this could lead to biases.

Researchers have to be very careful with the manner in which the questions are worded. Some societies resent being asked direct questions on sensitive issues like income and lifestyle. In most Latin American cultures, tax evasion is very common and so questions regarding income are viewed with a great deal of suspicion. In such cases, researchers should phrase the question in a subtle manner. Demographic and psychographic data may vary considerably. What is considered a lower working class in one country may be the middle class in another country. The researcher should determine the class structure in the country before looking for information in the appropriate segments in that culture. Language plays a very important role in qualitative research. A lot of vital information and subtle nuances can be lost in translation. In some countries with multiple cultures, differences in usage in a single language can add to the complexity of the task.

Chivas Regal carried out an international qualitative study in 1990 to help its managers evaluate a number of global advertising concepts for Chivas Regal whiskey. One of the aspects of this study was the treatment of Japan as a special case. There were 14 in-depth interviews and two group discussions that used one local moderator and three other researchers as unobtrusive observers. The interviews and groups progressed through a stage of building rapport to the actual research topics. The moderator and two observers were Japanese while one observer was an American bilingual. This was done to ensure that the researchers were in tune with the cultural significance of responses.[12]

BIASES IN QUALITATIVE AND OBSERVATIONAL RESEARCH

International marketing research involves researchers belonging to one culture or country studying the lifestyles, attitudes, values, and beliefs of consumers in another culture. There are vast differences between countries and between cultures even within one country. There is a very high possibility of the researcher misinterpreting the words and actions of consumers in another country. In any research study the interpretation of the data collected ultimately rests with the researchers and any misinterpretation on their part could lead to erroneous results; hence, it is very important to know what the different sources of biases are and how to avoid them.

One of the major sources of biases in international marketing research is the research design and approach taken by the researcher. The researcher allows their own values, beliefs, and attitudes to affect the way in which they interpret the verbal and nonverbal cues of respondents in a foreign culture (self-reference criterion). This effect is even more pronounced when the researcher is conducting a study in a culture that is vastly different from their own. For instance, an American researcher conducting a study in Canada might have a mistaken notion that geographic proximity implies similarity in habits and attitudes. This would be a blunder, especially if the researcher were to approach respondents with the business-like attitude that most Americans approve and practice. Canadians like to take their time in getting to know the person and establishing a rapport before getting down to business. If researchers keep an open mind and try to spend some time familiarizing themselves with the foreign culture, the study will be more effective.

Another major source of bias is communication. A lot of vital information is lost in translations, and international marketing research is heavily dependent on translations and back translations. First, the survey instrument has to be translated to the native language so that the respondent may understand it. Then the response has to be translated to the language used by researchers in the study. It is very important that the right message be conveyed in each of the translations. This could prove to be tricky because some languages have many dialects and are used differently in different regions. An example would be Hindi, the language spoken by many in northern parts of India. There are many versions of this language depending on the region that it is spoken in. Most studies use professional translators. Even so, a lot of miscommunication occurs at every stage of the translation process. This contributes significantly to the bias.

The third source of bias is interpreting the results. This is a major aspect of qualitative and observational techniques. Interpretation is entirely dependent on the researcher and this is where self-reference criterion comes into play once again. The researcher may have problems attributing the right reasons for a purchase behavior. If, for instance, in a developing country, a consumer were to choose a product that has been packaged in an aluminum container instead of a plastic carton, the reason could simply be that the consumer plans to use this container for storage purposes after the contents have been used. An American researcher could not be faulted for attributing reasons of efficient recycling as the motive for this purchase. This error in interpretation could mean a big blunder when it comes to positioning the product.

Avoiding biases in international marketing research requires a lot of effort from the researcher. The first step would be to try and understand the research problem from the perspective of the foreign country. This is easier said than done because the root of the problem may be the researcher's lack of sensitivity and understanding to such cultural nuances. A feasible alternative is to include researchers from different cultural backgrounds in the research team so that the team as a whole can consider all of the different facets of the research problem. At every stage of the research process, the researcher who is familiar with that specific culture takes the lead in conducting the study and the results are then compared across countries. In some cases, researchers find it easier to develop research instruments specific to one country and then coordinate and compare across countries. Here again, both researchers who are familiar with the country and those who are not examine the instruments and the data and draw conclusions. This second method of considering one country at a time and then comparing is preferable even though it is time consuming. This method also poses a number of interaction problems, as researchers from different cultural backgrounds have to be in constant touch with one another. Another means used to avoid biases is to use many different instruments to measure the same variables. Convergent results for any given variable would indicate absence of biases.

LANDMARK DEVELOPMENTS

International marketing research has come a long way in the area of qualitative and observational research. This section examines some of the landmark developments that have occurred in this decade.

Measuring Minds in the 1990s

A decade ago, lifestyle segmentation schemes were the latest addition to marketing research. A thick cloud of hype covered the Values, Attitudes, and Lifestyles (VALS) program and its competitors. Psychographics—the study of values, attitudes, and lifestyles—was anticipated to replace demographics as the one essential marketing tool, but today, SRI International's refurbished VALS 2 is competing for clients, and former agency executives are looking into other parts of the consumer's psyche to increase revenues. Techniques like benefits probes, role playing, and photo collages compete with large-scale psychographic segmentations at advertising agencies. Learning about consumers and emotions regarding specific brands holds the key to good advertising. Combining lifestyle segmentation with other psychographic techniques is the smartest way of getting closer to the customer.

The marketplace has become increasingly complex in the 1990s. One can no longer explain markets using four or five segments. Twenty-five segments must be used and it is impossible to keep all of them straight. In the beginning, the ability to generalize while fragmenting the mass market was the salient feature of psychographics. It grew from sociology, psychology, economics, and anthropology to facilitate understanding of large consumer groups. Sociological inquiries began when Harvard-educated psychologist Daniel Yankelovich and market researcher Florence Skelly noticed that societal changes influenced markets greatly. In the early 1960s, Playtex asked Yankelovich, Skelly, and White to ascertain the reason for the downturn of the girdle market. It was found that women, wanting a more natural look, had changing perceptions of their bodies and did not want girdles anymore. Another study for Chrysler confirmed that people were buying cars less for status than as a means of personal self-expression. These researchers cofounded Yankelovich Lifestyle Monitor. Yankelovich is currently president of DYG Inc. in Elmsford, New York. The Monitor was developed in 1970 as a way to chart changing societal attitudes and their impact on businesses. The

Monitor still identifies changing trends on the basis of annual interviews with 2,500 American adults, though Yankelovich Clanchy Shulman, a subsidiary of Saatchi & Saatchi, runs it.

Computers have made possible the cross-tabulation of large numbers of survey questions. Combining statistical theories, psychographics provides a quantitative way of studying customer qualities. It gives researchers a market segmentation method that goes beyond demographics. In an attempt to incorporate the realities of the 1990s, researchers have placed more emphasis on brand or product-specific attitudes and behavior. SRI International recognized that its VALS program needed updating and introduced a new version in 1989 that focuses on product use. When the original Values, Attitudes, and Lifestyles program was developed by Arnold Mitchell in 1978, many top advertisers and agencies embraced the typology as the newest microscope with which to understand the complexities of the U.S. marketplace. By the late 1980s, critics charged that it was too theoretical and not predictive enough of consumer behavior. There was also alleged to be too much variation in the size and homogeneity of the groups for them to be useful.

VALS 2, with its eight consumer types, answers these criticisms, according to Bruce MacEvoy, VALS senior research psychologist. Each consumer type now accounts for between 8 percent and 17 percent of the population, compared with between 2 percent and 38 percent in the original VALS. The new types are based on the consumption of 170 different categories of products. While the original VALS was intended as a model of social behavior, VALS 2 tries to predict consumer behavior by defining segments on the basis of product use. According to MacEvoy, about 65 psychological dimensions are reduced to 15 attributes that, in unison, are consistently more predictive of consumer behavior than selected demographic characteristics. VALS 2 evaluates consumption tendencies of people, says MacEvoy, rather than their style of relating to other people, their spiritual goals, or their ethnic values.

How They Feel

Agencies are reusing old projective techniques to get at the emotions that influence brand choice. For this, BBDO Worldwide uses a trademarked technique called Photosort. "Consumers express their feelings about brands through a specially developed photo deck showing pictures of different types of people from executives to college students," says Karen Olshan, executive vice-president and director of research services. Respondents connect people with the brands they think they use. A Photosort for General Electric revealed that consumers associated the brand with conservative, older, business types. To change that image GE adopted the "Bring Good Things to Life" campaign. Another Photosort for Visa found the card had a wholesome, female, middle-of-the-road image in customers' minds. The "Everywhere You Want to Be" campaign strove to interest more high-income men. Another trademarked technique developed in 1989 by the same agency uses photos of actors portraying 26 categories of emotions to determine how consumers feel after viewing commercials.

When D'Arcy, Masius, Benton, and Bowles Inc. (DMB&B) conducted a test for Clearasil to see how teenagers felt about acne, it used the Thematic Apperception Test (TAT). By describing the feelings of the person in a picture who had a blemish, they supposedly revealed their own feelings about having pimples. Says Hank Berstein, director of consumer information services at DMB&B, "We got a very clear image that a blemish meant social isolation and difference and all those things that a teenager fears most." The agency developed a series of ads, the theme of which was to get back into life as quickly as possible. Such information could not have been obtained by simply asking teenagers to talk about acne and its remedies. An advantage is that these techniques help consumers express feelings and emotions that they would have had difficulty expressing otherwise.

Projective techniques have been in vogue for a long time. Freud defined projection as an ego defense mechanism that allowed an individual to relieve anxiety by attributing its causes to the outside world. Since the 1930s, clinical psychologists have sought insights into the unconscious through projective techniques such as Rorschach's inkblot tests, sentence completion, and Thematic Apperception Tests.

Motivational researchers led by Ernest Dichter introduced Freudian psychology to market research during the 1940s. Dichter, now in his early eighties, has conducted thousands of in-depth interviews and consulted for most major advertisers during the 46 years he has run the Dichter Institute International in Peekskill, New York. After fleeing pre-Nazi Austria in 1938, he created waves with his work for Procter & Gamble and Chrysler. For Procter & Gamble he interviewed young girls who used their product before dates. He concluded that when they had a bath, they were also washing their sins away. The campaign, "Be Smart Get a Fresh Start" enhanced the virginal appeal of the product. For Chrysler, Dichter found that wives played a significant role in car buying decisions and helped equate convertibles with mistresses. He also put the tiger in Exxon's tank. By 1957, thanks to Dichter, motivational research became the subject of Vance Packard's best-selling book, *The Hidden Persuaders*. The new manipulation of consumers' unconscious motivations by marketers foreshadowed an America controlled by Big Brother. Subsequently, motivational research went out of vogue.

A part of the new emphasis on psychology may stem from pressure on advertising agencies to cut costs as advertisers trim their budgets and profit margins shrink. Says Marian Bockman, senior vice-president of the American Association of Advertising Agencies, "Research is adversely affected by such cost cutting measures. A good segmentation system can cost $50,000. Fewer agencies have the budgets for such research expenses. Much of the research is being farmed out to suppliers."

Brand Clutter

With increase in product categories and explosion in the number of similar brands, advertisers need to study how customers relate to their brands. As spending choices increase, agencies need to look for nuances in selling. Differentiation among brands has lessened. Ogilvy & Mather uses one-on-one interviews to focus on consumers' brand relationships. Agency researchers ask people to attach personalities to brands, get them into dialogues with the brand, and probe their feelings toward the personified brand. This is better than making use of attitude and attribute statements. A quantitative approach that preserves the original consumer language is preferred.

Grey Advertising has developed a process that identifies the characteristics people ascribe to brand name products. Executive vice-president Barbara Feigin believes that it helps develop an appealing character that strikes a strong emotional chord in consumers so that they feel that the brand is special and unique and just right for people like themselves. One copyrighted technique used by Grey to get an inner scoop on consumers' feelings is called a Benefit Chain. A self-administered probing technique, it uses layers of carbon paper. On the first layer, consumers use their own words to describe a product's two most important benefits. On the next, they write down the secondary benefits, and so on. This process allows consumers to express in their own words the benefits that they value and the level of consciousness at which these appear. A Benefit Chain done for Minute Rice, for example, revealed that the product's emphasis on perfect rice every time had outlived its effectiveness.

Another technique that Grey copyrighted is the Pictured Aspirations Technique (PAT) which gets at how a product fits into consumer aspirations. Consumers sort a deck of photos on the basis of how well the pictures describe their aspirations. For example, this technique helped to ascertain that Playtex's Eighteen Hour Bra did not correspond with potential customers' aspirations. Respondents chose pictures that depicted slenderness, youth, and vigor. The pictures they used to express their feelings about the product were comparatively old-fashioned, less stout, and less energetic looking. As a result, the "Good News for Full-Figured Gals" campaign emerged with Jane Russell as spokesperson with the fashionable concept of "The Fit That Makes the Fashion."

The Magic Yardstick

Advertising agencies have been using projective techniques for a long time. BBDO's Photosort, DMB&B's TAT, and Grey's Benefit Chains have also emphasized brand characterization. Most agencies now use projective techniques more often, while using less of broad segmentations. Young & Rubicam has been a steady subscriber to VALS. Though subscriptions to VALS 2 range between $12,500 to $50,000, getting a fix on the consumers is economical in the long run. VALS is now largely marketed to corporations instead of advertising agencies. The only competition faced by the Lifestyle Monitor is from in-house environmental scanning products developed by some agencies.

Large-scale custom research provides extra selling points with clients and exclusive market insights for agencies that can afford it. Grey has fielded major studies on the "ultra" consumer, the 50-plus market, and households of the 1990s in recent years. Backer Spielvogel Bates Worldwide has a program called Global Scan that currently segments markets in 18 countries by psychographics. NW Ayer has segmented the baby-boom generation based on psychographics and purchase behavior. Ogilvy & Mather has a consumer trend scanning program called New Wave that tracks major trends affecting consumption.

The longest running agency psychographic study is DDB Needham's Lifestyle Study, which has been conducted annually since 1975. Each year, 4,000 adults nationwide respond to a 1,000-question mailed survey that includes attitudes and opinions, activities, personal and family product use, product ownership, media habits, and demographics. Lifestyle analysis is used to profile target audiences and identify trends, according to William Wells, Chicago-based Needham's director of marketing research, who developed the Lifestyle Study. Both lifestyles and current product use are indicators of consumption behavior.

New Approaches

Agencies like Leo Burnett in Chicago and NW Ayer in New York pioneered evolutions in psychographic research. Formerly, computers were used to quantify personalities and lifestyles. They are now used to quantify emotions. Leo Burnett's Emotional Lexicon is an interactive computerized system that studies emotions derived from product categories. It leads the subject through an interview and contains words or phrases that represent 143 emotional dimensions that can be reduced to 15 key emotional points. For example, it is possible to study people who like low-calorie beer as opposed to regular beer and determine whether the difference is based on the rational level of calories. NW Ayer's version of the emotional lexicon consists of a questionnaire with phrases that rate according to 50 emotion brands, reactions to advertising, and feelings after using a product. The responses are cross-tabulated and can be graphically represented in perceptual maps. According to Fred Posner, executive vice- president of research, it is a quantitative approach that leads to a qualitative understanding of the consumer. Lifestyle research paved the way to both new emotional research and research into actual behavior coming from scanner data, according to Douglas-Tate.

It's All Semantics

Exhibit 8-2 lists the consumer categories obtained with one way of segmenting consumer markets. The criticism of psychographics arises largely due to semantics. Psychographics, once thought to mean segmentation by lifestyle, has now come to include product-specific attitudes, emotions, and behavior. The word *psychographics* was first published in the November 1965 issue of *Grey Matter,* an internal publication of Grey advertising. Even before the actual term was coined, the concept was used in its broadest sense. In 1964, Daniel Yankelovich published a paper in the *Harvard Business Review* in which he outlined what he called nondemographic segmentation. He recommended segmentation of markets be done according to consumer, product-specific values, and attitudes. Exhibit 8-2 summarizes the results of a consumer segmentation study. He warned that personality typologies were useless in predicting brand choice. He felt that personality differences are too deep to have much bearing on product choices that are rather superficial.

INTERNATIONAL MARKETING RESEARCH IN PRACTICE

Qualitative and observational methods are some of the most important means of data collection for Tasty Burgers. Qualitative methods involve informal or semi-structured interviews, focus groups, and projective techniques. Not all of these methods are equally

---

EXHIBIT 8-2

Global Segments

What is it that drives the consumer markets worldwide and the global strategies that arise as a result of this? There are several variables—nationality or culture, demographics, and personal values are some of them. The importance of each of these three variables relative to one another depends on the product or service category with which marketers are dealing. A Roper Reports Worldwide Global Consumer Survey in 1997 interviewed 1,000 people in their homes in 35 countries and classified adults into six global value segments.

The *Strivers* are the largest group and have a greater proportion of men than women. They place more emphasis on material and professional goals. One in three people in developing Asia and one-fourth of the population in developed Asia and Russia are Strivers.

Twenty-two percent of the population consists of *Devouts*, which includes more women than men. Tradition and duty are very important to this segment, which is most commonly found in developing Asia, Middle Eastern, and African countries. They are least common in developed Asia and Western Europe.

Altruists make up 18 percent of the people surveyed, with a slightly higher percentage of females. This group is interested in social issues and the welfare of the society. The average age of this group is higher and is found mainly in Latin America and Russia.

Intimates comprise 15 percent of the world's population and value personal relations and family above all else. This group has an equal proportion of men and women. One in four Europeans and Americans fall under this category, while only 7 percent of developing Asia can be called Intimates.

Fun Seekers are found in very high numbers in developed Asia and account for 12 percent of the global population. They are the youngest group, with 54 percent being males.

Creatives are the smallest group, with only 10 percent of the population falling under this category. This group has a strong interest in education, knowledge, and technology. They are mainly found in Latin America and Western Europe and are made up of equal numbers of women and men.

Source: From "Strivers to Creatives," by Tom Miller, *Marketing News* July 20, 1998, Vol. 32, No. 15, p. 11. Reprinted by permission of the American Marketing Association.

---

effective in all four countries. Focus groups work well in cultures where people are generally used to being frank and holding an independent opinion. It will be a very good method of data collection in the United Kingdom; however, in India, where most people succumb to peer pressure and do not want to appear very different from the rest of society, focus groups may not be the ideal method. Japanese consumers tend to be more hesitant to criticize a new product than their Western counterparts.[13] Individual semistructured interviews may be more effective in drawing honest responses. In Saudi Arabia, women are not allowed to talk to strange men and, hence, it may be necessary to have women moderators or interviewers to gather data from that segment of the society. It is important to ensure that the interviewers and focus group moderators are culturally sensitive and respect the religious beliefs of respondents, particularly those in India and Saudi Arabia, because the line dividing the social or political life and religion is very narrow.

Observational methods help researchers gather information that has not been voiced by the respondents. These methods will prove very helpful to Tasty Burgers in societies where people mask their true feelings in public in order to adhere to socially accepted roles. For instance, in India many people claim to be vegetarians because the religious beliefs of Hindus forbid them from eating beef; however, many of these people also consume meat unknown to their family and friends. These people will publicly deny trying any of the products that include meat. Observation unknown to the subjects will provide researchers better estimates of product sales. It may not be possible to engage in observational methods in all countries. For instance, in Saudi Arabia it may not be possible for researchers to observe the snacking habits of women, as restaurants have separate sections for women and families.

Summary

This chapter discusses the use of qualitative and observational methods in international marketing research. Qualitative methods include individual interviews, focus groups, projective techniques, and protocol. Direct observation, contrived observation, content analysis, physical trace measures, humanistic inquiry, and behavior recording devices come under observational methods. The chapter also discusses the advantages, disadvantages, and frequency and ease of use of these methods in international marketing research. Cultural influences make a big difference in recording and interpreting behavior, and researchers should be sensitive to the local culture in foreign countries.

The purpose of marketing research is to ensure that the company has not overlooked any major element of the problem or all alternative options available have been considered. Research is an iterative process wherein every stage is an improvement over the previous one. Qualitative and observational methods help researchers in exploratory research and in getting familiar with the international markets. The advantages and disadvantages of each method are also discussed here.

Questions and Problems

1. What are the significant differences between nondirective and semistructured individual interviews? In what circumstances would a nondirective interview be more useful than a semistructured interview?
2. You have conducted two group meetings on the subject of telephone answering devices. In each group there were seven prospective users of such devices, and in the two groups there were four users of telephone answering services. (These

services use an operator to intercept calls and record messages.) When the client's new product development manager heard the tapes and read the transcripts of the two meetings, the first reaction was, "I knew all along that the features I wanted to add to our existing model would be winners, and these people are just as enthusiastic. Let's not waste any more research effort on the question of which features are wanted." What do you say?

3. A local consumer organization is interested in the differences in food prices among major international markets. How should it proceed in order to obtain meaningful comparisons?

4. Toothpaste manufacturers have found consistently that if they ask for detailed information on the frequency that people brush their teeth, and then make minimal assumptions as to the quantity of toothpaste used on each occasion, as well as spillage and failure to squeeze the tube empty, the result is a serious overstatement of toothpaste consumption. How would you explain this phenomenon? Would it be possible to design a study to overcome these problems and obtain more accurate estimates of consumption? Describe how such a study would be conducted.

5. What difficulties might be encountered when conducting a qualitative interview in an international context?

6. When would you recommend observational methods in different countries? Why?

7. For each of the following scenarios, indicate whether qualitative or quantitative research is more appropriate. Also recommend a specific technique for each and justify your answer.

   a. A manufacturer of herbal teas in China wants to know how often and for what purposes consumers use herbal tea products in France.

   b. A multinational company starting to manufacture potato chips in India has two alternative package designs for the product and wants to determine which design will yield higher sales.

Endnotes

1. Adapted from V. Kumar, David A. Aaker, and George S. Day, *Essentials of Marketing Research* (New York: John Wiley & Sons, 1999).

2. Margaret Crimp and Len Tiu Wright, *The Marketing Research Process*, 4th ed. (Herfordshire: Prentice Hall, 1995) 60.

3. Rebecca Piirto, "Measuring Minds in the 1990s," *American Demographics* 12, no. 12 (December 1990): 30–35.

4. *Market Research*, (5 January 1998): 14.

5. This section adapted from David A. Aaker, V. Kumar, and George S. Day, *Marketing Research*, 6th ed. (New York: John Wiley & Sons, 1998).

6. Naresh K. Malhotra, James Agarwal, and Mark Peterson, "Methodological Issues in Cross-Cultural Marketing. A State-of-the-Art Review," *International Marketing Review* 13, no. 5 (1996): 7–43.

7. Peter Chisnall, *Marketing Research*, 5th ed. (Berkshire, England: McGraw-Hill Publications, 1997): 185.

8. Chris Robinson, "Asian Culture: The Marketing Consequences," *Journal of Market Research Society* (1991): 55–62.

9. Adapted from Thomas L. Greenbaum, "Understanding Focus Group Research Abroad," *Marketing News* 30, no. 12 (3 June 1996): H14.

10. Harold S. Kassarjian, "Projective Methods," in Robert Ferber, ed., *Handbook of Marketing Research* (New York: McGraw-Hill, 1974) 3–87.

11. Sydney J. Levy, "Dreams, Fairy Tales, Animals, and Cars," *Psychology and Marketing* 2 (summer 1985): 67–82.

12. Clive Nancarrow, Len Tiu Wright, and Chris Woolston, "Pre-testing International Press Advertising," *Qualitative Market Research: An International Journal* 1, no. 1 (1998): 25–38.

13. David B. Montgomery, "Understanding the Japanese Customers, Competitors, and Collaborators," *Japan and the World Economy* (1991): 61–91.

CHAPTER

Survey Research

INTRODUCTION

Survey research is one of the most popular means of collecting primary data. For instance, Ford Motor Company in Europe conducts regular tracking surveys to check on customer satisfaction with Ford cars. Previously, mail surveys were used; however, it was found that with mail surveys customers did not describe in detail the problems they faced with the cars; hence, Ford switched to telephone surveys to obtain more complete and accurate feedback from the customers. American Airlines and Continental Airlines frequently talk to customers to get feedback on service levels. Recently, American Airlines instituted a program where they offer bilingual services to customers from Latin American and European countries. Airline employees wear badges that indicate the languages they speak, making it easier for customers. This was the result of feedback received directly from customers.[1]

There are a number of different ways in which surveys can be conducted. As technology for communication progresses, the number of survey methods also increases. Fax and electronic mail have added to the many different ways in which the survey instrument can be communicated to the respondent. In international marketing research the choice of a specific survey method is a difficult one because of the difference in technological developments in different countries. This chapter considers in detail the three most popular forms of survey research and discusses the usefulness of each of these methods in various international settings.

TYPES OF SURVEYS

The three most prevalent methods of conducting surveys are personal interviews, telephone interviews, and mail surveys. This section discusses each of these methods.

Personal Interviews

Personal interviews can be classified into different types depending on the method by which the interviews are conducted. There are four entities involved in a personal interview—the researcher, the interviewer, the respondent, and the interview environment. The human factor affects the outcome of the interview since the researcher, the interviewer, and the respondent have certain characteristics, some acquired and some inherent. During a personal interview, the interviewer and the interviewee influence one another in the interview environment. The researcher decides on the interview environment depending on the type of data to be collected. The different methods of conducting a personal interview are discussed in the following paragraphs.

Door-to-Door Interviewing

In door-to-door interviewing, consumers are interviewed in their homes. This has been considered the best method due to a number of factors. The respondent is at ease in the home environment and is able to answer more freely. This type of interviewing also allows the interviewer to look out for body language and other nonverbal cues. This will add to the quality of the information collected. The interviewer's presence helps clarify difficult points for the respondent. This is the only viable method of conducting in-depth interviews and some in-home product tests.

Executive Interviewing

The industrial version of door-to-door interviewing is called executive interviewing. Business people are interviewed in their offices concerning industrial products or services. This method can prove very expensive. The first task is to identify the executives who will be able to contribute useful information to the survey. The next step is to get an appointment to meet with and interview the person. There could be a long wait for an appointment and last minute cancellations are very frequent occurrences. The interviewer must be very experienced, as the interview topic could be very complicated.

Mall Intercept Surveys

When funds are limited, researchers resort to mall intercept surveys. Interviewers are stationed at the entrances to malls and they approach shoppers in a random manner. The interviews are conducted either at that location or the respondents are invited to a special facility in the mall. The survey costs in this method are low, as the interviewers do not incur traveling expenses, and a high number of respondents can be contacted in a given time frame; however, the sample obtained from shopping malls is not representative of the general population. This method is very popular in the United States and Canada; however, it is not commonly used in either European countries or developing countries.[2]

Self-Administered Questionnaires

In self-administered questionnaires there is no interviewer involved. This contributes to reduction in costs. The other benefit with self-administered questionnaires is that interviewer bias is eliminated. The flip side is that there is no one available to clarify any doubts that the respondent may have. This method is used in malls, airlines, and other places where the researcher is assured of a captive audience. Businesses in the service sector, like hotels and restaurants, use this frequently to assess the quality of their service.

Purchase Intercept Technique

Another technique related to mall interception is called purchase intercept technique. This technique involves intercepting the customers while they are shopping and interviewing them about their purchase behavior. This is a combination of in-store observation and in-store interviewing to assess the shopping behavior of the respondents and the reasons for that behavior. The researcher usually observes the customers in a store unobtrusively while they are shopping and then interviews them as soon as the purchase has been made. This technique is superior because of better buyer recall. As very little time has elapsed between the purchase and the interview, the respondent is able to remember the details clearly; however, the interviewer can contact only people who make purchases and so the sample may not be representative. Researchers could also have problems gaining access to the stores.

Omnibus Surveys

Omnibus surveys are regularly scheduled personal interview surveys conducted on a weekly, monthly, or quarterly basis. These surveys are conducted for different clients on different topics. The questionnaire contains many question sequences, each provided by a different client. This method is very useful when the respondent needs to answer only a limited number of questions. The total cost is reduced because many clients share it. This method is particularly useful in continuous tracking studies because the procedure is standardized and the results can be tabulated very easily. Sometimes researchers use the split-run method to get better results. In a split-run method, some members of the sample survey receive one questionnaire and some receive another version. This method of survey has proved to be very useful in studying low-incidence activities, such as ownership of exotic pets.

Telephone Interviews

With improvements in technology in most parts of the world, telephone interviewing is gaining popularity among researchers, especially when the sample size required for the study is large. This is also effective in keeping costs down. Many respondents who may not be available for a face-to-face interview will be willing to do a telephone interview.

The process of conducting a telephone interview is very similar to that of a face-to-face interview. The process differs in selecting the sample. Researchers could use random dialing procedure or select numbers from a prespecified list, such as a directory or a customer list. In developed countries where most individuals or businesses are listed in a directory, picking numbers from a telephone directory has been the traditionally used method. For instance, in Sweden, the number of telephones per thousand inhabitants exceeds 900.[3] In such countries as the Netherlands, the number of telephone interviews far exceeds personal interviews;[4] However, in Finland only 11.2 percent of the interviews are conducted over the telephone.[5] Telephone interviews may not work very well in countries like Germany, where there is lot of resistance to telephone interviews.[6] This may not be possible in countries or states where the number of unlisted telephone numbers is very high. There is also the possibility that such a selection may not be representative of the general population, as people who have unlisted numbers tend to be significantly different from the rest of the population.

Random-Digit Dialing

To overcome this bias created by telephone directories, researchers resort to random-digit dialing. In a complete random-digit dialing method, all the digits of the telephone number (the area code, prefix, and the exchange suffix) are selected randomly. This implies that in a given country, all telephone numbers stand an equal chance of being called. The drawback in this method is that not all numbers may be in service and so many calls could be made to nonexistent numbers, which in turn leads to waste of time and money. Moreover, a completely random-digit dialing leads to telephone numbers which are of no interest to the researcher—outside the geographic scope of the study, government numbers, a business number when the research is on households, and so on. Exhibit 9-1 gives a list of countries for which samples are available.

Systematic Random-Digit Dialing

A variation of the random-digit dialing called systematic random-digit dialing (SRDD) is used in most cases. Here the researcher specifies the area code and the prefix for the telephone numbers to be called, thus avoiding sections of the population that are not useful for the study. The researcher determines a starting number (seed point) and a constant which is added systematically to the number generated. This produces the list of telephone numbers to be called. Not all of the numbers called will result in successful interviews; therefore, researchers have to generate at least four

---

EXHIBIT 9-1

Coverage Expands for Global Telephone Samples

Survey Sampling's random-digit dialing (RDD) telephone samples are now available for 13 countries. Five countries have been added since January 1998. Global random-digit samples can be ordered directly through SSI's Global Sales Department or through SSI SNAP™ Online Sample Ordering System. SSI SNAP™ has become the fundamental method for ordering and retrieving samples any time of the day or night. SSI SNAP™ is Windows-based software, available at no cost on a CD-ROM loaded with useful information. It can be installed on the PC and communicates with SSI's computer and databases via the Internet or a modem. Global representation, efficiency, and cost-effective sampling are built into SSI SNAP™. Geography file updates, mandatory for ensuring proper geographic representation, are immediately available for downloading.

The countries for which the sampling lists are available are: Australia, Austria, Canada, France, Germany, Italy, the Netherlands, Norway, Spain, Sweden, Switzerland, the United Kingdom, and the United States.

Source: Adapted from The Frame, Survey Sampling Inc., June 1998.

times as many telephone numbers as the sample size. The advantage in this method is that each telephone number has an equal chance of being called. At the same time, because the researcher controls the exchange prefix, it is possible to focus the study in a specific geographic area. If the study requires sampling with geographic dispersion, the researcher only needs to add more seed numbers and generate more lists. The list can be generated with the help of computers. A simpler version of the SRDD method is called plus-one dialing. This involves selecting random numbers from telephone directories and adding "1" to the last four digits in the number. These methods ensure that unlisted numbers are also included in the sample.

Telephone Prenotification Method

Telephone interviews are also being increasingly used in international marketing research as a method of screening and notifying the respondents. Surveys are very expensive in international markets and the costs can be justified only with very high response rates. Telephones are used in conjunction with other modes of survey to ensure excellent response rates. This was used in a survey conducted by the author for a software company to measure market potential in global markets for their products. Germany was one of the countries included in the study. The method adopted was to call up potential respondents and inform them of the purpose of the study and enlist their cooperation. The respondents were then sent a questionnaire either by fax or by e-mail. The respondents were once again contacted by telephone if they did not send in their responses within a specified time. This resulted in a very high response rate and as a consequence only a small sample size was required. This method of enlisting cooperation beforehand is found to work well among busy executives. Exhibit 9-2 gives some pointers on timing telephone calls.

The outcome of a telephone interview may be very different in international research. In the United States, interviewers are used to getting through to the number called more often than not. Most telephones are also hooked up to an answering machine or voice mail. The typical procedure is to leave a message and call back at a later time. In most other countries, the phone lines may not be functional for considerable periods of time. Even when they are in working order, the researcher could get a busy signal, as there is no concept of call waiting. It is very rare that the call is picked up by an answering machine. In case of industrial surveys, getting through to the decision maker could be very cumbersome because of bureaucratic management styles. The interviewer could at best secure an appointment from a secretary. The cost is also very high. There is a charge for most local calls and state-to-state calls are considerably more expensive than they are in the United States. There is the added complication of some cultures refusing to impart any information over the telephone. All of this has to be taken into consideration when considering the telephone as the medium of data collection.

It has been generally found that the reliability of the Mexican telephone network is questionable.[7] As a result, some companies chose to bypass it by using private satellite networks to provide their own telecommunication lines. In Argentina, one has to hold the phone for hours waiting for a dial tone. Hungary also has a telephone system that is not very efficient. In China there are no residential telephone directories. Many Chinese are not used to taking phone calls so there is no standard procedure for hanging up. Sometimes they give a warning before hanging up abruptly and other times

---

EXHIBIT 9-2

Timing the Telephone Call

The date, day, and time of telephone calls plays a very important role in the quality and rate of response. Analyzing telephone calls made to respondents during various days and times of the day, researchers have arrived at the following conclusions:

1. Interviewers displayed a high preference for working between Monday and Thursday and between 1:00 p.m. and 5:00 p.m.

2. There was a higher than expected correlation between times for the first and second call, particularly between 2:00 p.m. and 4:00 p.m.

3. Interviewers' patterns of working were more related to their preferences than the working practices of any marketing research agency.

4. There was a greater probability of achieving successful interviews by controlling the *time* at which interviewers called on any particular day, than by controlling the *day* on which they called on the respondents.

5. Encouraging interviewers to make evening calls may lead to better response rates and minimize costs.

Source: From *Marketing Research*, 5th Edition, Peter Chisnall, Berkshire, England: McGraw Hill Publications, 1997. Reprinted by permission of Professor P. M. Chisnall.

---

they hold the receiver farther and farther away from the mouth before finally fading away. These are some of the problems encountered in telephone surveys in international marketing research.

There are a few tips that come in handy when conducting a telephone interview. The introduction is a very important part because this helps establish a rapport with the client. It is absolutely necessary that the interviewer have a pleasant voice and sounds friendly over the telephone. The introduction to the topic of the study should be brief and precise. It is also important that the telephone call be made at a time when the respondent is most likely to be available. For instance, if the study requires that professionals be interviewed, they should be contacted at home after working hours or over the weekends; however, the call should not be made very late into the evening as it may intrude into their sleeping hours and the respondents may not cooperate. The interviewer should also make a detailed report of each call—the day and the time the call was made, the outcome, the length of the call, if the respondent should be contacted again, and so forth. This step is very important for collating the data.

Mail Surveys

This is a method of survey where the questionnaire is mailed to potential respondents who complete the survey and mail it back. In a mail interview the individuals to be sampled should be identified and their mailing addresses should be obtained. This is commonly used in countries where the literacy level is high.[8] Mailing lists can be obtained from various sources like telephone directories, organization membership

---

EXHIBIT 9-3

Great Britain: Great Market for Direct Marketers

With one-seventh the direct mail volume, but more than three times the average response rate as the United States, the United Kingdom is a ripe and growing market for U.S. direct marketers. The United Kingdom's 6.7 percent average direct marketing response rate compares to only 2 percent response rate in the United States, yet direct marketing volumes are low in the United Kingdom, with the average household receiving only 138 items of direct mail per year, compared to 972 items per year in the United States.

High response rate, low direct mail volume, and the increasing social acceptance of home shopping make the United Kingdom an enticing gateway for direct marketers seeking to expand sales. For U.S. companies, direct mail is the most cost-effective method of marketing in a foreign country. This is especially true in home shopping where the key to success is effective direct marketing—whether the business is financial services, magazines, or catalog sales.

A new study of consumer loyalty by the Direct Mail Information Service (DMIS), an independent organization that monitors the direct mail industry in the United Kingdom, has given fresh insight into how consumers view their relationships with direct mailers and reveals what types of communications they feel are appropriate. The DMIS research shows that loyalty includes both a qualitative and quantitative element; not just how much consumers buy, but also how they feel about the company. Their attitudes affect their judgment about what kind of communication is appropriate. The relationship that consumers have with their direct marketing companies can be categorized as follows:

- *Transactions-Only Relationships.* Consumers sometimes have no choice about the companies they deal with. When these companies make offers of products that are related to their core product, consumers may find this acceptable, but if the offering is not related to their core product, consumers are put off, especially if the direct mail is a blatant attempt at selling the product.

- *Added-Value Relationships.* As consumers have more disposable income, they are more willing to respond to special offers from direct marketers. These offers may include memberships, free information, or special sales. These offers may serve to strengthen the bond and lead to increased sales for companies and enhance customer attitudes toward the company.

- *Staying in Touch.* Consumers expect to receive periodic communication from direct mailers, but the level has to be appropriate to be effective. Too much direct mail can be irritating, while too little may be frustrating. Consumers like to be able to feel they are controlling the volume in some way, either by stressing their own particular interests or by regulating the frequency of offers.

- *Use of Data Consumers.* Consumers expect companies to tailor their mailings; however, they do not like direct references to personal information. In addition, they get especially upset when companies get information wrong— multiple mailings, misspelled names, inappropriate offers—all of which hurt the mailer's credibility and effectiveness.

- *Cross-Selling Brand Extensions.* Direct marketers need to be careful when extending their offers. Too big a leap from their core product will produce negative attitudes. Another important consideration is that existing customers often feel they should be told about new developments and should receive preferential treatment before new customers.

- *Soft-Sell Techniques.* DMIS found consumers were very responsive to informative communications without seeming to directly sell the product. Newsletters and company magazines that advised consumers were welcome, even though consumers realized they sometimes led indirectly to sales.

- *Reward Programs.* These programs increase consumer loyalty, especially for products they would buy anyway. For discretionary purchases, the level of reward has to be higher. All agree that rewards have to be realistic and readily available.

Source: Mail International—The Royal Mail Magazine for Customers in the United States, no. 1, 1998.

rosters, publication subscription lists, or other commercial sources. The only precondition is that the mailing list must be current and must closely relate to the group being studied. As can be expected, obtaining a valid mailing list that is current and representative of the general population is a cumbersome task. Exhibit 9-3 demonstrates the use of mailing lists in Great Britain.

There are other decisions that would have to be made before mailing a survey. Although they may seem relatively mechanical, these could affect the efficiency and quality of the mailing survey. Some of the aspects that need to be considered are the length of the questionnaire, the content, layout, color and format, the method of addressing the respondent, the contents of a cover letter, the incentive that would be given to the respondents, the type of return envelope, and postage. The choice of incentives is very critical to the success of mail surveys in cross-national research.[9] Researchers should also decide on the time and effort to be spent in follow up in the form of post cards, letters, or telephone calls. These decisions will have a significant impact on the response rates, the quality of information collected, and cost of executing the mailing survey. Respondents could be screened using a preliminary notification.

ADVANTAGES AND DISADVANTAGES OF SURVEY METHODS

Each of the three methods described above has both advantages and disadvantages. This section considers the benefits and drawbacks of each of these methods in the international context.[10]

The Personal Interview

Most researchers consider this to be the most flexible method of obtaining data. The interview is a face-to-face encounter and can put the respondent at ease. The interviewer will clarify any doubts that the respondent may have during the course of the survey. The rate of nonresponse error will be marginal. The interviewer has a high degree of flexibility to rephrase the questions on more comfortable grounds or probe the respondent on any aspect of the survey. This is the ideal method for studies that focus on complex topics or those that require a lot of information. The interviewer can also exercise the option of interviewing other members of the household if they can contribute significantly to the study. In countries where the literacy rate is very low, this may be the only way of gathering information from respondents. Even though the cost of personal interviews is very high, this is the most effective method of data collection in less-developed countries;[11] however, due to the high cost, this method is not commonly used in countries such as the United States and Canada.[12]

As contradictory as it sounds, the presence of the interviewer is also the biggest disadvantage of personal interviews. Respondents may provide wrong answers to some questions with a desire to appear prestigious and sophisticated. In some cases, the presence of the interviewer could make some respondents uncomfortable and reticent. It could be difficult to conduct personal interviews in certain parts of the world. For instance, interviewing housewives in Middle Eastern countries will be difficult if the interviewer is male. In many cultures, like Latin America, interviewers are treated with a lot of suspicion. For the interview to be fruitful, the interviewer has to put a lot of effort in winning the trust of the respondent. Studies have shown that there is a significant impact of the interaction effects of gender and ethnicity on the quality of response.[13] There is the possibility of interviewer bias, which is very pronounced in international marketing research. Exhibit 9-4 summarizes the results of a study on the effects of interviewer bias. The interviewer could misinterpret the response due to a lack of understanding of the foreign culture or language problems. Some countries have different dialects and differences in usage of the same language in different parts of the country. This makes the task of the interviewer more difficult. There could also be problems in interpreting nonverbal cues in a foreign country. An example would be shaking of one's head. While it means a negative reply in most parts of the world, the Japanese use it to indicate a positive answer. Last, but not the least of all, the cost of personal interviews is very high.

The Telephone Interview

Telephone interviews cost less than personal interviews and can be done in a very short period of time. The nonresponse rate is generally very low. If the respondent cannot be contacted on the first attempt, it is very easy to call back again at a later time. In countries that have a very good telephone network, it is possible to contact people who meet all of the specifications of the target population. Declining costs of telephone calls have made it possible for interviewers to cover a broadly distributed sample. It has also been observed that international calls produce better results consistently. The fact that they require no field staff serves to lower costs further. With advances in technology, interviewers can key in the responses directly into a computer, simplifying the task of data preparation.

Telephone interviews must be kept as short as possible as respondents fail to cooperate for very long interviews. The problem of interviewer bias is present, as in the case

---

EXHIBIT 9-4

Interviewer Bias

A study was conducted to investigate the effects of interviewer ethnic origins involving nonblack ethnic minorities. Elementary school children from four districts—Miami (Cubans), El Paso (Chicanos), NE Arizona (Native Americans), and San Francisco (Chinese)—were interviewed by 50 ethnic and 51 nonethnic interviewers. Twenty pairs of interviewers were randomly selected. Each pair consisted of one interviewer who did not speak the respondent's language and was not of the same ethnic group. The second interviewer in the pair was of the same ethnic group as the respondent but did not speak the respondent's language. The survey revealed that difference in ethnicity between interviewer and respondent did not affect responses to nonsensitive questions.

Another study, which focused on white respondents being surveyed by black interviewers revealed that respondents appeared anxious to avoid responses that might offend interviewers of opposing race. They tended to be more frank with their responses when interviewed by people of their own race. Other studies have also revealed that race of the interviewer did not affect responses to questions that were nonracial in nature; however, when the questions had racial overtones, respondents who were interviewed by people of a different race were more deferential to the race of the interviewer than those who were interviewed by people of the same race.

Source: From *Marketing Research*, 5th Edition, Peter Chisnall, Berkshire, England: McGraw Hill Publications, 1997. pp. 171–172. Reprinted by permission of Professor P. M. Chisnall.

---

of personal interviews. Telephone interviews do not permit the use of visual aids to aid the survey process. In developing countries the percentage of the population that owns telephones is very low. Telephone interviewers will be able to contact only the upper echelons of the society. The sample interviewed over the telephone will not be representative of the majority. Even if a telephone network exists, there may not be a reliable directory that lists the telephone numbers. Random-digit dialing will not be very effective because many telephones may not be in working order. In some countries, like Japan, people tend to think of telephone interviews as disrespectful. Respondents will cooperate only in personal interviews. Telephone interviews will not be cost effective in Europe because the charges are very high, especially in Germany.

The Mail Survey

Mail surveys can cover a broader respondent base and do not require any field staff. They are free from interviewer bias. The cost of mailing questionnaires to respondents selected from a sample tends to be low when compared to personal interviews or telephone interviews. This method can be used effectively for industrial surveys where the respondents are highly knowledgeable and the topic of the survey is very specific.

The nonresponse rate in a mail survey is very high and this causes some problems. Even though the cost of mailing questionnaires is relatively low, because of poor response, the cost-per-survey may be very high. The other problem is that there could be a significant bias because of low response rate. There is no control over the questionnaire once it has been mailed out. Respondents may answer questions selectively, ignoring personal issues. They could misinterpret some questions. In international marketing research, mail surveys are made difficult by the fact that current mailing lists may not be available. In many places, such as Hong Kong, people live on boats and have no formal addresses. There are no house or site numbers in Venezuela and addresses are identified by house names such as Casa Rosa or Casa Rio. Even if researchers were to look into magazine subscription lists, they tend to include citizens who are better educated and wealthier than the average folks. This introduces sampling biases in the survey. There could also be a significant loss of questionnaires and responses once they are mailed out. In Brazil, 30 percent of the mail does not get delivered. The postal system in many less-developed countries does not provide the service of forwarding mail. Low levels of literacy could also mean that even if it were possible to get the addresses, not all people would be able to respond. Including incentives in the mail to ensure cooperation is also not possible because of mail thefts. Conducting a multicountry mail survey also poses some practical problems for researchers—it is not possible to get return envelopes for such a survey. Researchers need to be aware of all these problems before deciding on a mail survey for international marketing research.

FREQUENCY AND EASE OF USE

In international marketing research, mail surveys are usually used for industrial products. The response rate is good and the cost per survey is low. Obtaining the mailing list for such products is easy. For consumer research, this method will be effective only in industrialized nations where the literacy levels are high and mailing lists are available. In most developing countries obtaining a mailing list will be expensive. Even if one were available, most potential respondents will not be able to respond because they are not literate. Other methods of survey research will have to be adopted in these countries.

Telephone interviews are dependent on the quality of the lines, which can vary substantially between countries. There are many countries where telephone connections are not widely available. Any survey conducted by telephone will be biased toward the upper classes in that country, therefore, this method is used if the population to be surveyed consists of lawyers, doctors, and other professionals who are in the upper income level. The second factor that decides the use of telephone surveys is the availability of telephone directories or lists that are valid and current. Cost per call is an aspect that researchers cannot ignore. In many countries, a hefty charge is levied on domestic or state-to-state calls. It may not be practical for the researcher to conduct lengthy surveys over the telephone.

Personal interviewing is considered the most flexible method of survey research. It is the most frequently used method of conducting surveys in international marketing research. Even though the cost of conducting personal interviews is very high, it can be cost effective in a foreign country because of the very high response rate. The preference for personal interviews arises because of the problems posed by mail surveys and telephone interviews. Telephone interviews are generally ruled out because of the high cost. Mail surveys are not very effective because most people do not mail the questionnaire back. Incentives do not help as most people in developing countries barely make ends meet and consider the incentive as a means of sustenance rather than as an obligation on their part to respond to the survey. There have been instances of mail thefts in cases where the postal employees become aware of the incentive included in the envelope. Besides, the cultural differences are so great that they can be captured only in personal interviews. In countries like India and China, the language, culture, and habits vary widely from region to region. Researchers will be able to gather all this data only by face-to-face interviews. In general, surveys for developing countries should be backed with observational studies because it may not be possible to obtain information from all classes of respondents.[14]

REQUIREMENTS

The researcher conducting the survey has to have three basic requirements:

1. Understanding of the research project.
2. Knowledge of the industry.
3. Familiarity with the national and cultural traits of the countries where the research is being conducted and fluency in the language.

Conducting a survey is a complex task of gaining trust and building rapport so that the respondent is comfortable with divulging information to a virtual stranger. This is a lot easier if the researcher is able to converse with the respondent in their own language. It is also better for the researcher to blend in with the culture rather than stand out. This can be achieved if the researcher is familiar with important customs and traditions in the part of the world where the survey is being conducted.

Industry knowledge and an understanding of the project are required because it will help the researcher design the survey better. It also becomes vital when the survey respondents are professionals and experts in the area that is being researched. They are likely to respect and respond better to someone who has a good knowledge of the technical aspects.

Audits & Surveys (A&S) conducts surveys on a regular basis for Coca-Cola Company to measure the awareness of Coke in all of the countries where it is being sold. The master plan for the research is designed by the headquarters in New York. The project is executed by researchers for A&S in all of these different countries. The questionnaire is originally designed in English and in each of these countries researchers translate it to the local language for the purpose of conducting the survey with the locals. The results are then translated back to English and sent to the New York office where the final analysis is completed. It is evident that researchers in all of these different countries should be fluent in English and the local language.

As many research companies point out, no one person can be an expert in all of the industries and all of the regions. People tend to specialize in a particular area and with experience gain insights into one or two cultures different from their own. A research company, however, will have the benefit of the combined knowledge and experience of all these researchers and is in a position to conduct surveys in any industry and in any part of the world.

APPLICABILITY

The chapter on primary research stresses the importance of establishing equivalence with respect to construct, measurement, sampling, and analysis. This is the stage in the research process where the researcher has to be concerned about establishing construct and measurement equivalence. The survey instrument used in surveys is a questionnaire, which has to be designed in a manner such that the data collected is comparable. This is better explained with the help of an example.

Consider a research study on car ownership among high-income homes in various countries. The researcher could formulate a hypothesis stating that the number of garages in a residence is an indicator of the number of cars owned. This would be a reasonably accurate estimation in the United States because almost every house comes with built-in garages. The problem arises when this questionnaire is used for surveys outside of the United States. In many countries most houses do not have garages. People use unconventional parking spots like the sidewalks and the front yard; hence, if the researcher wants the same hypothesis to hold true in other countries also, he should find all of the acceptable substitutes to a garage in these countries and incorporate all of these choices in the questionnaire. Only then will the results of the research be considered valid.

As can be understood from this example, it is very important for the survey instrument to be applicable in a given country, in a given situation, if the research is to be fruitful. Once again, it brings us back to the importance of cultural and national differences and the necessity for the researcher to be culturally sensitive.

CULTURAL INFLUENCES

There is a vast difference in the way different cultures react towards surveys. Personal interviews last longer in France, Germany, and Italy, as the interviewers provide elaborate descriptions for all of the terms that have no direct translation into that language. Therefore, care should be taken to ensure that the survey does not last more than 20 or 25 minutes in the United States because this would mean a 35 to 40 minute survey in any of the above-mentioned countries. There is also a high rate of refusal in these countries because a lot of people are subjected to too many surveys. The other factor that should be considered is that Germans are very conscientious about time. If they are told that the survey will last half an hour, at the end of the half-hour they ask you to stop. The French and the Italians are a lot more flexible with their time. The English are too polite to cut off the interviewer. People in the Scandinavian countries have lower refusal rates and are generally very cooperative. People in most Mediterranean countries, with the possible exception of Spain, like to converse. Among the Asian countries, the Japanese consider it impolite if they are surveyed over the telephone. They have to be interviewed personally. In Hong Kong, researchers are not allowed inside the residence. They will have to question the respondents through a small aperture in the front door of the house. In the Middle Eastern countries women cannot be interviewed in their houses without the presence of men. Researchers will have to bear all of this in mind while launching a survey. In most Middle Eastern countries lunch lasts for two to four hours and people have a relaxed attitude towards punctuality.[15]

The researcher must overcome problems of organization, sampling, fieldwork, untranslatable words, respondent unfamiliarity with the subject of research and lack of ability to provide information, in addition to gaining cooperation from governments, trade associations, respondents, and other agencies. Particularly salient is the problem that due to illiteracy and other socio-cultural factors, consumers in these countries are unable to respond to the information requested by the researcher using multipoint rating scales. Some of these problems are discussed in detail in the following section.

PROBLEMS SPECIFIC TO DEVELOPING COUNTRIES[16]

Language is likely to present a very big problem in conducting surveys, especially in countries where multiple dialects are spoken. Most of these countries are also characterized by low levels of literacy. Under these circumstances, written questionnaires are useless. Getting good research staff is also likely to be a problem in many of these countries. For instance, interviewers in India tend to be generalists and are not regarded very highly because the status of the marketing researcher is poor. Interviewers should be of the same racial group as the respondents. There could be a lot of respondent bias in developing countries. Thai and Indonesian women are not likely to talk to strangers, while Indian women require some known acquaintance to accompany the interviewer. Businessmen in some cultures view interviewers as industrial spies and refuse to divulge facts and figures. In many countries, like Hong Kong, China, and India, the best way to obtain an interview might be to just go knocking on the doors rather than trying to fix up an appointment over the telephone.

SOURCES OF BIAS IN SURVEYS

Bias in survey[17] research can be attributed to three major sources—the respondent, the interviewer, and the topic of survey.

Respondents in many countries, particularly in Asia, provide responses which they think would please the interviewer. The moral and cultural obligations of people in these societies imply that they will go to any extent to prevent the interviewer from getting upset. The norms of many societies demand that respondents be courteous to strangers, hence, more often that not, their responses are not indicators of their true feelings and opinions. To avoid this it may be preferable to conceal the sponsors of the study. Interviewers should be trained adequately to overcome these obstacles. The questions should be worded in a manner that will reduce courtesy bias. This could be achieved by phrasing the question as applicable to a third party—"People think that. . . ." rather than "What do you think. . . ."

Another source of bias is the respondents' desire to give socially acceptable answers. This occurs even more so with topics that are controversial. Many respondents answer in a manner that they think will make them socially or intellectually superior. Researchers have to try and understand values and topics that are likely to induce social desirability and make allowances for these. Cultural traits like modesty make a lot of difference in the survey. The Japanese are a modest society and tend to understate things while the Latin Americans tend to exaggerate their income and lifestyle. Even within a given country, factors like age, sex, and education play an important role in contributing to the bias. Respondents who are not well-educated try harder to please the interviewer.

Specific cultural traits can cause bias. It has been found that the Chinese in Malaysia tend to be more reticent than Malaysians or Indians and consequently give more "no" and "don't know" answers to open-ended questions. The Middle Eastern respondents tend to exaggerate, especially in aspects like class, income, position, and achievement. This can be overcome by using correlation techniques.

The presence of the interviewer adds to the bias in surveys. If the interviewer is not familiar with the country and its traditions, they could misinterpret the verbal and nonverbal responses given by the respondent. If the survey has open-ended questions, the interviewer may miss certain vital points. The research analyst could attribute wrong intentions to some of the responses or actions recorded during the course of the survey.

The topic that is being researched can cause bias. Some topics are socially sensitive in some countries. For instance, Latin Americans are touchy about alcoholism and Indians consider sex a taboo topic. In some surveys, respondents refuse to answer all of the questions, leading to nonresponse bias.

NEW APPROACHES TO SURVEY RESEARCH

Persuasibility research is becoming a very popular tool in survey research.[18] This method recognizes the fact that what people say initially is not what they say after some deliberation, and that their opinions change in response to the arguments to which they have been exposed. Theory of persuasion is based on two important factors:

- Most answers given in surveys are neither very thoughtful nor very stable. The attitudes that surveys seek to measure do not really exist in the respondent—they are created at the instant at which they are measured and dissipate almost instantly.
- Survey research treats respondents in a sterile atmosphere, divorced from any real context.

Survey research is a process of providing stimuli to respondents. Exhibit 9-5 demonstrates the use of surveys for gathering information. The response is said to be indicative of the mental state of the respondent. Individuals process information until they reach a satisfactory conclusion, hence, if people can be persuaded to process information or stimuli more thoroughly, a more valid conclusion can be drawn from the response. This can be applied in situations where additional information will provoke a more logical response, like a political or a theological survey.

EXHIBIT 9-5

Conducting Surveys

The *Financial Times* carries out a European Businessman Readership Survey every two or three years. In 1993 they surveyed 312,480 senior business individuals in 47,263 business establishments in 17 countries. This included establishments with 250 or more employees, head offices of companies employing 150 or more people, and head offices of banks and insurance companies, regardless of their size.

The main sources for industrial and commercial establishments are Kompass Directories or their local equivalents, supplemented by *Duns Europa*, an international source. Details of the financial institutions were derived from the *Banker's Almanac*, supplemented by the *Telerate Bank Register* and the *Assecuranz Compass Yearbook of International Insurance Companies*, which was merged with the *World Insurance Yearbook*.

The next stage in the survey involves telephone calls to obtain the names of heads of two departments or functions in each company. These people are then sent cover letters and questionnaires in their own language. The countries that are covered by this survey are Austria, Belgium, Denmark, Finland, France, Germany, Greece, Italy, Luxembourg, the Netherlands, Norway, Portugal, Spain, Sweden, Switzerland, and the United Kingdom. The questionnaire is translated into 21 languages.

Over a period of time these surveys have proved that the cover letter and the questionnaire affect the response rate. Some of the factors that aid in increasing the response rate are the content of the cover letter, the form of questions (structured versus unstructured), the style of print, the use of cartoons or symbols in the margins of the questionnaire, and the quality of paper used (color, texture, weight, scent, etc.).

Source: From *Marketing Research*, 5th Edition, Peter Chisnall, Berkshire, England: McGraw Hill Publications, 1997, p. 145. Reprinted by permission of Professor P. M. Chisnall.

A survey was conducted to study the usage of cellular and mobile telephones in countries around the world. Because the survey was conducted for academic purposes, the least costly method—the Internet—was chosen as a medium for making the questionnaires available to potential respondents. The questionnaire that was used for data collection is given is Exhibit 9-6.

The survey results showed that approximately 60 percent of the respondents owned cellular phones. Of the remaining 40 percent, the majority responded by saying they might consider buying a cellular telephone in the next year. The majority of the respondents who own a cellular telephone also own two regular telephones. Most of the respondents rated convenience as the main reason for their owning the telephone. Security, instrument features, and service features followed closely. Most of the respondents use the phone frequently (more than 200 minutes in a given month). Sixty percent of the respondents use it for personal uses. Only 15 percent of the respondents were satisfied with the service levels that they were currently receiving.

EXHIBIT 9-6

Wireless Phone Survey

We would like to know about your usage behavior regarding wireless phones. Please take a moment to fill out this brief survey. Your participation in this survey is greatly appreciated. The data collected from this survey will be used to better understand the needs and wants of the wireless phone customer. Your responses to this survey will be kept completely confidential. This is your opportunity to make your opinions heard, so please let us know how you feel. Please fill this survey out as soon as possible, thank you for your input.

1) *Do you currently own a wireless phone?* ◯ Yes   ◯ No

(If you answered yes please go to question #3)

2) *Do you plan on purchasing a wireless phone in the next year?* [_____ ▼]

(If you do not use a wireless phone please skip to question #17)

3) *How many wireless phones do you own?* ◯ One   ◯ Two   ◯ Three or More

4) *What was the major reason behind your purchase? (Please check your top two)*

☐ Attractive cost ☐ Convenience ☐ Security ☐ Phone features ☐ Service features

☐ Others (Please specify) [_____]

5) *Approximately how many minutes per month you use your wireless phone:* [_____ ▼]

6) *You primarily use the phone for:*

       Business Use   [_____] %

       Personal Use   [_____] %

       Total Use   100%

7) *Is your wireless phone:* ◯ Analog   ◯ Digital   ◯ Don't know

8) *Do you use your wireless phone outside your local calling area?* ◯ Yes   ◯ No

9) *What type of rate plan do you currently have?*

[_____ ▼]

10) *How satisfied are you with your current wireless service provider?* [_____ ▼]

11) *How did you purchase your wireless phone? (Please check one)*

◯ Retail Chain   ◯ Independent   ◯ From Your Service Provider   ◯ Provided
              Retailer   by Employer

◯ Others (Please Specify) [_____]

12) *How satisfied are you with your wireless phone?* [_____ ▼]

13) *What brand of wireless phone(s) do you use?* [▼]

[   ]

14) *Would you purchase the same brand in the future?* [▼]

15) *What features do you have on your wireless phone? (Please check all that apply)*

☐Voice Mail ☐Caller ID ☐Call Waiting ☐Paging ☐Online Services

☐Back-lit Display ☐Ring/Vibrate

☐Others (Please specify) [   ]

16) *What level of importance do you place on these features? (Please circle one for each feature)*
(1 = most important to 5 = least important)

	1	2	3	4	5
Voice Mail	○	○	○	○	○
Caller ID	○	○	○	○	○
Size/Weight	○	○	○	○	○
Battery life	○	○	○	○	○
Local calling area	○	○	○	○	○

17) *Rank the following features in order of importance to you (1 = most important to 5 = least important)*

Voice Mail	[ ]
Caller ID	[ ]
Size/Weight	[ ]
Battery life	[ ]
Coverage of calling area	[ ]

18) *Do you currently use a paging device?* ○Yes ○No

19) *Sex:* ○Male ○Female

20) *Age:* ○Under 18 ○19–25 ○26–35 ○36–50 ○Over 50

21) *How many years of education have you completed? (starting with first grade)*

○Less than 6 ○7–12 ○13 or more

22) *What country do you currently reside in?* [   ]

23) *What is your occupation? (Please check one)*

○Professional/Technical ○Self-Employed ○Administrative/Managerial ○Clerical

○Sales ○Homemaker

○ Other (Please specify) [   ]

24) Which of these activities do you enjoy? (Please check all that apply)

☐ Watching TV   ☐ Hiking/Camping   ☐ Sports   ☐ Reading   ☐ Travel

☐ Others (Please specify) [   ]

Thank you once again for participating in our survey. If you would like to receive a summary of the survey results please leave us your E-mail address. [   ]

[Submit Query]

This survey illustrates the latest survey technique—Internet-based surveys. The questionnaire was posted on the Web and respondents would have to fill in the responses online. They would then have to click on a "submit" icon and the response would be mailed to the e-mail address specified in the form.

This proved to be a cheap way to collect valuable information. The only investment was the time taken to set up the Web-based questionnaire. The disadvantage is that a majority of the cellular phone owners may not have access to the Internet. Even that segment that has Internet connectivity may not take the time to answer the questionnaire. Hence, this sample can by no means be considered representative.

INTERNATIONAL MARKETING RESEARCH IN PRACTICE

Data gathered from secondary research, observation, and qualitative methods would help Tasty Burgers identify the questions that need to be asked of potential clients. The design of the questionnaire will be discussed in chapter 11. This chapter deals with modes of conducting surveys. As discussed in this chapter, there are three methods of conducting a survey—personal interviews, telephone interviews, and mail surveys.

It has already been mentioned that the mail survey provides the lowest response rate. Generally, this method is not employed in international marketing research as the cost per returned response tends to be very high. The telephone is usually a very good means of conducting surveys. It provides better response rates and the interviewer can clarify any doubts that the respondent might have. It is the method that will be used by Tasty Burgers in the United Kingdom. In Brazil, Saudi Arabia, and India the penetration of telephones is very low and only a very small segment of the population can be reached. More often than not, the lines will not be functional, and even if they were, telephone calls work out to be very expensive. People are also reluctant to impart personal information over the telephone. The best survey method in these countries will be personal interviews.

Summary

This chapter deals with personal interviews, telephone interviews, and mail surveys. The advantages and disadvantages of each method and the applicability in international marketing research are discussed in detail. In international marketing research, one encounters a lot of constraints in terms of nature and complexity of problem, lack of adequate knowledge and information, and available budget. The researcher has a few basic data collection methods at his or her disposal and international marketing research calls for a great deal of adaptation of these methods. These methods could be used in combination in a given country. In a multicountry study, different methods could be used in different countries. The stress is on the comparability and usefulness of data rather than on the use of identical instruments. This is a judgment call that has to be made by the researcher. It has been generally found that survey methods are the most popular means of collecting primary data in international marketing research—the personal interview, in particular. Improvements in technology, like e-mail, have made surveys a lot easier and faster.

Questions and Problems

1. What kind of data collection procedure would you recommend to research the question of why female shoppers choose a particular retail store, in the Middle East, to buy clothing?

2. What are the advantages of the telephone prenotification approach over a conventional mail survey?

3. You are a senior analyst in the marketing research department of a major chemical company. Your company has a patent on a chemical that, when combined with plastic, gives it near metallic properties. You have been asked to find out international users for this chemical and also forecast its total market potential.

   a. What information, if any, that could be obtained from respondents, would be useful for this research?

   b. What techniques are applicable for obtaining each item of information?

   c. Design a survey to obtain the information desired. Prepare all instructions, collection forms, and other materials required to obtain such information.

   d. Estimate the cost of conducting the survey you have designed.

4. What are the problems faced by researchers when they are conducting research in developing countries?

5. You are the manufacturer of a major consumer product in the United States. You plan to enter the following countries with your products within the next two years: Russia, France, South Africa, Brazil, China, Japan, Mexico, Canada, India, and Germany.

   Based on the demographic data and the infrastructural data about these countries, determine the best survey method to be adopted in each of these countries.

6. Idaho Ideal Potatoes, Ltd., a U.S.-based firm, developed a new guacamole-flavored potato chip and wanted to ascertain the national sales potential for this unique product offering. However, they found the response rate to be extremely low (10 percent) and found that many of the returned surveys had been incorrectly completed.

   a. How might the company have more effectively collected the relevant data?

   b. What are the advantages and disadvantages of using telephone surveys and focus groups for this kind of study?

   c. Due to stringent budget constraints, the marketing research director decides to limit the survey to residents of San Antonio, Texas. What possible biases could be reflected in the survey results?

   d. Idaho Ideal Potatoes, Ltd. has decided to simultaneously offer their new potato chip in foreign markets and wishes to survey potential sales demand for the product in the United Kingdom. How is the choice of survey method altered to suit the company's research of foreign markets?

Endnotes

1. Laura Goldberg, "American Reaches out to Latin Fliers," *Houston Chronicle* (13 October 1998): 3C.

2. B. P. Kaiser, "Marketing Research in Sweden," *European Research* (February 1988): 64–70.

3. Jack Honomichl, "Survey Results Positive," *Advertising Age* 55 (November 1984): 23; D. Monk, "Marketing Research in Canada," *European Research* (November 1987): 271–74; and B. P. Kaiser, "Marketing Research in Sweden," *European Research* (February 1988): 64–70.

4. J. C. J. Ososteveen, "The State of Marketing Research in Europe," *European Research* (1986): 100–135.

5. T. Vahvelainen, "Marketing Research in Finland," *European Research* (August 1987): 62–66.

6. D. N. Aldridge, "Multi-Country Research," 365.

7. "Dialing For Dollars, Far From Home," *Business Week* (13 January 1992); Ray Converse and Shelley Galbraith, "Eastern Europe," *Business America* (18 June 1990); and "China's Budding Phone Market, Industry Still Has Its Wires Crossed," *San Jose Mercury News* (6 March 1994).

8. T. Vahvelainen, "Marketing Research in the Nordic Countries," *European Research* (April 1985): 76–79; T. Vahvelainen "Marketing Research in Finland," *European Research* (August 1987): 62–66; E. H. Demby, "ESOMAR Urges Changes in Reporting Demographics, Issues Worldwide Report," *Marketing News* 24, no. 1 (8 January 1990): 24–25.

9. David Jobber, Hafiz Mirza, and Kee H. Wee, "Incentives and Response-Rates to Cross-National Business Surveys: A Logit Model Analysis," *Journal of International Business Studies* 4 (1991): 711–721.

10. D. Monk, "Marketing Research in Canada," *European Research* (November 1987): 271–274; Jack J. Honomichi, "Survey Results Positive," *Advertising Age* 55 (November 1984): 23.

11. Naresh K. Malhotra, "A Methodology for Measuring Consumer Preferences in Developing Countries," *International Marketing Review* (autumn 1988): 52–65.

12. D. Monk, "Marketing Research in Canada," *European Research* (November 1987): 271–274.

13. Cynthia Webster, "Hispanic and Anglo Interviewer and Respondent Ethnicity and Gender: The Impact on Survey Response Quality," *Journal of Marketing Research* (February 1996): 62–72.

14. Naresh K. Malhotra, "Administration of Questionnaires for Collecting Quantitative Data in International Marketing Research," *Journal of Global Marketing* 2 (1991): 63–92.

15. Sak Onkvisit and John J. Shaw, "International Marketing—Analysis and Strategy,"

3rd ed. (Upper Saddle River, NJ: Prentice Hall, 1997): 224.

16. Joanna Kinsey, *Marketing in Developing Countries* (London, England: Macmillan Education Ltd, 1994).

17. Ibid.

18. James L. Gibson, "A Sober Second Thought: An Experiment in Persuading Russians to Tolerate," Working Paper, University of Houston, 25 April 1997.

C H A P T E R

Scale Development

10

INTRODUCTION

Globalization has led to increased competition among domestic and multinational firms in both domestic and foreign markets. Researchers have the challenging task of developing measures that will be useful in assessing customer attitudes and preferences for both domestic and foreign products.

The attitudes of customers shape their behavior and attitudes are based on the information they have about the product. What companies are really trying to do in the marketplace is to understand and ultimately influence customer behavior. It is, however, very difficult to follow the target segments and try to observe their behavior and come to reasonable conclusions. Instead, marketers try to work on understanding their attitudes, as attitudes are thought to be windows to behavior. It is easier to talk to potential consumers and get insight into the attitudes they have toward a product or concept. Favorable attitudes can translate into purchases and unfavorable attitudes will mean that the product or concept needs to be modified to suit their tastes better. It is possible to measure customer attitude with respect to specific features of a product. This chapter deals with measurement of attitudes and the tools used for this process. In international marketing, the main method used is the survey, which has already been discussed in an earlier chapter. This chapter deals with development of scales that are used to measure attitudes.

ATTITUDES

Attitude is defined as *an overall evaluation that enables one to respond in a consistently favorable or unfavorable manner with respect to a given object or alternative.*[1] Attitudes are mental states used by consumers to perceive their surroundings and are composed of three parts:

- The *cognitive or knowledge* component represents the information that a person has about an object. This represents awareness of the object's existence, beliefs

184

about the object's characteristics, and judgments about the relative importance of each characteristic.

- The second component is the *affective or liking* component that is an overall feeling of liking or disliking that a person has toward the object. This component causes consumers to prefer one object or concept to others and, hence, measure of preferences is a good indicator of the attitude.
- The last component is the *intention* component that represents the person's expectations of future behavior toward the object. Intentions are restricted by time periods that depend on the buying habits and planning horizons.

Consumer perception varies substantially among cultures. In the country of origin studies, it was observed that most consumers perceived Mexican products to be inferior to those made in Japan and the United States. Over time, Japanese products have developed a significant advantage over U.S. products in terms of perceptions of better quality.[2]

MEASUREMENT AND SCALING

Measurement is defined as the process of assigning numbers or other symbols to certain characteristics of the object of interest, according to some prespecified rules. Usually, numbers are assigned because of the ease of handling them in mathematical and statistical analyses. Certain rules should be followed while assigning numbers for measurement. There should be a one-to-one correspondence between the number and the characteristic and this assignment should be constant over time. Scaling is the process of creating a continuum on which objects are located according to the amount of the measured characteristic they process.

One important aspect of measurement is the level of measurement.[3] Level of measurement defines the relationship among values that are assigned to the attributes of a variable. Interpretation of data is simplified if the level of measurement is known. Based on the level of measurement, four categories of scales can be defined as follows.

Nominal Scale

If a number has been assigned to establish the identity of an object it is called a nominal scale. The section numbers of different courses offered at the University of Houston is an example. These numbers help distinguish one section from all others and any comparison between these numbers would be meaningless. The objects are mutually exclusive and there are no necessary relationships among categories. The numbers do not imply any order among the variables. An example would be labeling all respondents who are single as 1, all respondents who are married as 2, and all who were married but divorced as 3.

Ordinal Scale

If objects are ranked and arranged in a particular order with regard to some common variable, it is called an ordinal scale. This scale merely tells us which object has more of the characteristic we are interested in and which object has less of it. There is no information on how much difference there is between the objects. For example, graduate students from the University of Houston could be asked to rank courses offered by the marketing department. Ratings that one course gets would be on an ordinal scale. Some students would rate this course the best, some others would rate it the second best, and so on. It is not possible to compute a mean ranking for the course because the difference between the best, second best, and so on, are not known. Hence, statistical computation is limited to median and mode calculation.

Interval Scale

The problem of computing the difference between two categories is taken care of in the interval scale. Here the numbers used to rank the objects also represent equal increments in the attribute being measured and differences can be compared; however, there is no fixed zero point, as it does not indicate absence of the attribute. The Fahrenheit and Celsius temperature scales are examples of this kind of scale that have different zero points. With this kind of scale it is possible to calculate the mean, standard deviation, and correlation and conduct regression analysis, t-tests, and analysis of variance tests.

Ratio Scale

A further modification can be made to the interval scale. It is called the ratio scale and has a meaningful zero point. With this scale it is possible to say how much greater or smaller one object is than another. Absolute comparisons of magnitude are possible with this kind of scale. For instance, it is possible to say that a product costing $10 is twice as expensive as one costing $5.

Table 10-1 gives a summary of the types of scales and their applications.

TABLE 10-1 Types of Scales and Their Properties

Type of Measurement Scale	Types of Attitude Scale	Rules for Assigning Number	Typical Application	Statistics/Statistical Tests
Nominal	Dichotomous "yes" or "no" scales	Objects are either identical or different	Classification (by sex, geographic area, social class)	Percentages, mode/chi-square
Ordinal or rank order	Comparative, rank order, itemized category, paired comparison	Objects are greater or smaller	Rankings (preference, class standing)	Percentile, median, rank-order correlation/Friedman ANOVA
Interval	Likert, Thurstone, Stapel, associative, semantic differential	Intervals between adjacent ranks are equal	Index numbers, temperature scales, attitude measures	Mean, standard deviation, product moment correlations/t-tests ANOVA, regression, factor analysis
Ratio	Certain scales with special instructions	There is a meaningful zero, so comparison of absolute magnitudes is possible	Sales, incomes, units produced, costs, age	Geometric and harmonic mean, coefficient of variation

TYPES OF SCALES

A scale can have many dimensions depending on the attribute it is trying to measure and depending on how the construct is defined. This can be illustrated with an example. If we think that the choice of a specific brand of car is dependent only on price, the scale has to have only one dimension. Price is completely capable of explaining the purchase decision. In reality, however, this is not true. Customers look for various aspects like performance, style, name of the manufacturer, and price. Hence, the purchase decision has many dimensions, each of which has to be tested to determine the impact it has on the final decision.

Attitudinal scales can be broadly classified as single-item and multiple-item scales. Single-item scales are those that have only one item to measure a construct; however, attitudes toward most products are complex and cannot be measured completely with one scale question. There are many different facets that must be measured to get a complete picture of the true attitude of customers. Multiple-item scales are used in such situations. There are different types of single-item and multiple-item scales and some of them are considered in detail in this section.

Single-Item Scales

The most widely used single-item scale is the *itemized-category scale*. This scale gives the respondents options to indicate their opinions about the object being measured. There can be several different variations of this scale. The researcher can choose to label all the categories as shown.

Give us your opinion about the local newspaper.

____Very satisfied ____Quite satisfied ____Somewhat satisfied ____Not satisfied

It is also possible to label only the extreme categories.

Give us your opinion about the local newspaper.

Very satisfied				Very dissatisfied
+2	+1	0	−1	−2

As can be seen from the previous examples, there may or may not be a neutral point. The scale can be balanced, as in the second exhibit, or it can be unbalanced, tending toward more favorable or more unfavorable. There is no comparison with other newspapers; however, the scale can be designed in a manner such that a comparison is implied, as shown.

Give us your opinion about the newspapers you read regularly.

	Excellent	Very good	Average	Below average
The Times				
Bundes Post	____	____	____	____
USA Today	____	____	____	____

The same scale can be modified to include an explicit comparison in the statement. It is then called a *comparative scale*. The question used in the previous example would be modified as shown.

As compared to the *New York Times,* how would you rate your local newspaper?

____Excellent   ____Very good   ____Average   ____Below average

Another kind of single-item scale requires the respondents to arrange the objects in ascending or descending order with regard to some criterion. This is called the *rank-order scale.* Ranking has been used widely in international surveys as it corresponds to the choices that consumers would make in a shopping scenario; however, these require a lot of mental effort on the respondents' part and may not be very accurate if the number of objects to be compared is very high. Usually consumers have a very good idea about the best and worst in the list; however, if there are too many objects the differentiation for items in the middle becomes very obscure. The optimum number that can be used is five or six. If there are more than six objects, two-stage ranking can be followed. Respondents are asked to group the items into two or three groups. Within each group, the items are then individually ranked.

When the number of objects to be ranked is very high, say 89, ranking becomes very difficult even in two stages. In such cases, *Q-sort scaling* is followed. Consider the example of a car manufacturer wanting to study the most preferred features for a specific model. The product design team comes up with 89 different product concepts, each with minor variations. Respondents are given 89 cards, each containing one version of the product. They are then asked to sort these cards into eleven piles, such that one pile contains five of the most preferred versions and another pile contains five of the least preferred versions. The other nine piles contain versions of the product in the decreasing order of preferences. After this has been completed, researchers pick out the most preferred pile or some of the better-preferred piles and ask respondents to rank these versions. As the number of piles increases, the reliability of the results also increases. Figure 10-1 illustrates the plot of the number of cards in each pile.

Constant-sum scales ask respondents to allocate a fixed number of points among different categories such that the division of points reflects their relative preferences. This is illustrated in the following example.

Allocate 100 points among these factors so that the points indicate how important each of these factors is in your choice of a newspaper.

Regularity of delivery	_____
Cost	_____
Coverage of local news	_____
Coverage of national and international news	_____
Total	100

In international marketing research, researchers should be prepared for the event that the target population may be illiterate. There are also times when the study involves children who have not yet learned to read or write. Communicating ideas and concepts through written matter becomes a challenge. In such situations researchers resort to *pictorial scales* where the various categories are depicted pictorially. Respondents indicate their agreement or disagreement by indicating the corresponding position on the pictorial scale. The funny face scale is a very commonly used pictorial scale.

The type of scale used is dependent on the experience, preference, and judgment of the researcher; however, certain aspects have to be considered when using single-

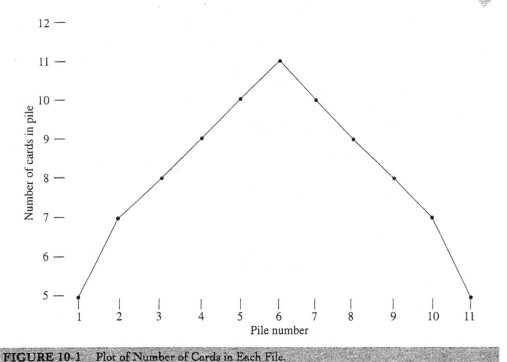

FIGURE 10-1 Plot of Number of Cards in Each File.

item scales. There cannot be too many scale categories in the questionnaire, even though, theoretically, the number can vary from two to infinity. In mail surveys and personal interviews, respondents can handle five to seven categories with reasonable accuracy. This number is further reduced in telephone interviews. The adjectives used to describe the categories are dependent on the country where the research is conducted. Some cultures require strong adjectives, whereas in others the adjectives should be suitably toned down. Depending on the country, researchers should also decide whether to use a unipolar or bipolar scale and whether to provide a neutral point or not. It has been pointed out that certain cultures, like the Japanese, tend to stick with the neutral when they have the choice. In such cases, researchers should avoid providing a neutral choice to force a decision from the respondent.

Multiple-Item Scales

When it is not possible for the researcher to capture the entire range of attitudes that the respondent might have toward an object using a single scale question, multiple-item scales are used. Figure 10-2 is a flow chart of the steps involved in multiple-item scale development. These scales obtain information about the respondent's attitude along different aspects of the object and then combine all these to form an average score indicative of the overall attitude of the respondent toward the object. Some of the frequently employed multiple-item scales are explained in this section.

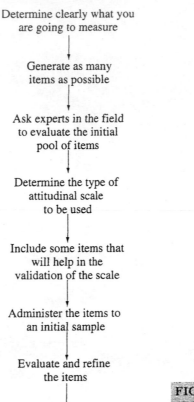

Determine clearly what you
are going to measure

↓

Generate as many
items as possible

↓

Ask experts in the field
to evaluate the initial
pool of items

↓

Determine the type of
attitudinal scale
to be used

↓

Include some items that
will help in the
validation of the scale

↓

Administer the items to
an initial sample

↓

Evaluate and refine
the items

↓

Finally, optimize the
scale length

FIGURE 10-2 Steps in
Multiple-Item Scale
Development

Likert scales require a respondent to indicate the degree of agreement or disagreement with a number of statements related to the characteristics of the object. The scale is designed such that there is a statement made about one aspect of the object and there is an evaluative part where a list of response categories is provided. Each of these statements represent a common construct (e.g., performance); otherwise, the scores cannot be summed up to produce an average score. An example follows:

	Strongly Agree	Somewhat Agree	Neither Agree nor Disagree	Somewhat Disagree	Strongly Disagree
Local paper covers local news very well	____	____	____	____	____
Local paper covers national & world news very well	____	____	____	____	____
Local paper is worth the price I pay	____	____	____	____	____
Local paper is delivered regularly to my residence	____	____	____	____	____

Thurstone scales help researchers obtain a unidimensional scale with interval properties and for this reason they are called the method of equal-appearing intervals. The procedure for administering a Thurstone scale is a two-step process. At first, researchers generate a number of adjectives, usually 100, reflecting all degrees of favorableness toward the object. A group of judges then classifies these according to their degree of favorableness or unfavorableness. Intervals between categories are treated as equal. The scale value for each category is the median value assigned by the judges. Adjectives for which there have been no consensus among the judges are discarded. This results in a scale consisting of 10 to 20 categories representing different degrees of favorableness. The second step is to ask respondents to rate different aspects of the object on different categories in this scale. This procedure is time consuming and very expensive to construct. It is also possible that the scale categories could depend on the judges selected for the process.

Semantic differential scales are used very widely in international marketing research to reflect the set of beliefs or attitudes the respondent has about an object. Different aspects of the object are presented to the respondent in the format described here and the respondents choose the one that matches closely with their opinions. There may or may not be a neutral point depending on the country where the questionnaire is being administered. Care should be taken to see that the adjectives used to describe the categories are relevant in the country where the survey is being conducted and respondents understand the implications of the categories. It is sometimes necessary to reverse the positive and negative poles of the scale to avoid halo effect, where the respondent allows previous judgments to affect subsequent judgments. It is possible to assign scores to the categories and provide an average score for different objects. A profile analysis is an application wherein the mean ratings for each category are plotted to get a visual comparison of the ratings. This aids researchers in getting a quick look at how different objects have been rated along different categories. Figure 10-3 gives a sample profile analysis.

Give us your opinion about your two newspapers—the *Wall Street Journal* and the *Financial Times*.

Low price	___ ___ ___ ___ ___	High price
Good local coverage	___ ___ ___ ___ ___	Bad local coverage
Good global coverage	___ ___ ___ ___ ___	Bad global coverage
Regular delivery	___ ___ ___ ___ ___	Irregular delivery

Stapel scales are a simpler version of semantic differential scales where the categories have only one pole. Respondents give a score to the category depending on their preference and a higher positive score implies higher preference.

A simple technique of multiple-item scaling called *associative scaling* is used frequently in international marketing research. This method overcomes the limitations of semantic differential scaling, where the respondent should be familiar with all of the objects to respond usefully. In associative scaling the respondent is asked to associate one alternative with each question.

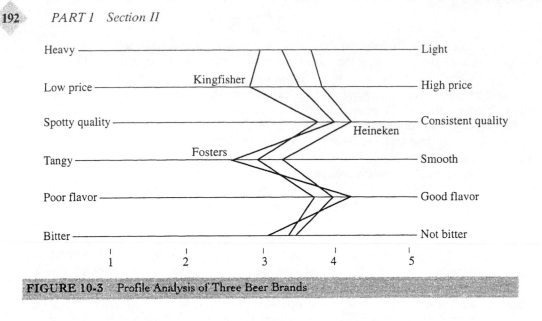

FIGURE 10-3   *Profile Analysis of Three Beer Brands*

SCALES IN CROSS-NATIONAL RESEARCH

The previous sections of this chapter discussed the various types of scales that are typically used in domestic marketing research. The question remains whether the same scales can be administered to respondents all over the world.[4] Low educational or literacy levels in some countries will have to be taken into account when the decision is taken to administer the same scale. Literacy and educational levels have a certain impact on the response formats of the scales employed. Moreover, culture in a country can also affect the responses and may induce some cultural biases. Likert and semantic differential scales are culture-bound and should be treated as culture-specific instruments.[5]

Research has been conducted to find out whether there is a pan-cultural scale. The semantic differential scale seems to come closest to being a true pan-cultural scale. It consistently gives similar results in terms of concepts or dimensions that are used to evaluate stimuli, and also accounts for a major portion of the variation in response when it is administered in different countries. An alternative approach that has been attempted is to apply techniques that use a base referent, a self-defined cultural norm. This type of approach is likely to be particularly useful in evaluating attitudinal positions where evidence exists to suggest that these are defined relative to the dominant cultural norm.

Another issue that is important in international research is whether response formats, particularly their calibration, need to be adapted for specific countries and cultures. For example, in France a 20-point scale is commonly used to rate performance in primary and secondary schools. Consequently, it has been suggested that 20-point scales should also be used in marketing research. In general, verbal scales are more effective among less-educated respondents, but a more appropriate procedure for illiterate respondents would be scales with pictorial stimuli. For example, in the case of lifestyle, pictures of different lifestyle segments may be shown to the respondents and they may be asked to indicate how similar they perceive themselves to be to the one in the picture. Some other devices such as the *funny faces* and *thermometer* scale are also used among the less-educated respondents.

GLOBAL OR PAN-CULTURAL SCALES[6]

Designing scales for international marketing research calls for a great deal of adaptation on the researchers' part. It has to be decided whether a single scale can be used in all of the countries or whether it should be customized to suit each country. Americans use a five- or a seven-point scale; however, people in many other countries, like France, are familiar with a 20-point scale. Semantics plays a very important role in the accuracy with which a scale measures any given attribute. Many cultures tend to overstate their feelings, while many others are more modest. The word "excellent" may connote very different levels of perfection to Japanese and Italians. Adjustments for these linguistic differences have to be made. It has been observed that verbal rating scales work the best in the international context. All respondents are accustomed to verbally expressing their feelings, irrespective of the country or culture they belong to. There could, however, be a problem with these scales. In some countries, 1 would be rated as the best while in others it would be the least-favored choice. The researcher should clarify this before asking respondents to rate attributes. The concept of the mid-point of the scale will have to be explained to respondents in many countries. Even if respondents understand the concept of mid-point or the neutral category, scales have to be modified to take into account the predisposition of many cultures to stick with the middle response category.

Bearing in mind the drawbacks of administering scales to respondents in other countries, the one scale that has consistently provided accurate results is the semantic differential scale. Because the adjectives on the polar ends of the scale are opposite in meaning, it is easy for the respondent to understand and answer the questions in a manner that is useful to the researcher.

MEASUREMENT OF EQUIVALENCE[7]

An important purpose of multinational research is to find similarities or differences among and between populations of interest to the researcher;[8] however, there are many problems associated with conducting cross-national research for comparative purposes. It is difficult to state with conviction whether the similarities and differences are real or if they are due to measurement problems. The issue of measurement equivalence must be addressed to reduce threats to measurement reliability and validity.[9] There is always the trade-off between capturing more variance more accurately by adding more categories and reducing the number of categories to make the scale less susceptible to response bias.[10]

It is important that data collected from various regions is comparable, otherwise it could lead to the researcher drawing erroneous conclusions. This is illustrated by the following example of a survey conducted in Europe to study the bathing habits of women.[11] Initial data suggested that the percentage of Belgian women taking baths was far higher than any other nationality; however, a closer look at the data revealed that the time period was not comparable. In Belgium the women were asked if they had taken a bath in the last seven days. In all other countries the question had been, "Have you had a bath in the last three days?"

Measurement equivalence relates to establishing equivalence in terms of procedures used to measure concepts or attitudes.[12] Three aspects will have to be considered to establish measurement equivalence

Calibration Equivalence

Equivalence has to be established with regard to the calibration system used in measurement. This should include monetary units, measures of weight, distance and volume, and perceptual cues like color, shape, or form. Various countries around the world follow different units of weights and measures. Americans are used to weighing things by the pound or ton. The British and most of the commonwealth countries use the gram and the kilogram. If the wrong terminology is used, responses will not be accurate. The same holds true for currency measures also. One billion in the United States may not mean the same amount in some other country (e.g., the United Kingdom). Researchers should also take care to establish equivalence in terms of interpretation of perceptual cues. Colors mean different things to different cultures.[13] White, for example, is considered a symbol of purity and peace in the Western world. The Japanese consider it a color of mourning.[14]

Translation Equivalence

The research instrument has to be translated such that respondents in all countries involved in the study understand it. The instrument should also contain equivalent meaning in each research context. This becomes more complicated when the researcher has to interpret and translate nonverbal clues. As has been pointed out earlier, the stress in this book is not on the equivalence of the instrument translated into another language. The stress is on the equivalence of the information collected. It may not be possible to translate a questionnaire verbatim into another language because of lack of equivalent words in the foreign language. For instance, there is no equivalent term for "husband" in Japanese. The researcher should focus on conveying the intent of the question to the respondent and obtain an answer that can be comparable across countries.

Metric Equivalence

Metric equivalence is the scoring or scalar equivalence of the measure used. The researcher has to ensure equivalence of the scaling or scoring procedure used to establish the measure. Care should also be taken to establish equivalence in terms of the responses to a given measure in different countries. The scales used in different countries may vary depending on the culture and education level of the respondents. In the United States, researchers typically use a five- or seven-point scale; however, there are countries where scales can have as many as 20 categories. When the sample consists predominantly of people incapable of reading, pictorial scales are used. The specific country also determines whether the scale should be unipolar or bipolar and whether there should be a neutral point in the scale. Researchers studying the Japanese market design scales with no neutral point, as the Japanese have a tendency to remain neutral if given a choice. The researcher should also ensure equivalence of the response to a given measure in different countries. For instance, researchers need to tone down income data from Latin American countries, as most managers in Latin American countries tend to exaggerate their income.[15]

Profile analysis can be used as a means of examining metric equivalence. This involves calculating the means for each measure and plotting it on a graph. The points are connected by lines. If these lines are not parallel it can be taken as an indication that differences between two data sets are not caused by systematic response bias. It must be noted that even if the lines are parallel, the differences between means could be caused by real differences and not necessarily by response set bias.[16]

ACCURACY OF ATTITUDE MEASUREMENT

Attitude measures, in common with all measures used in marketing, must be both accurate and useful. In this section, the focus is on those aspects of attitude measures that contribute to accuracy: validity, reliability, sensitivity, generalizability, and relevancy.

Validity

An attitude measure has validity if it measures what it is supposed to measure. If this is the case, then differences in attitude scores will reflect differences among the objects or individuals on the characteristic being measured. This is a very troublesome question; for example, how is a researcher to know whether measured differences in the attitudes of managers, consumer activists, and consumers toward marketing practices, regulation, and the contribution of the consumer movement are true differences? There have been three basic approaches to this question of validity assessment.

Face, or consensus, validity is invoked when the argument is made that the measurement so self-evidently reflects or represents the various aspects of the phenomenon that there can be little quarrel with it. For instance, buyers' recognition of advertisements is usually accepted at face value as an indication of past ad exposure. This faith typically is supported by little more than common sense, despite evidence that recognition scores are influenced by reader interest.

Criterion validity is more defensible, for it is based on empirical evidence that the attitude measure correlates with other "criterion" variables. If the two variables are measured at the same time, *concurrent validity* is established. Better yet, if the attitude measure can predict some future event, then *predictive validity* has been established. A measure of brand preference or buying intentions is valid if it can be shown through sales records to predict future sales. This is the most important type of validity for decision-making purposes, for the very nature of decisions requires predictions of uncertain future events.

Although face, concurrent, and predictive validity provide necessary evidence of overall validity, often they are not sufficient. The characteristic of these three approaches is that they provide evidence on *convergent validity*. That is, an attitude measure can adequately represent a characteristic or variable if it correlates or "converges" with other supposed measures of that variable. Unfortunately, an attitude measure may converge with measures of other variables in addition to the one of interest. Thus, it is also necessary to establish *discriminant validity* through "low correlations between the measure of interest and other measures that are supposedly not measuring the same variable or concept." Advertising recognition measures often fail this second test. While they correlate or converge with past ad exposure, which is what we want, they also are correlated with number of magazines read and product interest.

Construct validity can be considered only after discriminant and convergent validity have been established.[17] It is achieved when a logical argument can be advanced to defend a particular measure. The argument aims first to define the concept or construct explicitly and then to show that the measurement, or operational definition, logically connects the empirical phenomenon to the concept. The extreme difficulty of this kind of validation lies in the unobservable nature of many of the constructs (such as social class, personality, or attitudes) used to explain marketing behavior. For example, is occupation a good operational definition of social class, or does it measure some other characteristic? One way to assess construct validity is to test whether or not the measure confirms hypotheses generated from the theory based on the concepts. Because theory development is at a youthful stage in marketing, the theory itself may be incorrect, making this approach hazardous. This is one reason why little construct validation is attempted in marketing. A more significant reason is the lack of well-established measures that can be used in a variety of circumstances. Instead, marketing researchers tend to develop measures for each specific problem or survey and rely on face validity.

Reliability

So far we have been talking about systematic errors between an observed score (X_o) and a true score (X_t), which will determine whether a measure is valid; however, the total error of a measurement consists of this systematic error component (X_s) and a random error component (X_r). Random error is manifested by lack of consistency (unreliability) in repeated or equivalent measures of the same object or person. As a result, any measurement can be expressed as a function of several components:

$$X_o = X_t + X_s + X_r$$
Observed score = true score + systematic error + random error

To interpret this equation, remember that a valid measure is one that reflects the true score. In this situation, $X_o = X_t$ and both X_s and X_r are zero. Thus, if we know the measure is valid, it has to be reliable. The converse is not necessarily true. A measure may be highly reliable, $X_r = 0$, and still have a substantial systematic error that distorts the validity. But, if the measure is not reliable, it cannot be valid because at a minimum we are left with $X_o = X_t + X_r$. In brief, reliability is necessary, but not a sufficient condition for validity.

Although reliability is less important, it is easier to measure, and so receives relatively more emphasis. The basic methods for establishing reliability can be classified according to whether they measure stability of results over time or internal consistency of items in an attitude scale.[18]

Stability over time is assessed by repeating the measurement with the same instrument and the same respondents at two points in time and correlating the results. To the extent that random fluctuations result in different scores for the two administrations, this correlation and, hence, the reliability will be lowered. The problems of this test-retest method are similar to those encountered during any pretest-posttest measurement of attitudes. The first administration may sensitize the respondent to the subject and lead to attitude change. The likelihood of a true change in attitude (versus a random fluctuation) is increased further if the interval between the test and the retest is too long. For most topics, this would be more than two weeks. If the interval is too short, however, there may be a carry-over from the test to the retest: attempts to remember the responses in the first test, boredom or annoyance at the imposition, and so forth. Because of these problems, a very short interval will bias the reliability estimate upward, whereas longer periods have the opposite effect.[19]

The equivalence approach to assessing reliability is appropriate for attitude scales composed of multiple items that presumably measure the same underlying unidimensional attitude. The split-half method assumes that these items can be divided into two equivalent subsets that then can be compared. A number of methods have been devised to divide the items randomly into two halves and compute a measure of similarity of the total scores of the two halves across the sample. An average split-half measure of similarity-coefficient alpha can be obtained from a procedure that has the effect of comparing every item to every other item.

Sensitivity

The third characteristic of a good attitude measure is sensitivity, or the ability to discriminate among meaningful differences in attitudes. Such sensitivity is achieved by increasing the number of scale categories; however, the more categories there are, the lower the reliability. This is because very coarse response categories, such as "yes" or "no," in response to an attitude question can absorb a great deal of response variability before a change would be noted using the test-retest method. Conversely, the use of a large number of response categories when there are only a few distinct attitude positions would be subject to a considerable, but unwarranted, amount of random fluctuation.

Generalizability

Generalizability refers to the ease of scale administration and interpretation in different research settings and situations.[20] Thus, the generalizability of a multiple-item scale is determined by whether it can be applied in a wide variety of data collection modes, whether it can be used to obtain data from a wide variety of individuals, and under what conditions it can be interpreted. As in the case of reliability and validity, generalizability is not an absolute, but rather is a matter of degree.

Relevancy

Relevancy of a scale refers to how meaningful it is to apply the scale to measure a construct. Mathematically, it is represented as the product of reliability and validity.

$$Relevance = Reliability * Validity$$

If reliability and validity are evaluated by means of correlation coefficients, the implications are

- the relevance of a scale can vary from 0 (no relevance) to 1 (complete relevance)
- if either reliability or validity is low, the scale will possess little relevance
- both reliability and validity are necessary for scale relevance.

CULTURAL ISSUES

Communication depends, to a great extent, on the cultural background of the respondent, so designing scales also becomes culture-dependent. In certain cultures, communication is based entirely on explicit messages. The Swiss, for instance, talk very literally. The Japanese, on the other hand, are not as precise in their communication. Personal pronouns are not explicitly expressed and the number of tenses is largely reduced. In Japanese, both the spoken and written words have multiple meanings so that the listener needs to have some contextual clarification.[21] This becomes very important when deciding on the type of scale to be used. In certain countries, comparison between objects has to be made explicit. The scale ideas will also need to be conveyed with clarity.

The educational system of a country reflects the culture and heritage of the country significantly. Education, to a great extent, shapes the way people in a certain country think or act. It has also been proven that one of the most efficient ways of studying the national character is to observe the education systems and the child-rearing practices followed in the country. Education can also have a great impact on how receptive the people are to foreign products and concepts. This affects not just the researchers, but also the companies who plan to market their products in the foreign country. For the purpose of designing scales, it is very important that the researchers have an idea of the education levels of the target population. The knowledge and awareness of the respondent will decide the type of scale that can be used. A simple example would be conducting research in interior parts of the developing world where the population is mainly illiterate. Pictorial scales will have to be used so as to convey the intention to the respondents. It has been seen that people from China, Japan, and Hong Kong tend to use the middle category in the scale as opposed to people from the United States, Germany, and the United Kingdom. Hence, scales must have even numbered categories when they are being administered in China, Japan, and Hong Kong. This decreases the central tendencies and increases the variance in the questionnaire.[22]

INTERNATIONAL MARKETING RESEARCH IN PRACTICE

Tasty Burgers will have to design a questionnaire to collect information through the use of surveys. As discussed in the previous chapter, researchers can use telephone surveys in the United Kingdom and personal interviews in Brazil, India, and Saudi Arabia. The surveys are aimed at collecting demographic data of people who visit fast-food restaurants on a regular basis. Tasty Burgers would also like to know customer preferences in terms of food and beverages and average amount spent in a given visit to a fast-food restaurant. This will help them decide the ideal product mix for maximizing profits.

One of the concerns that researchers have will be the type of scales that can be used in the questionnaire. This is dependent on the country and type of survey mechanism that is used. Typically, in the United Kingdom five- or seven-point scales are used. Because telephones are used there, it would be better to use a five-point scale. This makes it easier for the interviewer to read out the scales to the respondent. The respondent will also be more comfortable remembering just five degrees of any attribute rather than seven. In Brazil, India, and Saudi Arabia personal interviews are used. Here the interviewer has more flexibility with the questionnaire script. For ease of comparison it may be better to retain a five-point scale; however, the interviewer could use examples to explain or clarify a certain point. For instance, the question could ask respondents to rate the burgers sold by a leading competitor on five levels: excellent, good, average, below average, and bad.

It is good practice in international marketing research to collect data on an absolute level and comparative basis. This can be done by setting one product as a basis for comparison and asking respondents to compare all other products to the base product. The basis for comparison should be a product that is positioned similarly in all countries. For instance, McDonald's is positioned as a fast-food chain affordable even by the lower income class in the United States; however, in India, their target market is the middle- and upper-income groups. Hence, Tasty Burgers should look for a product that is aimed at all of the segments, including the lower-income groups, and use that as a basis of comparison. This way the interviewer will be able to gain more insights into the fast-food market. This may not be possible with a telephone interview unless the question has been specifically worked into the script.

Care should be taken to use the currency of the country where the scale is being used. If required, the values could be translated back to dollars for easy comparison. An expert on the local culture should be involved while setting categories for the scales. As has been mentioned in this chapter, cultural differences play an important role in scale design.

Summary

This chapter deals with measurement of attitudes and development of scales that are used in this process. Attitude is defined as an overall evaluation that enables one to respond in a consistently favorable or unfavorable manner with respect to a given object or alternative. The three components of attitude are the cognitive part, the affective part, and the intention part. Measurement is defined as the process of assigning numbers or other symbols to certain characteristics of the object of interest, according to some prespecified rules. This chapter discusses four types of scales that are used in measurement: the nominal scale, the ordinal scale, the interval scale, and the ratio scale. Scales can be classified as single-item and multiple-item scales.

The focus of this chapter is on the modifications required to administer scales in different countries. It is important for researchers to remember that the objective should be to collect data that is comparable across countries. The scales that are being used should reflect this equivalence. In particular, researchers should ensure that scales meet the criteria for calibration equivalence, translation equivalence, and metric equivalence. Researchers should also take care to see that validity, reliability, and sensitivity of scales are maintained across different countries.

Questions and Problems

1. What is measurement? What are the scales of measurement and what information is provided by each?
2. Identify the type of scale and justify your answer.
   a. During which season of the year were you born?
      ____Winter ____Spring ____Summer ____Fall.
   b. How satisfied are you with the Ford Taurus that you have bought?
      ____Very satisfied ____Satisfied ____Neither satisfied nor dissatisfied
      ____Dissatisfied ____Very dissatisfied.
   c. On an average, how many cigarettes do you smoke in a day?
      ____Over 1 pack ____1/2 pack to 1 pack ____Less than 1/2 pack
   d. Rank the following laundry detergent according to your preference.
      ____Tide ____Surf ____Cheer ____Wisk ____Bold
3. How would you select a set of phrases or adjectives for use in a semantic differential scale to evaluate the image of banks and other consumer financial institutions in Australia, Japan, India, and Germany? Would the procedure differ if you were going to use a Likert scale?
4. Under what circumstances can attitude measures be expected to be good predictors of subsequent behavior? Is there any value to measuring attitudes in situations where attitudes are likely to be poor predictors?
5. Explain the concepts of reliability and validity in your own words. What is the relationship between them?
6. Carter Toys, the U.S.-based manufacturer of the popular PollyDolly, feels that a strong sales potential exists for the doll in foreign markets. The management has identified the selection of suitable foreign country markets as being its first priority. Worldwide Research Corp. has been employed to conduct a survey of the three countries that are currently under consideration: the United Kingdom, Japan, and Kenya.
   a. Can the same questionnaire be used to survey all three countries? Give reasons for your answer.
   b. What factors must be considered in selecting a suitable scale to be used in each country?
   c. Recommended the most suitable scale for use in each country.

Endnotes

1. Marieke de Mooij, *Global Marketing and Advertising—Understanding Cultural Paradoxes* (Thousand Oaks, CA: Sage Publications, 1998), 144.

2. John R. Darling and Van R. Wood, "A Longitudinal Study Comparing Perceptions of U.S. and Japanese Products in a Third/Neutral Country: Finland 1975 to 1985," *Journal of International Business Studies*, no. 3 (1990): 427–450.

3. William Trochim, "Levels of Measurement," http://trochim.human.cornell.edu/kb/measlevl.htm, 1996.

4. Most international research studies conducted use different kinds of scales in their research. A few examples are Daniel C. Fieldman and David C. Thomas, "Career Management Issues Facing Expatriates," *Journal of Business Studies* (2nd quarter, 1992); Earl Newmann, "Organization Predictors of Expatriate Job Satisfaction," *Journal of Business Studies* (1st quarter, 1993): 61–81.

5. Julie H. Yu, Charles Keown, and Laurence Jacobs, "Attitude Scale Methodology: Cross-Cultural Implications," *Journal of International Consumer Marketing*, no. 3 (1992): 320–327.

6. Susan P. Douglas and C. Samuel Craig, *International Marketing Research* (Englewood Cliffs, NJ: Prentice Hall, 1983), 196–198.

7. Ibid.

8. Michael Mullen, "Diagnostic Measurement Equivalence in Cross-National Research," *Journal of International Business Studies* (3rd quarter, 1995).

9. Alma T. Mintu, Rojer Calantone, and Jule B. Gassenheimer, "Towards Improving Cross-Cultural Research: Extending Churchill's Research Paradigm," *Journal of International Consumer Marketing*, no. 2 (1994): 5–23.

10. Michael Mullen, "Diagnosing Measurement Equivalence in Cross-National Measurement," *Journal of International Business Studies*, no. 3 (1995): 25–41.

11. C. Min-Han, Byoung-Woo Lee, and Kong-Kyun Ro, "The Choice of Survey Mode in Country Image Studies," *Journal of Business Research*, no. 29 (February 1994): 151–162.

12. Margaret Crimp and Len Tiu Wright, *The Marketing Research Process*, 4th ed. (Herfordshire: Prentice Hall, 1995), 51.

13. Laurence Jacobs, Charles Keown, Reginald Worthley, and Kyung-II Ghymn, "Cross-Cultural Color Comparisons: Global Marketers Beware," *International Marketing Review* 8, no. 3 (1991): 21–30.

14. Ibid.

15. Ki-Taek Chun, John B. Campbell, and Jong Hae Yoo, "Extreme Response Style Cross-Cultural Research," *Journal of Cross Cultural Psychology* 5, no. 5 (December 1974): 465–480.

16. Michael Mullen, "Diagnostic Measurement Equivalence in Cross-National Research," *Journal of International Business Studies* (3rd quarter, 1995).

17. F. M. Andrews, "Construct Validity and Error Components of Survey Measures," *Public Opinion Quarterly* (summer 1984): 432.

18. J. Paul Peter, "Reliability: A Review of Psychometric Basis and Recent Marketing Practices," *Journal of Marketing Research* 16 (February 1979): 6–17.

19. Ravi Parameswaran and Attila Yaprak, "A Cross-National Comparison of Consumer Research Measures," *Journal of International Business Studies* (spring 1987): 35–49.

20. For a discussion of generalizability theory and its applications in marketing research see Joseph O. Rentz, "Generalizability Theory: A Comprehensive Method for Assessing and Improving the Dependability of Marketing Measures," *Journal of Marketing Research* 24 (February 1987): 19–28.

21. Jean-Claude Usunier, *Marketing Across Cultures*, 2nd ed. (Herfordshire: Prentice Hall, 1996), 147.

22. Steven X. Si and John B. Cullen, "Response Categories and Potential Cultural Bias: Effects of an Explicit Middle Point in Cross-Cultural Surveys," forthcoming *International Journal of Organizational Analysis*.

CHAPTER

11

Questionnaire Design

INTRODUCTION

Exhibit 11-1 is a humorous demonstration of the most important problem faced by researchers in international marketing research—difference in perceptions due to cultural and regional differences. Designing a questionnaire and translating it to several languages without compromising the intended objective of the question is a challenge. Figure 11-1 gives an example of a questionnaire that has been translated into French and German from the original English version. This chapter deals with some of the important issues in designing questionnaires for international marketing research.

Survey research plays a very important role in today's dynamic, need-to-know-right-away business environment. Survey results are often the primary, if not the sole, vehicle for making important decisions; therefore, it is very critical that surveys be conducted in an accurate, unbiased manner. An important component of survey research is the development of the survey instrument—the questionnaire—which is a set of questions designed to evoke useful answers. The questionnaire is the vehicle of communication between those seeking insight (the survey sponsor) and those from whom

---

EXHIBIT 11-1

Opinions

Four men, a Saudi, a Russian, a North Korean, and a New Yorker are walking down the street. A marketing researcher says to them, "Excuse me, what is your opinion on the meat shortage?" The Saudi says, "What's a shortage?" The Russian says, "What's meat?" The Korean says, "What's an opinion?" and the New Yorker says, "Excuse me? What's excuse me?"

Source: Adapted from *India Herald*, 22 May 1998, 27.

202

insight is sought (the respondents). It is the role of the researcher to ensure that the sponsor's inquiries are accurately translated into appropriate questions for respondents and that the respondents correctly interpret the questions. The researcher must then correctly interpret the survey results and translate the findings into meaningful marketing terms.[1]

Questionnaires make it possible for the researcher to quantify various aspects of the research that are being studied. Designing a good questionnaire is considered an art. Questionnaires are not merely a bunch of questions thrown in with the intention of eliciting some information from the respondent. The researcher must be very clear on the type of information that is needed for the research and the questionnaire should be tailor-made to collect this information.

Researchers follow a specific sequence of steps to design a questionnaire. Figure 11-2 gives a flowchart of the steps involved in questionnaire design. The first step is to

---

FIGURE 11-1   Sample Questionnaire

English, German and French Items

1. In general, I am among the *last* in my circle of friends to purchase a new wine
   Möglicherweise bin ich in meinem Freundeskreis eher einer/eine *letzten*, der/die einen neuen Wein kauft
   En général, je suis un des *derniers* parmi mes proches ou mes amis á acheter une nouvelle sort de vin

2. If I heard that a new wine was available through a local store, I would be interested enough to buy it
   Wenn ich davon höre, dass in meiner Gegend in einem Laden ein neuer Wein angeboten wird, dann bin ich so interessiert, dass ich ihn mir kaufe
   Si je savais qu'un nouveau type de vin était en rayon dans mon magasin habituel je serais suffisamment intéressé pour l'essayer

3. Compared to my friends, I do little shopping for new wine
   Im Vergleich zu meinen Freunden kaufe ich wenig neue Weine
   Par rapport á mes proches ou á mes amis, je fais peu d'achats de nouvelles sortes de vins

4. I would consider buying a new wine, even if I hadn't heard of it yet
   Ich würde einen neuen Wein kaufen, selbst wenn ich noch nichts über ihn gehört habe
   Je suis en général prêt á acheter un nouveau vin, même si je n'en ai pas entendu parler avant

5. In general, I am the last in my circle of friends to know the names of the latest wines and wine trends
   Normalerweise gehöre ich zu den letzten in meinem Freundkreis, der die Namen der neuesten Weine oder die neuen Weintrends kennt
   En général, je serais plutôt le dernier parmi mes proches ou mes amis á connaître les noms des nouveaux vins ou des derniers tendances en matière de vin

6. I know more about new wines than other people do
   Ich weiss mehr über neue Weine als andere Leute
   J'en connais plus á propos des nouveautés sur le vin que la plupart des gens

Eigenvalue
Percent of variance accounted for in the correlation matrix (%)

Source: From "Theory and Measurement of Consumer Innovativeness: A transitional evaluation" by Ronald E. Goldsmith, Francois d'Hauteville and Leisa Reinecke Flynn, in the *European Journal of Marketing*, Vol. 32, Iss. 3/4, 1998. Reprinted by permission of MCB University Press.

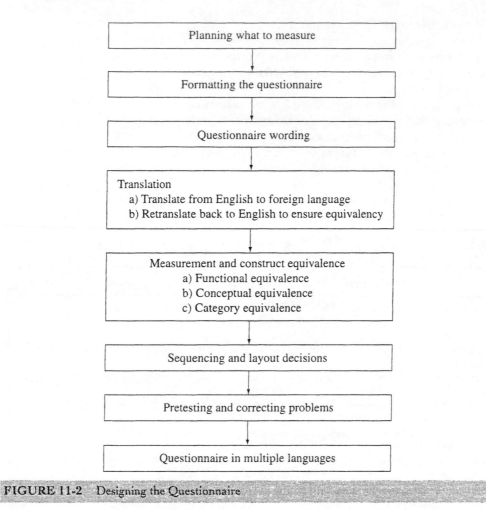

Planning what to measure

Formatting the questionnaire

Questionnaire wording

Translation
a) Translate from English to foreign language
b) Retranslate back to English to ensure equivalency

Measurement and construct equivalence
a) Functional equivalence
b) Conceptual equivalence
c) Category equivalence

Sequencing and layout decisions

Pretesting and correcting problems

Questionnaire in multiple languages

FIGURE 11-2   Designing the Questionnaire

decide what variables need to be measured. This involves going back to the research problem and the research questions. Researchers will also have to check back on the data collected during the course of secondary research and the hypotheses formulated when exploratory research was conducted. The next step is to decide on the content and format of each question. It is also necessary to work out the questionnaire's wording and its layout. The sequence of questions should be checked for logical continuity. The last step is to pretest the questionnaire and rectify any problems that may show up.

While designing the questionnaire, the researcher has to remember three factors that could have a great impact on the effectiveness of the questionnaire. First, the potential respondent should be able to understand the question. This implies that the language, the context, and the topic that is being investigated should be familiar to the respondent. Second, the respondent must have adequate knowledge to answer the question. The assumption behind survey research is that all of the responses are indicative of the true nature of the respondent's attitudes and feelings. This basic assumption fails if the respondent does not possess the knowledge required to give an intelligent answer. Finally, the respondent should be willing to participate in the survey without any external pressure. This is necessary to ensure unbiased responses that reflect the true feelings of the respondent.

QUESTIONNAIRE DEVELOPMENT

Table 11-1 gives the data organization of a typical questionnaire. The focus of international marketing research, as stressed in earlier chapters, will be on equivalence of information collected and not on equivalence of the instrument used to collect the data; hence, questionnaires do not have to be identical across all countries in a multi-country study. The objective is to ensure that the questionnaires convey the purpose of the study to the respondent and elicit responses that will be useful for the research. Information that can be collected by a questionnaire falls under three main categories: demographic data, psychographic data, and behavioral data.

Demographic data reveal information about the respondent, like age, sex, marital status, income, education, occupation, size of the family, and so on. This may not be a simple task in international marketing research. Some cultures support polygamy and so a person may have several spouses. There are societies where divorce and cohabitation of unmarried couples is common. This kind of data could be very difficult to capture in a questionnaire unless the researcher is aware of them and asks the respondent very specific questions. Income varies from country to country and the definition of classes—high income, middle income, and low income—also varies widely. Adequate data on this should be collected before designing the questionnaire. For instance, in some developing

TABLE 11-1   Organization of a Typical Questionnaire

Location	Type	Function	Example
Starting questions	Broad, general questions	To break the ice and establish a report with the respondent	Do you own a personal computer?
Next few questions	Simple and direct questions	To reassure the respondent that the survey is simple and easy to answer	What brands of personal computers did you consider when you bought it?
Questions up to a third of the questionnaire	Focused questions	Relate more to the research objectives and convey to the respondent the area of research	What attributes did you consider when you purchased your personal computer?
Major portion of the questionnaire	Focused questions; some may be difficult and complicated	To obtain most of the information required for the research	Rank the following attributes of a personal computer based on their importance to you.
Last few questions	Personal questions that may be perceived by the respondent as sensitive	To get classification and demographic information about the respondent	What is the highest level of education you have attained?

Source: Adapted from Aaker, Kumar and Day, *Marketing Research* 6e, Copyright © 1997, John Wiley & Sons, Inc. Reprinted by permission of John Wiley & Sons, Inc.

nations where the average annual income could be an equivalent of $500, it makes no sense for the questionnaire to include salary ranges from $25,000 upwards.

Education is another factor that varies widely between countries. There is a large disparity in the number of years spent in formative schooling and college education. The method and content of education also varies substantially. Definitions and product usage varies widely from country to country. Each country has a different definition for "urban" and "rural." Before conducting the research, this must be clarified for each country. The definition of "family" is dependent on the specific country. In Western cultures, nuclear families are the order of the day, while in many Eastern cultures, people continue to live in joint families. There could be differences in the place of residence. It could be a "house" in some parts of the world, "apartments" in some others, and "flats" in certain countries. The questionnaire will have to be designed in a manner such that respondents from all of the countries surveyed should be able to interpret it in a similar manner.

Psychographic, attitudinal, and lifestyle data prove to be the most difficult in terms of questionnaire design for a multicountry study. Many concepts that researchers may be used to in their home countries may not exist in other countries where the survey is being conducted. Even if the concepts exist, designing questions to convey the same meaning in a foreign language is a mammoth task that requires a lot of effort in terms of translations and back translations. A simple example would be the attitude of people towards credit. In the United States, credit cards, car loans, and mortgages are a part of daily life for most people; however, some cultures in Asia frown upon credit of any form and consider it an insult to be indebted to another person or organization. Purchase of durable goods and luxury items will be made only if the individual is capable of paying for the item in full. Another difference is in the role of women in different cultures. In the Western world, most women have careers and play an important role as an equal partner. In a lot of Middle Eastern countries, women are predominantly considered homemakers and are not included in making decisions; hence, if the study pertained to attitudes of women, the questionnaire and survey method will be different for women in the United States and women in the Middle East.

Behavioral data tracks the actual action taken by the consumer in terms of buying the product and the different ways in which the product is put to use. The researcher should be able to collect information on whether the behavior is dependent on a sociocultural or economic environment. There should also be adequate data on the various substitutes that could be used in a given country or culture. For instance, in the United States, most products are sold as specific brands. The questionnaire can ask the respondents to name the brand of pasta or rice that they use most frequently. The tradition of shopping at a grocery or department store chain is also very common; however, in some countries, people buy groceries from roadside vendors and stores. In India, for instance, it is very common to buy vegetables and greens on the sidewalks, where vendors sell them from mobile carts; therefore, asking the respondents the brand names for these items does not make practical sense. Chapter 1 talked about the survey results published by *Reader's Digest,* which stated that pasta is more common in Germany and France than in Italy. This is a classic case of designing the survey instrument without getting a thorough understanding of buyer behavior.

The research study determines the questions that should be included in the questionnaire and the order in which they should be asked. The researcher has to decide on the degree of freedom that can be given to the respondent in terms of answering the question. The question could be close-ended—the respondent has to choose among the alternatives put forth by the researcher. With close-ended questions the researcher may also decide to code the response—1 for "yes," 0 for "no," and so on. The other option is the open-ended question, where the respondent has the freedom of expressing independent opinions on the subject. With open-ended questions the researcher has to record the response verbatim. The questions could be direct or indirect. The researcher may also use visual cues to get an opinion from the respondent. The next section discusses the type of questions that can be used to design a questionnaire.

Question Format

The questionnaire design has to ensure data equivalence in international marketing equivalence. The format, content, and wording of the questions should be such that the respondent is able to comprehend and respond in a manner that is useful for the study. For example, in a developed country, a white-collar worker may be part of the middle class, whereas in a less-developed country, the same person would be a part of the upper class.[2] Hence, the questionnaire must be designed accordingly in different countries. The format, content, and wording of the questions must be decided after the respondent profile is understood.

In terms of format, content, and wording, questions can be categorized under the following types: open- versus close-ended, direct versus indirect, and verbal versus nonverbal.

Open- versus Close-Ended Questions

Close-ended questions offer a set of choices and the respondent has to choose one of the several alternatives available. Open-ended questions give the respondents the freedom to provide their own responses.

There are compelling arguments in favor of both open- and close-ended questions. Close-ended questions have the advantage of easy analysis. All the possible responses can be precoded and keyed into a computer prior to the survey; however, they also have a drawback in the sense that thorough research has to be conducted and all possible options must be included in the response set. Exhibit 11-2 gives an example of a complete list of options that can be used for close-ended questions. This poses quite a challenge in international research because the researcher first has to conduct an extensive study of buyer behavior and gather data on all acceptable uses and substitutes for the product in that country. Certain cultures tend to remain neutral when they are offered the option among different choices. This tends to cause significant bias in the survey. The other problem with close-ended questions is that respondents from different cultures may interpret the choices very differently.

In cases where the researcher is not sure about the purchasing behavior, it may be better to use open-ended questions. Open-ended questions do not impose any restrictions on the respondents and therefore eliminate cultural bias because of a lack of understanding on the part of the researcher. The researcher does not have to be familiar with the entire range of responses that can be obtained for that specific question. The limitation is obvious—these questions cannot be precoded. The process of coding and tabulating them once the data has been collected is very tedious. The length of the

---

EXHIBIT 11-2

Socio-Economic Classifications

1. Employers and managers in central and local government, industry, and commerce (large establishments)
2. As above (small establishments)
3. Professional workers (self-employed)
4. Professional workers (employees)
5. Intermediate non-manual workers
6. Junior non-manual workers
7. Personal service workers
8. Foremen and supervisors—manual
9. Skilled manual workers
10. Semi-skilled manual workers
11. Unskilled manual workers
12. Own account workers (other than professional)
13. Farmers—employer and manager
14. Farmers—own account
15. Agricultural workers
16. Members of armed forces
17. Indefinite
18. Other (please specify)

Source: From *Marketing Research*, 5th Edition, Peter Chisnall, Berkshire, England: McGraw Hill Publications, 1997, p. 102. Reprinted by permission of Professor P. M. Chisnall.

---

response and consideration given to the question before filling out the response are dependent on the time given to the respondent. If the respondent is pressed for time, the response may be hurried and half-hearted.

Some of the factors that affect the decision to design the question as open- or close-ended in international marketing research are level of literacy, education, and communication skills of the respondent. If the respondents are highly literate and very familiar with the survey topic, open-ended questions will enable the researcher to collect a lot of information. Similarly, open-ended questions will serve their purpose only if the respondent is very articulate and is able to communicate clearly to the researcher. These questions must be used with caution in international research to avoid bias due to differences in levels of education. The usefulness of these questions is also dependent on the interviewer's ability to record the responses thoroughly. Open-ended questions are used mostly in exploratory research where the primary objective is to gain insight into the research subject. Respondents are asked to list all possible options that come to their minds at the time of the survey. Responses that repeat very often are examined in greater depth.

Direct versus Indirect Questions

Direct questions avoid ambiguity regarding the question content and meaning. Indirect questions probe the respondent by asking them to list choices of their friends or peers rather than their own. Direct questions can be used when the topic is not controversial or it is not something that would make the respondent uncomfortable; however, for sensitive topics, it is more beneficial to use the indirect approach. In international marketing research, the researcher may have to spend some time finding out what is sensitive to people of a certain culture. For instance, while it is very common to discuss sexual preferences in the United States, this is a taboo topic in a lot of Asian cultures. Any information required on this topic should be asked in an indirect manner. Similarly, tax evasion is a very common occurrence in a lot of Latin American countries and respondents are extremely suspicious of anybody asking questions regarding income and taxes.

Verbal versus Nonverbal Questions

Most questionnaires are designed in a manner such that the questions can be read out to the respondents (interviews) or the respondent can read the questions (mail survey); however, in some cases, it may be necessary for researchers to use nonverbal cues, if the target sample consists mainly of children or the research is undertaken in countries where the literacy levels are very low. Interviewers administer the questionnaires; however, to assist the respondent in understanding the questions better, picture cards or other visual aids are used. In some cases, product samples may also be shown to the respondents. This may be necessary to ensure that the respondent is familiar with the product and its uses. This method is sometimes used even when the literacy levels are high. The researcher may want to subject one portion of the sample to nonverbal cues to ensure that the translation of the questionnaire is done correctly; however, allowance has to be made for the fact that the associations and uses that people have in different parts of the world vary widely. Therefore, nonverbal cues cannot be considered free of cultural bias. A side-to-side facial movement in Asian cultures indicates an agreement, whereas in many Western cultures it is considered a disagreement.

Wording and Translation

Wording of the questions is a very important aspect of questionnaire design. There are instances where different words could mean the same thing. In such cases, the researcher needs to make sure that the words used in the questionnaire are the ones that are commonly used in the country where the questionnaire is being administered. For instance, what Americans know as the baby carriage, the British call a pram. The British refer to Scotch tape as cellotape.[3] A question that is not understood by the respondent may be left unanswered or erroneously answered. Either way this causes a lot of bias in the survey. It is very important to remember the profile of the sample population. The respondent base should dictate the wording, tone, and structure of the questions. For instance, asking homemakers technical details about the air-conditioning in their residences will not make any sense. It is also necessary to keep in mind that respondents have limited attention spans, and asking long-winded questions will only result in them losing track of the question midway. A better option would be to break up the questions into smaller chunks that can be understood and responded to easily. If there are a lot of options that the respondent needs to consider before coming to a decision, these options must be presented in written form rather than having to listen to the interviewer read them. In a telephone interview, it is very important for the interviewer to make an oral transition from one type of question or subject area to another. This will help respondents anticipate change and shift them into a new mindset.

Questions have to be phrased in a manner such that they are free from bias and ambiguity. This becomes very important in international marketing research because of the different ways in which the same phrase can be interpreted. Consider the question, "Don't you think this advertising is appealing?" When an American answers "Yes," this usually means, "Yes, I agree with what you say"; however, in Asian countries this can mean a number of things. It could mean the other person is just acknowledging the fact that somebody is addressing them. It could also mean that the person understood what was being said but not necessarily mean agreement with what was being said. It could also mean complete agreement or complete disagreement. Some of the biggest blunders in marketing have been caused by using the wrong words or the right words in the wrong context. Exhibit 11-3 lists some examples that have made the headlines.

The most important aspect of designing the questionnaire in international marketing research is to get familiar with the local language, keep the language as simple as possible, and avoid lengthy explanations and instructions. This way the researcher can ensure that all of the respondents will be able to understand the questions and respond meaningfully. Care should be taken to ensure that there is no ambiguity for the respondent. As far as possible, the choices will have to be clearly specified. If, for instance, the researcher wants to find out how frequently the respondent indulges in a certain activity, specific options like "once a week" should be provided. Phrases like "often" and "usually" should be avoided, as respondents attach different meanings to these words.

EXHIBIT 11-3

What's in a Name?

Chevrolet launched its "Nova" in the Mexican market without giving any thought to the implications of the name, which, in Spanish, translated to "does not go." There were no takers for a car that was called "does not go."

A sign in a zoo in Hungary had the following to say: "Please do not feed the animals. If you have any suitable food, give it to the guard on duty."

Coors translated its slogan, "Turn it loose," into Spanish, which read "Suffer from Diarrhea."

"Nik Nak" potato chips failed dismally in the United Arabic Emirates because the word means aphrodisiac in Arabic.

A restaurant in Switzerland had the following sign: "Our wines leave you nothing to hope for."

Clairol introduced its "Mist Stick," a curling iron, in Germany, only to find that "mist" is slang for manure in German.

Pepsi's "Come Alive with the Pepsi Generation" translated into "Pepsi brings your ancestors back from the grave" in Chinese.

Dress shop in Hong Kong: "Ladies have fits upstairs."

"Cool-Piz" and "Pokari Sweat" tried to penetrate the soft drink market in Korea and failed for obvious reasons.

One airline ticket office in Denmark proudly advertised, "We take your bags and send them in all directions."

Sign in a hotel in Romania: "The lift is being fixed for the next day. During that time we regret that you will be unbearable."

Source: Adapted from the Internet and Mike Kelly, "Side-Splitting Translations: These Phrases Will Tickle Your Funny Bone." *The Milwaukee Journal*, 25 November, 1990, H5.

Exhibit 11-4 gives some tips on questionnaire design. Questions should not be clubbed together as this will cause a lot of confusion for the respondent and will make it difficult for the researcher to analyze the response. Consider a survey of recent car buyers to check for satisfaction levels. The question asked of respondents was "Are you satisfied with the design and performance of the car?" The customer could be satisfied with one aspect but not with the other, and there is no provision for the respondents to explicitly state that they are satisfied with the design but not the performance (or vice versa). Even if the respondent answers the question with "Yes" or "No," the researcher is not in a position to decide whether the response refers to the design aspect or the performance aspect.

The questionnaire should not in any way reflect the opinions of the researcher on the subject matter. This could be in the form of including choices as a part of the question, such as "What do you spend the most money on—clothes or dining out?" Here the choice is limited to one of the two choices offered by the researcher, whereas the

---

EXHIBIT 11-4

Tips on Questionnaire Design

Designing a questionnaire for international marketing research involves a lot of preparation by the researcher. Following are some of the pitfalls to avoid when designing questionnaires:

- Avoid using complicated words and long, complex sentences.

- Do not use words or phrases that are specific to one country or culture. They may not be understood by all respondents. This is particularly true of diverse cultures where the people speak many languages and dialects.

- Do not use double-barreled questions. A double-barreled question is one that combines two questions into one and creates ambiguity for the respondent. An example would be to ask respondents if they are satisfied with the price and quality of a product. Respondents who are satisfied with one but not the other will not be able to answer this question.

- Do not use questions that are leading or loaded. These questions convey the opinion of the researcher and force the respondent to answer one way or another. Consider the question, "Don't you agree that the Internet is a good source of information?" This is a leading question that forces the respondent to answer in a manner that is acceptable to the researcher. A loaded question introduces a very subtle bias. "What do you think is a good source of information—the Internet or some other medium?" Is an example of a loaded question. Avoid using words and phrases that convey strong emotions to the respondent.

- Instructions should not confuse the respondents. Keep the instructions short and precise.

- Avoid asking questions that are not applicable to respondents. Asking college students about desktop or laptop computer ownership in the United States is relevant. Asking the same question to college students in many developing countries may induce bias in the results.

Source: From Aaker, Kumar and Day, *Marketing Research* 6e, Copyright © 1997, John Wiley & Sons, Inc. Reprinted by permission of John Wiley & Sons, Inc.

respondent could be spending the maximum amount on some other activity. Any words that convey strong emotions or affect the self-esteem of the respondents should also be avoided. One way to avoid these pitfalls is to test the questionnaire on a small number of respondents from the target segment and rectify any mistakes at a very early stage.

Another important facet of international marketing research is translation of questionnaires and responses. Examples of blunders in the research study arising from errors in translation abound. For instance, alternatives for *Indian* in the Microsoft thesaurus include *cannibal* and *savage*.[4] It is important to note that accurate translation is important for both verbal and nonverbal stimuli and responses. The procedure normally followed in translating a questionnaire is very elaborate and involved. A professional translator translates the original English version of the questionnaire into the foreign language. This foreign version is then translated back into English by another person who is not familiar with the original version. This is done to ensure that the questionnaire is consistent in terms of content in both the languages. Though this process is very time consuming and expensive, many researchers use it because of its effectiveness. It should be noted that back translation assumes that equivalent terms and concepts exist in all languages that are of relevance to the researcher. This does not always have to be true.

There are several drawbacks with this method. The foremost problem is that the mental representations of verbal information is different in different cultures.[5] Professional translators may not be familiar with the idioms commonly used by the masses. Translators are usually not very conversant with the art of marketing and persuasion, and the translated version of the questionnaire often does not have a ring of authenticity to it.[6] Besides, in countries like India and China, where thousands of dialects are spoken, it is impossible for translators to be fluent in all of them. The original questionnaire is designed in a certain language and will carry the tone and style of that language and will be dominant in that language structure. The basic assumption in the method of back translation is that equivalent terms and phrases exist in all of the languages that the questionnaire is to be translated into. This may not always be the case. For instance, Japanese does not have an exact equivalent for the word "husband." Term selection is particularly problematic in the information systems industry, where Americans have invented a lot of words for which there are no equivalents in any other language. In circumstances like this, researchers have to settle for a colloquial equivalent. This is a strong argument in favor of focusing on the comparability of data collected rather than on the questionnaire itself. Researchers should concentrate on conveying the purpose of the survey and recording the responses in the best and most efficient manner possible. The instrument used to achieve this objective is secondary.

Pretesting the questionnaires is of utmost importance in international marketing studies. Pretesting is done to ensure that all versions of the questionnaire are interpreted in a similar manner by respondents from various countries. It is also important to check for clarity and fluency before the questionnaires can be used in the survey. In international marketing research, equal importance should be given to translating nonverbal cues and responses. Adequate time and effort should be invested in pretesting the perceptual and visual cues to avoid miscommunication arising as a result of difference in interpretations. It is also useful to have redundancy in the questionnaires to help researchers cross-check validity of responses.[7]

CULTURAL ISSUES

Even though the questionnaire has been designed and translated very carefully to meet the needs of several countries or cultures, there is still bound to be some bias in the responses because of cultural differences. Some of the factors that may lead to these biases are discussed in this section.

In drafting a questionnaire, knowledge of the social, psychological, and ethnic aspects of the society is essential.[8] This is a good indication of how people are likely to respond to certain topics, how they will react toward questions that are private, and the amount of time they will be willing to spend for an interview. The wording, length, and form of the questionnaire should depend on the verbosity, sophistication, credibility, conformity, and extremism of response of the sample population. The scales used, the language of the questionnaire, and the concept being tested should be comprehended by the respondents. As an example, if a questionnaire was to be designed for a national study of the Philippines, the questionnaire would have to be translated into nine different languages. In India, this would be several hundred. In regions where literacy levels are very low, pictorial scales have to be used and visual aids have to be provided to ensure that the respondents are clear on the concepts that are being tested. It has generally been found that open-ended questions provide better results and reduce cultural biases to a great extent; however, the trade-off is the difficulty in coding an open-ended question, which can generate thousands of responses in a multicountry study.

Translation is another major problem that researchers face in international marketing research. A study conducted to investigate trust and commitment and the importance of these attributes in relationship with management found that there are no direct translations of concepts related to trust in Japanese. *Amae* translates literally as indulgent dependency and *giri-ninjo* as an obligation to show compassion to those who show it to you; however, these ideas are not fully consistent with Western ideas of trust, and they apply only to Japanese-Japanese interaction.[9] This study focused on United States–Japanese interaction, and the lack of adequate terminology made it difficult for researchers to convey their questions accurately.

The desire to be socially correct or provide answers that may be felt to be desired by the interviewer is present in almost everyone. This is, however, stronger in some cultures than in others. The Japanese almost always try to respond in a manner that they feel the interviewer wants them to so that they do not upset or cause any distress to the interviewer. Respondents in several poorer countries consider the survey as an honor bestowed upon them and will go to any lengths to please the interviewer. The other factor that causes bias is the desire to give socially acceptable answers. This is common in many cultures where the respondents feel the need to live up to a certain lifestyle or appear sophisticated; therefore, the responses will be what they think they should answer rather than what they actually feel about the subject.

CONSTRUCT EQUIVALENCE

This concept has already been introduced in earlier chapters. The researcher has to establish that the constructs being studied in different countries are equivalent. There could be substantial differences in the way the same product is perceived in different regions. In the United Kingdom, Germany, and Scandinavia, beer is regarded as an alcoholic beverage, whereas in Greece, Spain, and Italy it is treated more as a soft drink and compared to Coca-Cola. It is necessary to establish construct equivalence in cases like this where the basic perception of the sample population differs. This consists of three parts: functional equivalence, conceptual equivalence, and category equivalence.[10]

Functional Equivalence

Functional equivalence involves establishing that a given concept or behavior serves the same purpose or function from country to country. We can consider the example of bicycles. While in the United States bicycles are primarily used as a means of recreation, in a lot of developing countries they serve as a mode of transportation. Hence, in the United States, the relevant competing products would be other recreational sports items, like roller blades and skiing equipment. In those other countries we would have to have a different set of competing products, like alternate modes of transportation. As far as activities go, people from different cultures do things differently. Shopping for groceries is a chore in the United States to be completed as efficiently as possible, and most food retailers make it easier with self-service aisles and shopping carts. In a lot of countries, this is considered a social activity and there is a lot of interaction between the grocer and the customer. Similarly, there could be differences in the way people perceive objects in various countries around the world. Cars are considered a necessity in the United States, while they are a luxury and status symbol in a lot of developing countries. All of these factors will play an important role in the design of the questionnaire. Researchers have to make sure that they ask the questions in the right context.

Conceptual Equivalence

Conceptual equivalence deals with individual interpretation of objects and stimuli. The focus in this aspect of construct equivalence is on individual variations in attitudes and behavior rather than societal norms and behavior (as was the case in functional equivalence). Researchers try to understand the extent to which people from different cultures exhibit personality traits, such as aggression, authoritarianism, or need for affiliation. Social interaction, rituals, and practices vary widely between countries. In the United Kingdom, engagement implies a commitment to marry, whereas in Italy or Spain, it merely means having a boyfriend or girlfriend.

Category Equivalence

The last aspect of construct equivalence is called category equivalence. This relates to the categories in which relevant objects or other stimuli are placed. In many countries beer is considered a soft drink. A lot of countries differ in the way they classify soft drinks, carbonated sodas, powdered or liquid concentrates, and so on. The same holds true for the dessert market. Many cultures consider sweets as a part of the meal; however, in China sweets are not included as a part of the meal. In many Middle Eastern and African countries, marital status could include several wives. Even occupations are placed in different categories in different countries. Less-developed countries give a lot of importance to professions like teacher or a religious minister.

Differences in culture, economic status, social structure, and product usage can cause wide variation in responses to the same given question. For instance, the American Customer Satisfaction Index (ACSI) represents overall satisfaction as a function of customer expectations, perceived quality, and perceived value.[11] The model is designed to take into account multiple indicators to measure customer satisfaction. This is done because the constructs used in the model represent different types of customer evaluations that cannot be measured directly. Using multiple indicators results in an index that is general enough to be comparable across firms, industries, sectors, and nations. This index is applicable in the international context also; however, special care needs to be taken when designing the questionnaire. Customer expectations and perceived quality and value are culturally and nationally sensitive constructs. They would depend on the product, its price in a given country, the substitutes available, and the usage methods.

Consider, for instance, the product category of passenger cars and measure of customer satisfaction in the United States and India. The average customer in the United States considers cars a necessity. There is ample choice and the cost of a car as a percentage of annual income is not very high; however, in many developing countries, cars are considered a luxury that is within the reach of only a small percentage of the population. As a percentage of the annual income, the cost of cars is very high and there is only limited choice; hence, the customer perception of value, quality, and their expectations of a car are bound to be different.

A questionnaire that does not take into account all of these differences will not capture the real picture. To start with the basics, translating the questionnaire will prove to be a problem. It is not possible to get a precise translation for the word "perceive" in many languages worldwide. Even if the meaning were conveyed adequately, there is bound to be differences due to differences of the perception of the product—the car itself in this case. Assume that Ford is conducting a customer satisfaction study for Escort. In the United States, Escort is a small car easily affordable by a middle- or lower-middle-income group; however, in India, it falls under the category of large and premium cars and is affordable only to a select few. The sample selected in both of these countries should be different. Asking the questions in an absolute sense does not provide accurate results. Questions have to be asked in comparative terms and researchers have to provide anchors that are comparable to obtain comparable results. One way to go about this would be to pick a model that is being used by a certain segment of the society and ask for satisfaction relative to this model. For instance, in the United States, the question could be phrased as, "Compared to the Geo Metro, how does Escort rate on all of the following factors?" (Provide a list of attributes that need comparison.) In India, the same question could be worded as, "Compared to the Maruti Suzuki, how does Escort rate on all of the following factors?" The only requirement is that the Geo Metro and the Maruti Suzuki should be positioned similarly in their respective markets.

There are certain aspects that are culture sensitive. For instance, Americans are used to speaking their minds and, hence, any dissatisfaction that they feel toward the car will be reflected in the response; however, Asians are not so candid and may hide any negative opinions for fear of hurting the feelings of the interviewer. In such situations, adjustments will have to be made to the scales and the interviewer will have to go to great lengths to convince the respondent of the importance of an honest response. This requires that the researcher have in-depth understanding of the foreign culture.

Designing the questionnaire in the correct manner is only solving half of the problem. Analyzing the results is the other major component, and it is always preferable to include researchers who are familiar with the foreign country or culture in the analysis.

INTERNATIONAL MARKETING RESEARCH IN PRACTICE

This section discusses the practical aspects of designing and administering a survey questionnaire for international marketing research. The first aspect that a researcher needs to look into is the population characteristics. It may be possible for the researcher to obtain a complete list of the people who make up the population; however, this would depend on the population and the location. A comprehensive list of all cardiologists in Houston is a reasonable goal; however, the same may not be available in a less-developed country. Even within developed countries, if the population were defined as all women who use shampoos and conditioners, in Houston it may be difficult to get a complete list. Even if the list were available, it would be difficult to contact all of these women. The population could be defined as all women who use shampoos in São Paulo. Obtaining this list is next to impossible, given that shampoo purchases are not usually tracked; hence, defining the population and deciding whether to go for the complete list or just choosing a representative sample is the first step in a survey.

Once the population has been defined, designing the questionnaire will depend on the population characteristics. It is safe to assume that any randomly selected women in Houston will be aware of the concept of shampoo; however, in Kenya, as in many parts of the less-developed world where cheaper and more traditional ingredients are prevalent, many women do not use bottled shampoos. Hence, the questionnaire must have a screening question at the start to ensure that respondents use shampoos. Language issues must be addressed in all international marketing research surveys. For the Houston area, the researcher may be better off designing questionnaires in both English and Spanish. For the survey in Kenya, questionnaires must be designed in English and the local language. Care should be taken when administering the questionnaire in Kenya; many cultures do not take kindly to strangers striking up conversations with women. There could also be substantial differences in the method of administering the questionnaire. Depending on the availability of time, telephone interviews, mail surveys, or mall intercept surveys could be used in Houston; however, mail surveys will produce poor response rates in many less-developed countries, as the postal systems are not efficient. Incentives may have to be offered in many countries to improve response rates.[12] It may also not be possible to obtain the mailing list. Hence, personal intercept or store intercept surveys seem to be the best way to collect information. The researcher needs to identify locations in various parts of the city that could give the best "hit" rates.

The type of questions that can be asked also varies widely from country to country. If an open-ended question were asked in the United States, most respondents would be verbose, telling the researcher exactly what they feel; however, many oriental cultures do not encourage verbosity, and an open-ended question in China and other Asian countries will not get very good results. For this reason, it may be better to opt for close-ended questions in these countries and ask respondents to choose from a pre-specified list of choices. The researcher will also have to watch out for various kinds of biases that are prevalent in less-developed countries. Many women in Asian countries may claim to use shampoos just so they can appear trendy and sophisticated. Respondents could also answer the questionnaire because they are too polite to refuse the interviewer.

Ultimately, all surveys are dependent on the resources available to the researcher. Hence, cost becomes a major factor in deciding the type of survey, length of the questionnaire, number of people to be surveyed, and the geographic coverage.

Summary

Surveys are an important source of primary information for researchers and questionnaires are used to collect information through surveys. Questionnaires make it possible for the researcher to quantify various aspects of the research that are being studied. There are three factors that are considered very important in using questionnaires: the respondent should understand the question, the respondent should possess adequate knowledge to answer the question, and the respondent should be willing to participate in the survey without any external pressure. Questionnaires gather data that fall under three categories: demographic data, psychographic data, and behavioral data. Questions in a survey can be open- or close-ended, direct or indirect, and verbal or nonverbal. The type of question used will be determined by the topic that is being researched and the country or culture where the research is being conducted. Questionnaires should always be pretested to make sure they achieve the objective planned by the researcher. A questionnaire has to meet the requirements of construct equivalence for it to be a valid data collection tool in international marketing research. Construct equivalence can be broken into three components: functional equivalence, conceptual equivalence, and category equivalence.

Questions and Problems

1. What are the translation problems encountered in designing an international marketing research questionnaire?
2. "Questionnaire design for descriptive research is more difficult than for exploratory research." Discuss this statement.
3. How does the general brand affinity of customers in international markets affect unaided-recall questions and aided-recall questions?
4. Evaluate the following questions and suggest improvements:
   a. Please check the following activities in which you participate as a private citizen interested in politics.

      Read books and articles on the subject   ____
      Belong to a political party   ____
      Attend political rallies   ____
      Write letters to legislators, newspapers, or government officials   ____
      Other (please specify)   ____

   b. When you eat dinner out, do you sometimes eat at the same place?
      ____Yes ____No

c. Is the current level of government regulation on environmental protection adequate or inadequate?

____Adequate   ____Inadequate

c. Where do you buy most of your clothes?

d. Do you think that Con Edison is doing everything possible to reduce air pollution from their electricity-generating stations?

____Yes ____No

e. Please indicate how much of an average issue of *Sunset* magazine you usually read:

1. Less than ⅓____   2. ⅓ to ½____   3. Over ½____

f. List the magazines you read regularly ("read" means read or look at; "regularly" means almost as often as the magazine is published).

g. What kind of hobbies do you have?

h. Everybody knows that teenagers and their parents have lots of arguments. What are some of the things you and your parents have argued about lately?

Endnotes

1. Kris Hodges, "Ask A Silly Question . . .," *Marketing 98/99*, ed. John E. Richardson (Guilford, CT: Dushkin/McGraw-Hill, 1998): 98–100.

2. Michael R. Czinkota and Ilkka A. Ronkainen, *International Marketing*, 5th ed. (Orlando, FL: Harcourt, Brace, and Company, 1998).

3. Sak Onkvisit and John J. Shaw, *International Marketing—Analysis and Strategy*, 3rd ed. (Upper Saddle River, NJ: Prentice Hall 1997), 214.

4. *Latin Trade* (September 1996): 16.

5. Bernd Schmitt, Yingang Pan, and Nader T. Tavossili, "Language and Consumer Memory: The Impact of Linguistic Differences between Chinese and English," *Journal of Consumer Research* 21 (December 1994): 419–31.

6. Simon Anholt, "The Problem of International Work: Why Copy Can't Be Translated," *DM News* (23 January 1995): 13.

7. Naghi Namakforoosh, "Data Collection Methods Hold Key to Research in Mexico," *Marketing*.

8. Joanna Kinsey, *Marketing in Developing Countries* (England: Macmillan Education Ltd, 1994).

9. Jean L. Johnson, Tomoaki Sakano, Kevin Voss, and Hideyuki Takenouchi, "Marketing Performance in U.S.-Japanese Cooperative Alliances: Effects of Multiple Dimensions of Trust and Commitment in Cultural Interface," Working Paper, Washington State University.

10. Susan P. Douglas and C. Samuel Craig, *International Marketing Research* (Englewood Cliffs, NJ: Prentice Hall, 1983), 78–82.

11. Claes Fornell, Michael D. Johnson, Eugene W. Anderson, Jaesung Cha, and Barbara Everitt Bryant, "The American Customer Satisfaction Index: Nature, Purpose, and Findings," *Journal of Marketing* 60 (October 1996): 7–20.

12. Charles Keown, "Foreign Mail Surveys: Response Rates Using Monetary Incentives," *Journal of International Business Studies* (fall 1985): 151–153.

C H A P T E R

Sampling

INTRODUCTION

The purpose of international marketing research is to study the characteristics and preferences of a population. *Population* is defined as the set of all objects that possess some common set of characteristics with respect to some marketing research problems. A survey that contacts all members of a population is called a *census.* In most research studies, it is not very practical to conduct a census because of limitations in terms of resources and time. Researchers choose a subset of elements from the population and from this subset obtain the *sample.* They then make an inference about the population based on the relevant information obtained from the sample. The critical assumption in this case is that the sample is representative of the population and any data collected from the sample can be applied to all members of the population.

It is important to bear in mind that using samples can introduce a bias in the research project. Even if the researcher is able to specify the population of interest, it may not be possible to access the entire population. The sample that has been selected may include some members who do not belong to the population. There is also the possibility that some segments of the population are left out of the sample. Also the members of the sample may not always give the correct response.

STATISTICAL BASIS FOR SAMPLING

It is important to familiarize the reader with some terms that are used frequently in conjunction with sampling.[1] A sampling unit that has been contacted by the researcher provides a *response,* which will be used as a basis for analysis. Any function of this response is called a *statistic.* A statistic can be described as the value obtained across all responses for a certain measure, like the sample mean or the sample variance. A *sampling distribution* is the probability distribution of the statistic. The total error in a survey can be split into two major components. If the difference between the population parameter and sample statistic is only because of sampling, this is called *sampling error.*

219

This could be mainly because of choosing a sample size that is smaller than the population. In most cases, the sampling error can be reduced to a great extent by using a relatively larger sample. Determination of the appropriate sample size is discussed later in this chapter. It must be remembered that the statistically determined sample size is the number of complete responses that must be received by the researcher. The response rate in a given country for a given method must be identified and an adequate number of people must be contacted.

If there is a difference between the population parameter and the sampling statistic that is not due to sampling error, it is called a *nonsampling error*. Nonsampling errors can be due to errors in measurement, errors in recording the responses, errors in analyzing the data, and nonresponse error.

THE SAMPLING PROCESS

Figure 12-1 represents the flowchart for the sampling process. The first step in the sampling process is determining the target population. The target population will have to be identified as clearly as possible. The narrower the definition, the better the results obtained through sampling. This is a very crucial step in international marketing research because of the differences in decision-making processes in various countries. This is discussed in detail under sampling equivalency. Deciding the target population and the sample size will be easier if the researcher has a good knowledge of the market. Domestic research relies heavily on prior research about the market. This will not be possible for most international markets, as there is not much prior research done about these markets. This is where secondary research and exploratory research play a major role. This will also help researchers establish the sampling unit. A sampling unit may consist of individuals, households, or organizations. The assumption behind the sampling unit is that all responding members of the unit provide information for the whole unit. Here again, the researcher needs to know the market well enough to decide this. For instance, if the family is considered as a sampling unit, the researcher needs to clarify the definition of a family in that country.

The next step is to decide on the sampling frame. The sampling frame is a list of population members used to obtain a sample. This frequently creates problems in international marketing research due to lack of documented information about businesses, industries, or consumer products. Researchers need to understand the system and the decision-making process involved before deciding the sampling frame. The decision-making process varies substantially in different countries. In Japan, for example, decisions are still made by consensus of every family member.[2] For instance, consider a drug manufacturer conducting a survey to find the number of kidney transplants done in a given country. In the United States, this information could be obtained by sampling a few leading Medicare and medical insurance providers; however, in other countries, where there is no concept of medical insurance, all leading hospitals will have to be sampled. The sampling frame in both of these cases is very different even though the objective is the same. This is one more area where international marketing research differs from domestic research. A list of members belonging to the sampling frame should then be obtained. Once again, in the United States and most of the developed countries there are professional organizations and database marketing companies that can provide a

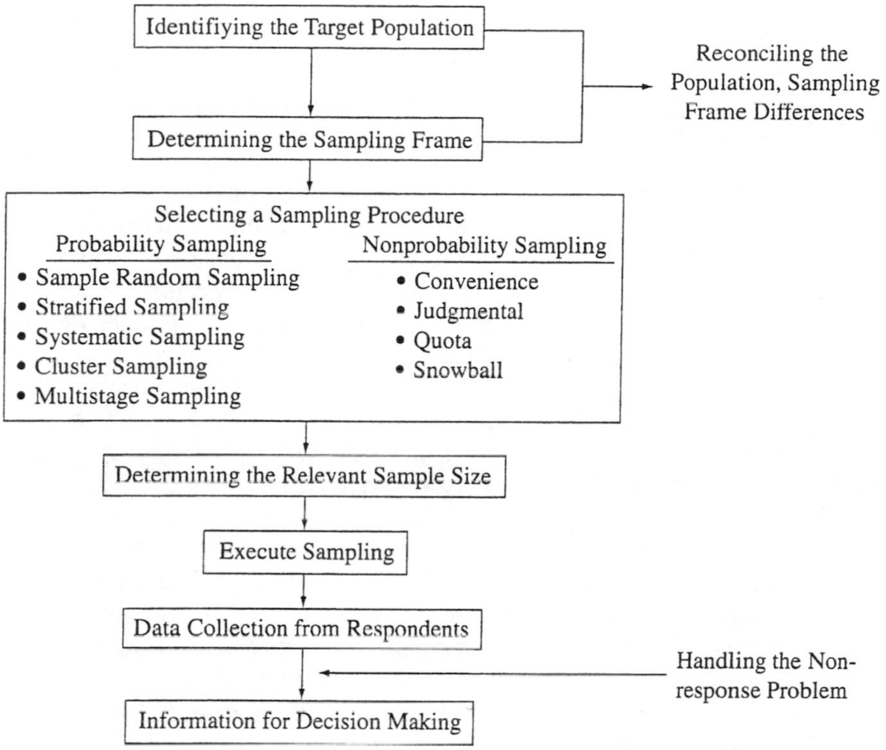

Identifiying the Target Population

Reconciling the
Population, Sampling
Frame Differences

Determining the Sampling Frame

Selecting a Sampling Procedure

Probability Sampling | Nonprobability Sampling

- Sample Random Sampling
- Stratified Sampling
- Systematic Sampling
- Cluster Sampling
- Multistage Sampling

- Convenience
- Judgmental
- Quota
- Snowball

Determining the Relevant Sample Size

Execute Sampling

Data Collection from Respondents

Handling the Non-
response Problem

Information for Decision Making

FIGURE 12-1 The Sampling Process

comprehensive list of the desired segment members. In some developing countries where marketing research is still in its infancy, finding a reliable source may prove to be a problem and researchers may have to opt for a less formal method.

Improper definition of the sampling frame can cause three types of problems for the researcher. If the sampling frame chosen is smaller than the population, some members of the population are not sampled and the research study does not consider their tastes and attitudes. This is called a *subset problem*. If, for instance, the population consists of all telephone owners in a given geographic area and the researcher looks into the telephone directory, this would be a subset problem, as the unlisted numbers will not be sampled. It has also been found that the people with unlisted telephone numbers are significantly different from those with listed telephone numbers. If the sampling frame is larger than the population, we have a *superset problem*. If the population consists of people using contact lenses and the researcher obtains a sample database from optometrists consisting of people using eyeglasses and contact lenses, this becomes a superset problem. The last and most serious error is the *subset/superset problem*. This occurs when the researcher leaves out some members of the sampling frame while including others that do not belong to the sampling frame. Assume a researcher is interested in contacting small business owners with at least $4 million in sales. If the researcher uses a business list which contains all businesses (not strictly small businesses) with over $5 million in sales, a subset/superset problem results.

TYPES OF SAMPLING

Selecting a sampling procedure is very crucial in international marketing research owing to uncertainties regarding the definition of the population and sampling frame. Theoretically, however, sampling methods can be classified under two broad headings: probability sampling and nonprobability sampling. In probability sampling, each member of the population has a known probability of being selected; however, the researcher needs to have a definite sampling frame and also have prior information on the objects or sampling units before getting started on the sampling process.

Probability sampling has several advantages. It permits the researcher to demonstrate the representativeness of the sample. It helps researchers state the variation introduced by using a sample instead of a census. It also helps researchers identify possible biases introduced due to sampling.

In international marketing research, it is not always possible to obtain a sampling frame. In such circumstances, nonprobability methods work best. There are no significant costs involved in developing a sampling frame; however, it is also not possible to guarantee the representativeness of the sample. The responses can contain hidden biases and uncertainties that cannot be explained. Increasing the sample size does not help overcome these biases, hence, researchers prefer to avoid nonprobability sampling methods whenever possible.

Probability Sampling

A sample can be obtained by using the principle of probability theory. In this procedure, researchers first specify the population to be sampled and the sample size. Generally speaking, the sample size depends on the accuracy required by the study, the resources available to the researcher, and the reliability of the sampling list collected by the researcher.

Simple random sampling is the method of sampling where a group of subjects is selected from the population entirely by chance and the probability of choosing any given member from the population is the same. This method is used when the population from which the sample is to be chosen is homogeneous. Small sheets of paper with names written out on them are mixed together in a bowl and the desired number of names are drawn out. This method works very well for small sample sizes; however, if a large number of people have to be chosen from a population, it becomes very tedious. Another way of picking out a random sample is by generating a random-number table. Exhibit 12-1 gives a list of computer generated random-number tables that can be used to pick out a sample. The researcher can start anywhere on the list and proceed horizontally or vertically. These numbers can then be used to generate a sample. In the recent past, computers have been used to generate random numbers. An example of random sampling could be choosing a set of teenagers from all countries across the world. Because teenagers worldwide are assumed to have similar opinions and exhibit similar behavior, this will be a random sample from a homogeneous group.

EXHIBIT 12-1

Computer Generated Random Numbers

99	55	62	70	92	44	32
95	17	81	83	83	04	49
39	58	81	09	62	08	66
50	45	60	33	01	07	98
33	12	36	23	47	11	85
63	99	89	85	29	53	93
78	37	87	06	43	97	48
59	73	56	45	65	99	24
52	06	03	04	79	88	44

Stratified random sampling, also called proportional sampling, is a two-step process in which accuracy and efficiency is improved relative to simple random sampling. There are factors that divide the population into clear-cut groups or strata and the first step in stratified sampling is to identify these strata. Each of these groups will contain members of the population who are homogenous to a great extent. The second step is to sample members from each of these relatively homogenous groups; however, there are marked differences between the groups themselves (e.g., males and females). These differences have to be accounted for when a sample is selected from a population. This can be achieved by stratified sampling. An example would be a car manufacturer trying to find out the factors that are considered most important to new car buyers. Assume that the manufacturer has conducted exploratory studies revealing that males and females have different criteria for evaluating cars. The population for this study will be all adults of age 18 and above who are interested in buying a new car in the next calendar year. The population could then be divided into males and females and simple random sampling could be employed for each of these groups.

Stratified sampling can be proportional, that is, the number of members chosen from each group is directly or inversely proportional to the size of the group; however, when the groups are very small, proportional sampling will not provide an adequate sample. In such instances, disproportional samples are used. Stratified sampling ensures that the sample will be representative of the population. It also goes one step further and guarantees that each subgroup in a given population is represented as well, no matter how small the subgroup may be. Stratified sampling is used very frequently in international marketing research. If the study involves understanding the breakfast cereal market in North America, the population would include Canada, the United States, and Mexico. The sample will have to include a proportional number of Canadians, Americans, and Mexicans. It is possible to go one step further and stratify the Canadian population based on the eating habits of the various ethnic groups. An international study conducted to survey the usage of cellular telephones used the stratified random sampling procedure. For conducting the survey in the United Arab Emirates, the demographics of the country were studied. It was found that there was a substantial percentage of expatriates living in the UAE—about 60 percent. The local population, which made up only about 40 percent, used cellular telephones for personal reasons. The expatriates mainly used them for official purposes. Because there is a significant difference in the product usage, researchers decided to go in for proportional stratified random sampling so that both of these groups are adequately represented.

Systematic random sampling is used in cases where the researcher knows that the list of population members to be sampled is in some order: random, cyclical, or monotonic. Systematic random sampling is used most frequently in telephone interviews. If the population consists of all people belonging to a given geographic territory and has telephone numbers starting with the same prefix, systematic random digit dialing could be used to obtain a representative sample. If the researcher is interested in conducting telephone surveys in an area where the first three digits of the telephone number (the area code) are 408 and the next three numbers are 560, the possible list of 10,000 telephone numbers that can be surveyed are (408) 560-0000 through (408) 560-9999. Assume that the required sample size is 1,000. Every tenth number in the list could be used starting with a randomly selected phone number between (408) 560-0000 and (408) 560-0010. It has been proven that households with unlisted numbers possess different characteristics from those with phone numbers that are listed in directories. This method eliminates any bias that could be created by ignoring the unlisted numbers in that population.

The one drawback with all of the random sampling methods discussed above is geographic coverage. If the population is spread over a wider area, it becomes difficult to obtain a representative sample. This problem can be overcome by using cluster sampling. *Cluster sampling* is a technique where the entire population is divided into similar groups, or clusters that are very similar, and each cluster represents a minipopulation. A random sample of these clusters is then selected. Once clusters have been selected for sampling, all members in these clusters are surveyed. This is different from stratified sampling in that all members of the cluster that has been selected in the sampling process are interviewed.

In international marketing research, owing to lack of information and the high cost of research, most researchers opt for multistage sampling. Consider a soft drink manufacturer conducting a study to find out the brand awareness of the beverage they manufacture. All the countries where the brand awareness study is to be conducted are first divided into regions that are similar on a predetermined set of attributes, such as per capita income or annual sales of the beverage. These regions are then broken down into countries and the countries are further broken down into cities. Clusters of residential areas are identified in each of these cities. Researchers then draw a random sample of a certain number of clusters depending on the sample size they need. All members in these clusters are surveyed. The results obtained for the selected clusters can be extrapolated to get the awareness figures for the whole region. Depending on the complexity of the information required and the geographic territory that needs to be covered, multistage sampling can involve as many as three or four stages. Exhibit 12-2 gives some national sources of sampling frames in Great Britain.

Nonprobability Sampling

In nonprobability sampling researchers typically do not develop a sampling frame. As a result, sampling efficiency and precision are absent in these methods; however, they are used in exploratory research, pretesting questionnaires, and surveying homogeneous population. In many international marketing research studies, nonprobability

---

EXHIBIT 12-2

Sources of National Sampling Frames in Great Britain

In the United Kingdom, there are two national address lists suitable for use as sampling frames. The Register of Electors is a list of individuals and the Postcode Address File is a list of addresses.

Registered electors' names appear in alphabetical order at their recorded addresses. It is usually possible to determine the gender, but the list does not provide any information regarding the age of the individual. This will prove to be a handicap if the research requires individuals in specific age groups. Another problem that could arise out of this list is that many members of a family are listed in different places in the register with the same addresses. If a sample of addresses is to be extracted this could prove to be a serious handicap; however, the sampling frame is validated by the fact that it will no longer contain names of those who are dead. In the United Kingdom, it is estimated that approximately 4 percent of the electors do not register; however, the bias introduced by this omission is considered negligible.

The list also contains names and addresses of people who have moved. This is estimated to be about 5 percent. This can bias the sampling frame as the category of people who move are predominantly in their 20s and 30s.

Postcode Address File (PAF) is a system used by the post office for mechanized sorting of mail. The largest geographical unit, there are 120 of them in the United Kingdom, is called the postcode area. Each of these is subdivided into districts, which are further divided into postcode sectors. The last two alphabets in the postcode denote the street. The postcode system is an ideal sampling frame for stratified sampling. It is possible to make use of PAF to survey all adults in a given area or select a random number of postcodes and survey all people living in that postcode. The only disadvantage is that PAF does not indicate the number of people living in a given address and further screening is necessary to obtain a list of people to be contacted for sampling.

Source: Adapted from *Marketing Research*, 5th Edition, Peter Chisnall, Berkshire, England: McGraw Hill Publications, 1997, pp. 77–79. Reprinted by permission of Professor P.M. Chisnall.

---

sampling methods are used frequently because of the novelty of the research process in these countries. For instance, the research project undertaken to study cellular telephone usage targeted countries like Egypt, Jordan, Saudi Arabia, and the United Arab Emirates. Even though all of these countries may have a very good penetration of cellular telephones, it is not possible to do a random sampling of the target population. It is socially unacceptable for strangers to go knocking on doors asking for information. Nonprobability methods are used in these cases. Some of the popular nonprobability methods are as followed.

Judgmental sampling is done when the researcher knows the market well enough to choose a sample using expert judgment. For instance, when conducting a survey in a mall to obtain the opinions of working women on a certain cosmetic, interviewers may decide to talk to women who appear to be employed. When conducting surveys in malls, interviewers usually talk to people who appear to be willing to respond. This is based on the assumption that all people coming to that mall have similar attitudes and opinions. This may not always be the case, and the survey may induce a bias. Judgmental sampling is used in cases where the researcher needs quick results. This method can be used with reasonable accuracy when the sample size is very small, like in an exploratory research or a questionnaire pretest.

Snowball sampling is used when the population consists of individuals in specialized areas. This method starts out with the researcher identifying one individual or unit that has all the population characteristics. This individual is then asked to give a list of names of all others who meet the population characteristics. This method is effective in sampling highly specialized population segments. This is an easy way of sampling segments like astronauts, deep-sea divers, and families with triplets. The drawback in this method is that people who are socially visible tend to get selected. The cellular telephone study that was mentioned at the start of this chapter used snowball sampling. This way, the interviewer would start with interviewing one respondent who fits the profile. This respondent would then be asked to provide names and addresses of acquaintances who also meet the requirements for the population. This is one of the more effective ways to interview women in the Middle East and many Asian countries.

Convenience sampling is used to obtain information quickly and inexpensively. Selection criteria could be as simple as the first few commuters getting off a local subway or students enrolled for a class in a certain university. This method is not very accurate and can be used only in exploratory research.

Quota sampling is judgmental sampling with the condition that a certain minimum number be included from each specified subgroup. The subgroups are typically formed on the basis of some demographic variable like age, sex, location, and income. Consider research that involves studying the television preferences of teenagers. The researcher wants to sample teenage boys and girls from local schools who visit a mall that is located in the same area. The researcher can work under the assumption that all teenagers who visit the mall attend local schools and are not visiting from another city. If it is known that the percentage of teenage boys in the area is 60 percent and the required sample size is 300, the researcher should interview 180 teenage boys visiting the mall.

In their haste to meet quotas, researchers sometimes ignore problems that are related to statistical principles. Consider the following example of a study conducted in the United States and Canada to evaluate the impact of the free trade agreement on employment. The study will be sampling male and female workers. The distribution of this population in two cities is given in Table 12-1.

The study requires a sample of 100 people, so researchers decide to go in for 50 Americans and 50 Canadians. Further, they decide to have a sample with 50 percent males. The quotas could then be as given in Table 12-2. It can be observed in the table that the marginal frequencies—50 percent and 50 percent—match; however, the joint frequencies in each cell—30 percent, 20 percent, and 30 percent—do not match. This type of error should be avoided when selecting quotas.

TABLE 12-1	Population Distribution			
	Male	*Female*	*Total*	*Percent*
United States	300	200	500	50
Canada	200	300	500	50
Total	500	500	1000	100
Percent	50	50	100	

Advantages and Disadvantages of Sampling Techniques

Simple random sampling is easy to conduct when the required sampling frame and the target population list are available. This is not always the case in international marketing research. Locating people, addresses, and streets can be a complicated task. For instance, in a lot of Asian countries, residences are identified by names rather than numbers. Even when numbers are used, there are not in a sequential order. Many parts of these countries do not have street maps, therefore, simple random sampling may prove very costly and time consuming in international marketing research.

Stratified sampling can be very effective in making the sample representative of the population by giving greater importance to segments of the population who have a more significant impact on the study; however, in the international context, identifying this segment of the population could present problems.

Systematic random sampling works very well with telephone interviews, even in countries that do not have most of the telephone numbers listed; however, it is very difficult to use for mail or personal interviews because obtaining the list of respondents and their mailing addresses could prove very cumbersome in some countries.

Cluster sampling involves surveying only certain subgroups of the selected sample. If the researcher was conducting a study in Germany and decided to sample only major cities like Frankfurt and Berlin, there would be significant savings in terms of time and cost; however, a critical assumption in this method is that the population characteristics of people living in Frankfurt and Berlin are similar. Otherwise, significant bias may be introduced in the study.

Judgment sampling provides an efficient way of obtaining the sample if done by an expert in the area of interest. This is particularly true of industrial marketing research, which calls for in-depth knowledge on the part of the respondent. In countries with low

TABLE 12-2	Population Quotas			
	Male	*Female*	*Total*	*Percent*
United States	50	0	50	50
Canada	0	50	50	50
Total	50	50	100	100
Percent	50	50	100	

levels of literacy, the researcher is free to sample educated people who are better informed than the general population. The flip side to this method is that, in the international context, the researcher may not always know the market very well. It is also possible that ignoring the vast majority of the population and selecting only a certain specific category of respondents may introduce bias in the research study.

Snowball sampling relies primarily on the initial respondents to obtain a list of more respondents. The problem with this technique is that the initial respondents tend to give names of people who are similar to them in terms of demographics. This could lead to the selection of a sample that is not representative of the population.

Convenience sampling is a very simple method where respondents who are willing or are easy to contact are surveyed. The advantage is the low cost of conducting the surveys and availability of information in a very short span of time; however, this method could introduce substantial bias as it may not be representative of the population.

Quota sampling is an appropriate method for surveying people from a specific industry. This method ensures that a representative sample is obtained quickly and with relatively low expense. Because the judgment of the researcher is involved, it is necessary that researchers be knowledgeable of the markets where the study is being conducted. Exhibit 12-3 summarizes a method developed to eliminate the disadvantages of quota sampling.

EXHIBIT 12-3

BMRB: GRID Sampling

The British Market Research Bureau (BMRB) has developed a method of sampling called GRID in order to eliminate the unsatisfactory features of quota sampling, while at the same time avoiding the costs and constraints attached to strict probability methods.

A small set of homogenous streets is taken as the starting point. Respondents are drawn from these streets using proportional sampling based on stratification by their ACORN characteristics. The characteristics required of the potential respondents are determined by the research study and quotas are set in accordance with the required characteristics.

GRID sampling differs from the traditional random sampling in the final stage where the streets are selected. The first stage of selection involves random sampling of wards and parishes listed within ascending order of ACORN neighborhood types. Within these selected wards and parishes, streets are selected at random. Because of this methodology, the sensitivity of this technique is increased due to cluster analysis performed on all of the districts listed in the ACORN neighborhood types and the increased scope and sophistication of technology used in selection of streets and potential respondents.

Source: Adapted from *Marketing Research,* 5th Edition, Peter Chisnall, Berkshire, England: McGraw Hill Publications, 1997, p. 98. Reprinted by permission of Professor P.M. Chisnall.

DETERMINING THE SAMPLE SIZE

The size of a sample can be determined either by using statistical techniques or through some ad hoc methods. Ad hoc methods are used when a person knows from experience what sample size to adopt or when there are some constraints, such as budgetary constraints, that dictate the sample size. This section discusses a few common ad hoc methods for determining sample size.

Rules of Thumb

One approach to determining sample size is to use some rules of thumb. Researchers suggest that the sample should be large enough so that when it is divided into groups, each group will have a minimum sample size of 100 or more.[3] Suppose that the opinion of people from various countries regarding a computer software package is desired. In particular, an estimation is to be made of the percentage who felt that some of the advanced features (which means that the package will be priced substantially higher) are required. Suppose, further, that a comparison is desired among those who (1) use these features frequently, (2) use these features occasionally, and (3) never use these features. The sample size should be such that each of these groups has at least 100 people. If the frequent users, the smallest group, are thought to be about 10 percent of the population, then under simple random sampling a sample size of 1,000 would be needed to generate a group of 100 subjects.

In almost every study, a comparison between groups provides useful information and is often the motivating reason for the study. It is therefore necessary to consider the smallest group and to make sure that it is of sufficient size to provide the needed reliability.

In addition to considering comparisons between major groups, the analysis might consider subgroups. For example, there might be an interest in breaking down the group of frequent users by age and comparing the usage by teenagers, young adults, middle-aged persons, and senior citizens. Sudman suggests that for such minor breakdowns the minimum sample size in each subgroup should be 20 to 50.[4] The assumption is that less accuracy is needed for the subgroups. Suppose that the smallest subgroup of frequent users, the experienced programmers, is about 1 percent of the population and it is desired to have 20 in each subgroup. Under simple random sampling, a sample size of about 2,000 might be recommended in this case.

If one of the groups or subgroups of the population is a relatively small percentage of the population, then it is sensible to use disproportionate sampling. Suppose that only 10 percent of the population watches educational television, and the opinions of this group are to be compared with those of others in the population. If telephone interviewing is involved, people might be contacted randomly until 100 people who do not watch educational television are identified. The interviewing then would continue, but all respondents would be screened, and only those who watch educational television would be interviewed. The result would be a sample of 200, half of whom watch educational television.

Budget Constraints

Often there is a strict budget constraint. A museum director might be able to spare only $500 for a study, and no more. If data analysis will require $100 and a respondent interview is $5, then the maximum affordable sample size is 80. The question then becomes whether a sample size of 80 is worthwhile, or if the study should be changed or simply not conducted.

Comparable Studies

Another approach is to find similar studies and use their sample sizes as a guide. The studies should be comparable in terms of the number of groups into which the sample is divided for comparison purposes. They also should have achieved a satisfactory level of reliability.

Table 12-3, which is based on a summary of several hundred studies, provides a very rough idea of a typical sample size. Note that the typical sample size tends to be larger for national studies than for regional studies. A possible reason is that national studies generally address issues with more financial impact and therefore require a bit more accuracy. Note, also, that samples involving institutions tend to be smaller than those involving people or households. The reason is probably that institutions are more costly to sample than people.

Factors Determining Sample Size

Sample size really depends on four factors. The first is the number of groups and subgroups within the sample that will be analyzed. The second is the value of the information in the study in general, and the accuracy required of the results in particular. At one extreme, the research need not be conducted if the study is of little importance. The third factor is the cost of the sample. A cost-benefit analysis must be considered. A larger sample size can be more easily justified if sampling costs are low than if sampling costs are high. The final factor is the variability of the population. If all members of the population have identical opinions on an issue, a sample of one is satisfactory. As the variability within the population increases, the sample size also will need to be larger.

Let us assume that we are interested in the attitudes of symphony season-ticket holders toward changing the starting time of weekday performances from 8:00 P.M. to 7:30 P.M. The population comprises the 10,000 symphony season-ticket holders. Of these ticket holders, 3,000 respond "definitely yes" (which is coded as +2). Another 2,000 would "prefer yes" (coded as +1), and so on. The needed information is the average, or mean, response of the population (the 10,000 season-ticket holders), which is termed μ:

$$\mu = \text{population mean} = 0.3$$

TABLE 12-3 Typical Sample Sizes for Studies of Human and Institutional Populations

Number of Subgroup Analyses	People or Households		Institutions	
	National	*Regional or Special*	*National*	*Regional or Special*
None or few	1,000–1,500	200–500	200–500	50–200
Average	1,500–2,500	500–1,000	500–1,000	200–500
Many	2,500+	1,000–	1,000+	500+

Source: From *Applied Sampling* by Seymour Sudman, Academic Press, 1976. Reprinted by permission.

This population mean is one population characteristic of interest. Normally, it is unknown, and our goal is to determine its value as closely as possible by taking a sample from the population.

Another population characteristic of interest is the population variance, σ^2, and its square root, the population standard deviation, σ. The population variance is a measure of the population dispersion, the degree to which the different season-ticket holders differ from one another in terms of their attitude. It is based on the degree to which a response differs from the population average response, μ. This difference is squared (making all values positive) and averaged across all responses. In our example, the population variance is

$$\sigma^2 = \text{population variance} = 2.22$$

and

$$\sigma = \text{population standard deviation} = 1.49$$

The problem is that the population mean is not known but must be estimated from a sample. Assume that a simple random sample of size 10 is taken from the population. The 10 people selected and their respective attitudes are shown in Table 12-4.

Just as the population has a set of characteristics, each sample also has a set of characteristics. One sample characteristic is the sample average, or mean:

$$\bar{X} = \frac{1}{10}\sum_{j=1}^{10} X_j = 0.5$$

Two means now have been introduced, and it is important to keep them separate. One is the population mean (μ), a population characteristic. The second is the sample mean ($\bar{X}$), a sample characteristic. Because $\bar{X}$ is a sample characteristic, it will change if a new sample is obtained. The sample mean ($\bar{X}$) is used to estimate the unknown population mean (μ).

TABLE 12-4 Attitude of Broadway Ticket Holders

Attitude

Nakamichi	$X_1 = +1$
John S.	$X_2 = +2$
Paula R.	$X_3 = +2$
Francois T.	$X_4 = 0$
Werner R.	$X_5 = +1$
Vinod K.	$X_6 = +1$
Amir K.	$X_7 = -1$
Jose F.	$X_8 = +1$
Spiros M.	$X_9 = -2$
Zhang T.	$X_{10} = 0$

Another sample characteristic or statistic is the sample variance (s^2), which can be used to estimate the population variance (s^2). Under simple random sampling, the sample variance is

$$s^2 = \frac{1}{n-1}\sum_{j=1}^{n}(X_j - \bar{X})^2 = 1.61$$

Note that s^2 will be small if the sample responses are similar, and large if they are spread out. The corresponding sample standard deviation is simply

$$S = \text{sample standard deviation} = \sqrt{s^2} = 1.27$$

Again, it is important to make a distinction between the population variance (σ^2) and the sample variance (s^2).

Of course, all samples will not generate the same value of $\bar{X}$ (or s). If another simple random sample of size 10 were taken from the population, $\bar{X}$ might be 0.3 or 1.2 or 0.4, or whatever. The point is that $\bar{X}$ will vary from sample to sample.

Intuitively, it is reasonable to believe that the variation in $\bar{X}$ will be larger as the variance in the population σ^2 is larger. At one extreme, if there is no variation in the population, there will be no variation in $\bar{X}$. It also is reasonable to believe that as the size of the sample increases, the variation in $\bar{X}$ will decrease. When the sample is small, it takes only one or two extreme scores to substantially affect the sample mean, thus generating a relatively large or small $\bar{X}$. As the sample size increases, these extreme values will have less impact when they do appear, because they will be averaged with more values. The variation in $\bar{X}$ is measured by its standard error, which is

$$\sigma_{\bar{X}} = \text{standard error of } X = \sigma_x/\sqrt{n} = 1.49/\sqrt{10} = 0.47$$

(σ_x can be written simply as σ). Note that the standard error of $\bar{X}$ depends on n, the sample size. If n is altered, the standard error will change accordingly, as Table 12-5 shows.

Now we are finally ready to use these concepts to help determine sample size. To proceed, the analyst must specify the size of the sampling error that is desired and the confidence level; for example, the 95 percent confidence level.

This specification will depend on a trade-off between the value of more accurate information and the cost of an increased sample size. For a given confidence level, a smaller sampling error will "cost" in terms of a larger sample size. Similarly, for a given sampling error, a higher confidence level will "cost" in terms of a larger sample size. These statements will become more tangible in the context of some examples.

TABLE 12-5 Increasing Sample Size

Sample Size	σ_x	$\sigma_{\bar{x}} = \sigma_x/\sqrt{n}$
10	1.49	0.470
40	1.49	0.235
100	1.49	0.149
500	1.49	0.067

Using the general formula for the interval estimate (recall that s and s_x are the same),

$$\bar{X} \pm \text{sampling error, or } \bar{X} \pm z\sigma_x/\sqrt{n}$$

we know that

$$\text{sampling error} = z\sigma/\sqrt{n}$$

dividing through by the sampling error and multiplying by $\sqrt{n}$

$$\sqrt{n} = z\sigma/(\text{sampling error})$$

and squaring both sides, we get an expression for sample size

$$n = z^2\sigma^2/(\text{sampling error})^2$$

Thus, if we know the required confidence level, and therefore z, and also know the allowed sampling error, then the needed sample size is specified by the formula.

Let us assume that we need to have a 95 percent confidence level and that our sampling error in estimating the population mean does not exceed 0.3. In this case, the sampling error = 0.3, and, because the confidence level is 95 percent, $z = 2$. The population standard deviation is 1.49, so the sample size should be

$$n = 2^2(1.49)^2/(0.3)^2 = 98.7 \approx 99$$

If the confidence level is changed from 95 percent to 90 percent, the sample size can be reduced because we do not have to be as certain of the resulting estimate. The z term is then 5/3 and the sample size is

$$n = (z\sigma)^2/(\text{sampling error})^2 = (5/3)^2(1.49)^2/(0.3)^2 = 68.5 \approx 69$$

If the allowed error is increased, the sample size will also decrease, even if a 95 percent confidence level is retained. In our example, if the allowed error is increased to 0.5, then the sample size is

$$n = (z\sigma)^2/(\text{sampling error})^2 = 4(1.49)^2/(0.5)^2 = 35.5 \approx 36$$

It should be noted that the sample size calculation is independent of the size of the population. A common misconception is that a "good" sample should include a relatively high percentage of the sampling frame. Actually, the size of the sample will be determined in the same manner, whether the population is 1,000 or 1,000,000. There should be no concern that the sample contain a reasonable percentage of the population. Of course, if the population is small, the sample size can be reduced. Obviously, the sample size should not exceed the population.

Determining the Population Standard Deviation

The procedure just displayed assumes that the population standard deviation is known. In most practical situations it is not known, and it must be estimated by using one of several available approaches.

One method is to use a sample standard deviation obtained from a previous comparable survey or from a pilot survey. Another approach is to estimate s subjectively. Suppose the task is to estimate the income of a community. It might be possible to say that 95 percent of the people will have a monthly income of between $4,000 and $20,000. Assuming a normal distribution, there will be four population standard deviations between the two figures, so that one population standard deviation will be equal to $4,000.

Another approach is to take a "worst-case" situation. In our example, the largest population variance would occur if half the population would respond with a +2 and the other half with a −2. The population variance would then be 4. The recommended sample size, at a 95 percent confidence level and a 0.3 allowable error, would be 178. Note that the sample size would be larger than desired, and thus the desired accuracy would be exceeded. The logic is that it is acceptable to err on the side of being too accurate.

Proportions

When proportions are to be estimated (the proportion of people with negative feelings about a change in the symphony's starting time, for example), the procedure is to use the sample proportion to estimate the unknown population proportion, π. Because this estimate is based on a sample, it has a population variance, namely,

$$\sigma^2_p = \pi(1 - \pi)/n$$

where
  π = population proportion
  p = sample proportion (corresponding to X), used to estimate the unknown
σ^2_p = population variance of p

The formula for sample size is then

$$n = z^2\, \pi(1 - \pi)/(\text{sampling error})^2$$

As Figure 12-2 shows, the worst case (where the population variance is at its maximum) occurs when the population proportion is equal to 0.50:

$$\pi(1 - \pi) = 0.25$$

$$\pi = 0.50$$

Because the population proportion is unknown, a common procedure is to assume the worst case. The formula for sample size then simplifies to

$$n = z^2(0.25)/(\text{sampling error})^2$$

FIGURE 12-2   A Graph of $\pi(1 - \pi)$

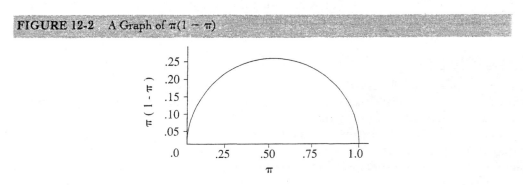

Thus, if the population proportion is to be estimated within an error of 0.05 (or 5 percentage points) at a 95 percent confidence level, the needed sample size is

$$n = 2^2(0.25)/(0.05)^2 = 400$$

since z equals 2, corresponding to a 95 percent confidence level, and the allowed sampling error equals 0.05. Figure 12-3 summarizes the two sample size formulas.

Sampling error (also known as *accuracy* or *precision error*) can be defined in relative rather than absolute terms. In other words, a researcher might require that the sample estimate be within plus or minus G percentage points of the population value. Therefore,

$$D = G\mu$$

The sample size formula may be written as

$$n = \sigma^2 z^2/(\text{sampling error})^2$$

where

$$c = (\sigma/\mu)$$

which is known as the *coefficient of variation*.

Several Questions

A survey instrument or an experiment usually will not be based on just one question—sometimes hundreds can be involved. It usually will not be worthwhile to go through such a process for all questions. A reasonable approach is to pick a few representative questions and determine the sample size from them. The most crucial ones with the highest expected variance should be included.

FIGURE 12-3 Some Useful Sample Size Formulas

In general

Sample size $= n = z^2 \sigma^2 \div (\text{sampling error})^2$

where

$z = 2$ for a 95 percent confidence

$z = \frac{5}{3}$ for a 90 percent confidence

$\sigma =$ population standard deviation

and

sampling error $=$ allowed sampling error

For proportions

sample size $= n = z^2 (0.25) \div (\text{sampling error})^2$

Cost-Benefit Analysis

Selection of the sampling procedure is an issue that needs a great deal of attention in international marketing research. Owing to the national differences, sampling procedures have different degrees of reliability in different countries, therefore, it is important for the researcher to use the procedure that is most effective in the country of interest. In a multicountry study, it is not necessary to use one method across all countries. It may be preferable to use different methods or procedures that provide equivalent sampling reliability. It is important for the researcher to focus on comparability in terms of response rates and quality of responses. The specific method that is used is secondary. There will also be a considerable difference in costs when different sampling methods are used. It is possible that standardizing the sampling methods results in centralized coding and analysis; however, the benefits of standardization may be far outweighed by the costs incurred in administering a specific sampling plan or due to loss of accuracy in sampling. For instance, if the research study called for random sampling in all countries, the cost of obtaining lists of potential respondents may be exorbitant in some countries. In such cases, the researcher should compromise on the sampling technique and opt for the method that is most cost-efficient while maintaining the accuracy and reliability of the study.

SAMPLING EQUIVALENCE

In international marketing research, it is important to make sure that the samples drawn from different countries are comparable. The stress is not on the equivalence of the method used or the profile from which the sample has been drawn, but rather on the equivalence of the information collected from the sample. Two different aspects need to be taken care of to ensure this.

The first step is to decide who should be contacted for the survey and whether the study needs to have a single respondent or multiple respondents within a household. This is typically dependent on the decision-making process involved and could vary widely among countries. A decision that is made by an individual in one country could be made jointly by two or more people in some other country. In the corporate world, decisions are made at different levels in the corporate ladder. The target segment could vary among countries. All of these differences have to be accounted for if the population sampled is to yield results that can be compared across borders. Examples for this aspect of sampling are numerous. For instance, the decision to make a large investment would be a joint decision with most married couples in the United States. In the Middle East, however, women are not consulted in such matters. If the study involves asking respondents about their investment habits, to get complete information we need to talk to both of the partners in the United States, while it is sufficient to survey the male partner in the Middle East. Children have a major say in a lot of purchase decisions in the United States, while this is hardly the case in many other countries. This goes to show that different categories of people will have to be surveyed to obtain similar information.

The second issue deals with the extent to which the sample is representative of the population. In most developed countries, information regarding potential markets and sampling frames is easily available; however, in Japan the residential list that was most popularly used in sampling studies has been made inaccessible to researchers.[5] Developing countries do not have such extensive databases and so obtaining the sampling frame to suit the needs of the research could be difficult. Researchers will have to employ different methods in different countries to obtain representative samples. In remote parts of certain developing countries where literacy levels are low, researchers have to survey folks who are reasonably well-educated. This automatically induces a bias, as the portion of the population not surveyed will be substantially different. In situations like this, judgment sampling or snowball sampling is more effective. The other part of this issue is whether the data from one segment or country can be extrapolated to other countries or segments. It is possible to group countries into clusters based on demographic and psychographic similarities. Sampling results can be extrapolated for such clusters. Many researchers use the Nielsen Regions for this purpose; however, extrapolation at national levels may produce significant bias in international marketing research.

CULTURAL ISSUES

Identifying the right kind of sampling and using the appropriate sampling method for an international marketing research project depends on a number of factors, the foremost of which would be the cultural differences in these countries. There are several practical problems faced by the researcher. A research study conducted for a software development company based in the United States highlights all of these issues. The study involved finding the market potential for software applications in Great Britain, Germany, Japan, France, and Belgium. The target sample was the chief information officers, system managers, and system development professionals of major companies in all of these countries. The main issue was to find the equivalent sample in all of these countries. There was the option of sampling people with identical or similar titles; however, this would not have provided information that could be compared across all five countries. The first step in this study was to understand the responsibilities and job descriptions of each of the categories that need to be sampled. The next step was to identify professionals who perform similar functions and carry similar job responsibilities in all of these countries, irrespective of the job titles. The responses from this sample could be compared across countries. In the end, it helps to pay attention to sampling design issues without getting too obsessed with them.[6]

MODIFICATIONS REQUIRED
FOR DEVELOPING COUNTRIES[7]

It is a lot more difficult for researchers to obtain samples in developing countries because of nonexistent or poor sampling frames. Most of these countries do not have registers, age and sex breakdowns, telephone directories, maps, or numbering on dwelling units. It is very difficult to get details of universal characteristics from which a meaningful sample can be drawn. Even if any of the above resources are available, they are very outdated and inaccurate. Due to lack of sampling resources, it is possible that large segments of the population are excluded from the sampling process. An example would be Brazil, where Rio de Janeiro and São Paulo have different sampling frames because sampling resources tend to be distributed differentially throughout the country. A "national urban sample" combining these different sampling frames in different cities is likely to yield less than perfectly accurate results. An additional problem in rapidly growing cites is maintaining adequate sampling frames. The expense involved in keeping them up-to-date is prohibitively high. In many cases, it becomes very important to specify terms, such as the exact meaning of a dwelling unit in the given research context. Consequently, coverage and comparability of existing sampling frames in developing countries often leave much to be desired and modifications in the sampling procedure are necessary.

An important fallout of this is that convenience, judgment, quota, and snowball sampling are used more frequently in developing countries than probability sampling methods. They are more cost effective and yield better results than probability sampling methods. Convenience sampling, though the cheapest method, is not likely to be very effective. Judgment sampling in these countries is based on the assumption that some members are better informed than others. An example would be asking the opinions of the village head, the priest, or any other local authority and assuming these opinions reflect that of the territory. Quota sampling requires that the researcher have some idea about the region to set aside quotas in a logical manner. Snowball sampling obtains a list of people to be interviewed from one interviewee. The best way to work out a sampling plan for developing countries is for researchers to observe and devise their own sampling frames.

Another important factor that needs to be considered for developing countries is that the markets are likely to be more fragmented, different markets within developing countries. Each sample should be representative of the population that represents a potential market. An example could be widely varying income levels in a given geographic territory. In this case it becomes necessary to choose an appropriate clustering procedure.

INTERNATIONAL MARKETING RESEARCH IN PRACTICE

Sampling is a very important aspect of the marketing research process and has a big impact on the validity of results. In the international scenario, this tends to be crucial because of the lack of information available to the researcher. This section attempts to help researchers avoid some common pitfalls of sampling with the help of examples from practical research problems conducted in the past.

A refrigerator manufacturer is interested in understanding the decision-making process involved in purchasing a refrigerator in several countries around the world. Some of the countries identified for the research process are the United States, Great Britain, and India. An appropriate sampling method has to be decided for each of these countries. In the United States and Great Britain, researchers decide to opt for random sampling of households in a geographically dispersed manner such that the sample is representative of these countries as a whole. The logic behind this decision is fairly clear—almost every household in these two countries has a refrigerator and so the probability of reaching a household that does not own one is negligible. It is also very easy to obtain a list of names and phone numbers in both of these countries. Let us consider the sampling process in India. The sheer size and cultural diversity of the country makes random sampling impossible. A more important factor that rules out random sampling is the fact that the majority of households do not own a refrigerator. A more appropriate method will be snowball sampling or convenience sampling. There is also the problem of obtaining the names and addresses of all the people to be contacted.

Selecting a sampling frame could also be a complicated decision in many countries. Consider the case of a financial services company wanting to evaluate customer satisfaction in various countries. For a researcher in the United States this would be a simple task—design a questionnaire that would allow customers to rate the company on different aspects of customer service. This questionnaire could then be administered to customers; however, in some countries, this simple procedure could prove very difficult to implement. In Brazil, the survey will be completely unsuccessful because any survey pertaining to personal finances is perceived as an audit by the tax department. In some Middle Eastern countries, the male members of the household make all the investment decisions, so even if the records indicate a female client, it would be useful to contact the spouse or the guardian. The sampling frame has to be redefined depending on the decision-making process. In most third world countries the concept of service is alien to customers and companies. Anything beyond basic service is considered a favor bestowed upon the customer. In such situations, questioning customers on service aspects does not make any sense.

Anticipating changes in economic, political, and social set up in different countries is very important to research studies, especially to sampling. A survey conducted to study public opinion in the former Soviet Union is an example.[8] Researchers anticipated the break-up of the Soviet Union and that the Baltic States would leave the Union. As these states were too small to make a major impact on the results, researchers decided to exclude them from the study. A thorough understanding of the country is required even before the decision to choose a sampling method is considered.

In this section we present a practical research problem with emphasis on the sampling method adopted for an international market.[9] Psychographics is an approach used to define and measure the lifestyles of consumers. It is a popular method employed by advertisers and marketers because it can provide more detailed information about consumers than basic demographic variables. Psychographic research involves two phases: the first phase includes determining the appropriate psychographic statements; the second phase focuses on developing a typology of consumers. A key factor is to capitalize consumer differences by identifying segments of consumers who differ significantly within the population, while also identifying consumers who display similar behavior.

This study had two objectives. The first was to generate the psychographic dimensions of female consumers in Greater China (The People's Republic of China, Hong Kong, and Taiwan), and the second was to develop a typology of female consumers based on their psychographic patterns. The chosen sample was restricted to working females between the ages of 18 and 35. The reason for selecting this age group is that it constitutes a relatively large percentage of the female population in the three regions, as well as appearing to be a very lucrative market segment.

Previous studies conducted in Hong Kong identified five distinct segments on the basis of respondents' attitudes and beliefs. These are listed in Exhibit 12-4. Similar studies conducted in Taiwan provided eight different segments, listed in Exhibit 12-5.

There were no published studies for China; however, consumers in mainland China are characterized by geographical factors and their consumption pattern varies widely across the country. It was observed that consumption power is generally higher in the South, while the consumers in the North tend to be more selective, and that Southerners are heavily influenced by Hong Kong and have greater access to foreign products.

The questionnaire design was completed after reviewing a lot of literature. The final version of the questionnaire consisted of three parts. The first part comprised interest and opinion statements, the second part contained frequency of participation activity statements, and the third part consisted of items relating to demographic information. The selection of lifestyle statements was based on three criteria: they had to be relevant to females, valuable to marketers, and measurable.

The target population was working females in the age group of 18 to 35. The objective was to obtain three groups of females who were matched in terms of age characteristics rather than in the representativeness of the working female population in each

---

EXHIBIT 12-4

Segmentation in Hong Kong

Segment	*Characteristics*
Traditionalists	Adhere closely to old attitudes and beliefs; resistant to change: reluctant to try new and premium products; tend to remain strongly loyal to brands frequently purchased; account for 41% percent of the population.
Strivers	Very materialistic; immersed in an aggressive pursuit of achievement; impulse buyers looking for instant gratification; want change of roles in their lives but most not likely to achieve this; population with an average of 31 years; make up 20 percent of the population.
Achievers	More successful than strivers, even though they also value achievement and materialism; can be described as "yuppies"; constitute 23 percent of the population.
Super-Achievers	A smaller sub-segment of Achievers—make up 7 percent of the Achiever population; very keen on luxuries and the first to latch on to new trends, products, and premium brands.
Adapters	Generally older people; comfortable with their achievements in life, but open to new experiences: make up 13 percent of the population.

Source: Adapted from "Research note: Psychographic segmentation of the female market in Greater China," by Jackie L. M. Tam and Ms. Susan Tai in *International Marketing Review*, Vol. 15, Iss. 1, 1998. Reprinted by permission of MCB University Press.

EXHIBIT 12-5

Segmentation in Taiwan

Segment	Characteristics
Traditional Homebodies	Less affluent, had little interest in buying or trying new products; about 16 percent of the population.
Confident Traditionalists	Middle-aged, predominantly male group; had a high self-image and a keen sense of social norms and expectations. (12 percent)
Discontented Moderns	Relatively affluent and younger; tended to follow Japanese and Western trends but maintained a number of traditional attitudes. (17 percent)
Rebellious Youths	Generally aged between 15 and 24 with a strong sense of individualism; impulsive buyers when it came to things that aroused their interest. (7 percent)
Young Strivers	Average age of 29; competitive and materialistic natures; appeared to be the most likely group to succeed in future. (13 percent)
Middle-Class Hopefuls	Averages 31 years; moderate spenders and willing to take a few risks with their finances. (8 percent)
Family Centered Fatalists	Primarily females aged 42 years. Not particularly affluent; tended to live slower paced lives. (13 percent)
Lethargics	Average age of 32; did not stand out in any way but were buyers of mass consumer products. (14 percent)

Source: From "Research note: Psychographic segmentation of the female market in Greater China," by Jackie L. M. Tam and Ms. Susan Tai in *International Marketing Review*, Vol. 15, Iss. 1, 1998. Reprinted by permission of MCB University Press.

---

region. The samples were drawn independently from the office districts of Guangzhou, Hong Kong, and Taipei. The respondents were approached randomly in high traffic office districts so as to make the samples drawn from the three cities comparable. The researchers employed the quota sampling method. The questionnaire was self-administered to respondents in Taipei and personal interviews were conducted in Guangzhou and Hong Kong. After a preliminary analysis it was found that there were 182 usable questionnaires from Guangzhou and 188 each from Hong Kong and Taipei.

The majority of the respondents from Taiwan and Hong Kong were found to be single. In contrast, more than half the respondents from China were married, even though the age distribution across the three groups was very similar. The education level of respondents from China and Taiwan was very similar—more than 60 percent had attained university education; however, only 19.1 percent of the respondents from Hong Kong had attained university education. This could be accounted for by the fact that job markets in China and Taiwan are very competitive. The researchers performed factor analysis and cluster analysis on the data. Each of these methods is explained in detail in chapter 15.

Summary

This chapter deals in depth with the sampling procedures that can be made use of in international marketing research. Researchers choose a subset of elements from the population and this subset is called the sample. A sampling distribution is the probability distribution of the statistic. If the difference between the population parameter and sample statistic is only because of sampling, this is called sampling error. If there is a difference between the population parameter and the sampling statistic that is not due to sampling error, it is called nonsampling error. If the sampling frame chosen is smaller than the population, some members of the population are not sampled and, hence, the research study does not consider their tastes and attitudes. This is called a subset problem. If the sampling frame is larger than the population, we have a superset problem. Sampling methods can be classified as probability sampling and nonprobability sampling. In probability sampling, each member of the population has a known probability of being selected. The chapter discusses in detail many different probability and nonprobability sampling methods and the advantages and disadvantages of each of these methods. The chapter also explains the statistical basis for the selection of a sample size and the means of achieving sampling equivalence in international marketing research. It is important to note that defining the population, choosing a sampling frame, and selecting a sampling procedure are very country-specific and are constrained by the resources available.

Questions and Problems

1. Develop a population list or sampling frame for an attitude study when the target population is
   a. All those who rode on a public transit system during the last month in New York
   b. Retail sporting good stores in London
   c. Stores that sell tennis rackets in India
   d. High-income families in Brazil
2. a. How does the sampling procedure employed in an international environment differ from that used domestically?
   b. What issues are relevant to a researcher's decision to use the same sampling procedure across countries?
3. A telephone survey is planned to determine the day-after recall of several test commercials to be run in Sydney, Australia. Design a telephone sampling plan.
4. A concept for a new microcomputer designed for use in the home is to be tested. Because a demonstration is required, a personal interview is necessary. Thus, it has been decided to bring a product demonstrator into the home. The city of Rome has been selected for the test. The metropolitan-area map has been divided into a grid of 22,500 squares, 100 of which have been selected randomly. Interviewers have been sent out to call on homes within the selected square until five interviews are completed. Comment on the design. Would you make any changes?
5. Discuss the differences between stratified sampling and cluster sampling.
6. Identify a situation where you would be in favor of using a nonprobability method over a probability sampling method.

7. Discuss the differences between proportionate and disproportionate stratified sampling.

8. Jane Walker is the founder and CEO of Sport Style, a sporting goods manufacturing company based in Louisville, Kentucky, that specializes in leather goods. The company currently is under contract to exclusively supply one of the leading sporting goods companies with Sport Style accessories. That large multinational company markets the products under its own major company label as part of its "Made in the USA" promotional campaign. Sport Style has expanded its product line to include golf gloves; premium quality leather grips for tennis, squash, racquetball, and badminton rackets; and sports bags. The contract for exclusive supply will expire within the next year.

Ms. Walker has recently felt that Sport Style specialized products may not be best served by this method of distribution, and she believes that her company's sales revenue could drastically increase if Sport Style were to market its goods under its own label as a specialty good. This would allow the company to eliminate the intermediaries and their portion of the selling price. The specialty goods could be offered at the same price as is currently being asked, but without the intermediary Sport Style would get a larger proportion of the final retail sales price. Ms. Walker has decided to undertake a marketing research study to determine whether a market exists among retail outlets and sporting goods distributors for these specialty items, under the Sport Style brand name.

a. Define the target population for this study.

b. Suggest a suitable sampling frame.

c. Recommend a sampling procedure for this study and support your answer.

Endnotes

1. William Trochim, http://trochim.human.cornell.edu/kb/sampstat.htm, 1996.

2. Edward Leslie, "Some Observations on Doing Business in Japan," *Business America.* (10 February 1992), 2–4.

3. Seymour, Sudman, *Applied Sampling* (NY: Academic Press, 1976), 50.

4. Ibid.

5. Kazuaki Katori, "Recent Developments and Future Trends in Marketing Research in Japan Using New Electronic Media," *Journal of Advertising Research* (April/May 1990): 53–57.

6. Uma Sekharan, "Methodological and Theoretical Issues and Advancements in Cross-Cultural Research," *Journal of International Business Studies*, no. 4 (1991): 711–721.

7. Joanna, Kinsey, *Marketing in Developing Countries.* (London: Macmillan Education Ltd, 1994).

8. James L. Gibson, "Mass Opposition to the Soviet Putsch of August 1991: Collective Action, Rational Choice, and Democratic Values in the Former Soviet Union," *American Political Review*, 91, no 3 (September 1993).

9. Jackie L. M. Tam, and Susan H. C. Tai. "The Psychographic Segmentation of the Female Market in Greater China," *International Marketing Review* 15, no. 1 (1988): 61–77.

Part II
Section IV

C H A P T E R

Asia-Pacific
17

INTRODUCTION

The countries that comprise the Asia-Pacific region tend to be extremely diverse in terms of culture as well as market characteristics. Several countries in Asia can be categorized as high-context cultures where there is significant emphasis placed on authority figures to endorse or suggest product usage. While advertising and marketing serve as effective means to determine consumer interest and purchase, the role of word of mouth and of role models is to be noted as well. Most Asian countries can be classified as collectivistic, where familial decision-making patterns as well as group interaction tend to be high as compared to the United States.

The differences in purchasing power and infrastructure are to be noted when trying to reach the entire Asia-Pacific market. The newly industrialized economies of Taiwan, Singapore, and South Korea are markedly different from the South Asian economies, India, Pakistan, and Bangladesh, as are some of the Association of Southeast Asian Nations (ASEAN) countries composed of Malaysia, the Philippines, Indonesia, Thailand, Myanmar, Brunei, Vietnam, Cambodia, and Laos. The economic volatility of these countries implies that companies should consider not only the demographic and psychographic characteristics prior to marketing, but look into the chief aspect of affordability. There is also a significant difference in tastes that should be taken into account. In the Philippines, while McDonald's used their standard menu, a rival company adapted its menu to suit the local tastes. McDonald's soon found that they had only 16 percent of the market share and the rival's business was booming.[1]

REGIONAL CHARACTERISTICS

The World Bank estimates that over 1.8 billion people live in the Pacific Rim today, representing almost one-third of the world's population. Regional trade agreements help to bring these consumers together into cohesive trade blocs, further encouraging and facilitating international trade. U.S. companies are able to reach these consumers in a manageable fashion by targeting surveys to the appropriate respondents. The economic transformation occurring throughout most Pacific Rim countries has been called an "Economic Explosion." The Gross Regional Product (GRP) in 1992 was over U.S. $14 trillion. Of the U.S. $7 trillion in world trade last year, 33.6 percent was generated in the Pacific Rim. With the exploding economic growth, consumers' standards of living and their ability to purchase U.S. goods and services through the mail will grow as well. As large multinational companies invest and begin operating in the Pacific Rim, more and more Americans are moving there. In Japan alone, there are over 47,000 U.S. citizens on business assignments (and over 24,000 in Hong Kong). Many of these potential consumers live on comfortable expatriate compensation packages, enjoy receiving mail from home, and like buying American products.

Education and overall industrialization is increasing throughout most Pacific Rim countries. This trend results in more sophisticated consumers who have a greater proficiency in the marketplace, and are more likely to buy through nontraditional marketing channels. In many countries, people are moving away from agricultural employment to manufacturing and service-oriented jobs. This means consumers have a higher disposable income per household, and also have less time to shop in retail shops.

Figures 17-1 and 17-2 illustrate the growth of Internet users and Internet commerce in the Asia-Pacific region. As can be seen from the various graphs, the scope for international marketing research on the Internet is quite high. Table 17-1 gives the reader a brief glimpse of some of the country characteristics for marketing in Asia and the Pacific Rim. Credit cards make it easier for companies to establish direct marketing channels. Increasing use of Internet and Web-based technologies to set up payment mechanisms require high credit card proliferation in the market of interest. Domestic list availability is of particular significance to marketing researchers. The ease with which mailing lists can be obtained to a large extent will decide the method used for data collection. This will also help in direct marketing. Import restrictions will determine the mode of doing business in any of these markets. China, for instance, has very high import requirements; however, the size of the market is favorable for companies to go in for direct investment and establish manufacturing bases in China. It is apparent from the table that the countries are vastly different in these characteristics. This makes it necessary for marketing researchers to adopt different methods in each of these countries to gather data that is comparable.

CULTURE

It has been repeatedly emphasized in the previous chapters that cultural sensitivity is important, especially when conducting a research survey. Each Asian country has a unique culture and history, and if U.S. companies neglect these issues, the results can be disastrous. This can lead to decision makers obtaining erroneous information and making wrong decisions that could cost the company millions of dollars. There is a greater fear that the company could have its reputation compromised and lose all the goodwill that it has built up over the years. (It must be noted that Australia and New Zealand are in the Pacific Rim; however, they are not considered Asian countries.) Sometimes little things that are overlooked can make a huge difference. For example, if an advertisement campaign were to show an automobile driving down the road in Thailand or

The Net Economy In Asia And Japan

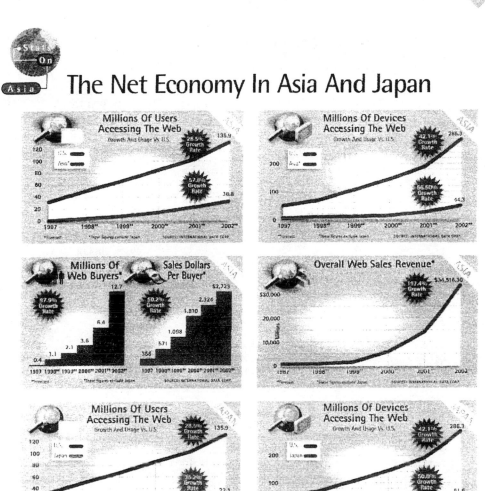

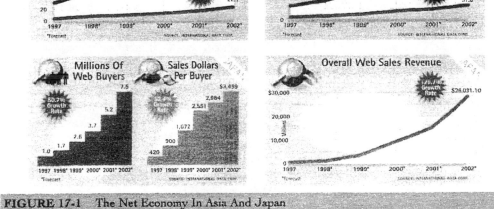

FIGURE 17-1 The Net Economy In Asia And Japan

Source: Inter@ctive Week. Nov. 30, 1998 p. 42.

Rapid Growth Throughout Asia And Pacific Region I-Commerce Revenue (In Millions)			
Country	1997	1998	2002*
Australia	$79.32	$403.25	$4,974.30
China	1.63	7.71	1,872.90
Hong Kong	14.72	59.74	1,621.45
Japan	437.05	1,720.00	26,030.00
India	.63	2.96	454.26
Indonesia	.43	1.25	167.05
Korea	14.45	56.35	2,000.41
Malaysia	3.34	13.09	646.86
New Zealand	9.93	43.29	546.85
Philippines	1.68	6.88	383.66
Singapore	8.34	35.18	898.91
Taiwan	9.36	44.23	1,278.77
Thailand	2.44	9.11	506.01

*Projected

FIGURE 17-2   Internet Commerce

Source: International Data Corp.; Reprinted by permission from *Inter@ctive Week*, November 30, 1998. Copyright © 1997 ZD, Inc.

TABLE 17-1   Country Characteristics for Marketing

Country	Credit Card Proliferation	Domestic List Availability	Import Requirements
Australia	High	Expanding	Light
Brunei	High	Nominal	Moderate
China	Low/Growing	Nominal	High
Hong Kong	High	Moderate	Light
Indonesia	Low/Growing	Nominal	Moderate
Japan	High	Moderate	Moderate
Malaysia	Moderate	Nominal	Moderate
New Zealand	High	Expanding	Light
Philippines	Low/Growing	Expanding	Moderate
Singapore	High	Expanding	Light
South Korea	Moderate	Nominal	High
Taiwan	High	Nominal	Moderate
Thailand	Low/Growing	Nominal	Moderate

Source: United States Postal Service, *Marketing Resource Guide to the Pacific Rim*, ed. William A. Delphos (Washington, DC, 1993). 5.

EXHIBIT 17-1

Optimism Makes Asia Stand Out

What are the values that made Asian economies so successful until recently? One of the simpler explanations that stand out is the optimism of the people. Asian popular optimism shines through in the results of one of the largest international pollings. The poll was conducted in 29 countries for *The Economist* by Angus Reid Organization, a Canadian polling company. 15,669 adults were questioned and data was collected between May and June of 1998. The target sample size was 500 for each country, with the exception of a 1000 sample size in urban China and the United States. In 23 of these 29 countries, full nationality probability sample was used. In six countries—Brazil, China, Colombia, Russia, South Africa, and Thailand—urban-only sampling was used. The list of questions asked included:

1. On a scale of '1' to '7,' where '1' means you are completely dissatisfied with the overall quality of your life and '7' means you are completely satisfied with the overall quality of your life, how would you rate your satisfaction with your life?
2. Over the next year, do you think your personal economic situation will improve, remain the same, or get worse?
3. All things considered, do you think you will be better off or worse off in ten years than you are today?
4. All things considered, do you think your children will be better off or worse off than you?

The poll asked a battery of questions designed to measure optimism in terms of people's expectations of their future prosperity. Asia stands out as the most optimistic region in the world. Of the ten most optimistic countries, five are Asian. Next comes Latin America, with two out of the ten most optimistic countries. The results are more interesting because of the hard times that have befallen most Asian economies in the recent past. Equally interesting is the exception to the rule—Japan. Only 9 percent of the Japanese expect to be better off in a year's time and only a quarter of them expect that their children will be better off. This puts Japan in 29th place, behind struggling Russia and pessimistic France and Germany.

Asian optimism is a potent contributor to economic growth, but even more potent is the fact that Asians are not satisfied with their existing circumstances. The picture that emerges of Asia is that of peoples who both believe that the present circumstances are unsatisfactory and that the future will be better.

The poll also provided insights into other attributes of Asians. They are not as suspicious of their governments as the Americans and Europeans. Fewer numbers believe that their governments are trying to regulate businesses.

Source: From "Optimism makes Asia stand out," in *The Economist*, August 1–7, 1998 p. 36. www.economist.com.

Hong Kong, it would do well to remember that people in these countries drive on the left side of the road. While this certainly would not violate any major cultural norms, it may show the audience that a researcher does not fully understand the marketplace or has not paid sufficient attention to details.

While each specific marketplace is unique, the following general issues can be applied to the region as a whole:

- In most Asian cultures, trying to solicit an immediate response from a potential consumer is contrary to traditional buying habits. For example, running a television advertisement which ends, "operators are standing by now" will fall on deaf ears. The advertiser should carefully word the "offer" in a mailing and generally steer away from "hard sell" approaches.
- A majority of Asians generally put their family names before their given names. Thus, Soung Chi Lan should be referred to as Mr. Soung. Be aware of these issues when developing a database or while mailing a survey questionnaire.
- Name/brand recognition is paramount throughout the region and helps create a comfort zone to facilitate the buying process. Consider using testimonials and providing a list of local or regional clients.
- Asians are generally more conservative than their Western counterparts and place a great deal of importance on loyalty, respect, age, and gender. Relationships are key throughout the region and must be developed accordingly.
- Regionally speaking, using a teaser on the envelope is not as popular as in the United States.

When designing the survey, researchers should consider that numbers, shapes, and colors may have very different (sometimes negative) connotations in some Pacific Rim countries. Some examples are listed here. In Japan, the numbers 4 and 9 signify death and odd numbers are considered unlucky. Black and white are funeral colors and bright red and other bold colors are inappropriate for a mailing campaign. People in Hong Kong believe that the number 8 signifies prosperity or good fortune, the number 4 signifies death, and the number 3 signifies life. Red and yellow are considered lucky colors, blue and white are the Chinese funeral colors, and triangles have a negative connotation. Blue, black, and white are negative colors in Singapore. In South Korea, the number 10 and red ink are said to bring bad luck. As with the Chinese, South Koreans and Taiwanese associate triangles with negative feelings. Exhibit 17-1 summarizes the results of a survey conducted by *The Economist*, which highlights the optimism of many Asian economies.

SEASONALITY AND HOLIDAYS

The timing of a mailing can have a significant impact on its success or failure. This fundamental truth holds as much water in the Pacific Rim as it does in the United States. The holiday charts in the country chapters should help companies develop mailings (by showing an awareness of the reader's specific culture) as well as help to determine when (and when not) to schedule the mailings. In general, Exhibit 17-2 lists some of the major holidays and seasons that are not recommended times to mail into the Pacific Rim.

EXHIBIT 17-2

Holidays

Season/Holiday	Months	Countries
Ramadhan Feast	Late March	Muslim Countries like Malaysia, Indonesia
Chinese New Year	Late January	Most Asian Countries
Summer months in Southern Hemisphere	December–February	New Zealand/Australia
Golden Week	Late April to early May	Japan
Obon Festival	Late July to late August	Japan

Source: United States Postal Service, *Marketing Resource Guide to the Pacific Rim*, ed. William A. Delphos (Washington, DC, 1993), 150.

LANGUAGE AND TRANSLATION ISSUES

There are over 1,000 different languages spoken in the Pacific Rim today, including English, so it is important to consider the following points:

- The long history of British influence in the region has resulted in a number of Asians who speak English.
- Many Asian business executives (and consumers) have studied in English-speaking countries and therefore know and/or speak this language.
- In some Asian countries, the English language carries with it an intrinsic value that can be used as a marketing tool.

THE MAILING LIST ENVIRONMENT IN THE PACIFIC RIM[2]

Researchers have to take into consideration some unique challenges that relate to mailing lists in the Pacific Rim. Asian lists are usually smaller than those available in the United States and are generally more expensive than U.S. lists, costing between U.S. $200 per thousand and U.S. $400 per thousand. If a list contains Asian names, it will be difficult to conduct a merge/purge and de-dup. While computer programs are being explored for this service, no cost-effective technologies are yet available to the direct marketing industry.

Professional list brokers are not the only place to locate a Pacific Rim list. There are many reliable sources from which researchers can obtain mailing lists. Consider contacting a major multinational publishing house operating in the region. In the past few decades, the publishing industry has made significant inroads into these countries and many have subscriber databases that can be rented by researchers.

SECONDARY SOURCES OF INFORMATION

There is a significant amount of published information specially designed to help companies compete in global markets. Many of these resources go unused because executives cannot locate the pertinent information. Listed in the following paragraphs are some of the possible avenues that can be looked into for obtaining secondary data.

U.S. Department of Commerce

The U.S. Department of Commerce provides a PacRim Hotline called FlashFacts. This service is available free-of-charge, seven days a week, 24 hours a day. By calling (in Washington, DC, United States) (202) 482-3875, (202) 482–4975, or (202) 482-3646 (from a touch-tone telephone), companies can receive reports of one to seven pages directly to their fax machines. A complete directory of all available reports can also be ordered by calling the hotline and following the directions or by visiting their Web site.

National Technical Information Service

Many useful U.S. government publications are available by contacting the National Technical Information Service (NTIS). During the earliest stages of a market research process, companies should contact the NTIS and have them send a directory of available publications covering the Pacific Rim. The address and phone numbers are:

National Technical Information Service
5285 Port Royal Road
Springfield, VA 22171
Telephone: (703) 487-4650
Facsimile: (703) 321-8547

Computerized Information

A number of market research resources are now available through electronic media. This greatly facilitates keeping information up-to-date, as well as disseminating the information to the business community. The following services can provide valuable, timely information on Pacific Rim markets:

- The National Trade Data Bank (NTDB) maintains trade and export promotion data on the Pacific Rim, which is collected from 14 different federal agencies. Additional information and ordering instructions are available by calling the NTDB offices in the United States at the following telephone numbers:

  (703) 487-4630 (for annual subscriptions)
  (703) 487-4650 (for single issues)

- The Commercial Information Management System (CIMS) coordinates the information resources of the Commerce Department's worldwide network of trade specialists to provide U.S. businesses with timely, accurate, and in-depth Pacific Rim marketing data.

AUSTRALIA

Country Characteristics[3]

Population: 18,438,824 (July 1997 est.)
Land Area: 7,617,930 sq km
Language: English (though several indigenous Aboriginal languages exist)
Literacy Rate: 99 percent
Religion: Anglican (26 percent) and Roman Catholic (26 percent)
GDP—purchasing power parity: $430.5 billion (1996 est.)
GDP per capita—purchasing power parity: $23,600 (1996 est.)
GDP—real growth rate: 3.6 percent (1996 est.)
Inflation Rate—consumer price index: 3.1 percent (1996 est.)

Business Characteristics

While Australians tend to be friendly and easy going, this behavior does not carry over to business relations. Most expect a code of etiquette with emphasis on the verbal as well as nonverbal aspects. For instance, it is considered appropriate to offer your business card, but you need not receive one in return because most Australians do not carry name cards. It is customary to shake hands when greeting, as it is at the conclusion of a meeting. It is also acceptable for people to introduce themselves without waiting to be introduced and most Australians would perceive this as informal and outgoing.

Market Research in Australia

The Australian market is extremely urbanized—85 percent of the people live in cities. Targeting such markets involves the foreign concern to evaluate the ease of access to the markets. The mass majority of Australia lives in the southern region in the major cities of Sydney, Melbourne, and Canberra. Table 17–2 gives readers an idea of the infrastructure that is available in Australia and New Zealand.

The Australian Internet Market is large with roughly 2 million users and growing. Even Crocodile Dundee would have an Internet account today.[4] However, conducting marketing in Australia is often more effective through telephone and mail rather than

TABLE 17-2 Market Research—Intrastructural Analysis

Country	Telecommunications per Capita	Newspapers/Circulation per 1000	Number of Telephones
Australia	TV—1 per 2.0 persons Radio—1 per 0.8 persons	68 daily papers 465 non-daily, 258 per 1,000 pop.	8.7 million 1 per 2.0 persons
New Zealand	TV—1 per 2.0 persons Radio—1 per 1.0 persons	297 per 1,000 pop.	2.1 million 1 per 1.4 persons

Source: Reprinted with permission from *The World Almanac and Book of Facts 1998.* Copyright. © 1997 PRIMEDIA Reference Inc. All rights reserved.

face-to-face/intercept. Perhaps one of the main aspects to be considered would be the size of the major cities in Australia. Though this is a significant problem, the accuracy and reliability of the secondary data available substantiates efficient marketing research ventures by foreign firms. Telecommunication in Australia and New Zealand is extremely efficient. Almost one in every two Australians owns a telephone and this ratio is 1 to 1.4 for New Zealand. Approximately 90 percent of Australians read newspapers regularly. In terms of estimating access to the consumers, this information is pertinent.

The Australian market is similar to that of the United States for technological progress. Media research is available for all media sources and this includes meter measurement of television audiences. Both Australia and New Zealand can be rated highly in terms of news awareness. Even though penetration of televisions and radios per person is not as significant as it is in the United States, high newspaper circulation levels keep the masses very well-informed. On the whole, the entire region is highly literate and media-conscious and on average has advanced methods of communication. This would translate to conducting effective market research in Australia.

Perhaps one of the main limitations of conducting research in Australia would be using mail as a mode of data collection. Postal questionnaires are not popular due to the low rate of return, which averages from 5 percent to 20 percent; however, telephone interviewing has made significant progress in Australia and is comparable to the United States in terms of reliability. In fact, the ability to reach most consumers has increased given the number of working women. While several refute the strike rate of telephone interviewing, it must be noted that consumers can be alternatively reached at another number rather than counting an answering machine as a void response.

Random sampling has been recommended as the most suitable research method because there is immense cultural diversity in the Australian market that needs to be captured. The influx of immigrants to Australia from several Asian countries implies that consumption patterns, as well as consumer characteristics, differ drastically between such groups.

CHINA

Country Characteristics[5]

Population: 1,221,591,778 (July 1997 est.)
Land Area: 9,326,410 sq km
Language: Chinese or Mandarin, Cantonese, Shanghainese, Fuzhou, Hokkien-Taiwanese, Xiang, Gan, Hakka dialects, minority languages
Literacy Rate: 81.5 percent
Religion: Taoism, Buddhism, Muslim (2 percent to 3 percent); Christian (1 percent est.); officially atheist, but traditionally pragmatic and eclectic
GDP—purchasing power parity: $3.39 trillion (1996 est.)
GDP per capita—purchasing power parity: $2,800 (1996 est.)
GDP—real growth rate: 9.7 percent (1996 est.)
Inflation Rate—consumer price index: 10 percent (1996 est.)

Chinese Marketing and Consumer Behavior[6]

China, potentially the world's largest consumer market, has in the last 20 years successfully created a lower-middle and middle-income class by adopting market-oriented economic policies. The Chinese seem to have a fascination for all things Western. Most department stores are modeled after American stores and carry lot of designer labels and very expensive merchandise. The mannequins used to display products are modeled after Caucasians. Brand names are westernized. Most shops are overstaffed, even though the level of customer service is not up to Western standards. An increasing number of department stores has not yet posed a serious threat to the roadside shops that sell clothes, shoes, and household items. Bargaining is a very common selling tactic in these smaller shops and they compete head-on with the larger stores using price as an effective tool. The same can be said of Western-style food courts, which are gaining popularity. However, smaller roadside shops still corner the bulk of the business. Many Chinese prefer buying their breakfast from eating stalls and restaurants rather than making it at home.

Most cars found in China are small—many smaller than the Geo Metro. Most cars are operated as taxis and private cars are less common. Bicycles and bicycle carts are very common and there are as many women on bicycles as there are men. Most Chinese seem to assume that foreigners have money, so vendors at tourists spots target foreigners and have no compunctions about overcharging them. Most Chinese women have adopted Western wear. Many supermarkets have cropped up in China that carry various international brands; however, the Chinese still prefer to shop at vegetable and meat shops for fresh produce and meat. English is becoming a popular language and many Chinese have been making a conscious attempt to learn written and spoken English.

Business Characteristics

Companies should be aware of the extreme political sensitivity in China and take great care to avoid stirring up political controversies. It is suggested that the companies get a good insight into various aspects of what is pertinent to specialize in before setting up a base in China.[7]

The Chinese give a lot of importance to the value of time and most meetings are started punctually. They place a lot of emphasis on precision and detail when designing contracts. They pay close attention to long standing relationships because it is believed that the culture of each company will be better understood by building long-term relationships. It does take a significant amount of time for a company entering China to understand the legal aspects as well as the culture in negotiating deals. In establishing business deals, the company that shows the greatest perseverance in securing the contract and a company that invests time in understanding Chinese culture often succeeds.

It is important that the Chinese counterpart is convinced of the company's prowess or the managers' technical expertise. The individual, however, need not try to prove his worth to the Chinese because they will surely acknowledge (in less explicit ways) the amount of respect they pay to the foreign party. In order to prevent "loss of face," most Chinese would prefer to work on a one-on-one basis with the party and not through an intermediary.[8]

In terms of nonverbal communication, it would help to assess the status of the officials who have convened to discuss the contract. Most Chinese meetings are devoted to pleasantries in order to wait for the most opportune moment to discuss formal aspects of the contract or the business. Also, most Chinese tend to get rigid in posture when their position is in jeopardy. It is important to understand the difficulty in establishing a nationwide strategy given the regional differences, which are similar to the vast differences that exist in India.

Product Positioning

A common concern for Western firms selling in China is the product pricing and positioning strategies that they should adopt. Chinese consumers are quickly becoming sophisticated, and they are now interested in both quality and value. It is important to try to produce products in China that combine Western quality and image at a Chinese price level. It would be beneficial to the company if the price level were to meet the local price point in order to boost sales beyond the initial level (which could have been geared due to the novelty effect). The distribution system in China is surely an aspect that most marketers would have to consider. It is extremely difficult to find a national system of distribution or a national system of transportation that can get goods from one part of China to another. It is also cumbersome because there are no set legalities surrounding product liability or return policy. The demographics of Chinese consumers according to a recent Gallup survey are explained in Exhibit 17-3.

There are several guidelines that stipulate factors that should be looked into by a party entering China. First of all, one should consider specific regions in China that are

---

EXHIBIT 17-3

Collecting Information on Chinese Consumers

Collecting information on the Chinese population requires some effort, according to the Gallup polls, which targeted 3,400 households. Covering almost every province in China, the researchers used almost every mode of transportation, including by foot, bicycle, and camel in order to obtain as diverse an opinion as possible. Most of the surveys conducted previously have been in metropolitan areas and the large economic zones and this is not an adequate gauge of the kind of consumption in the large country.

The most frequently owned durable in the household are bicycles (81 percent) and perhaps the most important aspect of the Chinese household is that only a quarter nationwide have refriger-

ators as compared to two-thirds of urban households. This difference in the standard of living has to be accurately noted by researchers in order for marketing decisions (in terms of pricing and positioning) to be effective.

The recognition of the multinational brands is an indication of the effectiveness of the strategies that are implemented. In the fast-food line, McDonald's had to come in second to Kentucky Fried Chicken, while in the beverages category, Coca Cola reigned over Pepsi Cola and Seven Up. It is interesting to note that Japanese brands tend to have better brand recognition as compared to American or European brands.

Source: From "Opportunities in China: Balancing Risks and Rewards," *Latin Trade*, 1998. Reprinted by permission of Latin Trade.

of interest and the kind of infrastructure that exists in those regions. It would be beneficial to consider the customers' expectations in this respect; that is, what kind of organizations they consider to be satisfactory. Perhaps one of the main prerequisites to functioning in China, is to understand the business culture. This would be facilitated if consultants were approached for suggestions. Exhibit 17-4 explains the attitude of workers in China. It would also be appropriate to obtain a list of government and financial institutions in order to understand the dealings that need to be done, as well as groundwork that would have to be accomplished prior to functioning in China. The concept of "guanxi" is prevalent in China and refers to the favors given and owed, as well as the equivalent of bribing.

Market Research in China

One of the biggest problems in conducting primary research in China is the language, which tends to impede a consistent transposing of strategies. Most often it is not adequate to have a literal translation of the questionnaire, which would not capture the full essence of the research. It would be valuable for the company to invest in translators who can interpret the jargon specific to the industry and appropriately relate to the audience. The issues concerning the various jargons in China are explained in Exhibit 17-5.

There is very little market research data available for China, which is a benefit as well as a problem. The current research being conducted by social scientists and professionals is often not done in the context of pricing analysis and/or brand equity.[9] One executive from Survey Research Group (SRG), which has been operating in China since 1984, mentioned that carrying out custom-designed research for Western or Japanese clientele has been a virtually impossible task. This is particularly true because there are insufficient training organizations that would be able to help hone the companies to suit the research to be conducted. Perhaps one of the main problems in conducting research would be the size of the market. This creates an immense reliance on the country's infrastructure, which may not be sophisticated enough.

The level of bureaucracy encountered while conducting research in China is also to be considered. Those surveys sanctioned by authorities lead to higher response

---

EXHIBIT 17-4

Attitude of Workers in China

The Chinese have a habit of telling a person whatever they believe he or she wants to hear, whether or not it is true. They do this as a courtesy, rarely with malicious intent, although it can be a real problem in the workplace. If bad news needs to be told, Chinese will be reluctant to break it. Sometimes they will use an intermediary for communication, or perhaps they will imply bad news without being blunt. To cut through such murkiness, it is best to explain to your Chinese coworkers that you appreciate direct communications and that you will not be upset at bearers of bad news.

Source: China Business: World Trade Press Country Business Guide (1994), 164.

EXHIBIT 17-5

Dialects and Idioms

Mandarin, or *pu tong hua* in Chinese, is the official national language in China; however, the problem is compounded by the existence of several dialects that are somewhat similar but exist as separate entities. In terms of the script the individ-ual dialects are exactly the same, though the phonetic usage, as well as the accent, could affect the usage. If a person who speaks Cantonese meets a person fluent in Hokkien or Hakka, it is most likely that they would converse in Mandarin.

Source: China Business: World Trade Press Country Business Guide (1994), 174.

---

rates.[10] As SRG discovered, it was forced to obtain permission for each individual survey (that is, submit the questionnaire as well as the relevant documentation in each city). While this has been changing gradually, the process is still elaborate and requires government approval at every step. In order to meet the deadlines stipulated, it is often necessary to pander to government officials and, while this does affect the cost and time allocated, it would ensure that there is a smooth collection of data. Exhibit 17-6 gives some useful tips on Chinese negotiating habits.

There are several international marketing research companies offering customized research services in China.[11] Focus groups and semistructured, in-depth interviewing are the popular qualitative research methods. Probability sampling and quota sampling using face-to-face interviews, central location study, and in-home placement study are popular quantitative methods. There are many omnibus surveys that can be of help to researchers. China omnibus covers three to five cities every six months providing companies with exclusive information on a shared cost basis and companies are charged on a per question basis.

The sampling method used most in China is random probability sampling. The research organization first decides on the sample coverage in terms of urban, suburban, and rural populations. Resident committees are selected randomly in each administrative district covered. From this sample of resident committees, households are selected randomly from the committee's records utilizing a random starting point and a fixed interval. Respondents are selected from each household by random number table.

EXHIBIT 17-6

Useful Tips (China)

When the Chinese counterpart refers to you as "a friend of China," this is a means of initiating an exchange with the foreign party. Also, by "softening up" the party, it will allow them to renegotiate the terms of the deal.

Source: "What Is Working for American Companies," *International Sales and Marketing* (March 1998).

Another way of selecting respondents could be to go by categories, say, housewives. The researcher usually makes three separate visits to contact the selected respondent. This method yields response rates of over 90 percent in China.

Interviewers for conducting surveys in China can be from both sexes and are typically between 25 and 45 years of age (relatively older than Hong Kong interviewers). Most of them are high school or university graduates and the majority of them work full time. The predominant attitude toward interviewing is that it provides them an opportunity to learn and is not really viewed as a means of earning extra money. Given a well-designed questionnaire and clear instructions, they produce high-quality work.

Respondents are cooperative and open and eager to try new products. They are also very candid in their feedback. This reaction is mainly because of their higher enthusiasm to try new products and the favorable image of foreign goods and not out of courtesy. Chinese respondents are a lot more patient than Hong Kong respondents and can tolerate longer discussions and interviews.

There is also a very good procedure for quality control. Interviewers are briefed and debriefed by supervisors and there is also field supervision. Ten percent of each interviewer's work is back-checked and the whole assignment of a given interviewer is rejected if any problem is detected.

There are some other aspects of conducting research that have to be noted. The biggest difference in researching Chinese would be in methodology. There is very little telecommunication penetration—about 7 percent versus a strong 95 percent in the United States. While mail would serve as the best alternative, response rates to mail surveys are dismal. Hong Kong has a telephone penetration of 96 percent; however, given the culture, this is not a very suitable method for conducting surveys.[12] The method that has been successful to date has been personal interviewing. The Chinese do not immediately respond to the questionnaire, because they believe that a connection or a tie has to be formed before any personal (even consumption) information is divulged.[13] It becomes necessary to reevaluate the kind of tools or information gathering methods that most interviewers employ. For example, when questioned on family relationships and financial aspects, most Chinese tend to get rather uncomfortable as compared to their U.S. counterparts. The unique features in doing research in China are explained in Exhibit 17-7.

EXHIBIT 17-7

Unique Features in Doing Research in China

- Vast differences between regional markets
- Industry is fragmented and widely dispersed
- Discrepancy in data sources—reliability of secondary data
- Volatility of the economic system in terms of investment influx
- Interviewing techniques are arduous because a significant amount of time is spent in familiarizing the customer (allow for warm-up)
- Ad-testing—emphasis on voice-over, visual, and audio
- Telephone interviews are often not feasible given reach and representation
- Taboo topics—politics and bourgeoisie

INDIA

A country of close to a billion people, India offers a fascinating insight into the manner in which marketing research is to be performed. This is especially true because India is such a diverse society, with vast differences in economic levels, caste, and religion-based composition, as well as a multiplicity of languages.

Country Characteristics[14]

> Population: 966,783,171 (July 1997 est.)
> Land Area: 2,973,190 sq km
> Language: English is used for most national, political, and commercial communi-cation. Hindi is the national language and primary tongue of 30 percent of the peo-ple. Other major official languages include Bengali, Telugu, Marathi, Tamil, Urdu, Gujrathi, Malayalam, Kannada, Oriya, Punjabi, Assamese, Kashmiri, Sindhi, and Sanskrit.
> Literacy Rate: 52 percent
> Religion: Hindu (80 percent), Muslim (14 percent), Christian (2.4 percent), Sikh (2 percent), Buddhist (0.7 percent), Jain (0.5 percent), other (0.4 percent)
> GDP—purchasing power parity: $1.538 trillion (1996 est.)
> GDP per capita—purchasing power parity: $1,600 (1996 est.)
> GDP—real growth rate: 6.5 percent (1996 est.)
> Inflation Rate—consumer price index: 10.3 percent (1995)

Business Characteristics

Conducting business in India requires considering certain cultural aspects and nuances. Hinduism dominates every aspect of Indian life, and often seeps into relation-ships and culture. Although not strictly adhered to in the big cities and amongst the westernized circles, the role of religion should be considered. Use of the first name for address should be avoided. An American business person in India will be considered an equal and, among equals, the usual method used is to press one's palms together in front of the chest and say "namaste," meaning "greetings to you." The attitude toward women is one of respect and the distance between men and women is one that should be maintained when addressing them. For instance, a young woman should not take the hand of a man who is not her husband. Women who have been educated generally do not perceive this to be objectionable, though it is preferable to extend a verbal greeting. Attitude toward time is lax in India, with most people being complacent about the provision of service. In conducting business, it would be appropriate to chart the dimensions of the contractual agreement in order to have a document to refer to over an extended period of time. Bargaining for goods and services is considered to be part and parcel of the Indian business environment. Though a significant number of retail outlets have sprung up in the past few years, most of the business dealings with small business owners tend to be dominated by bargain transactions. Indians usually consider business to be separate from personal life, though when inviting people to their homes their hospitality extends to trying to make the guest more at home either through cultural exchange or divulging personal information.

Market Research in India

Generally, in India the biggest problems are with accuracy and reliability, which are lacking in marketing research studies.[15] The role of market research as a tool in determining the feasibility of product innovations and applications has increased in the case of India. It has taken a significant amount of time for companies to realize the importance of market research in the allocation of funds and human resources in carrying out the activities of the corporation effectively. Methods to conduct research in terms of the tools used would be an area that the researcher should look into in terms of effectiveness as well as feasibility. Exhibit 17-8 gives some pointers on the cultural aspects of conducting marketing research in India. Exhibit 17-9 explains the manner in which McDonald's has adapted its business style to suit the Indian culture.

Telephone

The problem with telephone data collection is that the infrastructure is often inadequate and expensive to construct or develop. Furthermore, the problem with "reach" also exists because the research to be conducted tends to focus only on metropolitan cities. India is a large country with an immense consumer base that is relatively untapped. Given the rural and urban differences, it would be ideal to get information regarding purchase behavior. However, the infrastructure does not support a consistent national research to be conducted. Telephone penetration in India is less than 1 percent of households.[16] The cost of conducting such a nationwide study of the population would also be rather high given that local calls cost 1 to 2 rupees for the first 3 minutes (as of December 1998).

Facsimile (fax)

Similar to telephones, this mode of collecting consumer responses has not extended beyond business dealings. The problems with power outages, telephone lines, and inconsistent connections prove to be major hurdles to this otherwise effective

---

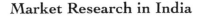

EXHIBIT 17-8

Cultural "Do's" and "Don'ts" in India

- Although many languages are spoken in India, most Indians speak excellent English, so language is not generally a problem.

- While it is acceptable for men to shake hands with men, men shaking hands with women may be frowned upon.

- The caste system is a complicated system and is difficult to understand. This is also a sensitive area to many Indians

and, hence, it is best to stay away from this topic.

- Hospitality is an outstanding feature of the Indian society. All guests, whether they are expected or not, are welcomed into the home and given some refreshments. Indians expect this to be reciprocated.

- While dining with Indians it is important to remember that only right hands are used for eating.

Source: Adapted from *The Cultural Gaffes Pocketbook* by Angelena Boden, *Management Pocketbooks,* 1997. Reprinted by permission of Management Pocketbooks.

EXHIBIT 17-9

McDonald's in India

In order to appeal to the Hindus in India, McDonald's has embarked on adapting its strategy, which is centered around the Big Mac, to the Maharaja Mac (which comprises two lamb patties, special sauce, lettuce, cheese, pickles, onions, and a sesame seed bun replacing the beef patties which are central to its product positioning). In fact, McDonald's has introduced the vegetable burger and nuggets with chili and masala sauces as part of its menu to cater to the Indian palate. The first McDonald's opened in India in 1997 with two outlets at Bombay and New Delhi. Since then, they have added four in New Delhi and two more in Bombay and plan to open several outlets across India.

The selling point for the Indian success is that McDonald's represents all things American. Despite the crowd that gathers around these outlets paying steep prices for a taste of the American icon, this represents the growing trend toward fast foods. This trend has seen entrants like Kentucky Fried Chicken and Domino's, which not only offer the product, but present the service, so far unexplored in India. The average price for a burger at McDonald's in India is 31 rupees, which is an equivalent of 80 cents in the U.S. As mentioned by Elizabeth Rozin, author of *The Primal Cheeseburger*, "the nature of the food exchange . . . explains the acculturation of the burger." The concept of fast food, as well as the appeal of the burger in itself, dictates the degree to which cultural sensitivity should be used to adapt the corporate strategy.

Source: L. S. Kadaba, "McDonald's Has No Beef in India," *Houston Chronicle—Dining Guide* (10 April 1997).

---

mode of data collection. The major metropolitan cities have a good reach to the consumer base and, because there has been a growth in the use of faxes, this method has a fairly bright future.

Mail Surveys

The biggest problem with having mail surveys would be the size of the population and the lack of a good database of consumers that can be used as a means of targeting the population. The size of the market is large and diverse enough to warrant such a method of data collection; however, the reliability of the postal system further complicates the issue with irregular delivery of mail, as well as postal strikes.

E-mail and the Internet

The development of the Internet as a tool in market research has not significantly impacted India. This is partly due to the telecommunication infrastructure as well as the cost of setting up such a system on a home-to-home basis. The average computer in India costs anywhere from Rs. 35,000 to Rs. 40,000 (1 US $ $\approx$ Rs. 43 in 1999) and the cost of establishing the network connection could range from Rs. 3,000 to Rs. 10,000. Furthermore, Web surfing in itself is charged by the hour, which means that individuals do not have the privilege to stay online for extended periods of time.

Resistance to Market Research

There are several aspects that impede market research in India and they are discussed below in detail.[17]

First, the sellers' market situation in the country is cited as being the reason why market research is not conducted. The basic idea that demand exceeds supply should in itself spur marketers, unless there is competition, which would then warrant market research to be conducted. Second, businesses in India do not realize the integral role of market research and believe that it is a cost best not undertaken; however, the availability of inexpensive tools for research, as well as the risk incurred in making a rash marketing decision, justify the need for market research. Third, the emphasis on secondary data collected by trade associations is considered to be adequate. In order to face competition and growing levels of technology, it is vital that the company step out of the complacency and conduct extensive primary research. Fourth, some executives perceive marketing research to be the answer to the firm's problems. The role of market research is to serve as a tool to gauge consumers' preferences and obtain a composite profile in order for the manager to translate it into executive decisions.

It is extremely important to see market research as an ongoing process rather than a problem-solving tool that is sporadic in application. As the company grows in the industry, it is required to reinvent itself and attempt to gauge from market studies if there is a potential for growth.

An Insight into the Indian Consumer Market[18]

The Indian market has a massive middle class of approximately 250 million people. The peril in marketing to Indian consumers as a whole is that this middle-income class varies significantly in terms of level of education, purchasing power, and consumption (based upon the geographical location). Considering just income as a determinant is often misleading given that the scale ranges from low-middle to upper-middle income levels. Marketing in India would require the company to tailor its product design and pricing strategies in order to address the differences between India and the Western world. It would help the company to understand the shifts that are currently taking place in India, the mobility between classes, the rural-urban migration, and the impact of new media (via satellite). For instance, Table 17-3 illustrates the differences in the market for consumer durables across India.

Even though there is a significant difference in the levels of income, most Indian households have the same pattern of expenditure as this market research effort uncov-

TABLE 17-3 Regional Differences in Penetration of Consumer Durable Goods

Product	North	East	South	West
Refrigerators	40	18	15	27
Color Televisions	18	17	23	28
Washing Machines	13	1	4	5

Source: Pathfinders Market Research Firm, "Venturing in India: Opportunities and Challenges" cited in *Business Today* (February 22–March 6, 1993).

EXHIBIT 17-10

Marketing Research in India

India has a population of 900 million people spread across 26 states, with 17 different languages and more than 1,700 minor languages and dialects and many different religions. With such a large population and vast regional differences, selecting an appropriate sample of the population is a mammoth task. There is also ample scope for misunderstandings or misinterpretations because of the numerous languages and dialects.

The postal system in India is not very efficient, so mail surveys are not effective. Telephone interviews are expensive. Besides, the telephone is rarely used for lengthy conversations, so telephone interviews do not produce very good results. The best method of data collection would be personal interviews. Labor is cheap and people are usually receptive to the idea of being interviewed in public or in their homes.

Many additional factors need to be considered when conducting surveys in India. During the rainy season, it pours in most parts of the country and conducting surveys becomes impossible. There are many religious festivals and Indians celebrate them with a very high level of devotion and fervor. Fieldwork in India requires very good scheduling and significant juggling skills.

Source: Sue Bunn, "Now That India's Got GATT, A Massive Market Beckons," *Research Plus* (April): 10–11.

---

ered. The Marketing and Research Group (MARG) Poll taken in 1995 reflected that most Indian households spend 46 percent of their household expenditure on food. Despite the high level of inflation over the past few years, which makes affordability an important issue, there has been a consistent rise in the spending levels. Increase in the credit facilities offered, as well as price competition, has resulted in a boost to consumer spending in India. This is a specific aspect that market researchers should address in trying to collect information by attempting to obtain data on the various segments of the diverse population. Exhibit 17-10 gives a brief overview of conducting marketing research in India.

JAPAN

The Japanese market has been considered insurmountable for most market researchers. However, the success stories of consumer products like McDonald's and Coca-Cola and high technology categories like IBM and Apple, indicates that there is an immense openness which can be utilized.

Country Characteristics[19]

Population: 125,732,794 (July 1997 est.)
Land Area: 374,744 sq km

Language: Japanese
Literacy Rate: 99 percent
Religion: Shinto and Buddhism (84 percent), other (17 percent, including Christian, 0.6 percent)
GDP—purchasing power parity: $2.85 trillion (1996 est.)
GDP per capita—purchasing power parity: $22,700 (1996 est.)
GDP—real growth rate: 3.6 percent (1996 est.)
Inflation Rate—consumer price index: 0.3 percent (1996)

Cultural Characteristics[20]

The Japanese's purchasing behavior is centered more on the vendors selling the product than on the product itself. Product purchase is dictated by the association to the company rather than for the usage of the actual product. Price-quality association is prevalent. The significant emphasis on after-sales service and long-term use of the product (i.e., brand loyalty) means that the company should assess the importance placed on quality and reliability. Despite being a competitive environment, the Japanese believe that intercompany dealings are advantageous and often relate to competition on a personal basis. Exhibit 17-11 gives a brief description of the complex interrelationships between organizations.

Business Characteristics[21]

Japanese are familiar with the culture of the people with whom they are dealing. The role of the purchaser is important and the retail industry should be able to cater to this need. The concept of "losing face" is crucial to understand in the Japanese culture. When approaching the Japanese one should take caution in not being too direct, because this would mean that if they are not able to answer or accommodate the query, they would lose face in front of the foreign party. Given the level of collectivism in the Japanese society, it translates to such a system in the workplace. Most executives convene as a group and often it is difficult to determine who is at the top of the hierarchy. The Japanese perceive uncertainty to be part of their business culture. While in the United States this would imply a lack of assertiveness, as well as lax planning, most Japanese do not pose resistance to the idea of not defining the boundaries of the business relationship.

Exhibit 17-12 explains the role of family in business relationships in Japan. The concept of time to the Japanese extends to the number of years they spend in the company. The long-term orientation relates to the length of the employment, their approach to the business dealings, as well as consumer loyalty. The construction of the contract in the Japanese environment is not based on the written agreement but on the verbal agreement. The rigidity of the written contract would not give sufficient space for the exchange of words between the parties. The ease at which the Japanese conduct business is misleading because they are sensitive to the actual business deal; however, a significant emphasis is placed on the actual interaction with the clients, which may deter from the business atmosphere in the U.S. setting. Exhibit 17-13 lists some data sources for Japan.

EXHIBIT 17-11

Japan's Corporate Culture

Look at the shareholders of NEC Corporation, the world's largest manufacturer of computer chips—Sumitomo Life Insurance Company, Sumitomo Trust and Banking Company, Sumitomo Bank Limited, Sumitomo Marine and Fire Insurance Company, and Sumitomo Electric Industries Limited—all giant companies themselves. This is no coincidence. NEC and Sumitomo belong to what the Japanese call *keiretsu,* meaning corporate group. The keiretsu system defines the unique business culture of Japan. It links the already powerful companies, banks, and insurance firms into even more powerful groups that can dominate markets in good times, drive out competition in bad times, and provide protection from hostile takeovers and stockholder demands for quick profits that plague American companies. The keiretsu system is one of the most important obstacles to foreign companies trying to penetrate Japanese markets.

Sumitomo Trust is a "stable shareholder" of NEC, as are most other Sumitomo Group Companies and some additional firms from other keiretsu. Sixty to 70 percent of the stock in publicly traded companies in Japan is held by stable shareholders. The result is that a Japanese company can forget about the pressures of constantly producing "good" earnings and sacrifice profits by lowering prices to gain market share. It can endure years of losses, if required, to drive competitors out of business. It can reinvest heavily because it does not have to worry about dividends.

The crucial question then becomes, which system will win—the Japanese keiretsu system or the American system of openness? The Japanese are aware of the importance of maintaining good relations with their trading partners, the biggest of them being the United States. They are trying to bring more foreign companies into their keiretsu system, although their demands for quality and delivery are stringent. On the other hand, a number of American companies impressed by the keiretsu system are emulating some of its aspects.

Source: T. Bettina Cornwell, *Global Exchanges, The Washington Post International Marketing Companion,* The Washington Post Writers Group (Allyn & Bacon Publishers, 1993) 82.

Myths about Dealing with Japanese Business Organizations[22]

Over the years some fallacies have emerged about the way Japanese conduct business. Some of the more common ones follow:

- The companies in Japan have more to gain from the foreign concern than vice versa.
- The on-the-job training of American managers abroad can be combined with their simultaneous roles as trainers of our Japanese staff.
- There is no need for a local expert on Japan; an American "Asian expert" is the best person to handle company relations with Japan.

EXHIBIT 17-12

Useful Tips (Japan)

It is a good selling point to ensure that your database reflects the family members of your clients. When addressing the Japanese party, it helps to re-ascertain your interest in the overall well-being of the person by inquiring about the family (even though this should be done outside of business hours).

It is important to maintain a long-term relationship with the Japanese because this is the "sole" criterion that is favored. Rather than using lower prices or better deals as means to determine their business ventures, the Japanese prefer to have a consistent management style to work with.

Source: "What is Working for American Companies," *International Sales and Marketing* (April 1998).

- All that is needed to deal with problems with the Japanese language would be to employ an interpreter who can handle company relations with the Japanese subsidiary and government officials. This would also be adequate when it comes to converting advertisements from English to Japanese.
- Transplant the Japanese from the subsidiary to the home office in the United States for management training and study tours. This would orient the employee in the management practices and help application in the Japanese context.
- The Japanese need our management skills, so the best way to transplant them is by direct investment.
- Management requires that employees have some awareness of the religious aspects of the Japanese culture. Workers are sent to learn about the art of Zen mediation and Buddhism or Shintoism.

EXHIBIT 17-13

Sources of Data for Japan

Kaigai Shinsutsu Kigyou Soran is published by Toyo Keizai Shinposa. This company also publishes *Tokyo Business Today.* Toyo Keizai publishes more than 100 volumes annually, as well as a variety of corporate and economic data covering economic conditions, stock markets, and Japanese corporations. The corporate quarterly handbook (published in Japanese as Kaisha Shikiho) contains data on more than 2,500 firms and has a circulation of more than four million.

Kaigai Shinsutsu Kigyou Soran (Japanese Investments Overseas) provides information on affiliates of Japanese companies listed on the major stock exchanges in Japan, as well as on the overseas subsidiaries of other Japanese companies.

Source: From "Japanese Firms and the Decline of the Japanese Expatriate," from *Journal of World Business* Vol. 32, No. 1, 1998, p. 38. Reprinted with permission from JAI Press, Inc.

- The perquisite (perk) system will equate to the employee's loyalty to the company. This is the manner in which the Japanese company ensures employee retainment.
- Japanese dealings would have to be based on monetary transactions.
- Japanese men are more involved in the business environment as compared to women. Given the scenario of a meeting, it is more feasible to address the men, given the social hierarchy in the country.

MARKET RESEARCH IN JAPAN

The differences in survey research in Japan further complicate the cultural issues that can impede conducting market research. While these represent significant areas that have to be addressed by the company, they also reflect on the problem in trying to conduct research in a similar manner as in the United States. Some of the common practices to be followed and some others that ought to be avoided are listed in Exhibit 17-14.

Door-to-door interview is a major data collection method in Japan, although there has been a gradual tendency toward the use of telephone and the Internet. The cultural aspect is intrinsically tied with this method. A growing number of women are now working or spend a significant amount of time away from home, reducing their accessibility for phone surveys or door-to-door interviews. The use of interphones in several apartment complexes has also affected the degree to which the potential respondents can filter and block out the researcher.

The application of a telephone survey has become difficult given that municipalities have an increasing number of unlisted subscribers, in which case the marketing research company may not be able to randomly sample a group. The problem with telephone interviews is that, if the cohort involves managers, they may not be willing to discuss matters pertaining to the company or its employees. This is particularly due to the space constraint in Japanese offices that forces them to work in cubicles.

EXHIBIT 17-14

Cultural "Do's" and "Don'ts" in Japan

- The Japanese are an extremely group-oriented and community-based people.

- Avoid making too much direct eye contact as it can be interpreted as challenging and can make most Japanese uncomfortable.

- Many Japanese are not comfortable with shaking hands, so it is best to take the cue from them before offering your own hand.

- Generally, the Japanese prefer the use of title and first names should be avoided.

- "Yes" from the Japanese does not always mean acceptance. It could merely be an acknowledgement of the fact that they are listening. Most Japanese do not say "no" directly. They phrase it more politely such as, "we will think about it."

- Silence is considered golden, so there is no need to try to fill it up.

Source: Adapted from *The Cultural Gaffes Pocketbook* by Angelena Boden, *Management Pocketbooks*, 1997. Reprinted by permission of Management Pocketbooks.

Several Japanese companies are looking at cost efficiency as a main prerogative in determining the kind of survey research method to employ. The emphasis is more on the ease of access to the sample as well as the speed with which the results are obtained and tabulated. The growing reliance on qualitative means of measurement versus the quantitative aspect would mean that companies rely on the provision of value-added services by marketing research firms.[23] The various predominant tools used for television ratings in Japan are explained in Exhibit 17-15.

Facsimile (Fax)

The use of fax machines in reaching the Japanese customers is facilitated by having a home reporter who has access to several respondents who fit the criteria for personal interviews. Benefits of this method include large reach, speed, low cost (though this would depend upon the installation charges and equipment), volume of the questionnaire (two-pronged benefit in which it has the reach of a telephone survey and the feasible length of a mail survey), and visual aids (words and figures).[24]

Disadvantages of conducting surveys through fax machines, as applicable to Japan, are also many. This method results in low penetration amongst residents and is used mainly as a tool to reach business respondents. The cost in installing machines in selected respondents' houses is very high. Given that there is such low diffusion of fax machines, the selection of the sample cannot be categorized as random. User ability may restrict the full usage of the fax machine.

Videotex

The increased growth of Videotex has stemmed from the benefit in reach due to the link between television, telephone, and personal computers. The questionnaires are entered into a database that is accessed by the subscribers of the media service. The respondents will then enter the data upon invitation to participate in the study. The benefits of this method would be cost (given that the cost is only for the link) and reach to a large sample size; however, the problem is that currently, only a few respondents have access to the terminals. The limitation is that the volume of the questionnaire can be affected given that the number of incomplete responses would be high if the questionnaire is too long or ambiguous. The other problem lies in the tabulation of the data

---

EXHIBIT 17-15

Research Methods in Japan

In Japan, peoplemeters (PM) are usually only available in urban centers or metropolitan cities (chiefly Tokyo). The alternative for other cities is a metered minute-based rating scale that can also be used, though the peril is that it is hard to obtain. So far, the main "tools" that are being used include PM data of Tokyo, metered scale (household data), individual diaries, and secondary data analysis.

Source: C. Ocada, *Dentsu Inc.*, (1998) (e-mail).

that is collected from the respondents. As the type of questionnaire design allows for a flexible response, it takes times to gather this information and present the results.

Electronic Media Options

While video-conferencing attempts to draw focus groups in Japan together, the main growth is in the use of the Internet as a survey tool. The level of technology is superior in Japan and this has surely translated in their optimization of electronic mail, list groups, and Web surveys to reach the audience. The increased diffusion of personal computers with relevant network connections suggests that the average consumer has access to the e-mail system, if not the company Web site, in order to address satisfaction or disgruntlement toward the party concerned.

Summary

This chapter presents an overall outlook of Asia-Pacific and provides data about personal and business habits that will be useful to the marketing researcher. Specifically, the countries of Australia, China, India, and Japan are discussed. Some of the topics that have been covered include the infrastructure available in these countries, the penetration of media, cultural habits, and sources of data.

Endnotes

1. Hugh Filman, "Happy Meals for a McDonald Rival," *Business Week* (1 July, 1996): 19.
2. U.S. Postal Service, *Marketing Resource Guide to the Pacific Rim*, ed. William A. Delphos (Washington, DC, 1993), 1–7.
3. CIA World Factbook 1997, http://www.odci.gov/cia/publications/factbook/
4. Randy Barrett, "Off the Beaten Track: Unexpected Net Hot Spots," *Inter@ctive Week* 5, no. 47 (30 November 1998): 44.
5. CIA World Factbook 1997, http://www.odci.gov/cia/publications/factbook/
6. Eugene Sivadas, "Watching Chinese Marketing, Consumer Behavior," *Marketing News,* (20 July, 1998): 10.
7. Philip R. Harris and Robert T. Moran, *Managing Cultural Differences* 4th ed. (Houston, TX: Gulf Publishing Company, 1996), 255–257.
8. Ibid.
9. Cyndee Miller, "China Emerges as the Latest Battleground for Marketing Researchers," *Marketing News,* (14 February 1994): 1–2.
10. Henry C. Steele, "Marketing Research in China: The Hong Kong Connection," *Marketing and Research Today* (August 1990): 160.
11. *The China Market and SRG China,* 1994, SRG Report.
12. R. W. B. Davies, C. J. W Minter, M. Moll, D. T. Bottomley, "Marketing Research in Hong Kong," *European Research* (May 1987): 114–120.
13. C. Miller, "China Emerges as the Latest Battleground for Marketing Researchers," *Marketing News* (14 February 1994): 1–2.
14. CIA World Factbook 1997, http://www.odci.gov/cia/publications/factbook/
15. D. D. Sharma, *Marketing Research: Principles Applications and Cases* (New Delhi, India: Sultan Chand & Sons, 1992), 2.
16. D. Sopariwala "India: Election Polling in the World's Largest Democracy," *European Research* (August 1987): 174–177.
17. S. Neelamegham, *Marketing in India: Cases and Reading* (New Delhi: Vikas Publishing House, 1998), 325.
18. "Venturing in India: Opportunities and Challenges," *Global Business White Papers,* The Conference Board No. 18, April 1996.
19. Ibid.
20. Philip R. Harris and Robert T. Moran, *Managing Cultural Differences* 4th ed. (Houston, TX: Gulf Publishing Company, 1996), 267.

21. Jean-Claude Usunier, *Marketing Across Cultures* 2nd ed. (Hertfordshire: Prentice Hall, 1996), 346–347.

22. Philip R. Harris and Robert T. Moran, *Managing Cultural Differences* 4th ed. (Houston, TX: Gulf Publishing Company, 1996), 273.

23. K. Katori, "Recent Developments and Future Trends in Marketing Research in Japan Using New Electronic Media," *Journal of Advertising Research* (1990): 53–57.

24. Ibid.

CHAPTER

18

Europe

INTRODUCTION

The basic fact to remember when targeting Europe is that it is a mesh of several nations rather than a geographically homogeneous group. People in such countries are used to local markets and specify the research based upon the kind of companies that exist within the confines of the continent. This has changed dramatically with the influx of U.S. investment. Exhibit 18-1 illustrates the operation of a business deal in Sweden.

Market research in the United States starts with referring to demographic data,[1] while a significant portion of European research is initiated with information from governmental or public-based data. The problem becomes acute when the researcher assumes that the national institute handling such output is consistent across Europe. For example, as mentioned by Cutler, INSEE in France is markedly accurate in its estimations of consumer profiles, while Italian sources tend to be raw in their presentation.

REGIONAL CHARACTERISTICS

Analyzing data on consumer behavior in terms of purchase habits will be easy in Europe because this is similar to the kind of research that is being conducted in the United States. The use of consumer panels and peoplemeters, for example, help translate the usage rates as well as perspectives, which will make sense due to the relative comparison made. Table 18-1 lists the television viewing culture of certain European countries.

Perhaps one of the biggest concerns for an American marketer working in Europe would be in the kind of emphasis being placed on obtaining quantitative information as a substantiation for the inferences being made on the local markets. Unlike the Japanese and Korean marketers, the degree to which numbers and raw data is placed higher on the list of priorities compared to analyzing the business culture is much higher by the Americans as compared to their European counterparts.

EXHIBIT 18-1

Useful Tips (Sweden)

Though known for its excellent communication network, as well as its advanced infrastructural system, the biggest problem in Sweden is the lack of reciprocation. In order to okay a deal or to confirm the terms of the deal, one should expect the Swedes to not call or reply. It is ideal that the foreign party calls in order to establish the status of the deal after every meeting.

Source: "What's Working for American Companies," *International Sales and Marketing* (March 1998).

The figure below illustrates the difference between the response rates across the world. While a continent like Europe is represented only by its Eastern section, Table 18-2 reflects the response rates for market research through mail surveys in selected regions. The results indicate that South Africa yields the highest return rate, but the inference should be viewed with caution because of the sample size.

One of the main problems that faces marketers trying to establish themselves in Europe is that there is a significant difference between obtaining information on the Western region as compared to the Eastern region within the continent. The maintenance of the databases has become exceedingly difficult because political influxes have rocked countries like the Czech Republic and Slovakia, which now have to reorganize their data collection. If a database uses a transliteration of the local language, it would have to restructure it to take into account any major changes.[2] Exhibit 18-2 gives an idea of the difficulty in getting authentic information for Europe.

Perhaps another aspect that should be noted is that financial information may not always be reliable. In Europe, there has been a push to ensure that financial reporting conforms to a certain standard as stipulated for the European Union (EU); however,

TABLE 18-1	Television Viewing Culture (minutes per day of television watching, per capita)
Culture	*No. of Minutes*
Spanish	207
French	188
Irish	145
Dutch	140
German	137
Belgian	132
Italian	129
Danish	132

Source: Sanchez Pacheo, "Market: Europe," *El Mundo* (February 1991).

TABLE 18-2 Response Rates in the ESOMAR 1992 Price Study

	Sample Selected	Effective Returns	% of Responses
North America	22	11	50.00
Latin America	17	16	94.12
Eastern Europe	17	10	58.82
Turkey	11	10	90.91
North Africa	6	4	66.67
Middle East	9	6	66.67
Australasia	9	6	66.67
India	5	4	80.00
Pacific Rim	12	11	91.67
Japan	12	5	41.67
South Africa	3	3	100.00
Total	123	86	69.92

Source: From *European Society for Opinion and Marketing Research Prices Study*, 1992. Copyright © ESOMAR® 1999. Permission for using this material has been granted by ESOMAR® (European Society for Opinion and Marketing Research), Amsterdam, The Netherlands. For further information please refer to the ESOMAR® Publications Website: www.esomar.nl.

EXHIBIT 18-2

Where in the World is Eastern Europe?

A common problem faced by marketing researchers trying to study Eastern Europe is the paucity of information for that region. Researchers stumble at the very first step—*Where in the World is Eastern Europe?* Which countries are actually in Eastern Europe? In the cold war days, this definition was fairly straightforward. Nations such as the USSR Comecon countries, or the Warsaw Pact were synonymous with Eastern Europe. With the fall of the Berlin Wall and the breakup of the USSR came the concept of Commonwealth Independent States or CIS; however, most of the countries that were a part of the Soviet Union are more Asian or Middle Eastern than European. Russia straddles two conti- nents. In terms of its population, however, it is decidedly European.

Another common problem faced by researchers in trying to gather secondary data about Eastern Europe is the spelling. Belarus is spelled Bylorussia in many databases. Information about Romania can be found under Roumania or Rumania in many databases. Researchers should also be aware of the history of many of these countries. Some databases still use Czechoslovakia, while many others have changed to the Czech Republic and Slovakia.

The solution to this problem is to decide beforehand with the client the definition of Eastern Europe in terms of the scope of the project.

Source: Marydee Ojala, "The Dollar Sign," *Online* (September/October 1996): 44–49.

East European countries have few regulations of their companies. One method to overcome this lack of accurate and reliable material is to search the Emerging Markets Database at http://www.securities.co.uk, operated by Internet Securities, Inc. There are several commercial databases that provide information on Eastern Europe, as well as a list of corporate financial data. They include:

1. KOMPASS Central/Eastern Europe
2. Dun & Bradstreet International Dun's Market Identifiers
3. Company Intelligence
4. Dun & Bradstreet Eastern Europe Directory
5. BizEcon News Russian Business Directory
6. ABC Europe: European Export Industry

EUROPEAN STATISTICAL SOURCES

There are some very good secondary data sources available for Europe, some of which are the following:[3]

1. *European Official Statistics: A Guide to Databases.* Almost 100 publicly accessible databases within the field of official statistics are listed. Information contained here covers virtually all social and economic sectors.
2. *European Official Statistics: Sources of Information.* Provides a list of over 250 government bodies, organizations, ministries, and banks that publish information.
3. *Eurostat-Your Partner for European Statistics: A Guide to the Statistical Office of the European Communities.* Contains information on where relevant statistical data can be obtained about the European Union.
4. *Europe in Figures.* Provides information on the process of European integration and the present state of the Union. It is an excellent source of information for understanding current and future developments in Europe.
5. *Eurostat Yearbook.* Contains information on the people, land and environment, national economy, and trade and industry in the Union.

EUROPE—ONE ECONOMY?

When trying to perceive the European Union (EU) or the European Economic Community (EEC) as a large bloc, a market researcher has to exercise restraint in standardizing across the continent. Operating a chain of retail outlets from Great Britain to the Czech Republic requires careful attention to the piquancy in the individual markets. Widely different infrastructures and varying economic growth rates and cultures makes this continent extremely deceptive for the unsuspecting marketer trigger-happy to target consumers in the EEC. For example, consumers from Eastern Europe and the former USSR are used to entering stores to find nothing stacked on the shelves. It is also very common to find that retail outlets may not extend service that is similar to that of the West and that product offerings may not include reasonable price and quality.[4]

Despite the fact that members of the EEC portray themselves as connected by a currency as well as heightened trade relations, the biggest problem is that the national identities are maintained as separate and distinct. Depending on the markets (countries), the population ranges from 320 to 800 million people and this intimidatingly large figure has a diverse population with vastly different needs.[5]

There are many ways that one can approach marketing research in Europe. One would be to address the consumers geographically. When the foreign concern tries to enter any country in Europe, it needs to evaluate the kind of consumer behavior in terms of the differences to the company's country of origin. Exhibit 18-3 shows how Russia is unique in terms of the beverage industry.

The EU is committed to eliminating all internal economic barriers to trade and creating a single market. These 12 countries have a combined population of 340 million and constitute one of the wealthiest markets in the world. In fact, Europe is home to 8 of the world's 15 richest countries. Collectively, the gross domestic product (GDP) is U.S. $6 trillion, with per capita income of U.S. $18,600. By comparison, the U.S. GDP is U.S. $5.5 trillion, with per capita income just over U.S. $21,400.

The European marketplace consists of more than just EU-member countries. The European Free Trade Association (EFTA) countries, Austria, Finland, Iceland, Liechtenstein, Norway, Sweden, and Switzerland, also represent excellent opportunities to U.S. direct marketers. These countries increase the market size by 32 million potential customers and U.S. $868 billion in combined GDP. The market structure of the EFTA members is closely aligned to the EU because many member countries are currently applying for EU membership. To support this, EFTA countries have agreed to work with the EU in the creation of a European Economic Area (EEA). This agreement is widely viewed as a preliminary stage for the incorporation of the seven EFTA countries into the EU.

Economies and marketplaces are also quickly evolving in many EU associate-status countries: the Czech Republic, Slovakia, Hungary, Poland, Bulgaria, and Romania. By including these countries, the European marketplace grows by another 38.5 million

---

EXHIBIT 18-3

Beverage Industry in Russia

In a world that is reigned supreme by the two soft-drink giants, Coca-Cola and Pepsi-Cola, Russia is perhaps the only country that has still not been "conquered." Along with Cadbury, these two companies have succeeded in capturing only 20 percent of the overall market.

The rest of the business is made up of local soft drinks, U.K. imports, and imports from East European countries like Poland. One of the main aspects of the market is that there is very little consumer loyalty to such large brands, as well as a lack of brand identity. Pricing in itself is based upon the number of middlemen involved in the retail chain, as well as the volatility in the currency value. The role of price in determining the beverage consumed suggests that it is necessary to measure the amount of importance consumers place on quality and ease of access.

Source: "Where Price is King," *Beverage World* (April 1995).

people and U.S. $440 billion in GDP. Other countries seeking EU membership include Turkey, Cyprus, and Malta. This "New Europe" represents a total market of over 536 million people with a combined GDP of over U.S. $7.7 trillion. Although each country is unique, there is a common denominator—lucrative sales opportunities for U.S. direct mailers.

CULTURE

Despite the vast size and wealth of this New Europe, it is important to realize that Europe should not, and cannot, be considered a single marketplace. For example, the 12 nations of the European Union have 14 official languages, 9 separate VAT tariffs, numerous payment options, 12 currencies, and 12 national cultures; however, starting January 1, 1999 the Euro dollar is in place. To communicate effectively with European customers, researchers must understand their culture. This requires a significant amount of cultural sensitivity and is especially important when developing an advertising campaign and writing copy. Europeans have unique cultures and histories, and if these issues are neglected, a researcher's reputation can be tarnished.

At the 1993 USPS-sponsored DM News Conference entitled "Profiting from the New Europe," one speaker commented on major European cultures, saying, "The Germans are serious, the Spaniards are serious with style, the Italians are serious about style, the French are stylish and entertaining, and the English are serious about wit." In other words, there is no (nor will there ever be) a single European culture.

Sometimes it is the little things that should be incorporated into a campaign. For example, when writing dates in Europe, the day (numeric) is placed first, followed by the month, and then the year. Thus, 7/2/99 is February 7, 1999 in the United Kingdom, but July 2, 1999 in the United States. A mistake in this area would not violate any major cultural norms, but may show the target audience that a U.S. company does not fully understand the marketplace. Some of the cultural aspects that need to be remembered are listed in Exhibit 18-4.

SEASONALITY AND HOLIDAYS

As a general rule, Europe is "Closed for Business" during the month of August when many people take their vacations and companies tend to run on a skeleton staff. U.S. companies should also realize that Christmas holidays are sometimes celebrated differently in Europe. For example, in the Netherlands gifts are exchanged on St. Nicholas Day, almost two weeks before December 25th, and in Spain gifts are exchanged on Epiphany—two weeks after Christmas.

LANGUAGE ISSUES

One of the most important decisions that a researcher will make is whether or not to translate the questionnaire. This decision depends on several factors, including the target audience, the type of product, and the nature of the survey. In general, translation is recommended unless it is certain that the target audience reads English. In the end,

---

EXHIBIT 18-4

Cultural "Do's" and "Don'ts" in Europe

- The French are proud of their language and they prefer to speak it. They may know some English but may be reticent about using it.

- The city-based Germans speak good business English, but they are not comfortable conversing in English.

- Italians and Spaniards are tactile and get physically close when talking.

- Meetings with the French tend to be formal and lengthy. They also consider it impolite to start a business conversation in French and revert to English.

- The Germans are very keen on punctuality and to be on time is everything. Business atmosphere is formal and a working knowledge is greatly appreciated.

- The British are less demonstrative and expect a reserved manner. They prefer to start with neutral topics on the first meeting. In any case, it is best to avoid religion and politics.

- The British do not appreciate physical proximity and they avoid using hand gestures when trying to make a point.

- The British society is still class-based and people are judged by their education and the newspapers they read.

- When doing business with the British they expect printed cards to be exchanged.

Source: Adapted from *The Cultural Gaffes Pocketbook* by Angelena Boden, *Management Pocketbooks*, 1997. Reprinted by permission of Management Pocketbooks.

---

however, the language issue should be addressed on a case-by-case basis. Many companies find it acceptable to translate only certain parts of the questionnaire (i.e., the incentives, the return instructions, and so on). Additionally, English can be written alongside the local language to ensure that the widest possible audience is being reached.

Many international researchers contend that companies can successfully mail survey over 100 countries in English. In Europe, however, there is no "Lingua franca." While English and French are generally considered the business languages of Europe, many business executives also speak German. In fact, over 100 million people in Europe (both East and West) consider German their primary or secondary tongue. It is spoken by 100 percent of Germans and Austrians, 88 percent of the Swiss, 85 percent of Luxembourgs, and 67 percent of the Dutch. Table 18-3 gives the percentage of English proficiency among adults.

The English language is also received differently in many European countries. For example, if mailing into France it is generally recommended translating materials into French; however, it may be acceptable to mail in English to the Netherlands and Germany. Remember that translated copy may take more space on a page than the English copy. For example, the same message requires 20 percent more space in French, 30 percent more space in German, and up to 40 percent more space in Finnish.

Most importantly, do not cut corners when it comes to retaining translation services. It is a necessary cost of doing business and the price should not be the sole criterion for choosing one firm over another. Quality adaptation is the key to successful translations.

TABLE 18-3 Percentage of English Proficiency Among Adults	
Austria	24
Belgium	53
Denmark	49
Finland	31
France	33
Germany	26
Greece	19
Italy	23
Netherlands	55
Norway	51
Portugal	19
Spain	20
Sweden	48
Switzerland	36

Source: Mardev List Service, England, 1993.

MAILING LISTS

The type of list being utilized also affects the translation decision. If using an internationally compiled list and targeting affluent consumers throughout the region, it may be acceptable to mail in English. On the other hand, if conducting a mass mailing to a domestically compiled list, translating the copy is advised. Talk to list brokers about the language issue; they can be valuable partners during a mailing effort.

The domestic list environment is different within each European country. In many cases, a country's data protection laws significantly affect how personal data can be compiled and segmented. In some countries there are regulations requiring that list owners remain informed (or even directly involved) with regard to their lists. Additionally, many European list owners require a sample mailing before releasing a particular list. In other countries, laws stipulate where a mailing must originate and whether the actual list can leave the country. Table 18-4 gives the domestic and business-to-business lists available for various countries in Europe. The average price for a consumer list works out to U.S. $95 to $140 per 1,000 and for a business-to-business list is approximately U.S. $140 to $250 per 1,000.

COMPUTERIZED INFORMATION AND SERVICES

Figure 18-1 illustrates the Internet economy in Europe and as the data indicates, the scope for international marketing research is on the rise. As a result of advances in the information technology field, a number of market research resources are now available through electronic media. This greatly facilitates keeping the information up-to-date and disseminating the information to the business community. Some of these sources are listed in Exhibit 18-5.

TABLE 18–4 Selected Domestic List Environments

Country	Consumer	Business-to-Business
Belgium	200	25
Finland	100	30
France	1,100	700
Germany	1,100	2,150
Italy	200	150
Norway	350	NA
Sweden	400	250
Great Britain	850	1,520
Switzerland	600	750

Source: Adapted from European Direct Marketing Association (EDMA) research and compiled data from national direct marketing associations and Mardev List Brokers in England, 1998.

National Trade Data Bank (NTDB)

The National Trade Data Bank holds a compilation of over 100,000 trade-related documents, including U.S. Government export and import trade statistics, the complete *CIA World Factbook,* and many other reports.

Country Marketing Plan (CMP)

CMPs are annual planning documents prepared by commercial officers at U.S. Embassies and Consulates in Europe. They assess the competitive position of U.S. products in a foreign market, analyze trade and investment issues, and forecast a list of best prospects for U.S. exporters.

The cost of conducting research in various European countries varies because of difference in overhead costs.[6]

Commercial Information Management System (CIMS)

CIMS coordinates the information resource of the Commerce Department's worldwide network of trade specialists to provide U.S. businesses with timely, accurate, and in-depth marketing data. A trade specialist creates an information package for the key industry, product, and/or country specified.

FRANCE

Country Characteristics[7]

Population: 58,609,285 (July 1997 est.)
Land Area: 545,630 sq km
Language: French
Literacy Rate: 99 percent
Religion: Roman Catholic (90 percent), Protestant (2 percent), Jewish (1 percent), Muslim (1 percent), unaffiliated (6 percent)

The Internet Economy In Europe

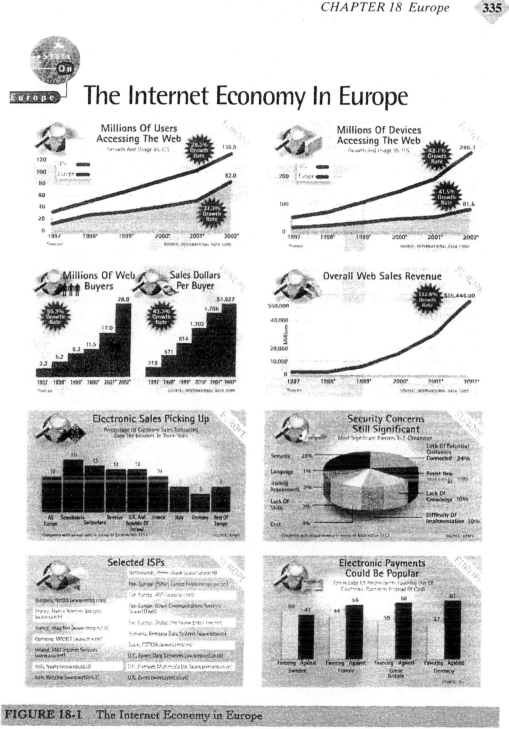

FIGURE 18-1 The Internet Economy in Europe

Source: Reprinted by permission from Inter@ctive Week, November 30, 1998. Copyright © 1997 ZD, Inc.

EXHIBIT 18-5

Electronic Information Sources on EU

Eurobases is an Internet service that provides access to bibliographic, legal, and statistical databases offered by the European Commission. Many databases are available on Eurobases, including *RAPID, SCAD, EUROCRON,* and *ECLAS. RAPID* provides full text of press materials issued by the commission every day, the council of ministers, weekly summations of court actions, and speeches by commission members. It also provides the list of items that can be downloaded every day. *SCAD* is a bibliographic database with references to official legislative documents and publications, as well as secondary periodic literature on the EU. *EUROCRON* provides a menu-guided presentation of general macroeconomic statistics and farm data. *ECLAS* is an online catalog of the Central Library of the Commission.

The Statistical Office of the European Communities (*EUROSTAT*) offers information on diskettes, tapes, and CD-ROMs. *COMTEXT* is a CD-ROM product with the detailed internal and external trade statistics of the EU based on the Harmonized System of product classification. An annual subscription includes 11 updates with monthly data. Each update contains the most current monthly data and two years of annual retrospective data. *COMTEXT* offers software for graphs and other presentations as well as downloading into standard spreadsheet programs. The Electronic Statistical Yearbook of the European Community, offered by Eurostat, has micro, macro, and regional economic data for the EU and individual member states, including map and graph capabilities. *EUROFARM,* a Eurostat CD-ROM database, has statistics on farm structure, wine cultivation, and orchard fruit trees.

EPOQUE is the documentary database of the European Parliament. It operates with a user-friendly menu. Its files cover the status of legislation in progress; citations for session documents, debates, resolutions and opinions; bibliographic references to studies done by the Parliament and national parliaments; and a catalog of the Parliament's library.

More information is available at http://www.Europa.EU.INT/

Source: Michael R. Czinkota and Ilkka A. Ronkainen, *International Marketing,* 5th ed. (Orlando, FL: Dryden Press, 1998), 249.

GDP—purchasing power parity: $1.22 trillion (1996 est.)
GDP per capita—purchasing power parity: $20,900 (1996 est.)
GDP—real growth rate: 1.3 percent (1996 est.)
Inflation Rate—consumer price index: 1.7 percent (1996 est.)

Business Characteristics[8]

The French believe in status and often do not mingle between the groups; for example, the upper bourgeoisie will not attempt to mix with the upper-middle or the middle income classes. There is often little motivation for the person to move up the social ladder since there is a belief that one is born into a class.

While conversing with the French, it is necessary to be able to distinguish their sardonic comments from humor. Most French are interested in discussions where there are no points of agreement and as the arguments grow more heated, tend to enjoy them better. This is seen to be reflective of a person's character and feelings, as well as their thought processes. The "I" centered conversations in American business tend to be perceived as individualistic and self-centered. Most French tend to view their personal achievements as aspects that should not be shared with visitors. It would be better to direct the conversation away from personal topics into more general subjects, like politics and art.

The French attitude to work ethics in the public sector is that there is little motivation to strive for excelling in their field. The strength of the union helps in ensuring that these workers maintain their jobs despite lax performance levels; however, in smaller companies there is significant emphasis placed on quality and performance. Also as an incentive to the workers, there are significant opportunities to scale up the ladder and gain the respect of fellow workers.

French management is rather centralized in structure, with a significant amount of emphasis placed on decision making by managers from the top levels in the company; however one aspect that should be considered is the manner in which the French view personal characteristics as reflective of the individual rather than his or her performance in sales or position.

Time consciousness is still important at business meetings because it reflects a pride in conducting business with the French. The French tend to take pride in purchasing products made locally. Products manufactured by the United States tend to come in third on the priority list, with Europe being the second-favored.[9]

Market Research in France[10]

France has a very established and updated infrastructure system that supports its direct marketing ventures. Currently, it has the second largest direct mail market in Europe (next to Germany). There are close to 1,000 mail-order buying lists in France and these include some 18 million families (consumer list) while the business-to-business list includes close to 4 million French companies.

Telemarketing is considered to be a booming area that foreign firms can opt for when trying to reach the French consumers. The development and standard of telecommunication services in France has been excellent over the past few years. There are several laws that limit the overall success of this medium, such as return policies that exceed a week for orders made. Television home shopping is popular in France and this has increased the reach of the medium to the average consumer.

It is ideal to conduct primary research by reviewing individual segments of the French population. This is because there are several differences between the classes within the society and this affects the purchasing pattern per household. Even though the telephone system in France is extremely advanced, it would be better to have personal interviews rather than over the telephone. The French value their personal time at home and often are not receptive to questions being posed. It is recommended that mall-intercepts be used because they are more relaxed in such a social setting and will be more willing to offer their perspectives. It is important, however, to note that the French are rather idealistic in their vision of current lifestyles and often skew their responses to reflect a better state rather than an actual state. The researcher should discount this bias in response and weigh the relevance of the answers.

GERMANY

The Germany of today is a united market, immersed in the democratic system. The cultural characteristics, which we shall explore, reflect the commonality between the East and West Germany of yesteryears. This is in line with the thought that regardless of political influence, culture pervades the society and is slower to change and adapt.

Country Characteristics[11]

Population: 82,071,765 (July 1997 est.)
Land Area: 349,520 sq km
Language: German
Literacy Rate: 99 percent
Religion: Protestant (38 percent), Roman Catholic (34 percent), Muslim (1.7 percent), unaffiliated or other (26.3 percent)
GDP—purchasing power parity: $1.7 trillion (1996 est.)
GDP per capita—purchasing power parity: $20,400 (1996 est.)
GDP—real growth rate: 1.4 percent (1996 est.)
Inflation Rate—consumer price index: 1.5 percent (1996 est.)

General Characteristics[12]

Germans are considered to be precision-oriented with immense emphasis on the exactness of the job. This translates into their working behavior, which is meticulous and driven toward goal-oriented philosophies (where efficiency is the primary prerogative). The Germans are not spontaneous in their dealings with people, tending toward being private in their approach. Their company dealings are based upon the etiquette demanded of a position held. It is often that business dealings do not stretch beyond the office working hours and recreation is almost strictly spent in personal endeavors.

Business Characteristics

The Germans are well-versed in their fields and are extremely knowledgeable. Their concept of business dealings involves formal interaction with the clientele where it would be advantageous to the client to maintain the professional distance. Most often, personal life is never discussed as part of a business meeting. The individual never mentions his achievements or offers insight into his personal matters. In Germany it is important that the dealings are made specific either in writing or verbally. This is specifically because Germans pay attention to detail and anything that is not specified will be considered in breach of trust.

The forms of address tend to be formal as well and the use of first names should always be avoided. A good option would be "herr" or "frau." English is taught in German schools and most people are aware of the nuances of the English language; however, the language used most often is "high German"[13] rather than several dialects.

Even though English is prevalent in most business spheres, Germans tend to resent that they have to use a foreign language to communicate (though this has changed dramatically, given the number of investments and business partnerships).

The German perception of time is an aspect to note. They value punctuality as an essential work ethic and do not take very well to clients who fail to show up on time for meetings or who do not specify a time-line for a certain project to be completed.

For the Germans, greeting is almost always a firm handshake. This is regardless of the meeting being for personal or business reasons. There is significant emphasis placed on the seniority of one employee over another and this inadvertently also relates to the formality of relationships within the company. Some of the aspects of dealing with Germans are listed in Exhibit 18-6.

Market Research in Germany

The availability of good secondary research information enables a thorough analysis of the consumer perspectives.

Germans are intensely private and tend to keep their opinions to themselves. In particular, the northern part of Germany tends to be a rather difficult area to elicit responses. There is a reasonable amount of resistance to responding to surveys at malls or in answering queries over the telephone. This is perhaps more in the former East Germany where surveys were conducted by government agencies, giving rise to speculation regarding the purpose of the study or the company behind the research venture.

Generally, German women are aware of all media forms and reaching them is perhaps easiest through magazines and other print media. In order to elicit responses, it would be useful to consider providing incentives to the public, such as a discount (coupon) on purchases or anything in kind.

The one misunderstanding that marketers have in targeting consumers in Germany is in assuming that most of them live in urban areas. There is a strong difference in perception as well as lifestyles between rural and urban Germany. Evidence proves that it would be beneficial for the marketer to consider different strategies and operationalize in order to cater to the specific region in Germany rather than a homogenization. Exhibit 18-7 explores the scope for direct marketing Germany.

EXHIBIT 18-6

Useful Tips (Germany)

In order to talk to the German representative, it is better to meet him or her in person rather than engage in a discussion over the phone. Most Germans feel comfortable seeing the deal on paper and prefer that proposals are drafted for them to review as opposed to finalizing the intricacies of the deal over the phone.

Source: "What is Working for American Companies," *International Sales and Marketing*, (February 1998).

EXHIBIT 18-7

Scope for Direct Marketing in Germany

Compared to other European countries, Germany has the highest per capita average mail-order rate. It is estimated that over 420,000 German corporations use direct mail as a means to reach their consumers. There are (as of 1997) 1,100 consumer lists and 3,500 business lists in Germany which may form a useful guide to conducting market research.

The problem with conducting market research is that the German culture is protective of consumer privacy and without the consent of the consumer, telemarketing is not conducted (and is considered illegal). This has markedly reduced the means of informing consumers with the regular media tools, though the incidence of direct marketing has grown. This is related to the fact that compared to other European countries, Germany has fewer protective laws regarding direct mail address lists. In order for database owners to legally use the information of new consumers, update, or delete data, they have to comply to the rule of notifying the consumer first. However, only 0.5 percent of the population is resistant to receiving direct mail and this is a consumer trend that most marketers can utilize to better reach their consumers.

Source: Adapted from United States Postal Service. *International Marketing Resource Guide,* ed. William A. Delphos (Washington, DC: Braddock Communications, 1994), 106–107.

GREAT BRITAIN

Country Characteristics[14]

Population: 57,591,677 (July 1997 est.)
Land Area: 241,590 sq km
Language: English, Welsh (about 26 percent of the population of Wales), Scottish form of Gaelic (about 60,000 in Scotland)
Literacy Rate: 99 percent
Religion: Anglican (27 million), Roman Catholic (9 million), Muslim (1 million), Presbyterian (800,000), Methodist (760,000), Sikh (400,000), Hindu (350,000), Jewish (300,000)—1991 est.
GDP—purchasing power parity: $1.19 trillion (1996 est.)
GDP per capita—purchasing power parity: $20,400 (1996 est.)
GDP—real growth rate: 2.4 percent (1996 est.)
Inflation Rate—consumer price index: 2.6 percent (1996 est.)

Business Characteristics

Although the entire United Kingdom can be classified as proud of their heritage, the English, Welsh, and Scottish cannot be confused to be from the same "land." Although British is preferred, it is ideal that one's "region" in the country is known prior to any generalized remark.

As in Germany, a good handshake establishes confidence in the other party and a willingness to conduct business. Although it is improper to end a meeting without an affirmative handshake, it is ideal to follow the cue of the British counterpart.

Concept of time in the United Kingdom is valued. Punctuality is seen as a virtue, as an awareness of how important the company or relationship is perceived by the client. Though most of the contracts drafted address the long-term aspects,[15] most British tend to look at the short-term benefits that the company can achieve.

It is essential to draw or rather adhere to the strict line drawn between friendship and business relations. Very seldom do the British intrude upon the personal life of the client; in fact, it is rare that the British counterpart would refer to the foreign representative by his first name, unless stated. Exhibit 18-8 explains the differences between the United Kingdom and the United States.

The British are very aware of the language differences within their own country as well as with the United States; however, the fact that English is a common turf for conducting marketing ventures is a trap that one should refrain from falling into. Not only are the connotations different for several words, as well as different in usage, it is necessary to refer to the kind of cues that would stir the consumer in the British. This impacts the manner in which advertising would have to be constructed as well as the way in which the British consumer would be addressed. Also, it is important to note the differences in nonverbal communication that affect the interpretation of attitudes.

Market Research in the United Kingdom

There are several detailed sources of secondary data available for conducting preliminary research in Great Britain.[16] *Guide to Official Statistics* and *Regional Statistics* published by the Government Statistical Service offer detailed data that is very useful in secondary research. The Central Statistical Office (CSO) publishes *Government Statistics: A Brief Guide to Sources* on an annual basis. This booklet lists the various ministries and departments responsible for specific economic and social data. The CSO has formed a partnership with Taylor Nelson AGB (TNAGB) to publish a report series *UK Markets*. The 91 Annual and 34 Quarterly Reports produced by TNAGB from data collected by CSO, which includes 28,500 manufacturers, covering 90 percent of U.K. manufacturers' sales and 4,800 types of products. Some other sources include:

EXHIBIT 18-8

Useful Tips for English Usage

Commonality between the United Kingdom and the United States is often assumed, given that they both speak English; however, the difference in usage, the types of jargon, and vernacular should be taken into account. For example, sleeping "on the job" in the United States connotes that one is lax in his or her work ethic, while in the United Kingdom this translates to having sex in the workplace.

Source: "What is Working for American Companies," *International Sales and Marketing* (February 1998).

- *Annual Abstract of Statistics:* provides information on population, housing, manu-factured goods, and so on
- *Abstract of Regional Statistics:* main statistics for Scotland
- *Digest of Welsh Statistics:* main statistics for Wales
- *Social Trends:* collection of key social statistics covering demographic trends, income and wealth, education, employment, households and families, leisure, and so on
- *Financial Statistics:* key U.K. monetary and financial statistics
- *Family Expenditure Survey:* annual detailed report presenting income and expenditure by type of household for the United Kingdom

There are several non-official sources of data available for the United Kingdom. *Sources of UK Marketing Information* by Elizabeth Tupper and Gordon Wills, *Sources of European Economic and Business Information* compiled by the University of War-wick Business Information Service, and *The European Directory of Trade and Business Journals* published by Euromonitor are a few.

The United Kingdom is a highly diverse country, which makes it a very complex country to understand despite its sometimes homogeneous appearance. The British have not been responsive to the opportunities posed to the European Community in general. In terms of responsiveness to purchase or participating in international mar-ket research activities, the United Kingdom lags behind countries like Finland, Den-mark, France, and Italy. In the U.K. market, a significant number of buyers refer to the common research tools that include anything from focus groups to omnibus surveys, which is more than other countries embark on.[17] Telephone penetration is only 80 per-cent in Great Britain and telephone interviews are not a very popular method of sur-vey research.[18]

Telemarketing in the United Kingdom has grown as a means to service the direct marketing needs of several companies. With several advertisers using the opt-out clause,[19] consumers are more assured that their names would not be used for other promotions without a formal consent. Exhibit 18-9 talks about selecting samples in the United Kingdom.

The growth of mailing lists in the United Kingdom is specifically useful, with 1,300 lists currently available, though a significant number are business mailing addresses.

EXHIBIT 18-9

Selecting the Sample

When determining the sampling method to be random, the postal code or the zip-code is often correlated to the geo-demographic means of classifying consumers. This helps when analyzing consumers taking part in a huge sample.

With the use of the two methods, ACORN and MOSAIC, the marketers would be able to understand the con-sumers who took part in the study, as well as obtain a general profile of those who did not.

Source: N. Bradley, Harrow Business School, University of Westminster, U.K., 1988.

While consumers are open to answering queries directed by telephone or through mail, there has been a concern regarding the manner in which the consumers' identities are available to marketers outside the country. Exhibit 18-10 explains the tools for catalogs' targeting strategy.

One of the major aspects to think about in terms of addresses of consumers is that most of the houses have names rather than street numbers or house numbers. A large number of the houses are termed as "Mansfield Manor" as opposed to street addresses.

It is important to note that the British take more to telephone calls than direct marketing programs. While the usual response of international marketers is that the British are reserved and secretive of their actual purchase need, the scenario is not much different than the lack of responsiveness that one gets in the United States. One benefit of conducting research in the United Kingdom is that the distribution system is similar to the United States and approachability to the consumer is equally effective.

Direct Marketing[20]

The United Kingdom has more than three times the average response rate as compared to the Unites States toward direct marketing efforts. While the U.S. average was around 2 percent, the response rates in the United Kingdom peaked at 6.7 percent. The point to be noted, however, is that the volume of direct marketing is low, with the United States at close to 1,000 items of direct mail annually and the United Kingdom at 138.

EXHIBIT 18-10

Catalogs — Targeting Strategy

It is important to note that there are close to 15 million upper-class consumers in the United Kingdom. This consumer base is extremely tempting for niche catalogs to target since these consumers form close to half the wealth in the country.

One of the main problems with catalogs is dispelling the myth regarding the kind of product being advertised or marketed. As mentioned by Forbes, from Sterling Marketing Limited in the United Kingdom, the following represent means to counter the problem of association:

1. Establish the history of the company and the kind of products being sold. It is important to be able to gain the trust of the consumers as well as to try to instill the notion that the company is in good standing and represents quality and reliability.

2. Provide prices in sterling instead of dollars to help to recover "lost consumers" who are not able to relate to the currency in dollars.

In advertisements, the emphasis is not so much on "in your face strategies" which speak for themselves. There is a need to explain and translate the merits of the product in terms of copy. It is therefore recommended to adapt to the local culture by transcribing the product attributes in significant length.

Source: Euromarketing Insights, Market: Europe, February 1991.

There has been an increase in social acceptance to direct mail and this has proved to be an advantage for the United States as well as other foreign investors who can extrapolate the response rate to mean an eagerness to purchase through direct marketing methods. The net benefit, in terms of cost effectiveness, is high and the atmosphere of acceptability to direct mail has boosted several ventures. The society's concept of individuality is also to be considered as one of the motivating elements to consumers' preference for direct mail.

Summary

This chapter deals with marketing research in Europe. With the fall of the Berlin Wall, the breakup of the Soviet Union, and the collapse of communism in many European countries, the primary difficulty would be in defining the boundaries of a given country and then trying to obtain reliable data for these countries. This is discussed in detail in this chapter. The chapter also deals specifically with France, Germany, and the United Kingdom. Relevant statistics, business characteristics, and cultural norms are provided for each of these countries.

Endnotes

1. Blayne Cutler, "Reaching the Real Europe," *American Demographics* (October 1990): 38–43.
2. "The Dollar Sign," *Online* (September/October 1996): 44–49.
3. Tony Proctor, *Essentials of Marketing Research* (London: Pitman Publishing, 1997), 57.
4. "East or West, Europe a Dynamic—But Mostly Closed—Market," *National Petroleum News* (November 1992): 26–30.
5. "Inside the Information Industry: Regional Marketing Skills Needed in Europe," *American Demographics.* (October 1990): 20–23.
6. J. Bigant and Y. Rickebusch, "Marketing Research in France," *European Research* (January 1985): 4–11.
7. *CIA World Factbook 1997* http://www.odci.gov/cia/publications/factbook/
8. Philip R. Harris and Robert T. Moran, *Managing Cultural Differences* 4th ed. (Hous-ton, TX: Gulf Publishing Company, 1996): 318.
9. U.S. Postal Service, *International Marketing Resource Guide,* ed. William A. Delphos (Washington DC: Braddock Communications, 1994), 101.
10. Ibid., p. 97.
11. *CIA World Factbook 1997* http://www.odci.gov/cia/publications/factbook/
12. Philip R. Harris and Robert T. Moran, *Managing Cultural Differences* 4th ed. (Houston, TX: Gulf Publishing Company, 1996): 321–325.
13. Ibid.
14. *CIA World Factbook 1997* http://www.odci.gov/cia/publications/factbook/
15. U.S. Postal Service, *International Marketing Resource Guide,* ed. William A. Delphos (Washington DC: Braddock Communications, 1994), 143.
16. Peter Chisnall, *Marketing Research,* 5th ed. (Berkshire, England: McGraw-Hill Publications, 1997): 53–63.
17. K. Gotton, "Moving in on More Markets," *Marketing* (10 March 1997): 26–29.
18. R. M. Worcester, "Political Opinion Polling in Great Britain: Past, Present, and Future," *European Research* (August 1987): 143–151.
19. U.S. Postal Service, *International Marketing Resource Guide,* ed. William A. Delphos (Washington DC: Braddock Communications, 1994): 138–148.
20. *Mail International*—The Royal Mail Magazine, 1998.

CHAPTER

19

Latin America

INTRODUCTION

The varied cultural influences that have impacted the 12 countries in Latin America have resulted in varied business patterns and strategies to be taken by the foreign concern. Not only the differences in language (Spanish or Portuguese) affect the degree to which the company has to adapt to the local climate, other factors such as the diversity in ethnicity and religion would be applicable, too.

THE MERCOSUR

The benefit of conducting business in Latin America is boosted by the MERCOSUR, which is a common market formed by Argentina, Brazil, Paraguay, and Uruguay. From January of 1995, this free trade zone has been successful in increasing international business activity and in the process enabling the markets to be reasonably stabilized. Table 19-1 compares the geographic data of selected Latin American countries.

CONDUCTING RESEARCH IN LATIN AMERICA

Attitudinal Differences[1]

In the United States, consumers are more experienced and with the amount of exposure, tend to be critical of market research. People in Latin America, however, do not view market research in that light. Rather, it is an area that is new to them, which attends to their needs and desires and serves as a means to evaluate their opinions.

In trying to obtain information from the Latin American population, it is important to note their candor and eagerness to respond. They believe that their opinions

345

TABLE 19-1   MERCOSUR—Basic Data (1997)

Country	GDP (billions of US $)	Area (millions of sq. km.)	Population (millions)
Argentina	319.9	2.8	35.5
Brazil	720.3	8.5	164.6
Paraguay	9.9	0.4	5.1
Uruguay	19.0	0.2	3.2
Total	1069.1	11.9	208.4

should be given because they were asked to respond. Contrary to the assumption that their motivation is based on the respondent fees of $40 to $50, it is the cultural dictate to answer queries. In fact, most of them do not expect to be paid in cash, and prefer in kind or *cariñito* (a small token of appreciation). The offering of cash may offend the respondents and they may not accept because this would turn an otherwise informal and pleasant arrangement into a transaction. Latin Americans place a great deal of importance on personal relations and the will and desire to help someone they know.

Other Differences

Culture and History

Argentina, Brazil, and Chile all share a common European history in terms of history, religion, culture, and people. In fact, people of these countries look up to Europe, while inhabitants of Mexico and Central America tend to be influenced by the consumer culture in the United States. Exhibit 19-1 explains the similarities in marketing between the United States and Latin America.

Language

Most of the Latin American countries use Spanish as the predominant language, except for Brazil where they speak Portuguese. In order to conduct market research in Latin America, it is necessary for the translator or the speaker to be aware of the nuances that exist within regions. The different dialects, word usage, and idiosyncrasies are aspects to look out for so that the lack of awareness of the language is not an impediment to the success of the market research venture. For example, in Argentina the usage of Spanish is interspersed with Italian. Furthermore, methods of addressing people vastly differs between countries, with *usted* being a common form in Colombia, while *tú* is widely used in several countries. Exhibit 19-2 gives some useful tips on people relations in Latin America.

Clothing Codes

In order to conduct a business-to-business focus group in Argentina, for example, it is necessary to maintain a formal setting. It is also important for the moderator to adhere to a formal dress code.

When addressing the head of the household in Bogotá, Colombia, as well as Brazil, it is important to note the differences. In Brazil, dressing is more casual, while in

---

EXHIBIT 19-1

Standardized Marketing?

Marketing in Latin America is considered to be easier for Americans as opposed to that being done in Asia or Southeast Asia, specifically. This is due to the cultural similarities, which transcend national boundaries. There is basically only one language, Spanish, which is spoken in most Latin American countries, except for Brazil, where Portuguese is more prevalent.

In Asia, one has to deal with a multiplicity of cultures and languages, which makes the undertaking of research tedious and subject to a lot of adaptation. It can be assumed that a greater proportion of strategies undertaken in Mexico would be functional in Venezuela and Argentina. Generally, most companies start off in Mexico, given its proximity to the United States, and then apply it to the Latin American scenario.

One of the biggest perils in targeting Latin America would be that there is no given means by which an effective strategy can be in place for the entire continent.

Source: "Latin America is a Marketer's Dream Come True," by D. Pert from *Marketing News*, 1994. Reprinted by permission of the American Marketing Association.

Bogotá a significant emphasis is placed on the kind of clothes. Exhibit 19-3 and Table 19-2 explain the differences in income levels and spending levels across countries.

Conducting Research—Do's and Don'ts[2]

Focus groups in Latin America tend to be misleading. When asking respondents if they would be interested, the cultural stigma in saying "no" often stifles them to refuse the offer. The best means is to offer a pick-up for them such that the respondents would

---

EXHIBIT 19-2

Useful Tips for Latin America

Asking for favors is common in Latin America, and one should not deny the favor requested because this is supposed to be a stepping stone to ensure a continued relationship. A refusal to comply with the "demand" would be tantamount to being perceived as uncompromising. It would be beneficial to say that "I shall try" rather than come upfront with a firm "no."

When paying respondents, it is important to know "how much is too much." It is recommended that some local partner is contacted in order to ascertain what needs to be offered for participation, since money is considered to be offensive for any responses given.[3]

Source: "What is Working for American Companies," *International Sales and Marketing*, (April 1998).

EXHIBIT 19-3

Income—Is It a Good Indicator?

The different methodologies between countries often leads to speculation regarding the kind of income being measured. As household incomes are being tabulated across the countries, it is still rather difficult to measure the purchasing power level of consumers in Latin American countries. While the Gross Domestic Product or the Gross National Product reflect the kind of spending and personal income allocation, it does not adequately measure the spending pattern of an individual consumer (refer to Table 19-2). The actual number of consumers who have income that they are willing to spend on foreign products is much lower than expected. The Strategy Research Corporation uses the following as gauges of the kind of spending or affordability gauges:

1. Number of durables in the household
2. Employment of domestic help
3. Education level in the household

Source: Chip Walker, "The Global Middle Class," *American Demographics* (September 1995).

---

feel more obliged to attend. The specifics about the demographics of Latin America are explained in Exhibit 19-4.

The redeeming aspect of conducting one-to-one interviews is that most Latin Americans are uncomfortable with the idea of talking over the telephone or responding to mail. The communication systems in these countries is often not up to par and this should be seen as a barrier to getting the desired "reach."

It is also necessary to have a good concept regarding the time-line to project completion. It takes a lot of time to conduct personal interviews and also to exercise a tremendous level of flexibility when dealing with Latin American partners. It is vital to note the

TABLE 19-2 Population Distribution by Class

	Upper Class (%)	Middle-to-Upper Class (%)	Middle Class (%)	Lower Class and Subsistence Level (%)
Argentina	2	9	35	55
Brazil	3	16	29	53
Chile	2	6	42	50
Colombia	2	8	37	53
Ecuador	2	15	22	61
Mexico	2	12	30	56
Paraguay	3	12	34	51
Peru	3	8	33	56
Uruguay	8	20	36	36
Venezuela	1	4	36	59

Source: Chip Walker "The Global Middle Class," *American Demographics* (September 1995).

EXHIBIT 19-4

Latin America—The Usage of Demographics

Data forms the basis of research in establishing the favorable segments to target in media and message executions. As several reports on Latin America refer to, the market cannot be segmented into specific niches, only because in such minute divisions, affordability is not drastically any different. Only 20 percent or less forms the core consumer (or as Kelly refers to it—the A/B segment).

It is important to select the media and relevant message based on a thorough evaluation of the opinions, attitudes, interests, as well as affordability of the consumers.

The dynamism of the global market lies in the younger generation in developing countries. Throughout Latin America, television has successfully penetrated close to 95 percent of the houses and with the advent of cable television (expected in the year 2000), it would be feasible to address this viable group.

The attitude of the Latin American youth tends to be more involvement based when seeing an advertisement on television. This enthusiasm and interest should surely be looked into.

Source: F. Kelly, "What Do You Do After Demographics?" *Inside Strategy* (FL.: Strategy Research Corporation, 1997).

---

seasonal differences that exist between the Latin American countries and much of the rest of the world. With some countries in the Southern hemisphere, the vacation time tends to fall in January or February and this would cause problems in trying to conduct research.

Direct Marketing

The direct marketing industry is growing rapidly in Latin America, at a rate of 40 percent to 50 percent, and this has been attributed mainly to the privatization of businesses in the continent. The business-to-business marketing is similar to that in the United States, where it occupies close to half the overall direct marketing efforts.

The different levels of direct marketing infrastructure pose a challenge to the marketer who would have to take into account, for example, Brazil's updated and sophisticated database as compared to that in Colombia or Chile. It is crucial that while language tends to be similar, one would have a better chance at success if the direct marketing effort were to be stylized and crafted to fit the appropriate country specifications.

The need to compensate for often lax systems in database management imply that the region has a desperate need to regularize both its consumer and business data systems. Table 19-3 compares the infrastructure across four Latin American countries.

The Use of the Internet[4]

Latin America is a continent that has been grossly underserved by the Internet. As shown in Figure 19-1, Latin American Internet users are affluent. If a general survey is conducted via Internet, biases may occur given the composition of the users. Internet

TABLE 19-3   Comparison of Infrastructure Across Select Latin American Countries

	Argentina	*Brazil*	*Chile*	*Peru*
Direct Marketing Agencies	10	72	10	1
Telemarketing Films	25	36	15	3
Toll-free Phone Lines	Yes	Yes	Yes	Available soon
Household Phone Penetration	65%	N/A	45%	19%

Source: L. Loro, "Zeroing in on Latin America," *Direct Marketing* (January 1998).

content is at least 95 percent in the English language and this makes it all the more crucial of an area to be considered for development. The translation services currently available help Web surfers to better understand the content of the Web site, immaterial of whether it is in Spanish or Portuguese. Exhibit 19-5 illustrates the activities of a Canadian telecommunications and Internet services provider in Latin America.

The problem in implementing any system in Latin America is in encountering the political framework that has the potential to impose restrictive communication policies. Exhibit 19-6 illustrates an alternative to this challenge. This can significantly limit the accessibility to the Internet for the Latin Americans. Argentina, Chile, and Brazil have achieved some degree of political stability, which has helped in fostering a positive climate for the growth of telecommunications.[5]

FIGURE 19-1   Latin America Internet Users Are Affluent

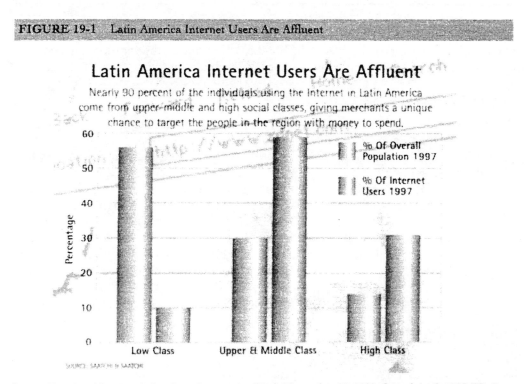

Source: Reprinted by permission from *Inter@ctive Week*, November 30, 1998. Copyright © 1997 ZD, Inc.

EXHIBIT 19-5

Telecommunications—Newbridge Networks

Newbridge Networks Corporation, Canada's telecom company, has been successful in Latin America (mostly Chile and Argentina, where it has captured 70 percent of the market) over the past decade. Its interest in targeting Brazil as its major market comes at the time of its recent acquisition of Coasin Chile S.A., which is a large telecommunications corporation in Latin America. As most people see it, this marks the beginning of the strategy that Newbridge is embarking on to ensure its growth and success in the region.

Perhaps one aspect that is crucial to its profitability lies in maintaining consumer confidence in the name of the manufacturer. Once that is set, it becomes imperative to ensure that the retail chain also carries with it the backing of the producer and the required reach.

The significant boost for Newbridge comes from the Internet and its growing usage in the region. With increased demand for links, as well as more companies insisting on installing local area networks (LANs), this would ensure the firm base in Latin America for Newbridge.

Source: Adapted from "Bridging the Gap," *Latin Trade* (February 1998): 72.

Several companies target the markets in Argentina, Brazil, Chile, and Colombia, which accounts for 15 percent of the overall population of 450 million. This is also because these countries have reflected a growing trend in telecommunications development as well as an increase in home computer purchases. The biggest challenge that faces Latin America is in trying to increase the relevance of content channels and also boost advertising online.

LATIN AMERICAN RELATIONS WITH ASIA

The paradox that describes Latin American trade with Asia is that while the current economic crisis has affected the level of relations, it has also prompted several Latin American countries to source and be sourced for investments. The trade levels of Latin American countries with the world are listed in Table 19-4. The Latin American economies grew by 5.3 percent over the last year, especially due to the growth rates in Argentina, Chile, and Mexico. As Table 19-4 indicates, the Latin American countries aggressively pursued their trade opportunities and took advantage of their economic growth, as well as declining inflation levels.

The demand for products in the Asian domestic markets has declined significantly and this has prompted several companies to consider the Latin American region. Similarly, the fact that this market poses a growth potential implies that it is worth investing in market research to better understand the consumers' requirements. As trade increases, this prompts a simultaneous requirement to have international marketing

---

EXHIBIT 19-6

The Franchising Alternative

Franchising is becoming the most employed "tool" in order to be able to gain better access into the market and, at the same time, study its consumers. For example, in Colombia, Tower Records has enjoyed immense success with sales soaring close to 25 percent over the expected level through an alliance with two local concerns, El Tiempo media group and Prodiscos.

The benefits of franchising are several, ranging from increase in the service or product offering (quality-wise and price-wise), the boost to the local economy, and the fostering of a healthy competition with local companies. Perhaps the largest benefit is that franchising provides a means to venture into an area with marketing conditions which are at best unfamiliar and diverse.

In Colombia alone, franchising has increased by 120 percent since 1997, and with more than 75 percent of these being foreign, they represent a growing trend toward this retailing concept. It is also necessary to conduct preliminary market research in order to determine the niche that the franchise would be targeting, as well as to identify the several segments in the population. In Brazil, most of the franchising chains are located in Rio de Janeiro and São Paulo state. The latter is considered excellent for its accessibility, infrastructure, and growth potential. In order to be able to change the lifestyles of the Brazilian population, companies like McDonald's had to conduct perception tests to determine the associations consumers make to fast-food restaurants. Once its results indicated that people viewed it more as a snack-bar than a full-fledged restaurant, it honed its marketing efforts more effectively.

The success of franchises in Latin America surely depends on the ability of the foreign concern to survey the market and adjust its offering, along with a local concern to address the host country requirements.

Source: Adapted from "Franchising Fever," *Latin Trade* (March 1998): 36–42.

---

research in order to capture the nuances of the individual markets. Refer to Table 19-5 for the trade between Latin America countries and Asian countries.

ARGENTINA

Country Characteristics[6]

Population: 35,797,985 (July 1997 est.)
Land Area: 2,736,690 sq km
Language: Spanish (official), English, Italian, German, French
Literacy Rate: 96.2 percent
Religion: Nominally Roman Catholic (90 percent—less than 20 percent practicing), Protestant (2 percent), Jewish (2 percent), other (6 percent)

TABLE 19-4 Latin America's Trade Levels (millions of $)

	USA	European Union	Asia	Latin America	Other	World
Argentina	6,967	12,406	4,738	19,177	4,252	47,540
Bolivia	553	473	90	1,717	69	2,902
Brazil	21,996	27,862	17,630	22,781	13,230	103,499
Chile	6,713	7,148	9,586	7,940	2,155	33,542
Colombia	9,234	5,195	1,865	6,285	1,374	23,953
Costa Rica	3,935	1,493	255	1,515	392	7,590
Dominican Republic	6,860	816	343	1,114	198	9,331
Ecuador	3,378	1,798	1,060	2,304	621	9,161
El Salvador	2,183	584	196	1,444	104	4,511
Guatemala	3,350	827	368	2,091	260	6,896
Guyana	266	335	45	173	208	1,027
Honduras	3,541	580	367	806	156	5,450
Mexico	130,872	10,332	10,621	8,024	7,451	167,300
Nicaragua	631	272	117	679	61	1,760
Panama	1,766	2,533	12,789	2,206	886	20,180
Paraguay	944	597	760	3,012	311	5,624
Peru	3,104	2,631	2,015	3,626	766	12,142
Trinidad & Tobago	1,771	741	138	820	192	3,662
Uruguay	757	1,395	581	3,429	430	6,592
Venezuela	18,460	4,277	1,052	8,976	1,536	34,301
Total	220,314	69,889	59,878	78,942	30,400	459,423

Source: From "Weathering the Storm," *Latin Trade*, April 1998. Reprinted by permission of Latin Trade.

GDP—purchasing power parity: $296.9 billion (1996 est.)
GDP per capita—purchasing power parity: $8,600 (1996 est.)
GDP—real growth rate: 4.4 percent (1996 est.)
Inflation Rate—consumer price index: 0.1 percent (1996 est.)

Argentina is a severe clash between European and Latin American Indian cultures; however, it is one of the most accessible of Latin American countries because its diversity has European overtones, which make it "homey" to U.S. and European visitors. The difference between the residents of Buenos Aires and the rest of the country is also an aspect of culture that should be noted.

Cultural Characteristics

The Argentines emphasize the individual's role in society and view the individual who is independent as capable. This affects the business culture, since the Argentines perceive one who takes orders from another as weak and inadequate. Exhibiting

TABLE 19-5 Trade Between Latin America and Asia

	Japan		Korea		Hong Kong	
	US $ millions	% change (1995/6)	US $ millions	% change (1995/6)	US $ millions	% change (1995/6)
Argentina	949	5.7	367	19.5	699	6.4
Brazil	5,735	−12.4	2,517	−13.6	1,602	−0.9
Chile	3,659	−11.3	1,980	17.5	764	5.5
Colombia	1,327	−12.5	242	10.8	82	−12.7
Mexico	5,431	7.4	1,443	15.4	587	−3.7
Panama	5,872	−19.0	4,039	61.3	1,088	−12.2
Peru	682	−19.7	370	0.0	97	0.0
Venezuela	587	−40.3	45	0.0	127	0.0
Total	22,915	−15.8	11,002	19.4	5,046	−2.3

	China		Taiwan		Singapore	
	US $ millions	% change (1995/6)	US $ millions	% change (1995/6)	US $ millions	% change (1995/6)
Argentina	667	3.5	540	17.1	194	−17.4
Brazil	2,353	19.4	1,650	47.1	934	17.3
Chile	865	34.9	950	5.0	659	104.1
Colombia	39	−41.4	120	8.1	25	4.0
Mexico	143	−63.3	800	5.3	764	120.3
Panama	424	−29.6	150	0.7	600	17.9
Peru	703	16.0	280	4.5	37	3.8
Venezuela	89	4.9	120	11.1	22	12.0
Total	5,282	5.2	4,610	19.7	3,236	35.9

	Malaysia		Total	
	US $ millions	% change (1995/6)	US $ millions	% change (1995/6)
Argentina	644	99.9	4,059	−13.2
Brazil	863	26.4	15,654	0.1
Chile	197	−16.1	9,074	−5.1
Colombia	17	0.0	525	290.0
Mexico	1,191	211.6	10,349	−15.0
Panama	199	19.0	12,372	1.1
Peru	238	−10.4	2,407	−23.3
Venezuela	25	−61.1	1,016	30.4
Total	3,364	57.8	55,455	2.1

Source: From "Far East Goes Deep South," *Latin Trade*, July 1997 pp. 62–63. Reprinted by permission of Latin Trade.

guachadas, or acts of generosity which manifest in helping someone in need is considered to be an exercise of free will.

When dealing with an Argentine it is important to note their frankness in voicing their opinions, though they take extreme care in being diplomatic. Their warm nature and friendliness is seen in situations when they try to establish a personal relationship prior to a business dealing.

It is also important to note the concept of space and time in dealing in this Latin American country. Most Argentines maintain little physical distance between speakers and tend to broach personal issues pertaining to the family in their conversation. Time is considered to be an asset to be enjoyed rather than utilized and most Argentines take this to be useful to establish relationships and to clarify situations better.

The role of the family in Argentine life is to be emphasized. Family is deemed central to the life of the average citizen and filial piety and bonds to elders are cherished; however, one of the main perils with working in Argentina would be in dealing with nepotism. Most positions are filled with family members first, and while there are specific rules that limit such incidents, this occurrence is significantly less than in other Latin American countries.

Business Characteristics

Argentine business people tend to differ from the stereotypical model of Latin Americans in the way they conduct business. They are seen as resourceful, highly educated, and motivated to form business networks and to boost the exchange between Argentina and the rest of the world.

Business style in Argentina is colored by the mixed heritage that it has. Generally, they are intensely competitive and this has been one of the redeeming factors that has increased the internationalization of its markets. Most often, the atmosphere at work is friendly and informal, though the attire is formal, as is the attitude toward work. There is a lot of emphasis given to specific aspects of any contract and most Argentines would be interested in getting their queries sorted out prior to furthering the business topic. It is ideal that the foreign party be aware of the Argentine culture as well as business environment before engaging in conversation. The usual tactic is to analyze the person in terms of his attitudes. To learn more about their culture before assessing their knowledge of Argentina.

It is also crucial to note that the practice of paying "propinas" (tips) and "coimas"(bribes) is part of the Argentine business culture. It is a rather delicate situation for a foreigner but a must-know if the ultimate goal is to function effectively in the country. They believe that while this expedites the process, periodic anticorruption campaigns also co-exist, which makes the business culture even more complex to function in. The business etiquette of Argentina is illustrated in Exhibit 19-7.

Market Research in Argentina

Similar to other Latin American countries, it is not considered appropriate to give respondents cash in reciprocation for their participation in surveys or focus groups. Most often a small gift (i.e., anything in kind) is far more appreciated because money slights their intention to voice their opinions, making it more of a transaction than an informal exchange of their sentiments.

EXHIBIT 19-7

Business Etiquette in Argentina

A researcher needs to understand the dialectic in Argentina between the old and the new, the European and the indigenous cultures. Slight nuances in nonverbal communication often help in this setting to determine the level of acceptability.

Business attire is most often formal and it is usually expected of the client to conform to the codes.

Small businesses tend to be more flexible with their work hours to incorporate the afternoon siesta. This is, however, not the case for most of the large corporations where, in fact, the working hours can stretch till 10 p.m.

In greetings, often the Argentines are warm and friendly, unless the circumstance calls for extreme formality (as in some business meetings). The usual greeting is a warm hug, though a firm handshake also connotes sincerity and a willingness to conduct business.

It is extremely important to recognize the power or status of the person with whom the company is dealing. The higher the person is in the organizational structure, the more likely he or she is to delay in keeping appointments. Regardless of the hierarchy, it is extremely important to establish closure for the business deal since Argentines tend to discuss the "appropriate" aspects, which may be for your benefit at the time of the dealing.

Source: Adapted from *Argentina Business: The Portable Encyclopedia for doing Business with Argentina,* Foundacion Invertir Argentina (World Trade Press, 1995).

BOLIVIA

Country Characteristics[7]

> Population: 7,669,868 (July 1997 est.)
> Land Area: 1,084,390 sq km
> Language: Spanish, Quecha, Aymara
> Literacy Rate: 83.1 percent
> Religion: Roman Catholic (95 percent), Protestant
> GDP—purchasing power parity: $21.5 billion (1996 est.)
> GDP per capita—purchasing power parity: $3,000 (1996 est.)
> GDP—real growth rate: 3.9 percent (1996 est.)
> Inflation Rate—consumer price index: 10 percent (1996 est.)

Business Characteristics[8]

The principle ethnic group in Bolivia are Latin Americn Indians, who make up an estimated 55 percent of the total population. Most of the population is concentrated in the 10 percent of Bolivia located on the cold and bleak Altiplano, which has been the center of Indian life since pre-Inca days. About half of the population live in rural areas, mostly by subsistence farming.

The Bolivian government is eager to attract foreign investment. Most members of Bolivia's private sector are experienced business persons with ample direct exposure to U.S. and West European customs and procedures. The local representative is a vital component in the successful operation of foreign-based firms.

With regard to product promotion and distribution, Bolivia's small market requires that most agents represent more than one line of merchandise. The amount of effort given to promoting a particular product line is determined in part by the interest and support expressed by the supplier, as well as the agent's ability and interest.

After a firm business relationship has been established, local distributors and agents generally expect to be extended an offer to visit the foreign company's plant facilities and head offices in order to become more familiar with the company's personnel and operating techniques.

Spanish is considered to be the official language of Bolivia, as well as the language of commerce. English is widely spoken among business and public officials, but most prefer to speak Spanish.

Marketing Research — Infrastructure Situation

Bolivia does not have a very good telephone network, with only three lines existing for every 100 Bolivians; some lines may come into service in the near future, but the country will still have a relatively low per capita level of phone lines.[9] As of 1992, Bolivia had only 207,823 telephone lines for an urban population of approximately 4 million. Given this condition, companies attempting to conduct research would have to take into consideration the reach of the targeted segment. Also, the cost consideration of convenience sampling would have to be taken into account, despite the problems in terms of accuracy and reliability of the segment.

The role of broadcast media is predominant, with television being one of the main media channels, while radio has continued to be a strong vehicle for advertising as well. Exhibit 19-8 indicates the price indices in Bolivian cities.

EXHIBIT 19-8

Bolivian Families Expenditures

In 1994, Bolivia's National Statistics Institute published results of the survey on family expenditures in the four largest Bolivian cities. The primary purpose of the survey was to establish a new market basket of goods to be used for a new Consumer Price Index (CPI). The survey team found that an average family in the three more affluent cities spend around U.S. $250 per month, while an average family in the poorer city of El Alto, near La Paz, spends only half that amount.

Source: Market Research Reports—Bolivia—Average Family Spending Statistics, USDOC International Trade Administration, 1994.

BRAZIL

Brazil is the largest and most industrialized nation of the Latin American countries with a vast size and diversity that often tempts marketers.

Country Characteristics[10]

Population: 164,511,366 (July 1997 est.)
Land Area: 8,456,510 sq km
Language: Portuguese, Spanish, English, and French
Literacy Rate: 83.3 percent
Religion: Roman Catholic
GDP—purchasing power parity: $1.022 trillion (1996 est.)
GDP per capita—purchasing power parity: $6,300 (1996 est.)
GDP—real growth rate: 2.9 percent (1996 est.)
Inflation Rate—consumer price index: 10 percent (1996 est.)

General Characteristics[11]

The tremendous problems with inflation have reduced the purchasing power by about 50 percent among the working and lower-middle classes and caused a major polarization of income. Exhibit 19-9 summarizes the results of a consumer trends survey in Brazil.

Most of the businesses in Brazil are operated via an agent or distributor. This is partly explained by the market peculiarities with which they are familiar, such as inflationary tendencies. Brazil's business community is highly educated and a significant portion of the population is well-versed in English as well as another foreign business language.

Market Research in Brazil

In a snapshot of the available telecommunication services in Brazil, this country has the largest telecommunications sector in all of Latin America. The Brazilian government has a monopoly in the provision of telephone, telegraph, data transmission, and other public services.

Telephone

Brazil at present has an installed base of 10.63 million telephones. With a rate of seven telephones for every 100 inhabitants, Brazil is ranked 42nd in the world. According to 1994 estimates, less than two percent of the rural population and only 19 percent of residences have access to telephone services. In bigger cities there is 30 percent penetration.[12] The biggest problem is that service congestion is worsening, which implies that while there was a 90 percent chance that calls were completed on the first attempt in 1980, this rate fell to 76 percent in 1991. Only 6.8 out of 100 people have phone lines and that becomes even smaller in the rural areas where only 2 percent of the population have phones.

Mail

As the growth of mail order catalogs (with companies like Sears Roebuck and JCPenney) indicate, the use of mail as a good survey tool has improved. The reliability of the mail service in terms of reach, as well as the number of undelivered or lost mail, is crucial to the effectiveness of this method of data collection.

EXHIBIT 19-9

Consumer Trends in Brazil

A recent study by the University of São Paulo (USP) revealed that less than 10 percent of Brazilian families (about 500,000) have annual incomes of U.S. $25,000 or more. Eighty-five percent of the national demand has concentrated in less than 10 percent of 5,000 cities surveyed throughout the country. It appears that lower income consumers are beginning to spend more on basic goods in the first quarter of 1994 compared to the first quarter of 1993; however, while Brazilian consumers are feeling more confident, large retailers are only maintaining stocks and paying off heavy debts. Yet, a boom in retail spending is anticipated and foreign investors are taking note.

The majority of the consumers with purchasing power in Brazil live in the southeastern part of the country. Considering a population of 140 million with an average size of 3.5, the USP study estimated 40 million families in Brazil of which 39.5 million are the so-called marginal consumers.

If the local retail outlets have been accurate in gauging, the low-income Brazilian consumer will begin spending more in the basic product categories in the following priority:

1. Meats and other basic foodstuffs with higher protein levels
2. Clothing
3. Household appliances and used cars

The biggest paradox is that as the base-level consumer spending in Brazil is poised to increase significantly, retail establishments, particularly the large ones, are only maintaining inventories while paying off large debts. As one retail sector consultant quipped in the *Gazeta Mercantil* (the national business newspaper), the sector is now living in a new boom of sales.

Source: Market Research Report, USDOC International Trade Administration, Brazil—Consumer Demand, 1997.

Facsimile (fax)

According to the 1994 study conducted, there are 210,000 cellular phones, which complemented the fax system. While the problem with faxes is similar to that of telephones (reliability on the telecommunications' infrastructure), the current operation of cellular phones has been restricted to the state-operated bandwidth. The result is an inadequate number of services and products.[13]

VENEZUELA

Bordering the Caribbean Sea between Colombia and Guyana in the northern part of South America, Venezuela (which means "Little Venice"—a reflection of early European connections) is a land of abundant resources, both natural and human.

Country Characteristics[14]

Population: 22,396,407 (July 1997 est.)
Land Area: 882,050 sq km
Language: Spanish, native dialects
Literacy Rate: 91.1 percent
Religion: Roman Catholic (96 percent), Protestant (2 percent)
GDP—purchasing power parity: $197 billion (1996 est.)
GDP per capita—purchasing power parity: $9,000 (1996 est.)
GDP—real growth rate: 1.6 percent (1996 est.)
Inflation Rate—consumer price index: 103 percent (1996 est.)

Cultural Characteristics

Roman Catholicism is the dominant religion in Venezuela, though a small number of people are of other denominations or tribal religions.

One out of four people live in Caracas, the capital of Venezuela, and though this is a fairly large metropolitan city, only a small portion of the population has high purchasing power. Approximately 4 million Venezuelans are considered to be truly economically active (in terms of producing and purchasing). When taking a cross-section of the Venezuelan population, 70 percent are less than 40 years of age, while close to 50 percent are less than 16 years of age.

Business Characteristics[15]

The Venezuelan business style is casual, with most of the address being informal. The manner in which they address each other in business is *tú*, which loosely translated is "you." Their greeting and saying goodbye to an acquaintance with a kiss is another cultural aspect to consider; however, in the first-time business meeting, in order to gauge the other side's responses, most Venezuelans would assume a more formal stance. The offer of coffee is considered to be normal practice and not an indication of the atmosphere becoming more lax. The first meeting may end in expression of interest, which may be primarily for the sake of politeness. The Venezuelans have a strong sense of independence and do not feel compelled to abide by the rules at all times. Overall, their laid-back attitude translates into the business environment.

Venezuelans have a great difficulty in saying "no." It would be to the advantage of the corporation if the conditions were not demanded or imposed. As the Venezuelans are coerced into a certain position, they would not want to compromise. It is important that the American businessperson is patient and probes to gain information on what the Venezuelan wants and how best to adapt to those needs.

It is interesting to note that retail outlets and other businesses are operated at the employees' convenience, rather than that of the shoppers. This reflects the attitude that the Venezuelans take toward service provision to their customers. The concept of refunds is usually unheard of and exchanging of garments as well as products with which the customer is unsatisfied is virtually impossible. Time consciousness is another area in which Venezuelans differ vastly from their American counterparts. Arriving at an appointment late does not carry with it the stigma that exists in the United States.

Patriotism toward their country is what most Venezuelans feel; however, most Venezuelans feel that the foreigners are not in the country to boost the growth of the nation or appeal to U.S.–Venezuelan friendship.

Drawing up contracts in Venezuela is never a reciprocal situation. Most of them are reluctant to commit things to writing, yet would appreciate it greatly if the information that they receive is specified.

Market Research in Venezuela

Telephone

Making telephone calls requires several attempts. It is time consuming and difficult to compile the research over a period of time. Many reference facilities and materials do not exist in Venezuela. The lack of infrastructure would mean that this might not be a dependable mode to conduct survey research.

Mail

The biggest problem is the reliability of the mail service in delivering the questionnaires to the specific sample homes. Most of the questionnaires are lost, almost 40 percent never reach the destination, and this may significantly affect the data collection. There are several private companies that address this problem by having the questionnaires delivered to major collection points.

Facsimile (fax)

These have become one of the more common tools used by businesses in order to get an expedient as well as detailed response to their questionnaires. The biggest problem with this method would be the cost in not only setting up the equipment but paying for the telecommunication link. Also, similar to the problem referred to for telephones as a viable means for research, faxes rely on the infrastructure that the country has set up, which has to make significant progress.

Personal Interviews

The problem in Venezuela is that there is no private time when conducting interviews at home. In a society where the involvement of the family extends to every realm, obtaining an individual response to a questionnaire or a product satisfaction query is virtually impossible.

As for business interviews, the working hours in most offices are from 9:00 a.m. to 1:00 p.m. and from 3:00 p.m. to 7:00 p.m. during the weekdays and some Saturdays. It is generally easier to obtain respondents among the business folk, mainly due to the fact that the work ethic is flexible. As for interviews in malls or on streets, this is not commonly practiced, primarily due to the irregular set-up.

For more information, please visit the Web site http://lcweb2.loc.gov/frd/cs/vetoc.htm

Summary

This chapter discusses Latin America from a marketing research perspective. It provides data about trade, culture, history, and the languages of Latin American countries in general. Special attention is paid to Argentina, Bolivia, Brazil, and Venezuela. The cultural norms, business habits, infrastructure, and data sources for these countries are discussed in detail.

Endnotes

1. Adapted from Strategy Research Corporation, *Household Buying Power Report*, 1996.
2. *Marketing News*, 1994—Research International Revelations #6.
3. "What's Working for American Companies" *International Sales and Marketing* (February 1998).
4. J. D. Zbar, "Latin America Gets Caught Up in 'net," *ComputerWorld* Global Innovators (9 June 1997).
5. C. Ryder, "Internet Opportunity," *ComputerWorld* (29 September 1997).
6. *CIA World Factbook 1997* http://www.odci .gov/cia/publications/factbook/
7. ibid.
8. *Marketing in Bolivia—Overseas Business Reports*, U.S. Department of Commerce (January 1989).
9. *Market Research Reports*—Bolivia Telecommunications, USDOC International Trade Administration, 1994.
10. *CIA World Factbook 1997* http://www.odci .gov/cia/publications/factbook/
11. *Market Research Report*, USDOC International Trade Administration, Brazil—Country Marketing Plan, 1994.
12. P. Pinhelro de Andrade, "Market Research in Brazil," *European Research* (August 1987), 188–197.
13. *Market Research Report*, USDOC International Trade Administration, Brazil—Country Marketing Plan, 1994.
14. *CIA World Factbook 1997* http://www.odci .gov/cia/publications/factbook/
15. *Market Research Reports*—USDOC, International Trade Administration, 1992.

CHAPTER

20

Middle East and Africa

INTRODUCTION

The Middle East is plagued with problems regarding inconsistent infrastructure and poor transportation. The biggest benefit for the countries is that their oil-rich sources boost their economies. The three countries of Saudi Arabia, Israel, and Lebanon have had immense improvements made to enhance their telecommunication systems and to modernize the current framework. The market research industry is relatively new to the Arab world, and in some countries the concept had not taken off to its maximum level until the 1990s. Table 20-1 explains the demographic profile of the Gulf Cooperation Council.[1]

The problem in conducting or gathering secondary research is that there is immense inaccuracy and most of the information is dated. This is also compounded by the government hesitating to release consumer information to the marketers (local as well as multinationals). It is also difficult to inculcate the culture of conducting market research and in the process infiltrating the barriers in terms of religion and social constructs to win respondents' trust (especially when it comes to Arab women).

PRIMARY RESEARCH IN THE MIDDLE EAST

The contrast between the level of importance given to the role of market research by local companies as opposed to foreign companies is extreme. Most local companies assume that they would have full awareness of the home market and the current trends in lifestyles and incomes; they do not believe in investing in intensive field research.

Conducting primary research has been mainly through observation and sample surveys. These can be seen as effective ways to gather information, especially regarding the psychographic profile of the average Arab. The method of observational research is through installing cameras and setting up consumer panels that will help gain some insight into consumer behavior; however, this has to be sanctioned first by the authorities and, of course, elicit a positive response from the consumers. Most often,

TABLE 20-1 Demographic Profile of Gulf Cooperation Council (GCC)*

Total Population	28 million	
Labor Force	9.1 million	
Population Growth Rate	3.5% p.a.	
Population Structure	0–14 years	43%
	15–64 years	55%
	Above 65 years	2%
Male : Female	1.3 : 1	
Literacy Rate	65%	
Economic Profile of GCC		
GCC GDP	$327 billion	
Inflation	4%	
Per Capita GDP	$15,750	
GCC Exports	$90 billion	
GCC Imports	$59 billion	
GCC Revenue	$58 billion	
GCC Expenditure	$70 billion	

*GCC comprises Bahrain, Kuwait, Qatar, Oman, Saudi Arabia, and the United Arab Emirates which was formed in May 1981.

Source: Compiled from several reports

they consider this to be an invasion of privacy and that the information regarding preference should be derived more from sales levels.

When having focus groups, the biggest disadvantage is that people are apprehensive of answering personal questions. It is necessary to ensure that the context or frame references are specified within the Middle Eastern countries in order to avoid cultural misunderstanding. Door-to-door interviews tend to be a problem because people are not receptive to the idea and tend to become suspicious of the intent behind the information sought. Also, interviewing women is considered to be difficult, and this skews the results since the actual decision maker for consumer goods does not reflect upon the purchasing process. This problem has been circumvented to a degree by employing women to ask the questions. Women respond well to the female interviewers, and recommendations and ideas have been positive.

One major aspect to note is the subtle dialects that exist due to class structure (dictated by economic status). This has been identified as a major barrier by marketing researchers. In dealing with the Arab population, a lot can be lost in the translation process (particularly for qualitative research). For example, personification—where the researcher asks the respondent to pretend that a particular brand name is a person—may not be effective. Translating the verbal as well as nonverbal communication elements requires expertise and familiarity with the Arab countries and the inherent culture(s).

The problem with mail service is that although the current system in Saudi Arabia is reliable, that cannot be applied across all of the Middle Eastern nations. The degree of reach to some of the population across Syria and Lebanon is limited and this may reduce the size of the sample to just the cities. Also, the difference in literacy and economic classes not only across the individual country but across the region make it a rather difficult method, though cost effective, to implement.

Telephone service is restricted to the metropolitan areas and, given the nomadic characteristics of some of the population, this would be extremely unreliable. Referring to Table 20-2, the ratio of telephones per person is unequal. Given that the infrastructure in some of these countries does not support such a means of data collection, this translates to the fact that perhaps only Saudi Arabia would be a "good" market to conduct research. Also, it is necessary to note that many Arabs are resistant to answering any queries over the phone. Exhibit 20-1 explains some of the cultural traits typical of Middle Eastern countries.

One of the most unique features of the Arab region is the number of expatriates in the different countries. This complicates the nature of the market and this multicultural characteristic makes conducting market research even more difficult. It would involve significant cost in trying to get a representative sample from the entire market. For instance, in the United Arab Emirates (UAE), a cross-section of the population reflects a composition of 40 percent locals and the rest, expatriates. It would be crucial for a company to analyze the degree of difference in consumer culture and level of affordability and accessibility to a select sample.

SECONDARY DATA SOURCES IN THE MIDDLE EAST

The sources of secondary market information can be broadly classified as:

1. Government publications
2. Commercial databases
3. Nongovernment agencies
4. Overseas sources

EXHIBIT 20-1

Cultural "Do's" and "Don'ts" in the Middle East

- Direct eye contact for too long is considered offensive. It is preferable to use titles and full names and avoid being too familiar.

- Open displays of affection toward the opposite gender are not appreciated. Private conversations and whispering while in a group is considered rude.

- Expressive hand gestures used to support conversation are considered as calling attention upon oneself and are frowned upon.

- It is best not to admire the possessions of one's host. They feel obligated to give the items to you.

- Meetings have to be arranged beforehand, and it is not unusual for the meeting to start later than the scheduled time.

- Though Arabs enjoy negotiating prices, once the price is fixed there is no going back.

- Some Arab men do not like doing business with women.

Source: Adapted from *The Cultural Gaffes Pocketbook* by Angelena Boden, *Management Pocketbooks,* 1997. Reprinted by permission of Management Pocketbooks.

5. Universities and research institutions
6. Newspapers and magazines
7. Miscellaneous sources (Internet, etc.)

Government Publications

The main secondary source in this region for a researcher is the publications from the local governments. The governments publish economic and demographic data as well as industrial and trade data including exports, imports, and reexports statistics annually. Though these publications prove to be reliable, in most of the cases the reports are published with a lag of over 2 years. In addition, the government publications from many countries in the region do not follow unified codes in presenting the trade statistics. Even within UAE, until recently the foreign trade statistics published by Dubai, Abu Dhabi, and Sharjah emirates followed different SITC and HS codes.

These statistics are available in hardcopy only. Electronic databases are not common in this region. Some of the publications from the local government are statistical year books, foreign trade statistics, and chambers of commerce.

Commercial Databases

There are almost no reliable commercial databases like ACNielsen's available in the region. Only a handful of companies, such as Kompass, offer statistics on trade and industry.

Nongovernment Agencies

A number of associations and special interest groups operating in the Middle East region offer valuable information. A partial list of the agencies and associations available in the region follows:

1. Arab Air Carriers' Organization (AACO)
2. Arab Authority for Agricultural Investment and Development (AAAID)
3. Arab Bureau of Education for the Gulf States
4. Arab Cooperation Council
5. Arab Federation of Petroleum, Mining, and Chemicals Workers
6. Arab Federation of Textile Workers
7. Arab Federation of Transport Workers
8. Arab Fund for Economic and Social Development (AFESD)
9. Arab Gulf Program of the United Nations Development Organizations (AGFUND)
10. Arab Iron and Steel Union (AISU)
11. Arab League
12. Arab Monetary Fund
13. Arab Organization for Human Rights (AOHR)
14. Arab Organization of Mineral Resources
15. Arab Society of Certified Accountants
16. Arab Sports Confederation
17. Arab Towns Organization

18. Arab Union of Railways
19. Association of Arab Historians
20. Association of Arab Universities
21. Center for Research in Islamic Economics
22. Center for Social Science Research and Documentation for the Arab Region
23. Cooperation Council for the Arab States of the Gulf (GCC)
24. Council of Arab Economic Unity
25. Federation of Arab Engineers
26. Federation of Arab Scientific Research Councils
27. General Union of Chambers of Commerce, Industry, and Agriculture for Arab Countries
28. Gulf Organization for Industrial Consulting (GOIC)
29. International Association of Islamic Banks
30. International Confederation of Arab Trade Unions (ACATU)
31. International Planned Parenthood Federation
32. Islamic Development Bank
33. Muslim World League
34. Organization of Arab Oil Exporting Countries (OAPEC)
35. Organization of the Islamic Conference (OIC)
36. Organization of the Petroleum Exporting Countries (OPEC)
37. OPEC Fund for International Development
38. Parliamentary Association for Euro-Arab Cooperation
39. Union du Maghreb Arabe (UMA)
40. Union of Arab Jurists
41. Union of Arab Stock Exchanges

Overseas Sources

Information on the Middle East markets can also be obtained from a number of sources published from outside the region, such as,

1. U.S. Reports on GCC: trade policies, import policies, and so on
2. The *CIA World Fact Book*
3. The European Community
4. The United Nations (UN)
5. U.S.–Arab Chamber of Commerce

Universities and Research Institutions

Other potential sources of secondary market data for the Middle East include universities and research agencies operating within the region as well as outside. A partial list of such universities and agencies follows:

1. European Association for Middle Eastern Studies (EURAMES), an umbrella organization for national and other Middle East studies associations, at the Centre for Middle Eastern and Islamic Studies, University of Durham, United Kingdom. It has a World Wide Web site at http://www.hf.uib.no/smi/eurames/

2. CANMES, the Canadian section of Middle East Studies Association (MESA), has a Web site at http://www.arts.mcgill.ca/programs/ICAS/CANMES/canmes.html

3. ARABIC-INFO is a new electronic bulletin board for announcements related to Arabic Studies (language, literature, culture, history, and so on), including calls for papers, announcements for conferences, new publications, notes on research in progress, abstracts of completed dissertations, book reviews, news of Arabic/Near Eastern Studies Programs, employment and funding opportunities, profiles of individuals associated with Arabic studies, and obituaries

4. The Jaffee Center for Strategic Studies at Tel Aviv University has a Web site at http://plato.tau.ac.il/jcssjb/

5. Amman University has a Web page at http://www.amman.edu/; the University of Jordan at http://www.ju.edu.jo/ and a regularly updated listing of Arab universities on-line at http://arabia.com/education/auni.html

6. Birzeit University (http://www.birzeit.edu), the first Palestinian university on the World Wide Web, maintains a regularly updated chronicle of events in Palestine and hosts a Palestine Archive at http://www.birzeit.edu:80/palarc/index.html plus a complete, updated guide to other Web sites in Palestine at http://www.birzeit.edu:80/links/index.html

7. Camel Researchers Database, maintained by the Animal Production Department of the United Arab Emirates University, at Al Ain, UAE. It has a Web page at http://www.uaeu.ac.ae/faculty/agri/camel.html

8. Directories for the Middle East and access to the Muslim organizations and organizations for Middle East and Islamic studies are available from the Columbia University libraries at http://www.columbia.edu/cu/libraries/indiv/area/MiddleEast/directories.html

9. The Arab Information Project at Georgetown University's Center for Contemporary Arab Studies focuses on information technology and electronic communications in the Middle East at http://www.georgetown.edu/sfs/programs/ccas/infotech/

Newspapers and Trade Magazines

A number of English and Arabic newspapers and magazines provide information on the Middle East market. A partial list of newspapers available on the Internet follows:

1. *Iran Weekly Press Digest* at http://www.neda.net/iran-wpd/, emphasizes political, social, and economic affairs

2. *Arab View* (http://www.arab.net/arabview/welcome.html) is a selection of editorial opinion on mostly political topics from the overseas Saudi-owned press (al-Hayat, as-Sharq al-Awsat, etc.)

3. *Al-Hayat*, the Arabic language daily from London, puts its complete edition online at http://www.alhayat.com/, in Arabic (Adobe Acrobat PDF format, requires Adobe Acrobat Reader, which is downloadable free from http://www.adobe.com)

4. *Al-Jazirah* is a Saudi newspaper published on the Internet at http://www.al-jazirah.com/, in Arabic graphics, multilingual browser not required

5. *Yemen Times* is online at http://www.y.net.ye/yementimes

6. *Ha'aretz* has select articles in English online at http://www.haaretz.co.il/eng with links to the Hebrew edition

7. *Economic Perspectives* (al-Ghad al-Iktisadi) from Jordan and the region, at http://www.arabia.com/ep/ offers news of business fairs, conferences, regional financial news, in English

8. *Business Today,* at http://www.arabia.com/BusinessToday/, is an online edition of the Egyptian business daily, in English

9. *Middle East Reports* is online at http://www.merip.org/ with tables of contents of the current issue and selections from previous issues.

Miscellaneous Sources

1. Centre d'Information Arabe Scandanavie (http://i-cias.com/index.htm) offers people interested in information on the Middle East the most comprehensive Web sites covering every possible subject. CiAS is a commercial company and is neutral in all political and religious questions

2. Internet MidEast lists "business opportunities on the World Wide Web" from *PC Magazine,* Middle and Near East edition, at http://www.pcmag-mideast.com /newsl.htm

3. Middle East Review of International Affairs (MERIA) is an electronic newsletter from the Begin-Sadat Center for Strategic Studies (BESA), Bar-Ilan University, with a news segment for short analyses of current developments, books, announcements of conferences and research queries, and a journal segment offering peer-reviewed scholarly articles. The scope of each includes culture, economics, politics, literature, history, archaeology, international and strategic studies, and peace and conflict studies. MERIA may be viewed on the World Wide Web at http://www.biu.ac.il /SOC/bera/meria.html

4. ArabPlex offers an extensive listing of World Wide Web sites on Arab art, music and film, ancient Egypt, and business and marketing sites in and for the Arab world at http://www.sage.net/~intercept/arabplex/cathtml/new.htm. ArabPlex is an offering of InterCept Trade Management (http://www.sage.net/~intercept/aboutus .htm) in Temple, TX

5. Privatization in the Middle East, at http://www.pmena.com/, targets organizations interested in the region with news about privatization in Arab countries, Turkey, Israel, and Iran

6. Arabseek, at http://www.arabseek.com/, offers an index of Arab country chambers of commerce, banks, and dialing codes, from Bahrain

7. The Jordanian General Intelligence Department has opened a World Wide Web homepage at http://petra.nic.gov.jo/gid/welcome.html

8. The Israel Defense Force has a World Wide Web homepage at http://www.israel-mfa.gov.il/idf

9. Information on the government of the state of Dubai, United Arab Emirates (UAE) can be found at http://www.dubai-ed.com; includes economic policy, foreign trade, customs, and tariffs

10. Palestine Central Bureau of Statistics, from the Palestinian National Authority, http://www.pcbs.org, collects and publishes demographic, economic, and census data

Table 20-2 gives the media outlook in some Middle Eastern countries. This will be helpful in deciding the research methodology to be adopted in each of these countries.

TABLE 20-2   Middle-East — Media Outlook

Country	Telecommunications Per Capita	Newspapers/Circ. Per 1000	Number of Telephones
Syria	TV—1 per 17	20 per 1000	512,600 37 per 1000
Lebanon	TV—1 per 3.4 Radio—1 per 1.3	201 per 1000	325,000 95 per 1000
Iran	TV—1 per 23	13 per 1000	2.14 million 35 per 1000
Saudi Arabia	TV—1 per 3.5 Radio—1 per 3.3	7 Arabic papers 2 English papers 49 per 1000	1.63 million
Israel	TV—1 per 6.9	357 per 1000	1.8 million

Source: Reprinted with permission from *The World Almanac and Book of Facts 1998.* Copyright © 1997 PRIMEDIA Reference Inc. All rights reserved.

SAUDI ARABIA

Country Characteristics[2]

> Population: 20,087,965 (July 1997 est.)
> Land Area: 1,960,582 sq km
> Language: Arabic
> Literacy Rate: 62.8 percent
> Religion: Muslim
> GDP—purchasing power parity: $205.6 trillion (1996 est.)
> GDP per capita—purchasing power parity: $10,600 (1996 est.)
> GDP—real growth rate: 6 percent (1996 est.)
> Inflation Rate—consumer price index: 1 percent (1996 est.)

Cultural Characteristics

Despite the stereotyping that all Arabs are Muslims, what is essential to note is that the religion complements the Arab way of life. Exhibit 20-2 discusses the curious mix of religion and cosmopolitanism among Saudi Arabian youth. Here, Arab means pertaining to Arabia and carries with it the cultural connotation and not the religious association.[3] Saudi Arabians tend to perceive business to be a means to gain understanding of the Middle Eastern methods of management. Often, in order to succeed, the following pointers are useful:

- Time is a major commodity, but patience is a virtue. It is beneficial for the foreign party to spend the time in getting accustomed to the Arab culture. Time is considered to be decided upon by God. It is important not to stipulate rigid time frames without giving allowance for the concept of God's will. Saudi Arabians are also fatalistic; they believe in fate and the "hand of God." Therefore, planning for contingencies is not something they frequently indulge in.

EXHIBIT 20-2

Saudi Arabian Youth

There has been an increasing interest in trying to understand the youth from the Middle East, what their perspectives are, what their tastes are, and most importantly, do they live up to the consumer interest figure that marketers are hoping for. Approximately 62 percent of the population in Saudi Arabia are under 25 years of age.

The recent survey by AMER World Research of 3,845 youth elicited a response that was justifiably a mix of all influences (both ethnic and religious). Traditional values and beliefs are still held onto despite the infiltration of western (European) influences. The new generation of respondents were conservative in their clothing styles, considered family and marriage to be strong institutions, and believed that while women should get more prominence, it is the family which takes precedence.

It is interesting to note that despite the changes that have been seeping through, the emphasis that they place on tradition, filial piety, and religion has not altered dramatically.

Source: Adapted from Saudi Arabia: The Youth of Today, Response Analysis (The Sampler), http://www.response-analysis .com/sampler/win985.html

---

- Arabs are considered to be people of great emotional depth who believe in expressing their loyalty and friendship as key to an ongoing relationship. In conducting business, they tend to be warm, hospitable, and when the party becomes more aware of the nuances of the culture, make it a very easy-going discussion. It is necessary to note that the dealings are with the person and not the company, so the role of fostering relations is emphasized.

- The concept of the individual is very important in Arab culture. One cannot afford to lose face or ruin his family's name in the process of dealing with others. There is a hierarchy in the society, whether stipulated or otherwise, and an individual who has been shamed loses his status in the eyes of the group.

- Negotiating is considered to be part of the average business deal, and one should ideally expect that it would take time for a unanimous decision to be reached.

- Nonverbal communication is especially complicated in Saudi Arabia. Most Arabs express themselves with a multiplicity of gestures that the foreigner should be able to recognize. This is particularly important when conducting market research in this country.

- When targeting all of the countries in the Middle East region, one falls into the stereotypical thought that all Arabs in that part of the world conduct business alike. Saudi Arabia has raced ahead in its modernization attempts while countries like Syria and Iran are catching up, slowly.

- The role of women in business was considered to be secondary; however, with women becoming more educated, their presence on the business front has become significantly prominent. The foreign party, however, has to be conscious of the physical distance that should be maintained with an Arab woman when conducting business.

Arabs like new things because they have a very restricted life at home. Burgerland used this to their advantage in Saudi Arabia by combining their fast-food operations with the sociocultural environment of the Middle East.[4]

MARKET RESEARCH IN AFRICA

Conducting research in Africa requires a thorough analysis of the reach into the continent's several countries. The actual research, analysis, and interpretation, as well as applicability, become difficult for the market researcher due to the extreme polarization that exists within the continent. From Tunisia to South Africa, Sudan to Ethiopia, the researcher needs to take on a country-by-country approach to targeting within Africa as compared to a standardized strategy. While the use of the Internet is relatively higher in other regions, Africa lags behind due to poor infrastructure facilities, regulations, and cost of Internet connection (see Figure 20-1). Although the majority of the countries are in the cyberdark ages, the Republic of South Africa is in striking contrast.[5]

SOUTH AFRICA

Country Characteristics[6]

Population: 42,327,458 (July 1997 est.)
Land Area: 1,209,912 sq km
Language: 11 official languages, including Afrikaans, English, Ndebele, Pedi, Sotho, Swazi, Tsonga, Tswana, Venda, Xhosa, and Zulu
Literacy Rate: 81.8 percent
Religion: Christian (68 percent), Muslim (2 percent), Hindu (1.5 percent), traditional and animistic (28.5 percent)
GDP—purchasing power parity: $227 billion (1996 est.)
GDP per capita—purchasing power parity: $5,400 (1996 est.)
GDP—real growth rate: 3 percent (1996 est.)
Inflation rate—consumer price index: 9 percent (1996 est.)

Exhibit 20-3 illustrates the bargaining atmosphere in South Africa. There has been a sudden surge in the income levels in South Africa, which has improved the consumer goods industry's feasibility of operations. South Africa surely represents the first world among the rest of the countries in the African continent.

Conducting business dealings in South Africa is rather tedious. Most Africans do not stand on formality and though that connotes a relaxed attitude, they do not fall into that category either. Personal matters are kept separate from business dealings. Similarly, it is considered impolite to discuss business at home. Exhibit 20-4 explores the cultural similarities and dissimilarities between whites and blacks in South Africa.

The concept of elders and their status in the society is also to be emphasized. Concepts like seniority play a big role and it is important to adhere to the word of the oldest member of the host party.

FIGURE 20.1 The Internet In Africa: The Cost of Connecting

Estimated Internet users and costs in selected African countries, 1998

Country	No. of Users	Cost of Internet Access Per Hour (in U.S. Dollars)
Angola	1,500	$6.00
Botswana	500	$0.60
Central African Republic	200	$6.90
Chad	50	$10.50
Congo	0	N.A.
Democratic Republic of Congo	100	N.A.
Egypt	20,000	$1.20
Ethiopia	3,000	$2.60
Gabon	1,000	$13.90
Ghana	4,500	$1.34
Ivory Coast	1,000	$4.80
Kenya	5,000	$1.36
Libya	0	N.A.
Mauritania	100	$6.60
Morocco	6,000	$0.85
Mozambique	3,500	$0.80
Namibia	2,000	$1.00
Nigeria	1,000	$0.40
Senegal	2,500	$1.90
Somalia	0	N.A.
South Africa	800,000	$1.60
Sudan	300	N.A.
Tanzania	2,500	$1.94
Uganda	2,000	$8.40
Zimbabwe	10,000	$4.00

N.A. - Not available

Source: Reprinted by permission from *Inter@ctive Week*, November 30, 1998. Copyright © 1997 ZD, Inc.

EXHIBIT 20-3

Useful Tips (South Africa)

In order to allow for a better atmosphere, it is advisable to not push the deal. Hard bargaining is not part of the culture and it is better to start a business deal by fostering some exchange along informal lines, which would reduce the resistance to arriving at the end decision.

Source: Anonymous, "Doing Business in South Africa," *International Sales and Marketing* (15 February 1998).

EXHIBIT 20-4

Cultural Clues in South Africa

- *Family structure* in the black community has been destabilized by past apartheid policies and its constraints; dislocation caused by job searches contributes to 7 million living in poverty. In the black extended family there is great respect manifested toward the elderly, and obedience to parents. The white community's family is nuclear, close-knit, and privileged.

- *Life-style* among the white community is comparable to that of the average European or American experience, relative to socialization, work and recreation. Afrikaners are very independent and nationalistic with a sense of superiority and pride. Among the blacks there is more vibrancy, naturalness, and brotherhood, sometimes marred by inter-tribal conflict and power struggles.

Market Research Analysis

The most reliable sources of information on this continent and in South Africa are from databases already constructed by the multinational corporations and international organizations. The problem, however, is that the information is dated and cannot be relied upon to provide an accurate estimate of the demographic constitution of the country or region. The availability of newspapers, as well as other media, tends to be inconsistent, with Cape Town being the sole exception.

When attempting to conduct primary research, it would be beneficial to note that interviewing the respondents may not necessarily represent the entire consumer base. A significant portion of the population lives in rural areas, though in relation to the consumption levels, it is rather miniscule. While it would help to isolate the respondents to a specific income level, it may defeat the purpose of asking questions.

Conducting personal interviews with probes as well as focus groups may be a better option when dealing with such a diverse population. The biggest problem would be in terms of the cultural differences, the languages, as well as the habits which tend to differ from region to region, across classes and races. The construct should be able to reflect an insight across the board rather than minute subtleties.

The telephone is an effective, but costly and unreliable means to obtain consumer response. The problem becomes more complex due to inconsistency and poor infrastructure across the continent. In South Africa, telephone interviewing is considered to be appropriate, though the main problem is that there is significant ethnic bias. Only 25 percent of black households have telephones as compared to 93 percent of white households. In order to have a better representation, it is recommended that focus groups or personal interviews be used.[7]

Mail is intrinsically linked with the literacy rate, which varies from region to region. The mailing system in Africa is also not reliable and does not always extend beyond the usual cities into the rural areas.

PROBLEMS IN CONDUCTING RESEARCH
IN SOUTH AFRICA

Perhaps one of the biggest problems with South Africa is that political uncertainty infiltrates even into the research to be undertaken. It is difficult to measure the actual population of South Africa with the most recent measurement being in 1991. The regions that surrounded the cities themselves have been counted into the population figures (though inconsistently). In terms of considering some black townships, such as Soweto, the "estimated" population is 43.6 million (as of 1994).

In terms of language, there are close to 11 official languages spoken and these tend to be vernaculars or dialects. In order for there to be some consistency, the researcher would have to fix the conceptual aspect and then adjust it in order to be able to convey the same idea and try to eliminate bias induced in translations. Also, when targeting the African population, it would be necessary to consider the rural-urban settlements. This would determine both the standard of living as well as provide a cross-section of the racial mix of South Africa.

Summary

This chapter deals with the Middle East and Africa. Data about these regions in general and tips on conducting marketing research in the Middle East and Africa are provided. Country information is provided about Saudi Arabia and South Africa. Some relevant statistics and sources of information, such as journals and Web sites, are also mentioned.

Endnotes

1. Some sections in this chapter were developed with the information provided by G. Balasubramaniam of Dubai, UAE.
2. *CIA World Factbook 1997,* http://www.odci .gov/cia/publications/factbook/
3. Philip R. Harris and Robert T. Moran, *Managing Cultural Differences,* 4th ed. Houston, TX: Gulf Publishing Company, 1996), 347.
4. "Will Sheiks Take to Burgers and Fries?" *D&B Reports* (January–February 1986): 10–13.

5. Randy Barrett, "Off the Beaten Track: Unexpected Net Hot Spots," *Inter@ctive Week* 5, no. 47 (30 November 1998): 44.
6. *CIA World Factbook* 1997, http://www.odci .gov/cia/publications/factbook/
7. J. Rice, "The 1994 South African Election— The Research Experience," 23rd MRSA (Marketing Research Society of Australia) Conference, 1994.

CHAPTER

North America

INTRODUCTION

In 1988 the governments of the United States and Canada agreed to enter into a free trade agreement, which went into effect January 1, 1989. The goal of the agreement was to eliminate all tariffs on bilateral trade between Canada and the United States by 1998. This was followed in 1991 by talks among the United States, Canada, and Mexico aimed at establishing a North American Free Trade Agreement (NAFTA). The talks concluded in August 1992 with an agreement in principle. The agreement became law January 1, 1994. It contains the following actions:

- Abolishes within 10 years tariffs on 99 percent of the goods traded between Mexico, Canada, and the United States
- Removes most barriers on the cross-border flow of services, allowing financial institutions, for example, unrestricted access to the Mexican market by 2100
- Protects intellectual property rights
- Removes most restrictions on foreign direct investments between the three member countries, although special treatment (protection) will be given to Mexican energy and railway industries, American airline and radio communications industries, and Canadian culture
- Allows each country to apply its own environmental standards, provided such standards have scientific basis—lowering standards to lure investment is described as being inappropriate

The new North America comprises Canada, Mexico, and the United States. NAFTA, with more than 362 million consumers, is larger than the European Union, but slightly smaller than the European Economic Area (which has a consumer population of over 380 million people). NAFTA's combined output is nearly $8 trillion or about 21 percent larger than that of the European Union. The agreement progressively eliminates almost all United States-Mexico tariffs over a 10-year period and also phases out Mexico-Canada tariffs at the same time. Such barriers to trade as import licensing requirements and customs user fees are eliminated. NAFTA establishes the principle of national treatment to ensure that NAFTA countries will treat NAFTA-origin products in the same manner as similar domestic products. Service providers of the member nation will receive equal treatment. To protect foreign investors in the free trade area, NAFTA has established five principles: (1) nondiscriminatory treatment, (2) freedom from performance requirements, (3) free transference of funds related to an investment, (4) expropriation only in conformity with international law, and (5) the right to seek international arbitration for a violation of the agreement's protections.

About 2.1 million or 28 percent of export-created jobs can be traced to U.S. exports to Canada and Mexico. It should be noted that export-related jobs pay 17 percent more than the average U.S. wage. Canada's focus of economic activity has always been along the U.S. border, which stretches some 4,000 miles. It is not too surprising that the natural axis of trade has always been from north to south rather than east to west. Canada is the largest single market for U.S. exports as well as the largest market for American manufacturers. In addition, the CFTA has opened the Canadian market to the American services. As a result, U.S. exports of services to Canada reached $18 billion in 1991, representing an increase of 98 percent over 1987. Canada-U.S. trade has continued to grow, and the total bilateral trade in goods reached $272 billion in 1995.

U.S.–MEXICO TRADE

The United States is Mexico's most important trading partner, absorbing about two-thirds of total Mexican exports worldwide. On the other hand, Mexico is the third largest U.S. trading partner, ranking after Canada and Japan. Approximately 70 percent of all Mexico's imports come from the United States, and 15 cents of every additional dollar of Mexico's GDP is spent on American goods and services. Mexico is purchasing most of its durable goods and industrial materials from the United States. Not surprisingly, Mexico is the fastest growing major U.S. export market.

By far, Mexico is the largest U.S. trading partner in Latin America, accounting for about one-half of U.S. exports to and imports from the region. The total bilateral trade reached $108 billion in 1995. The U.S. trade balance with Mexico was in deficit for most of the 1980s, reaching a peak of $7.7 billion in 1983. In 1993, the United States recorded a trade surplus with Mexico for the first time since 1981.

Exhibit 21-1 lists some of the cultural peculiarities of North America.

UNITED STATES OF AMERICA

Country Characteristics[1]

Population: 267,954,764 (July 1997 est.)
Land Area: 9,158,960 sq km
Language: English, Spanish
Literacy Rate: 97 percent
Religion: Protestant (56 percent), Roman Catholic (28 percent), Jewish (2 percent), other (4 percent), none (10 percent)
GDP—purchasing power parity: $7.61 trillion (1996 est.)

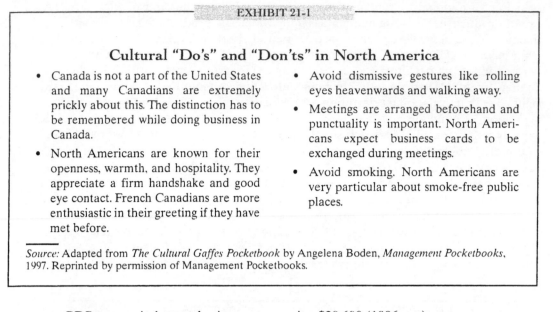

EXHIBIT 21-1

Cultural "Do's" and "Don'ts" in North America

- Canada is not a part of the United States and many Canadians are extremely prickly about this. The distinction has to be remembered while doing business in Canada.

- North Americans are known for their openness, warmth, and hospitality. They appreciate a firm handshake and good eye contact. French Canadians are more enthusiastic in their greeting if they have met before.

- Avoid dismissive gestures like rolling eyes heavenwards and walking away.

- Meetings are arranged beforehand and punctuality is important. North Americans expect business cards to be exchanged during meetings.

- Avoid smoking. North Americans are very particular about smoke-free public places.

Source: Adapted from *The Cultural Gaffes Pocketbook* by Angelena Boden, *Management Pocketbooks*, 1997. Reprinted by permission of Management Pocketbooks.

GDP per capital—purchasing power parity: $28,600 (1996 est.)
GDP—real growth rate: 2.4 percent (1996 est.)
Inflation Rate—consumer price index: 3 percent (1996 est.)

U.S. exports topped $650 billion in 1996, up from $448 billion in 1992, and the U.S. Department of Commerce expects exports to grow by nearly 10 percent per year through 2100. By comparison, the U.S. domestic market is expected to grow by 3.0 to 3.5 percent annually. Despite this rapid export growth, fewer than 50,000 U.S. companies actively export, with the top 250 exporting companies accounting for over 80 percent of all export revenues. U.S. companies that are not exporting should consider these reasons to look abroad for growth:

- The United States has less than 5 percent of the world's population and less than one-fourth of its gross domestic product. There are big opportunities beyond the border.
- The world's fastest growing markets are overseas—in Asia and Latin America. Companies that enter these markets in the early growth stages have the best opportunity to affect buying habits, brand identities, product standards, and distribution networks.
- Foreign competitors of U.S. companies are not only marketing in the United States, but in third-party countries worldwide. While it is not always necessary to compete in every market, forfeiting overseas markets to competitors will make it more difficult to compete—both domestically and abroad—in the future.
- It is becoming easier than ever to market and sell internationally. Trade barriers in most major markets are low and falling, and direct mail, the Internet, and telemarketing can minimize initial marketing investments.
- Many U.S. companies—indeed, entire industries—face a saturated, highly competitive U.S. market. For these companies, tapping into foreign markets can be the ticket to long-term growth.

Cultural Characteristics

For almost all cultures, it is important to understand how executives view power and authority. Many U.S. entrepreneurs are highly individualistic, time-conscious, goal-oriented people. The use of colors, numbers, and shapes can symbolize different things in different cultures. For example, in the United States, red, white, and blue are patriotic colors, but in China, blue and white are funeral colors, and red ink suggests bad luck in South Korea. A good way to avoid cultural missteps in conducting a research survey is to have the material reviewed by an individual from the target country.

The English spoken in the United States is different from that spoken in the United Kingdom and Australia. Portuguese spoken in Brazil is not the same as that used in Portugal. In France, natives speak French differently from Canadians. In Quebec, Canada, many residents speak English, but French is the official language. Product descriptions, labels, and warranties must be in French. If a Canada-wide mailing includes addresses in Quebec, the materials should be in both English and French.

MEXICO

Country Characteristics[2]

Population: 97,563,374 (July 1997 est.)
Land Area: 1,923,040 sq km
Language: Spanish, various Mayan dialects
Literacy Rate: 89.6 percent
Religion: Roman Catholic (89 percent), Protestant (6 percent)
GDP—purchasing power parity: $777.3 billion (1996 est.)
GDP per capita—purchasing power parity: $8,100 (1996 est.)
GDP—real growth rate: 5.1 percent (1996 est.)
Inflation Rate—consumer price index: 28 percent (1996 est.)

Cultural Characteristics[3]

It is important to note that Mexico has been undergoing significant changes in terms of its literacy rate, which has increased to 89 percent, as well as urbanization, which has been boosted to 65 percent. The Mexicans are seen to be a hospitable and warm group of people. When conducting business, it would be beneficial to have some time to talk to the Mexican counterparts and establish a personal relationship. Mexican attitude and behavior tend to be a combination of both European and Native American influences.

To the Mexican, the uniqueness of the individual should be recognized. Comparisons to the ways that others accomplish a task or in particular to the way it is done in the United States may be perceived as an insult. It is in this light that the Mexican society pays significant attention and respect to those who have had personal accomplishments in industry or in the arts.[4]

The family plays a chief role in an average Mexican's life and emphasis is placed on knowing one's family ties and connections prior to conducting business with them. Family relationships tend to be the basis upon which bonds are established and fostered. It is necessary for the foreign company to understand that questions posed regarding family are a means of ascertaining well-being rather than intrusion into privacy.[5]

Communication style is markedly different from that in the United States. Most Mexicans speak in a circumculatory manner and often avoid any direct references or conversations. In order to ensure that there is a pleasant atmosphere, Mexicans will tell their counterparts what they would want to hear, rather than mention anything harsh. This is not to say that they knowingly flatter in order to get their work done, the purpose is often to please the other party and to make them feel at home.

Mexicans tend to be fatalistic and try to attribute emphasis on the "right time" to conduct business. Time is perceived as relative and flexible to the Mexicans and the concept of *mañana* which means "tomorrow" filters into every aspect of business. This is not a means of procrastinating, but a way of evading a deadline or specific time.

When approaching the organizational structure, it is important to note the hierarchy within the company. The top-down system is very much in effect and seniority is considered to be a discriminating factor between levels. It is advisable for the foreign concern to be aware of the ranking of officials and alter its decision-making style based on the hierarchical differentiation.

One major aspect to note is machismo, the concept of masculinity that infiltrates business dealings as well. Though women are represented in several managerial positions, it is believed that only a man should earn the respect from society and demonstrate strong leadership qualities. This affects the manner in which business is conducted; assuming a woman represents the foreign concern, it would take a significant amount of coaxing before she is treated on equal terms to the male counterparts in the host country. Though this scenario is changing, the concept of machismo affects the manner in which market research is to be conducted.

Tangibility in presenting the results of a certain business deal is important to the Mexican. The style of the presentation is seen to be equal to that of the content. Contradicting their opinion on flexibility, Mexicans prefer to see their presentations in terms of visual aids and heavy word play. This becomes central to the market researchers in their effort to help understand or interpret Mexican interests and viewpoints.

Despite such emphasis on presentation, Mexicans prefer to give time in order to make a decision. Formality of agendas tends to suggest that the other party is not concerned over the overall well-being of the other. A business relationship to the Mexican is to be seen as an extension of the personal friendship that is to be formed prior to the deal. Time to them becomes a crucial element in order to establish that bond. Also, in order for them to avoid "losing face," they may avoid immediate commitment or direct conversation.

Market Research in Mexico

Providing the respondents with gifts is often seen to be more appealing as compared to paying money, which may be perceived as for services rendered. As for other Latin American countries, Mexicans tend to view the interviewing process to be one where they can express their ideas and contribute. Rather than paying them the equivalent of what would be given in the United States, it would be appropriate to contact a local representative to determine the ideal gifts.

The telecommunications system in Mexico is considered to be developing at a tremendous rate. This would imply that for the market researcher, contacting potential respondents over telephone or fax would not be too much of a problem; however, there are several impediments to this method of research. Chiefly, reliability of the connections cannot be guaranteed, and secondly, there is immense inconsistency in the degree of growth between major cities in Mexico. While the population of Mexico is concentrated around the cities, there is a significant number of people who live in smaller towns and areas with vastly different incomes, purchasing capacities, and culture.

The postal system in Mexico is not considered to be effective. This would hamper the use of mail surveys that would otherwise be a cost efficient way to conduct market research. This suggests that the best possible way to conduct surveys in Mexico would be personal interviews or mall intercepts. This allows the required reach to the consumers and at the same time provides the one-to-one interaction, which is extremely important in a country where nonverbal communication is high. Exhibit 21-2 points out some common Mexican gestures.

It would help the foreign company to select translators who would effectively communicate and help analyze the reactions of the consumers. This would be vital when conducting qualitative tests (such as focus groups), where reactions of the respondents forms a significant aspect of the questioning process. It is necessary to have some support from a local representative who is well-versed in Spanish and can also address the several dialects in Mexico.

As for secondary data, information regarding the 32 states and close to 2,403 municipalities are available. This would be data on age composition, income, housing, education, and sex, as well as information on specific industries including manufacturing, commerce, and financial services. One of the main sources of this information is the Insitituto Naciónal de Estadistica Geografía e Informatica (INEGI).

EXHIBIT 21-2

Mexican Gestures

1. Physical distance is relatively less in Mexico as compared to the rest of North America where members of the same sex may keep more than an arm's length when engaging in a conversation. This is not the case in Mexico where it is even common for close friends to embrace.

2. Mexicans tend to use their whole body when talking and use a lot of hand gestures in order to complement their verbal exchange. It is extremely useful to understand the implicit meanings of such gestures which will help the foreign concern conduct more in-depth research.

3. It is considered impolite to talk with one's hands in the pockets and if one places his/her hands on the hips, that is to be perceived as a form of challenge.

4. It is customary to greet the other person by shaking hands when entering or leaving the room.

Source: From *Business Mexico: A Practical Guide to Understanding Mexican Business Culture*, by Peggy Kenna and Sondra Lacy, Passport Books, 1994. Reprinted by permission of NTC/Contemporary Publishing.

CANADA

Country Characteristics[6]

Population: 30,337,334 (July 1997 est.)
Land Area: 9,221,970 sq km
Language: English, French
Literacy Rate: 97 percent
Religion: Roman Catholic (45 percent), United Church (12 percent), Anglican (8 percent), other (35 percent)
GDP—purchasing power parity: $721 billion (1996 est.)
GDP per capita—purchasing power parity: $25,000 (1996 est.)
GDP—real growth rate: 1.4 percent (1996 est.)
Inflation Rate—consumer price index: 1.4 percent (1996 est.)

Canada is composed of 12 provinces and territories that are extremely diverse. It is interesting to note that most of the major cities are located at the border of the United States and Canada. Despite the physical proximity, there are several differences that make the Canadian market distinct from the United States. Exhibit 21-3 talks about the attitude of Canadians when it comes to protecting their culture from American invasion.

EXHIBIT 21-3

Does Canadian Culture Need This Much Protection?

Some Canadians feel that their culture is too fragile to survive the threat of American cultural imperialism without government protection. Canada has long maintained some curbs on sales of American publications and textbooks and on the reach of the American radio. But Canada has lately been pushing the envelope of cultural protectionism.

Without protections for the Canadian media, the cultural nationalists fear that American magazines could soon deprive Canadians of the ability to read about themselves. American music and rude Yanks will dominate the airwaves. And Americans will sell the textbooks shaping young Canadian minds, possibly sans Canadian content.

Federal regulators handed down a requirement that at least 35 percent of the music played on local radio stations must be Canadian and officials plan to hike the Canadian share to 40 percent in the next five years. There have been proposals to include a stiff new magazine tax with subsidy for Canada-based products or a ban on Canadian ads in publications with less than 60 percent Canadian content. Meanwhile, a plan that could permit American textbook publishers to provide books for grades 1 to 8 in the province of Ottawa—with appropriate Canadian content—is meeting with fierce opposition in the legislature.

Source: Business Week (8 June 1998): 37.

Business Characteristics

Canadians do not take very well to comparisons made between the United States and Canada. When considering business ties with Canada, it would be advisable to view it as a separate country rather than assume it to be a replica of the United States. Also it would be beneficial to note the differences between the English-speaking Canada and the French regions, such as Quebec. For instance, this manifests in the manner in which they negotiate.[7] While the English Canadians adopt a more cooperative strategy in complying with the foreign party and business partner, the French Canadians compete in order to obtain the best possible strategy. These differences are represented in Table 21-1.

The Canadians are considered to be more aware of formality and decorum as compared to the United States. It is necessary for the foreign company to understand the patterns of communication and take note of the hierarchy within the Canadian concern.

The business culture thrives on establishing ties with the rest of the industry. It takes time to foster ties and this aspect becomes essential for a partner to note. Canadians tend to value relationships in business and tend to take time when choosing a business partner or deciding upon a strategy that will optimize industry relations.[8]

The culture in Canada is so markedly influenced by European norms that it becomes imperative for the marketer to address the regions separately. For example, direct marketing efforts for the French-speaking population should be different, not only in language but also in size and color.

Market Research in Canada

Because of common language and long-standing ties between U.S. and Canadian research firms, it is easier to conduct research in Canada than in Mexico.[9] The level of expenditure on marketing research in Canada is estimated at $1,700 million annually;[10] however, most business people consider this to be very small as compared to the amount that is spent in the United States. Exhibit 21-4 explains the differences in marketing research between Canada, Mexico, and the United States.

TABLE 21-1 Internal Variations in Canada

	English-Canadians	*French-Canadians*
Negotiation concept	Abstract arguments	Instrumental arguments
Selection of negotiators	Differentiation based on tangible aspects, such as age and social class	Differentiation given less emphasis—more tolerance to inequality
Bargaining strategy	Cooperation	Competition
Protocol awareness	Not much attention paid	High concern
Time management	More conscious	Flexible
Trust	Tend to trust those willing to communicate	Evaluate the level of trust to place on information
Language usage	Low-context	High-context (nonverbal emphasis)

Source: From *Managing Cultural Differences*, 4th edition by Philip R. Harris and Robert T. Moran.

EXHIBIT 21-4

North American Neighborhood

Nielsen Marketing Research's subsidiaries in Mexico and Canada reveal markedly different cultures in conducting research. The first being that after Nielsen, the other companies in Mexico are small and often gross between $1.5 to $2 million. In 1993, several research firms formed the Asociación Mexicana de Agencias de Investigación de Mercados y Opinion Pública (AMAI) which provides a directory of all the research companies in Mexico. Compared to this, the Canadian industry has two trade associations which handle the role of the marketing research societies more systematically. The Professional Marketing Research Society (PMRS) and the Canadian Association of Marketing Research Organization (CAMRO) publish a list of the research firms across Canada, the services rendered, and the size of the companies.

It is important to note that the infrastructural problem in Mexico often impedes its research industry. Given the lack of reliability on the telephone and mail systems, a great amount of emphasis is placed on personal interviews conducted from door-to-door. This is often concentrated on three or four markets: Matamoros, Monterrey, Guadalajara, and Mexico City. The biggest problem with survey research in Mexico is that in trying to capture the Spanish-speaking population, researchers overlook the Native Indian community. While this problem also persists for Canada, greater effort is placed in trying to ensure that the French or English-speaking population is not isolated.

The Nielsen subsidiary estimates its share of the Canadian marketing industry to be $44 million as compared to approximately $27 million in Mexico. Through panels at retail stores, as well as television audience measurement systems installed and gauged at Toronto, Vancouver, and Montreal, the Canadian marketing research industry seems to be more stable (while the Mexican industry has potential for immense growth).

Even though the Canadian marketing research industry feels familiar to the United States counterpart, it is important to address both Mexico and Canada as two distinct cultures with different potential for growth and development.

Source: "Research Cultures are Different in Mexico, Canada," by J. Honomichl from *Marketing News,* May 10, 1993. Reprinted by permission of the American Marketing Association.

Telecommunications infrastructure in Canada is considered to be extremely advanced and conducting surveys over telephone, fax, or the Internet is relatively expedient and accurate. Perhaps one of the main problems that several companies face is that consumer groups complain regarding the invasion of privacy. Telemarketers and catalogs tend to aggravate consumers when researchers face low response rates from a select sample and try to inflate it to a larger figure to get a better representation.

Conducting focus groups as well as personal interviews is feasible if a compensation (monetary or otherwise) is offered to the respondent. Most often, qualitative interviews help the researcher to arrive at a more specific niche in such a diverse market to target. In order to translate consumer's opinions more effectively, it would be helpful if a translator were available. A significant number of people speak English in Canada, yet certain terms or jargon which may add color to the perspective of the respondent should be duly noted.

Summary

This chapter deals with the practical aspects of conducting marketing research in North America—the United States[11], Mexico, and Canada. The three countries are geographically very close to one another and there is a lot of cross-border movement of goods, services, and personnel. Despite this, it would be a fallacy to assume that these countries are similar and the methods that work in one country will be just as effective in the other two. This chapter also presents some of the possible secondary data sources and the cultural peculiarities for these three countries.

Endnotes

1. *CIA World Factbook 1997,* http://www.odci.gov/cia/publications/factbook/
2. Ibid.
3. Philip R. Harris and Robert T. Moran, *Managing Cultural Differences,* 4th ed. (Houston, TX: Gulf Publishing Company, 1996), 226–231.
4. Peggy Kenna and Sondra Lacy, *Business Mexico: A Practical Guide to Understanding Mexican Business Culture* (Chicago, IL: Passport Books, 1994), 18–23.
5. Ibid.
6. *CIA World Factbook 1997,* http://www.odci.gov/cia/publications/factbook/
7. Philip R. Harris and Robert T. Moran, *Managing Cultural Differences,* 4th ed. (Houston, TX: Gulf Publishing Company, 1996), 217.
8. United States Postal Service, *International Marketing Resource Guide,* ed. William A. Delphos (Washington DC: Braddock Communications, 1994), 85.
9. Jack Honomichl, "Research Cultures are Different in Mexico, Canada," *Marketing News* 27, no. 10 (May 1993), 12–13.
10. J. G. Barnes, "Tracking a Growth Industry: The Development of Marketing Research Services in Canada," 1997.
11. For information on marketing research in the United States, please refer to David A. Aaker, V. Kumar, and George S. Day, *Marketing Research,* 6th ed. (New York: John Wiley & Sons, 1998), and V. Kumar, David A. Aaker, and George S. Day, *Essentials of Marketing Research* (New York: John Wiley & Sons, 1999).

the **Print** shop

**Algonquin College of Applied Arts
and Technology**

1385 Woodroffe Avenue
Ottawa, ON K2G 1V8
Tel: (613) 727-4723
Fax: (613) 727-7684
www.algonquincollege.com